JUDICIAL VETOES

How does the selection of judges influence the work they do in important constitutional courts? Does mixed judicial selection, which allows more players to choose judges, result in a court that is more independent and one that can check powerful executives and legislators? Existing literature on constitutional courts tends to focus on how judicial behavior is motivated by judges' political preferences. Lydia Brashear Tiede argues for a new approach, showing that, under mixed selection, institutions choose different types of judges who represent different approaches to constitutional adjudication and thus have different propensities for striking down laws. Using empirical evidence from the constitutional courts of Chile and Colombia, this book develops a framework for understanding the factors, external and internal to courts, which lead individual judges, as well as the courts in which they work, to veto a law.

LYDIA BRASHEAR TIEDE is an associate professor in the Department of Political Science at the University of Houston. Her current research focuses on constitutional courts in Latin America and Eastern Europe as well as comparative research on the rule of law, judicial independence, and democratic backsliding in developing countries.

COMPARATIVE CONSTITUTIONAL LAW AND POLICY

Series Editors

Tom Ginsburg *University of Chicago*
Zachary Elkins *University of Texas at Austin*
Ran Hirschl *University of Toronto*

Comparative constitutional law is an intellectually vibrant field that encompasses an increasingly broad array of approaches and methodologies. This series collects analytically innovative and empirically grounded work from scholars of comparative constitutionalism across academic disciplines. Books in the series include theoretically informed studies of single constitutional jurisdictions, comparative studies of constitutional law and institutions, and edited collections of original essays that respond to challenging theoretical and empirical questions in the field.

Books in the Series

The Fall of the Arab Spring: Democracy's Challenges and Efforts to Reconstitute the Middle East Tofigh Maboudi

Filtering Populist Claims to Fight Populism: The Italian Case in a Comparative Perspective Giuseppe Martinico

Constitutionalism in Context David S. Law

The New Fourth Branch: Institutions for Protecting Constitutional Democracy Mark Tushnet

The Veil of Participation: Citizens and Political Parties in Constitution-Making Processes Alexander Hudson

Towering Judges: A Comparative Study of Constitutional Judges Edited by Rehan Abeyratne and Iddo Porat

The Constitution of Arbitration Victor Ferreres Comella

Redrafting Constitutions in Democratic Orders: Theoretical and Comparative Perspectives Edited by Gabriel L. Negretto

From Parchment to Practice: Implementing New Constitutions Edited by Tom Ginsburg and Aziz Z. Huq

The Failure of Popular Constitution Making in Turkey: Regressing Towards Constitutional Autocracy Edited by Felix Petersen and Zeynep Yanaşmayan

A Qualified Hope: The Indian Supreme Court and Progressive Social Change Edited by Gerald N. Rosenberg, Sudhir Krishnaswamy, and Shishir Bail

Reconstructing Rights: Courts, Parties, and Equality Rights in India, South Africa, and the United States Stephan Stohler

Constitutions in Times of Financial Crisis Edited by Tom Ginsburg, Mark D. Rosen, and Georg Vanberg

Hybrid Constitutionalism: The Politics of Constitutional Review in the Chinese Special Administrative Regions Eric C. Ip

Constitution-Making and Transnational Legal Order Edited by Tom Ginsburg, Terence C. Halliday, and Gregory Shaffer

The Invisible Constitution in Comparative Perspective Edited by Rosalind Dixon and Adrienne Stone

The Politico-Legal Dynamics of Judicial Review: A Comparative Analysis Theunis Roux

Constitutional Courts in Asia: A Comparative Perspective Edited by Albert H. Y. Chen and Andrew Harding

Judicial Review in Norway: A Bicentennial Debate Anine Kierulf

Constituent Assemblies Edited by Jon Elster, Roberto Gargarella, Vatsal Naresh, and Bjorn Erik Rasch

The DNA of Constitutional Justice in Latin America: Politics, Governance, and Judicial Design Daniel M. Brinks and Abby Blass

The Adventures of the Constituent Power: Beyond Revolutions? Andrew Arato

Canada in the World: Comparative Perspectives on the Canadian Constitution Edited by Richard Albert and David R. Cameron

Constitutions, Religion and Politics in Asia: Indonesia, Malaysia and Sri Lanka Dian A. H. Shah

Courts and Democracies in Asia Po Jen Yap

Proportionality: New Frontiers, New Challenges Edited by Vicki C. Jackson and Mark Tushnet

Constituents before Assembly: Participation, Deliberation, and Representation in the Crafting of New Constitutions Todd A. Eisenstadt, A. Carl LeVan, and Tofigh Maboudi

Assessing Constitutional Performance Edited by Tom Ginsburg and Aziz Huq

Buddhism, Politics and the Limits of Law: The Pyrrhic Constitutionalism of Sri Lanka Benjamin Schonthal

Engaging with Social Rights: Procedure, Participation and Democracy in South Africa's Second Wave Brian Ray

Constitutional Courts as Mediators: Armed Conflict, Civil-Military Relations, and the Rule of Law in Latin America Julio Ríos-Figueroa

Perils of Judicial Self-Government in Transitional Societies David Kosař

Making We the People: Democratic Constitutional Founding in Postwar Japan and South Korea Chaihark Hahm and Sung Ho Kim

Radical Deprivation on Trial: The Impact of Judicial Activism on Socioeconomic Rights in the Global South César Rodríguez-Garavito and Diana Rodríguez-Franco

Unstable Constitutionalism: Law and Politics in South Asia Edited by Mark Tushnet and Madhav Khosla

Magna Carta and Its Modern Legacy Edited by Robert Hazell and James Melton

Constitutions and Religious Freedom Frank B. Cross

International Courts and the Performance of International Agreements: A General Theory with Evidence from the European Union Clifford J. Carrubba and Matthew J. Gabel

Reputation and Judicial Tactics: A Theory of National and International Courts Shai Dothan

Social Difference and Constitutionalism in Pan-Asia Edited by Susan H. Williams

Constitutionalism in Asia in the Early Twenty-First Century Edited by Albert H. Y. Chen

Constitutions in Authoritarian Regimes Edited by Tom Ginsburg and Alberto Simpser

Presidential Legislation in India: The Law and Practice of Ordinances Shubhankar Dam

Social and Political Foundations of Constitutions Edited by Denis J. Galligan and Mila Versteeg

Consequential Courts: Judicial Roles in Global Perspective Edited by Diana Kapiszewski, Gordon Silverstein, and Robert A. Kagan

Comparative Constitutional Design Edited by Tom Ginsburg

Judicial Vetoes

DECISION-MAKING ON MIXED SELECTION CONSTITUTIONAL COURTS

LYDIA BRASHEAR TIEDE
University of Houston

CAMBRIDGE
UNIVERSITY PRESS

CAMBRIDGE
UNIVERSITY PRESS

University Printing House, Cambridge CB2 8BS, United Kingdom

One Liberty Plaza, 20th Floor, New York, NY 10006, USA

477 Williamstown Road, Port Melbourne, VIC 3207, Australia

314–321, 3rd Floor, Plot 3, Splendor Forum, Jasola District Centre, New Delhi – 110025, India

103 Penang Road, #05–06/07, Visioncrest Commercial, Singapore 238467

Cambridge University Press is part of the University of Cambridge.

It furthers the University's mission by disseminating knowledge in the pursuit of education, learning, and research at the highest international levels of excellence.

www.cambridge.org
Information on this title: www.cambridge.org/9781316512319
DOI: 10.1017/9781009058254

First published 2022

A catalogue record for this publication is available from the British Library.

Library of Congress Cataloging-in-Publication Data
NAMES: Tiede, Lydia Brashear, 1965– author.
TITLE: Judicial vetoes: decision-making on mixed selection constitutional courts / Lydia Tiede, University of Houston.
DESCRIPTION: Cambridge, United Kingdom ; New York, NY: Cambridge University Press, 2022. | Series: Comparative constitutional law and policy | Includes bibliographical references and index.
IDENTIFIERS: LCCN 2022003215 (print) | LCCN 2022003216 (ebook) | ISBN 9781316512319 (hardback) | ISBN 9781009061025 (paperback) | ISBN 9781009058254 (epub)
SUBJECTS: LCSH: Constitutional courts–Chile–Decision making | Chile. Tribunal Constitucional–Decision making | Political questions and judicial power–Chile. | Constitutional courts–Colombia–Decision making | Colombia. Corte Constitucional–Decision making | Political questions and judicial power–Colombia.
CLASSIFICATION: LCC KH501 .T54 2022 (print) | LCC KH501 (ebook) | DDC 342.8/00269–dc23/eng/20220331
LC record available at https://lccn.loc.gov/2022003215
LC ebook record available at https://lccn.loc.gov/2022003216

ISBN 978-1-316-51231-9 Hardback

To David and Natalie

Contents

Figures

Tables

Acknowledgments

It is impossible to thank all the people who have helped me with this book, and I am indebted to all of them. The statistical part of the book relied substantially on data coding from my research assistants at the University of Houston with whom I had the good fortune to work, including Marina LaCalle, Amalia Mena-Mora, Margarita Ramírez, Susan Achury, and Samantha Chapa. Without their difficult work, this analysis could not have been undertaken.

The project benefited greatly from a small grant from the University of Houston, Division of Research, which partially funded interviews and archival research in Santiago and Bogotá in 2016. I am thankful for the time that judges and lawyers spent with me in Chile and Colombia explaining their respective constitutional courts. I gained fresh perspectives and insights from these interviews. I thank the following people for interviews or information provided to me in correspondence when I was in Chile: Rodrigo Pica Flores, Jose Cea Egaña, Marisol Peña Torres, Gonzalo García Pino, Sebastián López, and Jorge Correa Sutil.

In Colombia, my trip was greatly aided by Ana M. Ibague, Ana Isabel Gil Castiblanco, and José Albino Ibague, who helped me with many of my contacts, transportation, and opportunities to speak with people. I also thank Mónica Pachón, my colleague from the University of California, San Diego (UCSD), for her hospitality during my research visit. I am grateful to the following people for interviews and information provided to me when I was in Colombia: Dr. Maria Victoria Calle Correa, José Gregorio Hernández Galindo, Dr. Clara Inés Vargas Hernández, Iván Darío Gómez Lee, Hernán Correa Cardozo, Felipe Clavijo Ospinam Alonzo Sabria, Luis Diaz, Diana Salazar, Dr. Carlos Cárdenas Hernández, and Luis Bernardo Diaz Gamboa.

I am in debt to the following people who offered useful conversations or comments on prior drafts or presentations of various articles and chapters, some of whom even agreed to look over the work or speak to me more than once: Susan Achury, Richard Albert, Dan Brinks, Francisco Cantú, Joshua Fischman, John Golden,

Jennifer Horan, Daniel Lempert, Nicki Marinov, Mathew McCubbins, Susie Morse, Raul Sanchez-Urribarri, Patrick Shea, David Tiede, Jason Todd, and Georg Vanberg. Prior versions of several of the chapters benefited greatly from comments received at the Law and Courts Conference at Duke University (October 2017), the Works-in-Progress Roundtable in Comparative Law at University of Texas Law School (May 2019), the Texas Comparative Politics Circle (January 2020), and the University of Houston, Department of Political Science brown bag series (January 2020). I also thank anonymous reviewers and the editor of *Comparative Political Studies* who published my article in 2020, portions of which appear in the introduction, theory chapter, and chapter on individual choice. The manuscript was greatly improved by the anonymous reviewers of Cambridge University Press' series on comparative constitutional law and policy and its editors, Ran Hirschl, Tom Ginsburg, and Zachary Elkins.

I could not have moved forward with the project and the analysis of legislative histories and cases without the help of Patricia Dobaño, my friend and Spanish teacher of many years. Additionally, I am grateful for coach Greg Orphanides and my friends at Houston Cougars Aquatic Sports for over a decade of great swimming and encouragement in and out of the pool.

Although not connected directly with this study, I thank Stephan Haggard for his support and inspiration in my academic endeavors since my graduate school days. I also am thankful for my uncle William Truettner and dear friend Julie Deloria, who have supported me in so many ways throughout my life. I am fortunate to have had two wonderful parents, Lydia Rothman and William Brashear, who encouraged me in very different ways to always follow my heart. Finally, words are insufficient to describe the unwavering support of my husband, David, and daughter, Natalie.

1

Introduction

The increased judicialization of politics over time has rendered the institutional design of courts both contentious and significant. As courts play a larger role in shaping policy, citizens and policymakers increasingly grapple with the powers of courts, selection of their judges, and their role in society in both backsliding and more established democracies. Despite claims that independent courts are important for governance and the separation of powers, politicians, past and present, often seek to control the powers of courts and judicial selection to seemingly control policy outcomes. At times, politicians successfully manipulate these two facets of courts to achieve their own ends. At other times, the composition of political actors and public sentiment as well as the strength of certain courts defies such blatant methods for controlling courts.

The institutional design of courts, especially high courts, has become a salient political issue because courts often make extraordinary decisions invalidating laws approved by the elected branches. For example, in 1995, the South African Constitutional Court struck down a section of its Criminal Procedure Act of 1977 and abolished the death penalty.[1] In recognition of the values espoused by the post-apartheid period, the Court found that this section had violated the state's commitments to human rights found in its interim Constitution. Similarly, the Constitutional Court of Romania in 2010 found unconstitutional a lustration law that would have prohibited former communists from holding political office.[2] The Court reasoned that adopting such a law so many years after the country's democratic transition would violate citizens' rights to run for office or avoid punishment under ex post facto laws. In 2013, the United States Supreme Court issued a groundbreaking decision striking down the Defense of Marriage Act, because it

[1] S. v. *Makwanyane and Another Constitutional Court of South Africa,* (3) SALR 391 (CC) (1995).

[2] Decision No. 820 of June 7, 2010, Romanian Constitutional Court.

violated the due process and equal protection guarantees of the United States Constitution.[3] This decision was later referenced by this same court when it struck down discriminatory state laws and legalized same sex marriage nationwide.[4] In 2015, in response to technological innovations, the Indian Supreme Court struck down a section of India's controversial Information Technology Act, which had allowed the police to arrest individuals for making comments on social network sites that caused "annoyance or inconvenience."[5] The Court explained that this article violated the constitution's guarantee of free speech. All these examples show how high courts empowered with constitutional review powers check other branches of government, uphold provisions of the constitution, and create societies' laws and policies. The decisions are dictated in many ways by the composition of courts and their ability to exercise constitutional review. As used in this study, constitutional review refers to "the authority of an institution to invalidate the acts of government – such as administrative decisions, and judicial rulings – on the grounds that these acts have violated constitutional rules, including rights" (Stone Sweet 2000: 21).[6]

Although constitutional review tends to be viewed as normatively valuable, there is an inherent tension between providing high courts with enough freedom and power to hold elected politicians accountable to constitutional mandates and ensuring that courts, as oversight agencies, can also be held accountable if they misuse their power. Friedman (2004, 2005) notes that the institution of constitutional review provides citizens with both a "hope and a threat" (2005: 309). There is the hope that constitutional review will be used to constrain governments that overstep their powers or fail to respect citizens' rights. In contrast, there is the looming threat that constitutional review will be misused such that courts will inappropriately interfere with the work of the elected branches[7] or that courts' decisions will be biased by the preferences of individual judges. Relatedly, in more fragile democracies, delegating oversight of elected officials to non-elected courts may provide insurance and safeguards for outgoing politicians (Ginsburg 2003; Finkel 2004) but is just as likely to signal an "accountability deficit" (Moreno et al. 2003) or simply a means of "hegemonic preservation" (Hirschl 2004).[8]

3 *U.S.* v. *Windsor*, 570 US 744 (2013). The Defense of Marriage Act or DOMA defined marriage as a union between heterosexual couples only.

4 *Obergefell* v. *Hodges*, 576 US ____, 135 S. Ct. 2584 (2015).

5 *Singhal* v. *Union of India* (2015).

6 Similarly, Vanberg (2005) defines constitutional review "as the power of judicial bodies to set aside ordinary legislative or administrative acts if judges conclude that they conflict with the constitution" (p. 1).

7 These same arguments are found in popular discourse about judicial activism. Some classify courts as activist if they strike down laws that a segment of the population supports. Some classify courts as passive or deferential if they fail to invalidate policies that a segment of the population opposes.

8 Moreno et al. (2003) suggest that the proliferation of non-elected branches to supervise the elected branches will not make elected officials more accountable to the public for its transgressions.

Despite the "hope" and "threat" that constitutional review provides to governments, the majority of high courts worldwide have the power to review and find unconstitutional laws enacted by the elected branches of government. In exercising constitutional review, high courts prevent the elected branches from overstepping their powers and protect minority rights that may be overlooked by presidents, legislators, or other bureaucracies. In exercising constitutional review, courts also uphold the values found in a country's constitution. Even in semi-authoritarian regimes, high courts have been empowered with constitutional review to constrain, or give the appearance that they are constraining, the executive.[9] When high courts invalidate laws, they voice a stern objection to policies approved by the elected branches of governments past or present. When they uphold laws, high courts signal approval for agreements made by the elected branches. Despite the prevalence of constitutional review worldwide, we know very little about what conditions lead judges and high courts to invalidate laws and what aspects of the decisions themselves may make it more likely that they are influential and will be followed.

While most countries allow courts to review laws passed by legislators or decreed by executives, there is enormous variation in the constitutional review powers afforded to courts as well as how judges are selected. Some countries allow courts at all levels to review the constitutionality of laws, while other countries limit such review to their highest courts. Some governments provide their courts with broad powers to review legislation prior to enactment, while others limit their review to laws after enactment and in some only within a certain time period after enactment.[10] Some countries allow courts to review laws abstractly – allowing them the broadest powers most akin to those held by legislators, while other countries only allow courts to review laws within a case and controversy. Many high courts, within some procedural limits, are required to review all cases presented to them, although a few have broader discretion to choose what cases they will review (see Fontana 2011). In some countries, the effect of constitutional review is limited to only the parties to the action (i.e., *inter partes*), while in others this review has broader effects (i.e., *erga omnes*). Some governments further demand obligatory review by the courts of certain types of laws. Policymakers also may restrict constitutional review through rules regarding access to high courts and limiting it to certain political actors rather than all citizens. While these parchment descriptions of constitutional review may provide one way of evaluating a high court's strength or influence over the other branches of government, analyzing the variations in *use* of these powers in practice is another.

9 It puzzles many scholars as to why authoritarian governments would empower independent courts. Some reasons include the need to provide credible commitments to citizens and outside investors (Weingast 1997), and to provide insurance that an independent court exists to protect those in powers' interests once out of power (Ginsburg 2003).

10 For example, the Peruvian Constitutional Tribunal, when exercising its constitutional review function, is limited to reviewing laws that are not more than six years old (Dargent 2009).

Besides wide variability in the type of constitutional review available to most high courts in the world, there is tremendous variation in how judges are selected, although in most cases judges are selected by some elected officials. Judicial selection provides a means for elected and other political actors to choose agents who may serve the selectors' purpose, which is especially important considering the expansive powers that courts hold as well as the increasing judicialization of politics seen worldwide. Judicial selection methods also may enhance diversity and representation on the bench, such that different viewpoints or judicial philosophies are considered on a collegial court. One particular method for selecting judges on high courts that is quite prevalent, and the focus of this book, is mixed judicial selection of constitutional court judges whereby different political or other actors select specific portions of a high court. About 52 percent of high courts worldwide use a form of this selection method, which allows different selectors to fill some of the seats on the court with the type of constitutional adjudicator that the selecting institution believes is most appropriate. Further, this method, in some of its forms, allows all three government branches to choose a specific number of judges allowing for a balance of branch representatives to serve on the court.

While there have been a significant number of studies regarding the creation of constitutional courts (Hirschl 2000; Finkel 2004; Ginsburg 2003), their normative value (Bickel 1986), as well as a large number of single court studies that investigate the use of constitutional review outside the United States (see Garoupa et al. 2021a for a review of these studies), there are fewer empirical studies that evaluate how judges and courts respond to the preferences of elected officials from a comparative perspective, especially in high courts outside of the United States (but see, Kapiszewski 2012; Sadurski 2008; Schwartz 2000; Garoupa and Ginsburg 2015).[11] Interactions among elected branches and constitutional courts are vital for understanding what laws and policies a country ultimately adopts. If high courts are unable to constrain the other branches of government, then laws and policies simply reflect the decisions of the majority of those controlling the legislative agenda. In turn, if courts are effective in invalidating laws, then the ultimate policy that arises is based not only on the preferences of elected politicians but also those of non-elected, professionally trained judges who have been tasked with upholding the constitution. The decisions of all these various bodies and the individuals who work within them are of course constrained by institutions and the political context more generally. A richer understanding of the constitutionality of the laws a country adopts can be achieved by studying how individuals and courts make decisions within the broader political and legal context in which they operate.

[11] Alarie and Green (2017) study how institutional design affects judicial decision-making on appeals on several common law courts. As such, they do not deal specifically with constitutional review.

1.1 AREA OF INQUIRY AND SCOPE OF THE BOOK

The substantial variation in the propensity in which courts with seemingly similar powers choose to invalidate laws calls into question whether courts' powers alone determine how influential and independent courts are in the policy-making process.[12] For example, some courts are bold in confronting their government despite few powers granted to them. Indeed, the United States Supreme Court was never granted the power to review legislation, and some argue that the founding founders never intended it to have such powers (MacGregor Burns 2010). However, despite this limitation, the Court was able to create its own powers by invalidating the Judiciary Act of 1789.[13] In a more recent example, the Bulgarian Constitutional Court, created after the fall of the Berlin Wall in 1989, was provided with the power to review abstractly legislation a posteriori or after enactment when requested by a limited number of political actors, similar to a number of newly created courts in Eastern Europe. However, despite its seemingly ordinary constitutional review powers and the refusal to allow citizens to bring cases directly before it, this constitutional court has historically overturned around 50 percent of the laws it has been asked to review. Unlike the above examples, where courts that have relatively few powers are bold in confronting other branches of government, there are other examples of courts that are given broad powers to review legislation but are hesitant to use them. For example, the Japanese Supreme Court has the power to determine the constitutionality of any order, regulation, or official act (Japanese Constitution 1946, Article 81), but rarely strikes down laws (see Law 2011).

The above examples suggest that the powers afforded courts do not entirely explain when courts will choose to strike down laws. We do not know why some courts with seemingly similar powers more actively check the elected branches, while others do not. Likewise, it is unclear what conditions make it more or less likely that judges and high courts will exercise judicial vetoes, defined as striking down a law passed by the elected branches as unconstitutional. While it would be challenging to have one theory describing the determinants of striking down laws for all high courts, it is possible to broadly theorize some of the correlates of judicial vetoes on a subset of constitutional courts, namely those with abstract review powers who choose their judges by a mixed selection method, which seeks to staff these courts with representatives chosen by the different branches. As such, this book is concerned with a broad, but more limited, inquiry: *How does the mixed selection of*

[12] When discussing judicial independence, Feld and Voigt (2003) and Voigt et al. (2015) and others make the important distinction between de jure and de facto independence. De jure judicial independence refers to the written laws and rules of the game that define courts' powers and procedures and the rules regarding appointing, disciplining, and removing judges as well as defining judges' tenure, salaries, and immunity from prosecution. De facto judicial independence assesses whether judges themselves can make independent decisions in fact.

[13] *Marbury* v. *Madison*, 5 US 137 (1803).

constitutional court judges influence decisions to invalidate or strike down laws under abstract constitutional review? To answer this question, the book provides a general theory about how mixed judicial selection in its many forms influences judicial decision-making and tests this theory within the specific institutional configurations and political context of the Chilean and Colombian constitutional courts. As will be discussed in more detail in later chapters, these two mixed selection courts closely follow the Kelsian constitutional court model[14] originating in Europe and have similar powers and selection rules. Further, by studying two courts within Latin America, the comparison controls for many factors because these two courts share the same legal tradition and legal culture, and the Colombian Court even considered the Chilean Tribunal among others as a model for its own (Legislative History of Colombia's Constitutional Assembly April 8, 1991: 16). Furthermore, the debates surrounding the selection of judges to these courts were roughly similar in their aspiration to construct a balanced court that represented the various branches of government.

The scope conditions of the current study also limit it to an analysis of these courts' abstract review of legislation passed by the legislature currently in power in Chile and Colombia at the time of constitutional review. Such stringent scope conditions again allow for a more fruitful comparative analysis but, as discussed later in the book, limit the generalizability of the empirics. While a more comprehensive review of all types of constitutional review decisions may provide a better landscape of the power of constitutional courts to effectuate policy, it prevents me from focusing on judicial selection and quorum rule fluctuations[15] as other types of review mandate smaller court sizes and, in the case of the Chilean Tribunal, different voting rules. Indeed, the focus on the two courts on one particular type of constitutional review allows me to control for a host of factors and allows a closer examination of the arguments presented in this book.

1.2 BRIEF OVERVIEW OF THE MAIN ARGUMENTS AND APPROACH

What drives individual judges' and courts' decisions to strike down laws as unconstitutional? The theory I develop here diverges from a strictly attitudinalist viewpoint in which judges have policy preferences correlated with their political party

[14] Kelsian courts are those inspired by Hans Kelsen and are described later in more detail. According to Garlicki (2007), "[t]he centralized Kelsenian system of judicial review is built on two basic assumptions. It concentrates the power of constitutional review within a single judicial body, typically called a constitutional court, and it situates that court outside the traditional structure of the judicial branch" (p. 44).

[15] The study does not analyze concrete review cases in Chile or *tutelas* in Colombia, which also significantly influence policy, because these types of cases involve a reduced court size, which may drive decision-making.

allegiances and tend to vote those preferences sincerely constrained only by the law and the facts of the case (Segal and Spaeth 2002). Under such an attitudinalist approach, courts' decisions are based on the simple aggregation of individual preferences under a majority rule. Courts tend to strike down laws when the court's aggregated preferences diverge from those of the legislature and president (see Dahl 1957; Tsebelis 2002). This view has been criticized on several fronts. While judges may hold sincere preferences, scholars espousing approaches rooted in theories of strategic interaction and positive political theory (PPT)[16] posit that judges do not always vote their sincere preferences for several reasons. As part of the "strategic revolution," scholars have shown that while judges may want to make decisions in accordance with their political policy preferences or attitudes, they often need to vote strategically to avoid retaliation from other branches of government that may harm their own employment or the court's strength as an institution (Epstein and Knight 1998). Judges also may behave strategically to curry favor with a new government (Helmke 2002), to foster collegiality within the court (see Songer and Siripurapu 2009 on the highly consensual Canadian Supreme Court), to have more input in the majority opinion (Cameron and Kornhauser 2017a), or to strengthen the role of the court.

Scholars also have criticized attitudinalists for theoretic and methodological reasons. Theoretically, judges have a myriad of preferences unrelated to policy outcomes (Epstein and Knight 2013) and the myopic focus on policy outcomes misses the fact that judges have numerous other objectives that their votes may support. Methodologically, attitudinalists and others also have failed to demonstrate how "the ideological direction of a vote [usually liberal or conservative] determines the outcomes that a judge cares about" (Cameron and Kornhauser 2017b: 538).[17] Further, judges' political preferences or allegiances do not seem to drive all decisions as evidenced by the number of unanimous cases issued by judges with opposing party preferences (see Songer and Siripurapu 2009; Fischman 2015).

[16] McCubbins et al. (2007) state that like other strategic theories, "PPT assumes that individuals recognize that the consequences of their actions can depend on and affect the actions of others, and take this dependence into account when making decisions," and that PPT specifies "how choices and consequences are jointly determined by multiple actors, and characterizes people's choices as strategies within a game" (p. 1664).

[17] Cameron and Kornhauser (2017b) assert more succinctly that many judicial attitudinal scholars

> do not elaborate how the ideological direction of a vote determines the outcomes that the judge cares about. What is the relation between the dispositional vote and job satisfaction, external satisfaction, salary, and leisure; i.e., how does the judge's vote affect the arguments in the agent's utility function? How do judges value the direction of this disposition? Do they value it at all? (p. 538)

These authors' critiques apply to some attitudinalists who try to determine if the judges' political preferences influence the outcome of their vote, which in such studies is coded as conservative or liberal.

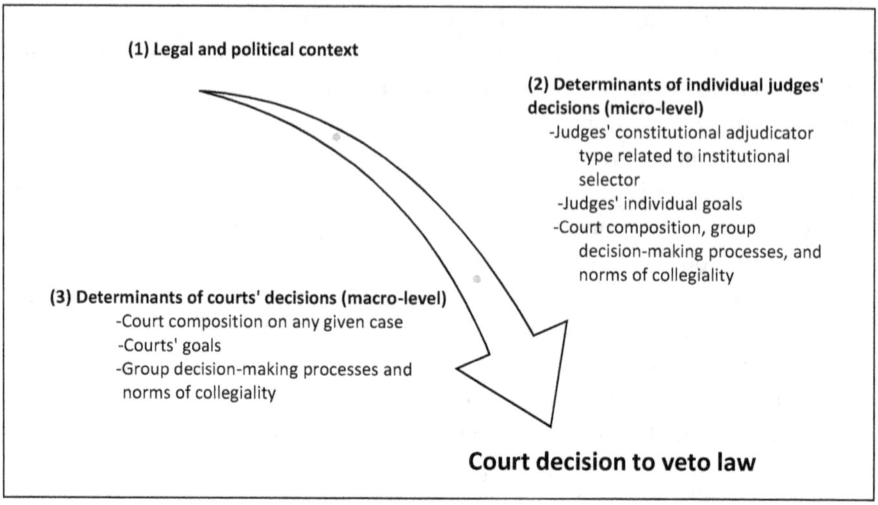

FIGURE 1.1 Conditions for judicial vetoes on mixed selection constitutional courts

Finally, attitudinal explanations may only explain a fraction of a court's decisions, such as those that are most salient (see Unah and Hancock 2006).

Diverging from an attitudinal approach focusing on judges' policy preferences, this book thus attempts to determine what drives judges' and courts' decisions in constitutional review cases. The micro (judge-level) and macro (court-level) arguments are summarized in Figure 1.1 and discussed more thoroughly in Chapter 2. The arguments apply to Kelsian constitutional courts in which the judges are chosen through some type of mixed selection method and that are empowered to review legislation abstractly. The empirical analyses in subsequent chapters focus on the Chilean and Colombian mixed selection constitutional courts. As depicted in Figure 1.1, correlates of judicial vetoes or a court's declaration that a law or part of a law is unconstitutional are derived from the following:

1. The legal and political context under which a law is drafted as well as the type of review triggered by the law and its subject matter;
2. Judges' constitutional adjudicator types informed by the institutions that select them and their individual goals; and,
3. Court composition, collegial norms, and the court's own goals.

I briefly discuss these below and provide a more detailed description in Chapter 2.

The legal and political context that a court finds itself in at the time of constitutional review shapes its response. What I mean by legal and political context is the character of the legislation under review (which depends on the composition of the enacting legislature and its voting rules, which may vary by type of legislation), the manner in which constitutional review is triggered, and the subject area of the law reviewed. Judges and courts do not set their own agendas but rather react to and review legislation previously written and approved by the elected branches.[18] Unlike the United States Supreme Court, many constitutional courts, including those in Chile and Colombia, do not have discretionary review and thus must review most cases that appear before them. Indeed, the laws under scrutiny themselves provide the fodder for constitutional judges' and courts' decisions and thus constrain how much influence judges and courts are likely to have in the policy-making process. The content of the laws reviewed reflects the characteristics and attitudes of legislators and the constituents they represent as well as the compromises that occur during the legislative process to ensure the approval of legislation – in short, politics. The content of law, shaped by the political process, is also determined by the legislative voting rules that inform the type of compromises legislators are able to make.

There are also distinct manners in which constitutional review is triggered, which vary by the features of the law itself and inform court decisions. Some laws require obligatory review by a tribunal as defined by their constitution or organic laws. Undoubtedly, the legislature's anticipation of the reviewing court's reaction also will shape the type of laws that are passed (see Langer and Brace 2005). Abstract constitutional review in some countries may only be triggered by certain political actors. In some countries review also may be triggered by citizen petitions.

Beyond constitutional review type, judges' and courts' decisions are also conditioned on the subject matter of the law being reviewed (see Scherer 2004; Amaral-Garcia et al. 2009). Certain subject areas are especially important or salient, while others have been traditionally avoided by courts, such as foreign policy issues by the United States Supreme Court or economic policy issues in other countries. Certain subject areas may be more controversial over time causing courts to revisit earlier decisions.[19] Further, high courts may act more deferentially when reviewing certain subject areas than others. Shapiro (2004) suggests, for example, that courts are better at confronting other branches of government about rights but are less instrumental when dealing with issues of separation of powers or federalism. Some subject areas also may lead to more divisions among judges, such as cases on abortion decided by the US Supreme Court or those dealing with separation of powers issues or rights in new democracies. As such, judges' and courts' decisions should be conditioned on the subject area of the law being reviewed.

Besides the legal and political context, understanding judges' individual choice requires a focus on judges' roles in constitutional adjudication, the decision-making forum within which they make decisions, and their attributes as influenced by their

[18] It is acknowledged that some constitutional courts may issue advisory opinions and have other tasks that are not related to constitutional review such as lifting the immunity of elected politicians or deciding conflicts between branches of government.

[19] For example, the US Supreme Court overturned its decision in *Bowers* v. *Hardwick*, 478 US 186 (1986) that had allowed states to criminalize sodomy with its decision in *Lawrence* v. *Texas*, 539 US 558 (2003), holding such action as a violation of the due process clause of the Constitution.

selectors and the selection process. With both the legislative and judicial roles of the Kelsian constitutional courts in mind, policymakers choosing mixed selection, the focus of this book, favor a process that selects a specific number of judges chosen by different branches of government to appear in a constitutional court's decision-making forum. In selecting constitutional judges, selectors are not simply looking for judges who will rubber stamp their policies, but rather those who will determine if a law is consistent with the values enshrined in the constitution (see Stotzky 2004). Institutions selecting constitutional court judges may not be especially concerned with whether judges' votes mirror their own policy preferences because the role of the court is to determine the constitutionality of a law, not whether it is a good policy prescription. Additionally, in most constitutional courts, judges do not have lifetime appointments and often judges' terms are not concurrent with their selectors. Thus, selectors are keen on filling constitutional courts with judges who are likely to represent an approach to constitutional adjudication that is most in line with the selecting institution's role in policy-making even when individuals within those selecting institutions are no longer in office.

In turn, judges' voting is highly correlated with their selecting institution, because the nominating institution has chosen a specific type of judge that it wants based on that judge's prior record in a myriad of decision-making posts prior to service on the bench. Judicial candidates are not an unknown quantity but prestigious lawyers, judges, or law professors within a nation. Many constitutional court judges have also served in politics in governmental or non-governmental institutions. They are thus selected for their approach to constitutional law and decision-making more generally (see Garoupa and Ginsburg 2015: 153). Individual judges on mixed selection courts use their votes to enhance their own reputation and that of the court when this serves them. Judges want to be considered expert constitutional adjudicators and carry out their role in a way that is consistent with the selecting institutions' conception of an expert constitutional adjudicator.

A key to solving the micro to macro problem relating to the mechanism from which individual choice is transformed into collective choice is understanding that the collegial forum itself provides judges with certain opportunities to maximize their influence on any case. In the mixed selection context, judges may have strategic concerns regarding their particular influence on the court in any decision. Policymakers choosing mixed selection systems generally, and in Chile and Colombia specifically, chose this selection method to have a specific balance of judges representing different institutions on the court at any one time. However, quorum rules and judges' individual schedules ensure that on many cases, the intended balance of judges by institutional selector is not found. Therefore, individual judges may use their votes to enhance their power on a particular decision when the court composition allows it. Judges' calculations about how to vote rely on the costs and benefits that the court composition, which fluctuates by case due to quorum rules, affords them. In certain compositions, judges selected by certain selectors (and in some cases parties) will be more influential than under other compositions. When certain cases are made up of an uneven balance of judges representing different institutions, judges of a type holding the most seats may seek to maximize their power and vote more readily in line with their type. In instances when they hold fewer seats on a particular case, they may agree with a different and more prevalent type of judge to help shape the majority opinion and to enhance the strength of the decision, which is increased if decided unanimously.

The above discussion focused exclusively on individual choice, rather than choices made by constitutional courts as a whole, to strike down laws. Although judges may individually have motivations to vote to invalidate legislation, scholars have historically been skeptical about whether courts as a whole can ever act as true veto players, defined as "individual or collective actors whose agreement is necessary for a change of the status quo" (Tsebelis 2002: 19) and manifested by courts that strike down laws approved by elected politicians. Literature on the determinants of courts as veto players is of two types. One strand of literature significantly emphasizes the composition of the elected bodies in relation to the composition of the court at the time of a court's review of the law (Dahl 1957; Tsebelis 2002; Rogers 2001; Brouard and Hönnige 2017). Another strand of literature emphasizes courts' collegiality as a main explanation (see Kastellec 2007; Fischman 2015; Grossman 2016; Alarie and Green 2017). If the collegial literature is also considered, it becomes apparent that courts' decisions do not simply reflect the direct aggregation of individual policy preferences, but instead there is a value to the court in judges who change their votes in agreement with others.[20] If contextual, presence or panel effects evidencing collegiality along with judges' individual motivations for changing votes are taken seriously, then courts' decisions should fluctuate with the composition of judge types appearing on the court on any case. A critical mass of certain types of judges on any particular case with certain adjudicating philosophies appearing on a case should influence the outcome of the decision. Thus, certain compositions of the court make it more or less likely that a law will be vetoed.

Although a discussion of judges' preferences and their indirect aggregation has been applied to theoretic arguments about the US federal courts (McCubbins et al. 1995; Gely and Spiller 1990), the impact of collective choices has been seldom explored quantitatively or comparatively in the context of non-American high courts (but see Alarie and Green 2017, focusing on individual judges' choices on appeals before Commonwealth high courts; Kapiszewski 2012). It is yet untested whether a constitutional court's fluctuating composition under quorum rules and mixed selection based on judges' type drives collective choice to issue a judicial veto.

[20] See Austen-Smith and Banks (2011: xii–xiii) for the difference between direct and indirect aggregation.

Cases that have judges with many different interests and connections to both political branches and parties may find it difficult to articulate preferences that are different from the enacting legislature and may also lead to dissent. The empirical chapters on individual and collective preferences that follow will explore in more detail the above briefly introduced arguments as well as analyze them in the context of the two constitutional courts.

To study decision-making empirically necessitates two levels of analysis. Only looking at individual voting may lead to inferences that overweight the decisions of any one judge. Only looking at aggregate choice will mask the mechanism that supports collegial behavior or disagreement. Thus, to understand judicial decision-making by courts and other collective bodies, scholars must develop theories that include a "micro" level explanation of individual choice, a "macro" level explanation of a court's collective choices, and a "micro to macro" theory that explains how the institution of group decision-making influences behavior.[21] Judges, like other individuals within a collective decision-making forum, know that their individual decision is not alone determinative (Austen-Smith and Banks 2010) and thus they may not only use their votes expressively to signal preferences for their own interests but also use their votes strategically or consequentially "if they care about the decision of the Court" (see Cameron and Kornhauser 2017b: 9) or the court's reputation.[22] Understanding individual choice is dependent on determining judges' strategies regarding whether to emphasize their individual goals relating to enhancing their own reputations or to focus on other goals related to the court's reputation. Understanding collective choice, in the form of a court decision, depends on understanding goals that the court wants to achieve, which may or may not overlap with individual goals. Courts' goals revolve around maximizing their power and stature to enhance their roles as a reputable institution and policymaker. Understanding how court decisions may vary from the preferences of any single judge depends on "the way in which votes are aggregated on the court or because of the process of deliberation (and compromise)" (see Kornhauser 1992: 442).

To accommodate the two levels of analysis, the dependent variable for investigating judge level determinants of vetoing laws is whether individual judges decide to strike down part of or an entire law and the dependent variable for the case level analyses is whether the court as a whole finds part or an entire law unconstitutional. These same dependent variables have been used as proxies for judicial independence (Iaryczower et al. 2002; Helmke 2002 for the Argentine Supreme Court; Ramseyer and Rasmusen 2001 for the Japanese Supreme Court) or for judicial assertiveness (Kapiszewski 2012 for the Argentine and Brazilian Supreme

[21] The micro and macro language is attributed to Coleman (1990).

[22] The language of expressive and consequential preferences comes from Cameron and Kornhauser (2017b: 9).

Courts; Von Doepp 2006 for the Malawian and Zambian Supreme Courts).[23] However, using judges' or courts' decision as a proxy for independence or assertiveness in this manner is not without its problems. Judicial independence is largely unobservable and, rather than being equated with votes or outcomes of cases, is best understood as judges' decisional discretion to state legal opinions without undue influence from political or other actors (see Tiede 2006). Further, judges may very well have decisional independence even when they defer to legislative drafters and uphold their laws and lack it when they find a law unconstitutional due to the quality of the legislation or due to outside political or other pressures (Prillaman 2000: 28; Rosenn 1992: 12).[24] Some laws are clearly unconstitutional and stating this is not necessarily a sign of judges' assertions against the elected branches but rather a sign that they are carrying out their professional duties and a proper reading of the constitution. Therefore, for simplicity's sake, this analysis defines the dependent variables as the act of striking down a portion of or an entire law enacted by the elected branches, and does not associate this a priori as a sign of independence or assertiveness. The act of striking down the law is seen as a judge's or court's exercise of a judicial veto because in choosing to find a law unconstitutional, justices are disagreeing with and potentially changing the policies established by elected politicians.

1.3 PREVIEW OF THE EMPIRICAL RESULTS

The empirical results from the two exemplar courts support my theories about decision-making on mixed selection courts and provide a more complete explanation regarding when judges and courts may exercise judicial vetoes on laws passed by the government at the time of constitutional review. A significant portion of the existing judicial politics literature demonstrates that judges make decisions based on their political preferences defined almost exclusively by party affiliations and that courts' decisions follow a simple aggregation or median justice model. The results from this study suggest that judges' institutional selector is a greater determinant of judges' behavior than their party associations in the context of the two mixed selection courts analyzed here. As suggested by the results, the influence of branch selectors on individual voting varies by country as well as what selecting branches are being compared. For Chile, after reforms enacted in 2006, appointing branches consisted of two elected branches (the legislature and the president) and non-elected branches (the Supreme Court and the Consejo de Seguridad de Estado (COSENA), the latter until 2010). The empirical analysis shows that the

[23] Kapiszewski (2012) defines high court assertiveness as a "court's issuance of decisions that challenge other actors' exercise of power – that seek to nullify, restrict or change their behavior" (p. 11) (see also Von Doepp 2006).

[24] Rosenn summarizes arguments against using outcomes of cases to define judicial independence (p. 12).

Chilean Constitutional Tribunal judges selected by the elected branches are more likely to strike down laws than those selected by the non-elected institutions. For Colombia's Constitutional Court, a specific number of judges are chosen by the president and two non-elected high courts (the Supreme Court and Consejo de Estado, the highest administrative court) and in Colombia all nominees are confirmed by the Senate. In Colombia, judges selected by the president and Supreme Court are less likely to strike down laws than those selected by the Consejo de Estado.

While the results show that judges' selection origin matters, changes in court composition due to institutional rules regarding turnover and tenure as well as quorum rules influence individual behavior. The individual judge-level results indicate contextual, panel, or presence effects. Judges change their votes when the composition of the court defined by the presence of judges with different selecting institutions fluctuates. Finally, changes in the courts' overall composition, which occurs periodically, and the type of review and subject matter of the case all influence individual and collective choice. Finally, the book analyzes judicial vetoes with significant dissent, which is a potential cost of the mixed selection method that explicitly seeks judges with different opinions who may disagree. Although there are few cases with a great deal of dissent on the two collegial courts, they provide a metric for determining some of the most contentious issues facing the societies where these courts are located.

1.4 PLAN OF THE BOOK

This introduction has focused the readers' attention on the main question to be addressed as well as the mixed selection context and a summary of the theory to be developed in this volume. Chapter 2 provides an overview of the extant literature, highlighting what we do and don't know about judicial decision-making and presenting an approach for understanding individual and collective choice on mixed selection constitutional courts. While much of the discussion is informed by prior insights from rational choice, positive political theory of law (PPT), and new institutionalism, as applied to the US Supreme Court, this chapter points out when assumptions made by that literature are inapplicable to the Kelsian constitutional courts analyzed here and suggests others. Chapter 3 discusses the prevalence and variation of mixed selection courts worldwide as well as an explanation for focusing the empirical analysis on the constitutional courts of Chile and Colombia. Chapters 4 (Chile) and 5 (Colombia) each provide the legal history and political context of the two constitutional courts examined in the book as well as their institutional rules. To analyze the insights presented in this introduction, the analysis takes a twofold approach, focusing on choices made by individual judges and then by courts collectively. As such, in Chapter 6, the determinants of individual decision-making are explored on the Chilean and Colombian

Constitutional Courts. In Chapter 7, the determinants of legal invalidation by an entire court are analyzed to determine how court composition and contextual factors influence the propensity of a court to strike down laws. Chapter 8 then turns to focus on cases with substantial dissent, which some imply may be a cost for using mixed selection. The book's conclusion in Chapter 9 focuses on the implications of the study to institutional design more generally and provides areas for future research.

2

The Implications of Mixed Judicial Selection on Decision-Making

2.1 INTRODUCTION

Much has been written about judicial decision-making on high courts from scholars from many different fields, including law, political science, economics, psychology, and anthropology. Constitutional courts have been a particular area of focus due to their broad powers and impactful decisions. While there have been many gains in studying decision-making on various courts, individual court-specific studies have tended to present empirical results that focus on the decisions of either individual judges or the court as a whole. As a result, scholars have rarely analyzed data on individual and collective choice for high courts concurrently. As mentioned in Chapter 1, an analysis of both types is important to show both what drives and constrains individual judges and how their choices are influenced by the collegial forum.

To provide a framework for the empirical analysis of individual and collective choice as it relates to judicial vetoes, this chapter first focuses on the difficulties that constitutional courts face in striking down laws, which require individual judges to assert their authority counter to the interests of elected officials and require the court as a whole to have a composition that has preferences for striking down a law that are outside those of legislators approving the law. After reviewing these challenges, the chapter argues that the contextual aspects of the law matter and that within the scope of mixed selection courts exercising constitutional review, *judges' decisions* are in part explained by their own selectors, which define their constitutional adjudicator type, and by the presence and number of judges with other selectors. An increase or critical mass of judges of a certain type on any case shifts the entire decision of the *full court*. In short, the court's composition defined by the percentage of judges with certain selectors influences collective choice more than judges' political affiliations, which are generally seen as a significant driver of court decisions on other courts with different selection mechanisms. The chapter provides a general theory, arguments, and general hypotheses. Subsequent chapters analyzing the constitutional courts of Chile and Colombia will provide hypotheses that align more with the specifics of these two courts.

2.2 THE DIFFICULTY OF STRIKING DOWN LAWS AS UNCONSTITUTIONAL

Several important strands of literature have emerged to explain court behavior, although this literature does not explicitly explain the mechanism by which individual choice is transferred into collective choice. This literature describes the challenges that courts face when overturning laws, especially those passed by the government currently in power. In general, this extant scholarship focuses on the composition of the government at the time of review and sometimes on the court's composition as well. While the studies on courts as veto players reviewed below are theoretical and do not relate to judicial selection specifically, they provide the groundwork necessary for understanding judicial vetoes on mixed selection courts.

2.2.1 *Court Action or Inaction Based on Retaliation*

Scholars, focusing on separation-of-powers games, emphasize that a court's issuance of a judicial veto relies heavily on the political environment in which the court operates, as this determines the likelihood that the court will be punished if it acts in a way that undermines elected officials.[1] Political actors can retaliate against courts' unfavorable decisions in several ways, including stripping courts of their jurisdiction, lowering or failing to raise the court's budget or individual judges' salaries, and changing the composition of the court through impeachment, removal, or court packing. Further, political actors can override courts' decisions through constitutional amendments or new legislation. In general, the likelihood that the court is punished by other elected actors is thought to fluctuate with a country's political context (i.e., unified and divided or fragmented government). Courts operating under fragmented governments are more likely to issue antigovernment decisions (McCubbins et al. 1995, 2006; Eskridge 1991a; Gely and Spiller 1990; Spiller and Gely

[1] Friedman (2005), in an analysis of positive political scholarship on separation-of-powers games related to Supreme Court behavior, suggests that these games share a common assumption, namely "(a)ll institutions (including the Supreme Court) have preferences as to policy outcomes, but in acting they also must take into account the preferences of other branches that play a role in the ultimate policy choice" (p. 311). As a result, "institutional actors think ahead to what response their action will engender and then modify their positions in light of the anticipated reaction in a way that moves policy closest to the preferred outcome, while avoiding trumping action by another branch" (p. 312). But see, Segal et al. (2011), comparing the preferences of the court in relation to the legislature, who find that there is no evidence that the Supreme Court is deferring to other branches due to a "rational anticipation" of an override of a specific decision.

1992; Bergara et al. 2003; Iaryczower et al. 2002) precisely because they are less likely to be punished due to the inability of a more divided government to coordinate on judicial punishment. The fragmentation argument has similarly been used to explain judicial independence in nondemocratic regimes (Epperly 2017).[2]

Since these earlier studies on the effect of political composition on courts' likelihood of striking down laws, scholars have grown skeptical of whether political fragmentation significantly drives courts to issue unconstitutional decisions. Herron and Randazzo (2003) find that political fragmentation in Eastern European democracies does not affect courts' proclivities to declare laws unconstitutional, and Hilbink (2012) finds that political fragmentation is neither a necessary nor sufficient condition for judicial assertiveness. For parliamentary regimes, Stone Sweet (2000) suggests that, unlike in presidential systems, constitutional courts under fragmented government may be *less* likely to strike down the resulting laws because these laws reflect a broad societal consensus on policy and compromises made by the minority government in power to get the law passed. As a result, a skepticism has arisen whether political fragmentation drives court decisions in cases other than those arising in two-party presidential systems, which provided the context for some of the examples in the earlier literature. Adding further critique, Vanberg (2015) states:

> Judges are aware of the conditional nature of their influence and are protective of their authority, but this does not imply that judges are unable to issue decisions that are genuinely unpopular, either with other officeholders or large swaths of the public. Because attacks on judicial independence are a blunt instrument, and the critical consideration for those in a position to attack the judiciary is the balance of benefits and costs derived from independent courts, judges have considerable latitude, particularly in isolated instances, to make decisions that impose significant costs on other actors. (p. 180)

While the political context may help define the likelihood that the government will retaliate against a court for unfavorable decisions, the above literature fails to suggest whether government actors will indeed take action against a court for any particular unconstitutional decision and whether the court is even willing to heed such potential actions or threats. Further, political fragmentation does not covary significantly outside of the election cycle and thus cannot explain how courts' decisions themselves vary within these cycles.

[2] In a variation of the above political fragmentation arguments, Helmke (2002) also focuses on how court decisions on the Argentine Supreme Court fluctuate with changes in the composition of the elected branches. However, rather than looking at political fragmentation within government, she instead finds that judges' propensity to strike down laws fluctuates with changes of the presidency. Judges strategically defect (i.e., issue more anti-government decisions) when presidents are about to lose power through elections or other means. Helmke (2002) and Helmke and Sanders (2006) show that judges become less risk adverse to opposing a government that will soon be out of power and are forward thinkers seeking to curry favor with new governments.

2.2.2 *Court Action or Inaction Due to Diverging and Sometimes Converging Preferences*

While strategic scholars suggest that court decisions are based on a court's anticipation of the likelihood of punishment by the elected branches (but see Segal et al. 2011), another group of scholars explains that courts strike down laws and act as veto players when a court's composition diverges sufficiently from that of the coalition that enacted the law under review (i.e., Dahl 1957; Rogers 2001; Tsebelis 2002; Brouard and Hönnige 2017). These scholars tend to leave the threat of punishment out of their arguments but still have a strategic component to their analyses.

Dahl (1957) argues that the US Supreme Court rarely serves as a check on the elected branches (and thus cannot protect minority rights), because of the fact that "the policy views dominant on the Court are never for long out of line with the policy views dominant among the lawmaking majorities of the United States," and thus it is "unrealistic" that the Court would "stand against any major alternatives sought by a lawmaking majority" for more than a few years (p. 285). While Dahl's argument applied only to the US Supreme Court, other scholars have presented similar arguments to be applied to a greater variety of courts (Abraham 1999; Flemming and Wood 1997; Landes and Posner 1975; Eskridge 1991a, b; Ely 1980). Further, Dahl qualifies his results by suggesting that older laws passed by previous enacting coalitions are more likely to be stricken down than laws of the enacting coalition in power at the time of the review because they are more likely counter to the prevailing public opinion at the time of review. Shapiro (2004), in agreement with Dahl that older statutes are easier to overturn than more recent statutes, suggests this is due to the difficulty of reconstructing the same enacting political coalitions at a later point in time.

Tsebelis (2002), like Dahl, but looking at constitutional courts outside of the United States, is similarly skeptical whether constitutional courts often act as true veto players. The ability of high courts to act as true veto players depends on whether they are able to *collectively* make decisions outside of what Tseblis calls the "unanimity core," requiring unanimous agreement among existing veto players, which ensures that policy remains stable and is not overturned. He claims that this is highly unlikely and that generally courts' preferences are "absorbed" into those of "existing veto players" (p. 227). However, a large part of the arguments of Tsebelis and Dahl are based on a view that courts rarely strike down laws because the legislature and the court rarely diverge in preferences.

Such views have been supported in part by separation-of-powers models (Marks 1989; Eskridge 1991b), which Rogers (2001) summarizes as "'distributive' models in the sense that the judicial veto can only stymie the ability of the legislature to attain its most preferred outcome as legislative and judicial preferences diverge" (p. 86). In these models, if the legislature and the court agree on preferred policy outcomes, or converge, "then the court has no independent effect on legislative choices" (p. 86).

Such views disregard institutional features of some constitutional courts, especially those selected by mixed selection methods, as well as a variety of the political contexts in which they work. Further, judicial preferences in these models seem to be confined to political party preferences along a left/right spectrum, rather than other preferences.

Much of Tsebelis' arguments against constitutional courts serving as true veto players are based on his assessment that judicial selection methods are highly politicized, ensuring that judges are chosen by existing veto players in the policy-making process. While Tsebelis admits that his description of constitutional courts as nonexistent veto players does not consider judicial tenure, he seems unaware of the wide variation of constitutional court selection systems. He suggests that the French Conseil Constitutional may be more likely to serve as a veto player because in his estimation it is the only country that comes to mind without a purely politicized appointment process, because judges are selected by a mixed system and there are no professional requirements to serve as a judge (p. 227). Tsebelis, however, fails to consider the prevalence of other courts that have mixed selection systems in which a significant number of judges are *not* selected by existing veto players but instead by non-elected institutions such as courts or bureaucracies or small bodies within the legislature that themselves are not empowered to independently draft laws or to strike them down (see Brouard and Hönnige 2017).

In contrast to Tsebelis (2002), Rogers offers an alternative model to explain judicial vetoes and uses it to explain case outcomes when the US Supreme Court and Congress converge or diverge in their preferences. First, he explains that courts may strike down laws even when their preferences converge with Congress due to the Court's "informational advantage" over the legislature derived from the Court's ability to review the law after enactment within a particular case and controversy, the doctrines of ripeness and standing, and the relative expense to the legislature in repealing a law as opposed to vetoing it with a court decision. Rogers' argument as to the Court's informational advantage is inapplicable to laws reviewed abstractly and a priori by Kelsian constitutional courts as the law is not tested within the facts of a specific case. Second, Rogers explains that the US Supreme Court may strike down laws when the Court's and Congress' preferences diverge because the Court has little fear of retaliation due to the benefits that Congress reaps from having an institution that can get rid of bad legislation (see also Whittington 2000). He concludes that, by looking at the informative value of the Supreme Court, there are plenty of instances in which the Court can vote sincerely against government interests, rather than strategically.

In recent comparative research, Brouard and Hönnige (2017) provide a more nuanced understanding of judicial vetoes by constitutional courts. These authors correct Tsebelis' misunderstandings of judicial selection on constitutional courts. They indicate that several institutions, which "frequently" select judges to serve on constitutional courts, are not themselves veto players. Rather, judges' selectors on these courts include "parts of the judiciary itself; heads of state in parliamentary systems; asymmetric second chambers; and supermajorities enabling the participation of minority parties" (p. 6). These authors then argue that whether constitutional courts can serve as veto players depends significantly on the political composition of courts as well as the ever-changing configurations of the elected branches that they face. For example, in some cases, constitutional courts are ineffective as veto players at a point in time closest to judicial appointments when judges are most clearly aligned with their appointers who are enacting legislation that the court reviews. Later, however, when appointers' terms end, the court may emerge as an effective veto player as its members no longer face a government with similar preferences or to which it owes much loyalty. Nonconcurrent terms between judges and their selectors, rules about replenishing a certain portion of the court at regular intervals, and limited tenure of judges may result in fluctuations in a court's ability or willingness to strike down laws when power is alternated. (See also Rodríguez-Raga 2011, asserting that the Colombian Constitutional Court's decisions from the period 1992 to 2006 were influenced by changes in presidential leadership.)

Courts' internal composition as well as the political context in which they find themselves drive courts' decisions to strike down laws as unconstitutional and depend both on the practicality of doing so as well as the cost and benefits that courts may incur in taking such an action. From a practical standpoint, courts' finding laws unconstitutional might be considered a rare event, as it is difficult for a group of judges to agree to change the status quo mandated by the legislature and issue a judicial veto. Constitutional courts may be especially hesitant to do so, because although Kelsian constitutional courts have a legislative role in policy making, nonelected judges on these courts may be hesitant to question legislation approved by elected politicians in the name of legislative deference. This may be especially true for younger courts or those created after or emerging from a democratic transition. After transitions, courts may be reticent to find laws unconstitutional, while they establish their legitimacy among political actors and the public. Couso (2004) suggests that the Chilean judiciary may have used a survival strategy due to historical interventions, such as the military coup of 1973, which left the regular judiciary untouched as long as it "limited itself to do its 'normal business' and did not interfere with 'political' issues of the time" (Couso 2004: 86). Specifically speaking of the Chilean Constitutional Tribunal (CT) prior to the 2006 constitutional reforms, Couso claims that the CT containing three justices chosen by and from the Supreme Court had deferential habits typical of the regular judiciary. Courts may want to avoid confrontations with elected politicians when they first start operating to build their strength and stature without interference from the other branches. Likewise, a preexisting court emerging from a democratic transition may want to be especially cautious in declaring laws unconstitutional, as democratic institutions may be especially fragile. The conjecture that newer or younger courts may have lower rates of finding cases unconstitutional is not without its exceptions (see Bagashka and Tiede 2018 on the Bulgarian Constitutional Court). Further, several more established and long-standing high courts in common law countries have exhibited low rates of finding laws unconstitutional, which may be explained by norms of legislative deference or their own weighing of the costs and benefits of issuing a judicial veto.

Despite the examples of some courts' willingness to veto laws, a court striking down a law is practically challenging for a collegial body, and the costs of doing so may well exceed the benefits. First, as discussed in more detail below, it may be difficult for a court, composed of judges who represent many diverse interests, to congeal on a decision that falls outside the preferences of the legislature that approved the law under review. This may be especially difficult on a mixed selection court in which judges represent many diverse selectors and have various party associations. Further, in countries where there are two or more viable parties represented in the legislature, approved legislation may embody compromises that are appealing to both parties as well as different institutions and thus appeal to a wide range of judges' interests.

Further, policymakers choose particular designs and rules for constitutional courts and lawmakers, because while acknowledging that in theory such courts provide an important check on improper government action, they do not necessarily want a court that thwarts their own legislative actions or can do so easily (Kiewiet and McCubbins 1991). Requirements mandating obligatory review may make it especially difficult for a majority of the court to find anything wrong with a law, because the nature of this type of review induces legislators to be especially careful when drafting legislation that they know must undergo court scrutiny. Anticipating the reaction of the reviewing court may cause legislators to pass laws that fulfill all constitutional requirements in order not to receive an adverse ruling from the court (Langer and Brace 2005). Additionally, other rules, such as the passage of certain laws by a supermajority of legislators, also may make it difficult for a court to hold a position outside such a high threshold of legislative agreement.

Figure 2.1 presents a simplified spatial description of five scenarios for a court to find a law unconstitutional considering the composition of the lawmaking bodies and the constitutional court and the voting rules that impact these two decision-making bodies. The figure demonstrates the difficulty of a court finding laws unconstitutional and is tied to previous scholars' work as indicated. In each scenario, the executive (E) and the legislature (L) appear on the left side, and the constitutional court (C) appears on the right side. The left/right location does not refer to ideology on a left/right spectrum but rather depicts the executive and legislature's policy positions along a continuum. The diagram also does not specifically note whether the executive and the legislature agree or not (i.e., unified or fragmented government) but simply depicts what is necessary for the court to overcome their preferences. As shown, the ability of judges to strike down laws depends on both the legislature's and court's voting rules. The space accentuated by the double line

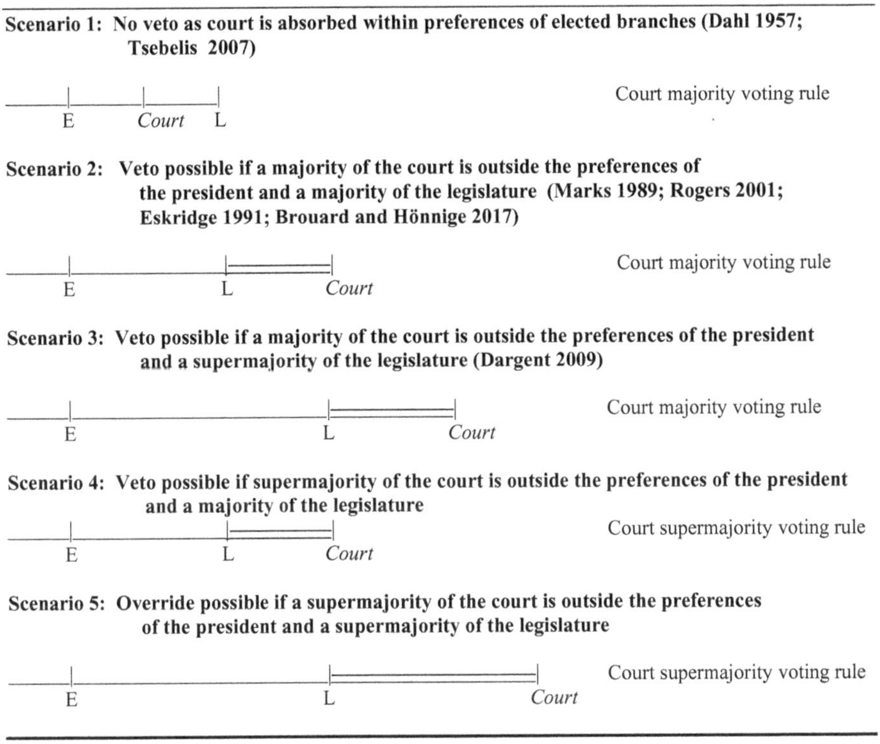

FIGURE 2.1 Court vetoes of legislation under different conditions
Note: For the Court to strike down a law, it needs to be outside of or to the right of the executive and legislature.

shows that the court's decision-making coalition must reside outside of the preferences of the elected actors in order to issue a judicial veto.

In Scenario 1, the court's interests are not divergent from those of the lawmaking bodies, and therefore a judicial veto is unlikely (see Tsebelis 2002; Dahl 1957). As such, Scenario 1 represents Tsebelis' conjecture that courts fall within the unanimity core of other veto players. Scenarios 2–5 differ as to the voting rule required by the legislative body to approve legislation and the voting rule required by the court to issue a decision. Moving from example 2 to 5, it becomes more difficult for the court to issue a decision that diverges from the elected branches. In Scenario 2, if both the constitutional court and the legislature have majority voting rules, a judicial veto is possible if a majority of judges' preferences are outside of those of a majority of legislators (Marks 1989; Rogers 2001; Eskridge 1991b; Brouard and Hönnige 2017). Scenario 3 represents courts that operate in countries in which supermajority voting rules are required for the legislature to pass certain types of laws, such as constitutional amendments, reforms, or treaties. In these scenarios, a majority of judges' preferences must lie outside those of a supermajority of legislators for the court to strike down a law. Scenarios 4 and 5 represent situations in which courts are required to make decisions under their own supermajority voting rules. For example, the Chilean CT requires that for concrete review cases (in which only half or five of the judges appear) to have *erga omnes* effects, four out of five of the Tribunal must agree (Chilean Constitution, Article 93.7). Similarly, the Peruvian Constitutional Tribunal has required since 2001 that five of seven judges must agree to veto a law (Dargent 2009: 270), and the South Korean Constitutional Court has required six of nine since 1988 (Hong 2019). In Scenario 4, a supermajority of judges' preferences must be outside a majority of legislatures' preferences, and in Scenario 5 outside a supermajority of legislative preferences. In these final two scenarios, it will be difficult for courts to strike down laws, especially if the court is composed of very diverse judges or the legislature has many fragmented parties.

Aside from the practicality of finding laws unconstitutional, courts must determine if the benefits of doing so exceed the costs. As indicated previously, younger courts may benefit from cautiously striking down laws in their early years in order to build public support and political respect in favor of the court and its role in the country. However, it is also likely that, to build a court's reputation and legitimacy, it must do so through the quality of the decisions it issues and the demonstration of its constitutional acumen and independence. Therefore, striking down laws that are indeed unconstitutional would strengthen the court's reputations, as would upholding legitimate laws. However, the latter are not seen as particularly difficult decisions for a court and may not have substantial reputational benefits. Courts are especially likely to forge their institutional reputation on difficult cases in which it is politically disadvantageous to strike down a law but legally correct to do so. In related work on understanding when courts are more likely to strike down laws, Vanberg (2005) finds that the German Constitutional Court is more likely to strike down laws as unconstitutional if the process for doing so is transparent, which would necessarily make legislative evasion of such a court's decision questionable, and the court garners public support. Further, he finds that the importance of a case makes courts act more deferentially (see also Staton 2010).

Despite the significant number of benefits to courts in making quality decisions to strike down legislation and thus oppose elected legislators, there are also significant costs that the court must consider. Recent examples across the world, such as in Venezuela, Poland, and Hungary, have indicated how powerful leaders have purged courts, changed judicial selection rules, and altered their powers after they are confronted with court decisions that seem to undermine their power. Apart from these more extreme forms of punishment, more likely in semi-authoritarian or authoritarian countries, courts still must consider the likelihood of other ways that the elected bodies might retaliate against unfavorable decisions. For example, legislatures and executives may limit courts' constitutional review powers through court-stripping measures. Such measures were proposed but not enacted as part of Roosevelt's judicial reforms in the 1930s, which sought to limit judicial review of

New Deal legislation.[3] Congressional court (CC) stripping has occurred several times in American history.[4] In Chile, debates about constitutional reform under President Bachelet's second term and more recently in 2019 after significant protests have supported the idea of constraining the powers of the CT (Ramos 2019). In Colombia, attempts were also made to reduce the powers of its CC. The governments of Ernesto Samper and Andrés Pastrana tried to remove the Court's powers to review economic and national security decrees (Merhof 2015: 728; Rodríguez-Raga 2011: 86). During Uribe's presidency, his interior minister, Fernando Lodoño, announced restrictions on the Court's powers and Senator Gómez Hurtado wanted to draft a law abolishing the Court (Merhof 2015: 728). Not only do court stripping provisions in fact limit a court's ability to act, the threat of such measures also may diminish a court's use of its power in practice. Judges may limit or alter their decisions on especially controversial issues in anticipation that the elected branches will retaliate by limiting the court's ability to review important policies in the future (Helmke 2002; Iaryczower et al. 2002; McCubbins et al. 1995).

While court stripping provisions are indeed extreme curtailments of a court's review authority, other rules may in practice limit a court's ability to use its powers. Most courts and judges are highly dependent on the legislature and executive for approving national budgets for courts to run efficiently. One of the best ways to curtail the work of a court and its judges is to cut judicial budgets. Even for countries that have constitutional mandates that allow courts to recommend how much money they receive or allow a certain percentage of the national budget to be used for the judiciary,[5] such provisions do not necessarily safeguard courts from budget cuts. Not only do courts rely on funding from the other branches to survive, but individual judges must feel secure in their salaries such that they are not threatened with a reduction in their income if they make decisions that are unappealing to others. In the United States, the Constitution prohibits the reduction of federal judges' salaries. This provision is thought to enhance judicial security and independence.[6] Most countries,

3 MacGregor Burns (2009) discusses the historical context and implications of Roosevelt's attempts to reform the judiciary in order to support his New Deal programs.

4 Dobkin (2007) indicates that as early as 1830, Congress proposed court stripping measures and that since 1953 many bills have introduced measures to strip the federal courts of judicial review. In 1996, the government succeeded in enacting court stripping provisions preventing federal courts from judicial review of certain immigration decisions (Dobkin 2007). See Antiterrorism and Effective Death Penalty Act of 1996 (AEDEPA) (eliminating judicial review for certain criminal aliens); the Immigration Reform and Immigrant Responsibility Act of 1996 (IIRIRA) (eliminating review of non-final immigration orders to remove aliens in removal proceedings).

5 For example, the Costa Rican Constitution of 1949 as revised in 2011, states that in the budget bill "an amount no less than 6% of the ordinary revenues calculated for the economic year will be allocated to the Judicial Power" (Costa Rica Constitution, Article 177).

6 The compensation clause in Article III, Section 1, of the United States Constitution states that "[t]he Judges, both of the supreme and inferior courts . . . shall, at stated times, receive for their Services a Compensation, which shall not be diminished during their Continuance in Office."

however, do not have constitutional safeguards protecting their salaries and thus this possibility poses more of a threat to judges and courts outside of the United States.

Courts also may be concerned about legislative overrides. Courts are well aware that their institutional legitimacy depends on public opinion and how other political actors, including lower courts, perceive the strength and relevance of the court. If a court's decision is easily overridden when it is unpopular, a court's reputation will suffer. Further, if the court is seen as easily subverted, its decisions, even those not overridden by the elected branches, may be given less credence. In the case of older laws, the likelihood of legislative override is quite slim as the enacting legislative coalitions are out of power and their interests may not correspond with those of the sitting legislature (Shapiro 2004). For constitutional courts that review many cases a priori or close to the time when they were approved, such as in Chile and Colombia, legislative override by the enacting legislative coalition may be more feasible. Still, some may argue that legislative override is such a rare occurrence that it is not a reasonable constraint on court behavior. However, its rare use points to how effective a threat it may be, as argued by Howard and Segal (2004) speaking about the US Supreme Court.

The above discussion shows that it may be difficult for practical and strategic reasons for courts to issue a judicial veto. Practically, it may be hard for a court majority to agree on a position that opposes legislation passed by Congress especially if that legislation involves compromises among diverse parties or needs to be approved under supermajority rules. Strategically, courts may face considerable damage to their legitimacy and powers when issuing decisions that run counter to the interests of elected politicians and their constituents. The damage from such decisions may be amplified for the majority of constitutional courts in which judges have no job security and for those courts that are reviewing laws drafted by elected politicians still in power at the time of the court's review, which is the subject of the empirical analyses in Chapters 6 and 7. Judges' and courts' strategic calculations rely, in turn, on the context of the case before the courts, such as the subject matter of the law and how a case arrives, which set the stage for the court's overall decisions. Additionally, the composition of the court at the time of constitutional review shapes the courts' strategic decisions about when it is more advantageous for the court to issue a judicial veto.

2.3 LEGAL AND POLITICAL CONTEXT FOR INDIVIDUAL AND COLLECTIVE CHOICE

As indicated in Chapter 1, judges' and courts' decisions are conditioned on the legal and political context of the law under review. The laws substance, in turn, reflects compromises made by the individual legislators enacting the law as well as voting rules, which constrain their ability to disagree. The type of constitutional review that the law triggers determines who may access constitutional review, the timing of the review, and the scope of the decision. Depending on the court, type of review may also be linked to the subject matter of the case and both constrain judges' behavior and alter the lens through which they view a law's constitutionality. Although not taken up in this study, it has been suggested that courts may be more willing to strike down cases it reviews under concrete as opposed to abstract review because such cases are less risky to judges as they do not involve broad and direct confrontations with elected officials (see Couso et al. 2011; Shapiro 2004).

Within the area of abstract review, there are also significant variations (see Ríos-Figueroa 2011), which constrain the behavior of judges. One variation is the timing of the review, whether it is a priori or a posteriori. In a priori review, judges are called on to take a highly legislative role because they are able to veto the law as unconstitutional before it is enacted. In a posteriori review, courts can strike down laws that are already operating within a country, some of which have been enacted by prior governments. There may be distinct costs and benefits to judges and courts depending on when they confront elected officials.

Abstract review also may be obligatory or mandatory or may be brought to the court's attention by other means. In the case of mandatory review, legislators are well aware that the law will come under constitutional court scrutiny and may induce legislators to work especially hard in making the law meet constitutional mandates in anticipation of the court's reaction. In non-obligatory review cases, the legislature lacks such information. When the review is not obligatory, policymakers have chosen which actors are allowed to bring cases before it. Some courts only allow certain political actors to refer a case to the court, while others allow courts to review cases forwarded to them from other courts in the country or from citizens directly.[7] While each of these different types of review may influence judges' behavior as noted above, many of the types of review overlap or are applied together (see Ríos-Figueroa 2011 for an analysis of these combinations of types of review on Latin American constitutional courts).

While scholars have theorized how one specific type of constitutional review may influence judges' decisions, they have done limited theorizing on how combinations of different types of constitutional review influence judges' behavior. This may be because it is difficult to disentangle the influence of a type of review with other rules that define whether certain types of constitutional review are available only for certain subject areas or whether certain types of constitutional review are only applicable to certain laws that require supermajority passage in the legislature. From a practical standpoint, it is therefore difficult to test statistically the influence of any one of these rules as they usually occur concurrently with other rules. Further, it is difficult to compare and hypothesize about the exact influence of

7 A final variation is the reach or scope of the court decision. In some countries, the decision is *inter partes*, only affecting the parties to the case. This generally applies to concrete cases although some courts have the power to allow concrete cases to have *erga omnes* effects as well.

constitutional review type across courts because each court has distinct and individual rules governing each review type. Due to the overlapping rules of abstract constitutional review described above, the prediction regarding impact of type of review is intentionally vague. It posits that review type matters and creates variations in judges' decisions, but it does not specify the directionality or exact effect of the review type due to the above mentioned overlapping features of each type. The foregoing discussion leads to the following general prediction:

H2.1: Judges' and courts' propensities to strike down laws should vary by type of constitutional review.

In any empirical examination of judges' voting behavior, it is important to bring "the law back into the study of courts" as urged by Cameron and Kornhauser (2017a) and Friedman (2006). The laws being considered provide the context for which judges may agree or disagree.[8] In the context of abstract constitutional review, judges do not have case facts or 'a case and controversy' in which a plaintiff or defendant disputes the application or interpretation of a statute within a specific factual scenario. Instead, under abstract review, the dispute concerns whether the law being reviewed complies with the country's constitution. In abstract review, the subject area of the law and how it is worded provide the context within which judges decide if certain aspects of the law comply with the constitution. The subject matter of the law should influence individual judges' decisions with certain areas of the law leading to more disputes regarding their constitutionality than other areas. As with other judicial studies, the subject matter of a case or law analyzed has been shown to be an important determinant of judicial decision-making (see for example Scherer 2004; Segal and Spaeth 2002). In the context of courts in developed democracies, Shapiro

[8] Cameron and Kornhauser (2017b: 548) advocate the "case space approach" for understanding judicial behavior. In this approach

> [A] case is a vector (a point) in a metric space and a policy is simply a partition of that case space. In the typical context of adjudication, a policy partitions the case space into a set in which plaintiff prevails and a set in which she loses. Actors may then have preferences over the best partition of the case space. All the actors may agree on the best partition of the case space ... or they may not ... Specifically, the case space approach represents each judge's view of the law as a partition of case space; the partition identifies how the judge would ideally rule on a case. (p. 548)

The above approach allows for judges to disagree both "in accordance with law, just somewhat different understandings of law as captured in the different versions of the possible partitions of the case space" (Cameron and Kornhauser (2017b: 548). These authors suggest that case by case decision-making applied above may not apply to Kelsenian constitutional courts, studied here, because they are engaging in abstract review and thus making "policy embedded in the statute" (see p. 548, fn. 21). Despite Cameron and Kornhauser's proviso about Kelsian courts, constitutional judges still may similarly disagree over understandings of the constitution for each reviewed law.

(2004) considers three important subject areas: separation of powers, rights review, and federalism. In the case of the US Supreme Court, he shows that historically, the Court was more successful or "changed public policy in the direction the court wants public policy to go" (p. 7) in federalism cases and had less influence in cases involving separation of powers issues. As to rights cases, the US Supreme Court had a reputation of defending property, specifically corporate property rights, and then used "the institutional support for these efforts to further 'individual' or 'human' rights," reaching an apex under Chief Justice Earl Warren in the 1950s (p. 8). In the case of Kelsian courts, the record for "success" in certain subject areas has been less clear than that of the US Supreme Court, although many courts outside the US have been considered more successful in changing policy in their preferred direction in rights and federalism cases than the US Supreme Court. Furthermore, the creation of Kelsian courts was born out of concerns for protecting separation of powers more generally, and presumably these courts have a higher stake in such cases.

From the above discussion, it follows that certain subject areas of law provide judges with different contexts for assessing the costs and benefits of striking down laws and certain subject areas may result in more diverse interpretations of the constitution. First, judges on mixed selection constitutional courts may find that cases involving the review of laws related to the separation of powers or rights are some of the most important and contentious that the court decides. The subject areas that make these cases more salient than others may influence judges' calculations. Judges may want to show their independence by striking down these important laws or may want to steer clear of conflict with the elected branches by simply deferring to Congress' approval of a reviewed law. For some judges, striking down important issues involving separation of powers or rights or other salient cases will benefit their reputation by highlighting their independent thinking in a high profile way. For other judges, the costs of doing so may override revealing preferences for finding such laws unconstitutional.

Second, while the laws reviewed may provide unique contexts for judges to weigh the costs and benefits of striking them down, certain areas of the law may invite more variations in judges' understanding of whether a law complies with or violates the constitution. Judges may have strong and divergent views regarding the constitutionality of laws involving separation of powers because these laws define the powers on the branches of government that are represented on the constitutional court itself. Judges chosen by different branches of government may have very specific understandings about the constitutionality of legislation that defines or limits the powers of some branches of government in relation to those of other branches either because they want to protect the branch that chose them or more likely their constitutional adjudication style, related to deference to the elected branches, varies.

While laws involving separation of powers may seem especially important and result in more debates among judges on mixed selection courts, laws related to states' rights in federal systems or subnational governments in unitary systems may be seen as less risky for judges to strike down. Laws on subnational governments may favor one region over another and may have resulted from particular legislators successfully lobbying the national government to favor a particular region. Mixed selection judges, chosen by national political actors, may be more likely to strike down laws implicating subnational governments because individual judges tend not to have strong affiliations with subnational governments.[9]

Judges' decisions also may be influenced by whether the law reviewed involves individual rights. For many judges, such laws are often especially political, contentious, and lead to divisions within society. Furthermore, one of the justifications of empowering courts is to protect the rights of minorities from the majority although Kelsen himself warned against allowing separate constitutional courts to adjudicate rights disputes because they were so political (see Shapiro 2004: 16). Despite this warning, over time, Kelsian courts have consistently reviewed laws involving rights and European constitutional review of these types of cases has resulted in the protection of minority rights. As such, rights cases provide a context in which judges are deciding the constitutionality of important laws that make the case particularly salient. In some newer or emerging democracies, constitutions also may be particularly focused on rights. For example, Colombia's constitution includes many rights, while Chile's constitution, constrained by a pacted transition, tends to emphasize property rights over others. Judges' review of legislation involving rights also emphasizes an important tension within democratic governance involving the will of the majority and the protection of minority interests – an area in which judges may have unique and varied understandings of what types of rights-related laws comply with the constitution. Despite the importance of rights cases, predictions regarding the directionality, rather than the significance, of a covariate that controls for rights cases are difficult to make as they depend not only on the judges' constitutional adjudication type and perhaps their political associations, but also on the specifics of the law in question. It cannot be assumed that courts are always reviewing laws that seek to broaden individual rights. Rather, the substance of the rights legislation depends on the laws that Congress (with acquiescence of the president) agree on which in turn depends on the composition of the legislature, voting rules, and compromises to pass a law in this area as well as societal demands for rights legislation. The above discussion leads to the following general predictions:

H2.2: Judges' and courts' propensities to strike down laws should vary by subject area of the law reviewed.

[9] This is different than the court striking down laws passed by subnational, rather than national governments on subnational issues. It has been shown that constitutional courts may be more likely to strike down laws passed by subnational governments compared to those passed by national governments (see Tiede and Ponce 2014; Pellegrina and Garoupa 2013).

2.4 INDIVIDUAL CHOICE AND GENERAL PREDICTIONS

2.4.1 *Judges' Preferences*

Until recently, judicial scholars insisted that judges' decisions were driven primarily by their preferences for policy outcomes, which they exhibited either by voting sincerely (Segal and Spaeth 2002) or strategically (Epstein and Knight 1998). Judges whose votes follow their policy preferences, in which their or their appointers' political orientation or party serves as a proxy, have been shown on the US Supreme Court (Segal and Spaeth 2002; Epstein et al. 2013, but see Cameron and Kornhauser 2017a)[10] as well as on several high courts outside of the United States (see Iaryczower et al. 2002; Ostberg and Wetstein 2007). In this literature and its strategic variations,[11] there is a strong correlation between judges' party (or the party of their appointer) and decisions that are coded as having a conservative or liberal outcome. According to attitudinal and strategic scholars, judges vote consistently with their policy preferences due to their sincere beliefs, loyalty to their appointer or to curry favor with parties during and after service on the bench. Attitudinal voting of this type generally applies to the most salient cases (Unah and Hancock 2006).

For many studies, especially those concerning US federal courts, policy preferences have been inferred from the party of the president that appoints the judge (Segal and Spaeth 2002 on the Supreme Court; Cross and Tiller 1998; George 2001; Brudney et al. 1999; Gotshall 1986, but see Ashenfelter et al. 1995 on the US Court of Appeals and Rowland and Carp 1996; Schanzenbach and Tiller 2008; Tiede et al. 2010 on district courts). A more nuanced approach by Goff (2005), suggests that judges should be characterized both by the party of the appointing president as well as the majority party in the confirming Senate (see also, Giles et al. 2001). Outside of the United States the party of the appointer has been ascribed to judges and has similar behavioral ramifications (see Ostberg and Wetstein 2007 for the Canadian Supreme Court, Iaryczower et al. (2002) for the Argentine Supreme Court and Von Doepp (2006) for the Malawi Supreme Court.)

Decisions driven by policy preferences defined by judges' party affiliations also have been found on mixed selection constitutional courts (see Garoupa and Grembi (2015) for Italy and Amaral-García et al. (2009) for Portugal). For Spain's mixed selection Constitutional Court, Garoupa et al. (2013a) find that judges' behavior on

[10] Cameron and Kornhauser (2017b) criticize studies that use judges' ideology, determined by the party of the appointing president to determine the effect on their vote coded as liberal or conservative, because such studies "do not elaborate how the ideological direction of a vote determines the outcomes that the judge cares about" and thus do not indicate whether or how "judges value the direction" of a case outcome (p. 538).

[11] Strategic variations assume that judges have preferences based on their ideological or policy preferences but do not always reveal these preferences for strategic reasons (see Epstein and Knight 1998; McCubbins et al. 1995). As a result, strategic models might be seen as an extension of attitudinal models.

abstract review cases is not completely explained by judges' party alignment "but subject to complex incentives and institutional influences" (2013a : 530). For the French Constitutional Council, another mixed selection court, Hönnige (2009) finds justices vote according to their political preferences, but this analysis is not based on judge-level data. While these analyses suggest that judges' party alignment is important, they do not concurrently explore the impact of judges' institutional selector on decision-making (but see, Garoupa et al. 2021b) which is a main contribution of this study.

There is good reason, however, to believe that judges' policy preferences (defined by the party affiliation of their appointers), are not the only or strongest predictors of judicial choice on mixed selection courts. Despite the ubiquity of the attitudinal explanation and its strategic variants, some scholars have questioned whether judges' preference revelations are always tied to policy objectives (see Helmke and Sanders 2006). Voeten (2008), studying international courts, shows that judges' preferences are based less on judges' political party orientation and more on preferences for legislative deference or activism. Additionally, Epstein and Knight (2013) have asserted that their previous ground-breaking work (i.e., Epstein and Knight 1998)[12] incorrectly adopted the "conventional (political science) party line," which argues that "maximizing policy is of paramount, even exclusive, concern" of judges (p. 12). As noted by these and other authors, judges have many preferences besides policy outcomes. For example, judges may have preferences for legislative deference (Peress 2009; Voeten 2008), upholding the role of a judge (Baum 2006), the legitimacy of a particular court (Couso 2004; Staton 2004) or the judiciary as a whole (Garoupa and Ginsburg 2015). Judges also may have preferences for making correct, quality decisions (Baum 2006) or getting it right (see Iaryczower and Shum 2012). These latter preferences may improve judges' own reputations or increase their pecuniary interests through career advancement or higher salaries (see Epstein and Knight 2013).

Constitutional court judges' preferences are unlikely to be predominantly oriented toward policy outcomes due to these judges' specific tasks as constitutional adjudicators, specifically to decide *abstractly* (or concretely) whether legislation is constitutional or not. Such decisions require that judges ensure that the law under review complies with the nation's constitution. Because the cases analyzed in the empirical chapters are decided abstractly in the "absence of litigation," the role of judges is to "read the legislative text against the constitutional law" (Shapiro and Stone Sweet 2002: 344–345). In the absence of case facts (so important in American style judicial review), there is "no storyline" (p. 345) and thus judges' decision-making tasks do not require a political policy preference per se. In other words, the

[12] Epstein and Knight (1998) extended the attitudinal model of Segal and Spaeth (2002) by showing that judges had policy preferences that were constrained when they accounted for the preferences of other political actors.

"function of a judge in a constitutional democracy is to give meaning and application to constitutional values, independent of political preferences" (Stotzky 2004: 199). As a result, judges' preferences in the context of abstract constitutional review are based on making the correct constitutional decision, which not only requires comparing the law reviewed to the constitution but also depends on judges' interpretation of the proper constitutional role of judges and the elected and non-elected officials that select them. In short, instead of preferences tied to policy outcomes, judges' preferences are tied to making the correct decisions based on their reading of the law under review and the constitution.

While judges prefer making correct constitutional decisions, judges themselves will diverge as to what they conceive is correct, which varies with what type of constitutional adjudicator they conceive themselves to be. In other words, judges' constitutional adjudicator type and their behavior are defined by the selecting institution's *characteristics and interests* as well as the *selection process* itself (see Goff 2005). In several courts with mixed systems, a specific number of judges are selected by different branches unilaterally or in combination with another branch and thus the institution that selects is a defining characteristic of the judge.

Policymakers, including those in Chile and Colombia, chose mixed selection systems to allow different political institutions a voice or representative on courts that have the power to veto legislation. Here, having a representative on the court does not mean that judges represent the selecting institutions' policy preferences on particular laws or serve as loyal agents for the selector as suggested by Epstein and Posner (2016)[13] (although this may occur in certain cases), but rather that judges are of a certain type that will represent the selecting institution's profile for a constitutional adjudicator who can effectively opine when a law is inconsistent with the constitution. Selecting institutions will select judges who fit their ideal of a constitutional adjudicator, who may be either active or deferential to the elected branches. Institutional selectors also will choose judges who they know will understand and voice opinions consistent with the selecting branch's own role in the policy-making process, which is predicated on the Madisonian idea that the ambition of different branches, here represented within constitutional courts, "must be made to counteract ambition" (Federalist 51).

Selecting institutions are distinguished by whether they are elected (i.e., by the executive and legislature) and thus vertically accountable or responsive to voters or non-elected (i.e., courts) and responsive to a counter-majoritarian institution with no vertical accountability to citizens. In more theoretical accounts, some scholars argue that judges selected by elected actors will be more assertive than those

[13] Epstein and Posner (2016) establish that judges exhibit a loyalty effect to the specific president who appointed them to the US Supreme Court. The results, however, are confined to cases in which the president appears as a litigant. In the current analysis, judges are conducting abstract review in which selecting institutions are not litigants to the case.

chosen by courts. Judges appointed by elected officials may see their role as like that of "legislators in robes," and thus are more likely to strike down laws (Stone Sweet 2011: 81). Elected institutions (i.e., the president and legislature) also may choose judges who are more willing to consider political factors in their decisions and play an active role in the policy-making process much the way that elected politicians do when enacting laws. This may result in judges selected by elected institutions who are more willing to strike down laws as unconstitutional or more interested in considering political factors in their decisions, but this depends on the political context.

In contrast, non-elected institutions may choose judges who value legislative deference and see their role as less political and more judicial, possibly taking a more deferential stance toward legislators who draft the laws they review (see Merryman and Pérez-Perdomo 2007). Just as likely, judges chosen by courts may be more willing to consider legal factors in their decisions than those chosen by the elected branches. Judges selected by non-elected institutions may exhibit a lower likelihood of striking down laws than judges selected by elected institutions. Even scholars of the US Supreme Court have conceded that despite voting their preferences, many judges on this court are constrained "by beliefs of what is normatively appropriate such as deference to the other branches of government" (Howard and Segal 2004: 133; see also Baum 1997). Similarly, courts that select judges to serve on constitutional courts may choose judges who embody this more deferential role. In the mixed selection context, judges chosen by courts often have judicial, legal, or academic careers prior to the bench and may be more comfortable applying well-established norms to cases rather than considering political factors in their decisions. Further, a reputation for judicial restraint claimed by judges selected by courts may be useful for post-bench employment in other courts or academia. Judges selected by courts may view interpreting the law, rather than voiding it, as the proper role for a judge. Anecdotal accounts of specific mixed selection constitutional courts have suggested that judges chosen by supreme courts in Bulgaria (Sadurski 2008) and Chile (Couso and Hilbink 2011) behave more deferentially than judges chosen by the elected branches in these countries.[14]

As discussed below, however, it is difficult to assert a priori that judges selected by elected institutions are always less deferential to policymakers than those selected by non-elected institutions. This depends decidedly on the interests of the selecting institution and the legal, political, and historical context in which judges operate within a particular court or country. Institutional selectors want to select judges who

[14] If more than one court selects judges, these distinct courts may also select different types of judges depending on each court's own distinct roles in the policy-making process defined by the constitution. A selecting court involved in appellate review, such as the Colombian Supreme Court may have a distinctly different role in the policy-making process than a court that has the ability to constrain political actors and advise government, such as Colombia's Consejo de Estado.

will decide cases in line with the goals that the selecting institution hopes will be achieved through constitutional adjudication. However, deciphering these exact goals in turn depends on the specific political context in which courts operate, which in turn may differ dramatically across time and place. As a result, while on the basis of selection, it is likely that judges with different selectors will decide cases differently, it is difficult to make absolute statements about whether or not judges selected by elected institutions will be more likely to strike down laws than those selected by non-elected selectors. There may be instances when judges appointed by elected presidents may themselves be more deferential than those appointed by non-elected actors in cases where selecting presidents have strong executive powers and significant influence over the legislature or judges appointed by courts who are adamantly opposed to the policies of elected officials as occurred in Turkey (Varol et al. 2017).

In short, different institutions select different types of judges who they entrust will carry out what the selecting institution believes is its own role and the role of a constitutional judge in the policy-making process. Judges selected by different institutions will have different propensities for striking down laws, which depend on the selecting institutions' own role in policy-making and the extent that this leads judges to consider political or legal factors in their decisions. The propensity of judges with different selectors to strike down laws also will depend on which selecting institutions are being compared to one another.

But how does the institution that selects judges influence judges' behavior in constitutional adjudication? Selecting institutions carefully choose judges because they know that there are few ways to control judges once on the bench as this would undermine aspirations of judicial independence.[15] The vigorous debates over selection in Colombia and Chile described in Chapters 4 and 5 attest to this. Institutions base their selections on signals that judicial candidates send through past performance (see Kiewiet and McCubbins 1991: 31) on a myriad of prior decision-making jobs. In some, but certainly not all cases, judges on mixed selection courts have worked for or closely with the institutions that selected them. While some scholars argue that judges' or even bureaucrats' past careers in and of themselves explain individual judges' voting patterns (see Pardow and Verdugo 2015 on the Chilean Constitutional Tribunal and Adolph 2013 for central bankers), judges on many constitutional courts including in Chile and Colombia have each worked in a wide range of legal, judicial, academic, and political posts. Instead, the selecting branch is aware of judges' prior posts and will select the judge whose complete background and profile best fits with what the selecting branch seeks in constitutional adjudication.

[15] Judicial independence is an important requirement for allowing courts to have constitutional review powers in the first place (Ginsburg 2003: 43).

Once on the bench, decisions of judges with different selecting institutions will diverge for several reasons. First, judges understand what type of constitutional adjudicator the selecting institution wants and the basic needs and mission of the selecting branch (see Nunes 2010; Whittington 2000), which vary by institution. Understanding that one of the needs of the selecting institution is to make decisions in line with the institution's perceived role in policy-making ensures that a judge behaves a certain way on a variety of tasks to fulfill that role (George 2008), and this "impacts the frequency with which he will pursue his preferences sincerely without consideration of other concerns" (p. 1356). Keck (2007) suggests that institutions "have a life of their own," which influences 'role conceptions' of those who work in them or by analogy are selected by them (p. 323). Judges in turn live up to the expectations of their selectors as they want to solidify their reputations as quality decision-makers, which may be useful for employment in academic, political, legal or other fields after short terms on the bench (see Garoupa and Ginsburg 2015).

Scholars of judicial politics may ask about the influence of judges' party associations within the mixed selection context. Unlike other types of selection systems in which the party of the judge is the same as their appointer, this is not always the case with mixed appointments. Under this system, judges may be selected in part for their party affiliation; however, whether that party is aligned with the appointer's party depends on several factors. While, the president may appoint judges who represent the party of the presidency or the governing coalition, presidents may strategically choose candidates with party preferences distinct from their own as described by Sadurski (2008). As far as legislative branch appointees, these also may not be clearly aligned with the majority party in the legislature in situations where there are multiple fragmented parties or supermajority confirmation rules requiring a compromise among diverse political interests. Further, appointing legislatures may agree beforehand to alternate the selection of judges from different parties or "horse-trade," as is well documented for Chile's legislative appointees on the post-reform CT.[16] In this case, alternating legislative appointees would not necessarily represent the party of a majority of legislators. As to judges chosen by non-elected collegial courts or other bodies, judges' party may reflect the dominant party or nonpartisanship represented by a majority of members on the appointing court or may represent a variety of different political preferences requiring a consensus.[17] Nonconcurrent terms of judges and their selectors as well as replenishment of the courts after certain time periods also may diminish judges' incentives for voting according to the party line. In mixed systems, judges may be influenced both by the type of institution that select them (elected or not) and the selecting institution's party preferences, if ascertainable. However, institutional selector should be a more influential driver

[16] See Chapter 4 discussing this.

[17] Sr. Valenzuela Somarriva pointed this out during debates on choosing CT judges (see Historia de la Ley N° 20.050: 540).

of judges' decisions than their party. Additionally, the impact of the selecting institution may be attenuated by a judges' party associations in certain circumstances.[18] The above arguments lead to the following predictions:

H2.3: *Judges' selecting institutions should influence individual judges' decisions to strike down laws more than their party associations.*

H2.4: *On constitutional review cases, fragmentation in voting will be based more on differences among judges' selecting institutions than differences due to their party associations.*

2.4.2 *Behavioral Implications of Variations in Mixed Selection Systems*

The arguments above posit that judges' individual decisions divide due to differences in their selecting institution. However, there are variations in types of mixed selection systems, and these may have distinct behavioral implications. According to judicial and other scholars, more veto players in the appointment of judges should result in judges who are more moderate or represent more diverse interests (Moreno et al. 2003; Driscoll and Nelson 2015; Nunes 2010). Just as likely, judges chosen by mixed systems, which require another veto player to confirm the selection, may also be more moderate as to their constitutional decision-making strategies as they must appeal to more selecting institutions and represent broader and more overlapping interests to be chosen in the first place. According to Ginsburg (2003), selection of judges by one institution and confirmation by another ensure "broad support (institutional or political) for those who are to interpret the constitution" (p. 44). Likewise, institutions that unilaterally select judges on mixed selection courts allow "theoretically, appointees who can be much closer to pure agents of the appointers" (p. 44). Besides selecting judges that are open to more interests, confirmation by the Senate may allow the confirming institution to assert some influence over all judges despite their diverse nominators. Moreno et al. (2003) have suggested that institutional designers that require congressional confirmation of appointments "have preferred to keep a body charged with reviewing the admissibility of their own laws on a somewhat shorter leash" (p. 106, citing Ecuador, which requires legislative confirmation of the country's constitutional court nominees). There are circumstances in which selection by more veto players does not necessarily lead to moderate judges. The key is whether the different veto players involved in selecting

[18] For example, evidence from elite interviews conducted by Lamprea (2010) suggests that this was just the case as to the Supreme Court nominees to the Colombian Constitutional Court. He argues that for the Supreme Court, "the fact that some candidate is liberal or conservative is not as important as the 'loyalty' that a candidate should be ready to show to her nominator – the Supreme Court – once appointed to the Constitutional Court" (p. 16). Lamprea notes that the Consejo was more interested in the party of its nominees. Although party associations may be a reason for selecting judges, this analysis attempts to determine if it is a determinant of judges' voting records.

judges truly represent different interests. For example, if both the president and legislature share the same party or other interests, having both branches involved in the selection process will have little moderating effect.[19]

2.4.3 *Implications of the Collegial Forum for Individual Choice: The Micro to Macro Explanation*

Besides judges' own characteristics, another strand of explanations involving individual choice on high courts focuses on how diversity on a collegial court may induce judges to vote in a way that is *distinct from their* constitutional adjudicator type. The influence of the group's characteristics on the individual is generally known as contextual, presence, or panel effects. Extant literature suggests that the diverse composition of a court hearing a particular case should independently affect individual decision-making. Panel effects have been found based on judges' race (Kastellec 2007), sex (Boyd et al. 2010), and ethnicity (Grossman et al. 2016).

Panel effects suggest that the mere presence of judges with *other* characteristics may cause judges to vote in a way that is different from how they would if surrounded by judges with similar characteristics. According to Fischman (2015), "contextual effects occur when an individual's behavior is influenced by the characteristics of the group members" (p. 811). In the context of courts, a theory based on pure contextual effects, claims that an individual judge is influenced by the *presence* of judges with different characteristics or the characteristics of the court as a whole. In other words, the heterogeneity of the group influences individual choice.

Scholars have offered numerous reasons why individuals may agree with others whom they do not share similar preferences or political backgrounds including saving time, social pressure (Songer 1982), and maintaining collegiality or consensus (Epstein et al. 2011). Another explanation is associated with avoiding the costs related to disagreeing (Conlisk 1980; Epstein et al. 2011). Judges may conduct a cost/benefit analysis regarding whether to disagree with the majority (see Epstein et al. 2011). Decision-makers, such as judges, know that their singular choices are not determinative on a collegial body but depend on the decisions of others (Austen-Smith and Banks 2010). As a result, judges that sincerely do not agree with the majority may benefit by voting with it to better shape the majority decision. Judges also may be concerned that the court issues unanimous decisions to enhance the reputation of the court (Garoupa and Ginsburg 2015) or strengthen the decision itself. Finally, judges may be concerned with making the correct decision that requires careful consideration of other judges' perspectives.

[19] Likewise, the number of actors involved in the removal process may also influence judges as well. While who is involved in removal is an important consideration, in many countries the threat and actual use of removal powers may pose no real constraint as judges are rarely removed. Further, removal of judges by actors who were not in office at the time of the judges' decision provide a weak *ex post* constraint on judges' behavior (Brinks and Blass 2017).

Other explanations of individual behavior on a collegial forum claim that diverse court compositions may have a deliberative effect by enhancing the quality of discussion ultimately leading to decisions that are different from those elicited from a homogenous decision-making body (see Spitzer and Talley 2011; Alarie and Green 2017). Accordingly, more diverse decision-making forums should lead to better decisions as a larger variety of positions and reasons for those positions are aired and considered (Gutmann and Thompson 1996). Judges may be influenced by the arguments made by judges with different characteristics and change their own positions accordingly. Contacts among diverse individuals in a collegial setting may change the behavior of individuals with the most extreme preferences (see Krackhardt 1998; Grossman et al. 2016) or the most prevalent.

A further proposition about how group composition influences individual choice relates to the influence of case features. As demonstrated by Fischman (2015), if judges are influenced by the characteristics of other judges with whom they deliberate, then the impact of case characteristics should vary depending on the context of the case decision including the case type, law being reviewed, and presumably case facts. However, if judges are influenced by other judges' behavior, rather than their characteristics, then decision-making is unlikely to vary in a meaningful way due to differences in the law and facts of the case (Fischman 2015: 809–810).

Unlike studies that focus on panel effects based on party or some innate characteristic (see Fischman 2015 for these references), on mixed selection courts, judges are predominantly defined by their selecting branch, and institutional design reinforces this emphasis by ensuring that there is a balance of judges who represent the different selecting institutions. Therefore, judges should be influenced by the presence and the votes of *other* judges who are selected by a diverse group of selecting institutions that diverge from their own.[20] Panel or presence effects based on institutional selectors should be more meaningful than those based on party associations. This leads to the following predictions:

H2.5: *Panel effects have an indirect and independent influence on judges' individual decisions to strike down laws as unconstitutional.*

H2.6: *Panel effects based on institutional selector have a larger effect on individual judges' decisions to strike down laws than panel effects based on party associations.*

While the above hypotheses focus on the influence of court composition that varies by the case due to quorum rules and judges' ability to take leave, many constitutional courts, including those in Chile and Colombia, additionally change a portion of their court periodically either because it is dictated by law to do so or because of nomination dates and term limits. Changing a portion of the court,

[20] While the empirical analysis tests in general for "panel" effects or group composition on individual choice, it is difficult to decipher and quantify endogenous effects – whether judges' votes change with the votes of other judges.

usually one-third or more in this way, allows new judges to enter the court while others exit. These compositional shifts influence individual behavior in two ways. First, as noted in the above discussion on panel effects, judges are influenced by the presence of other judges or the composition of the group. Thus, the presence of new judges on the court should alter these presence effects as new judges bring new characteristics to the court, new viewpoints, and new deliberative strategies, all which influence individual judge behavior. Second, and relatedly, new compositions of the court, which usually are not concurrent with changes in government and in any event only influence a proportion of the court, may result in the formation or the possibility of formation of new majorities, which in turn change how the court reacts to the political context in which it finds itself. As stated by Brouard and Hönnige (2017), due to the non-concurrence of judges' and elected politicians' terms and the changing nature of the composition of a constitutional court, the "VP [Veto Player] status of constitutional courts not only varies across systems, but also over time" (p. 19). Such changes or shifts in the courts' compositions vis-à-vis the elected legislature will in turn influence individual calculations regarding whether to vote their sincere preferences or to temper them to achieve other types of goals such as influencing the majority opinion, maintaining collegiality or increasing the legitimacy of the court. As a result, overall compositional changes should have an independent influence on judges' votes distinct from changes in the composition due to quorum rules. This leads to the following prediction:

H2.7: *Overall changes in court composition should have an independent effect on judges' decisions to strike down laws.*

2.5 COLLECTIVE CHOICE AND GENERAL PREDICTIONS

As indicated in Chapter 1, understanding collective decision-making requires understanding how individuals make choices as well as how individual choice is aggregated. One approach is direct in which judges' preferences are simply aggregated into a collective decision (Austen-Smith 2011). This direct approach involves sincere voting on the part of judges. A second approach is indirect and implies the possibility of strategic voting, which allows individuals to use their votes to serve some other goal. The following sections describe courts' preferences as well as how changes in the composition of a court and the benefits of collegial decisions provide a more complete understanding of decision-making on mixed-selection courts.

2.5.1 *Courts' Preferences*

What are the preferences of constitutional courts and how are they determined? Do institutions have preferences at all? It is commonplace in the social sciences to speak of institutions as having preferences because, although made up of individuals, institutions themselves take purposeful action. As a result, institutions are referred to as goal oriented, having "a life of their own" (Rogers Smith 1988: 95). It follows that courts as institutions have preferences that may be the same or distinct from those of individual judges. What are those preferences and what are they conditioned on? As with the discussion of individual judges' preferences, courts' preferences are multifarious and may vary depending on the case heard, law reviewed, legal issues implicated, and political context in which the court finds itself. Traditional attitudinalists, inferred court preferences as the aggregation (under majority rule) of individual preferences primarily oriented toward policy, constrained of course by the facts and law.

Independent of policy outcomes, courts have more fundamental preferences, which are related to sustaining or increasing their powers and stature as institutions. To achieve such preferences requires courts to avoid retaliation from the elected bodies, which may attempt to strip courts of their powers or budget or alter the composition of the court. This can be achieved through court packing, forced retirements or reduction of salaries.

Beyond avoiding retaliation due to a decision perceived by the legislature as adverse, courts may have interests in maintaining or increasing their powers in other ways, such as building their stature as viable, useful, and well regarded institutions (see Couso 2004). Indeed, courts are concerned about how others will perceive them through their decisions. As noted by Gilman (1993: 11, cited by Keck 2007: 328) speaking of the US Supreme Court, "judicial behavior – that is, writing opinions and making decisions – may be motivated by a set of interests and concerns that are relatively distinct from the preferences of particular social groups, the policies prescribed by particular economic theories, or the personal social and political loyalties and sympathies of individual judges." Institutions also have "institutional missions" (see Keck 2007: 328) and seek to maintain their power as well as sustain or improve their legitimacy and reputation. A court with a strong institutional reputation increases the costs to elected officials if and when they attempt to undermine the court. Substantial institutional stature also makes it more likely that other actors, such as non-governmental groups or the public, will severely criticize elected bodies if they attempt to punish or curtail the courts (see Vanberg 2005).

Courts may increase their powers by enhancing their own reputations in the eyes of other institutions or the public. Enhancing a court's collective reputation, shapes its "social and political influence" and may affect "overall judicial budget, salaries, pensions . . . as well the level of social prestige" (Garoupa and Ginsburg 2015: 23). To do this, courts need "to resolve legal disputes in accordance with their best understanding of the law" and by "maintaining coherent and defensible jurisprudential traditions" (Keck 2007: 328, citing Gilman 1993: 67–68, 79–80). As constitutional courts are tasked with upholding a nation's constitution, courts may achieve their goals, by doing just that in a legal and reasoned way (see Whittington 2000: 624).

Constitutional courts may strengthen or maximize their power through not only well-reasoned legal opinions but also strong opinions that are supported by as many judges as possible (Pritchett 1948; Danelski 1960; MacGregor Burns 2010; O'Brien 2011). It is especially crucial that decisions have much consensus when a court seeks to veto a law because such decisions are more controversial and more likely to illicit ire and retaliation from the other branches (see Kelemen 2013). Further, the public and non-governmental organizations are less likely to sound an alarm against government attempts to subvert a particular decision if the court itself seems divided or reflects conflict within the court itself. Weaker decisions are often those that appear to be motivated solely by judges' political associations, which could occur if judges associated with one party are seen to vote together. Issuing decisions that give the appearance of a politically biased court, such as split decisions based on judges' political associations could hurt the court's reputation, a concern that US Supreme Court Chief Justice Roberts seems well aware. Without strong opinions, the court's decisions will be questioned by other political actors, other lower courts, and the public.

2.5.2 *Implications of Selecting Institutions on Collective Decision-Making*

Courts' and judges' strategic calculations regarding whether to issue an unconstitutional decision not only depend on whether such an outcome is supported by a substantial number of judges on the court, but also on whether certain *types* of judges appear on a case together. Thus, the type of judges and their number dictates whether the court is more or less likely to veto a law. As indicated by the veto player literature, courts only serve as veto players (i.e., strike down laws) when, as a collective body, a majority of judges are willing to vote counter to or outside the preferences of the elected branches and there is a collective belief that the benefits of striking down legislation, which is more controversial than upholding it, outweigh any costs. A court's motivation for vetoing laws in some cases and not others is in part based on its desire to maximize its reputation and power, which is more possible when a case has a high percentage of judges of the type who are more likely to veto a law.[21] Conversely, vetoing laws will be repressed when there is a high percentage of judges of the type preferring legislative deference or when interests on the court are very diverse and there exists no anchor of like-minded judges on the court.

Additionally, in relation to panel composition, so important in individual choice, an increase in certain types of judges on any particular case will tend to induce other judges of a different type to support their position (see Beim and Kastellec 2014). The random variability of the exact number and type of judges appearing on any one

[21] Such a theory is similar to that presented by Austen-Smith and Banks (2011: 11) describing Myerson (1998, 2002) regarding individual voting behavior based on "the numbers of individuals of each type in the electorate" in large populations.

particular case requires that courts and judges constantly re-evaluate and make calculations about the composition of the court in which they find themselves on any particular case (see Myerson 1998 regarding population uncertainty in large groups). As noted above, courts have strong incentives to ensure that their decisions are supported by as large a number of judges as possible when they strike down laws as such decisions are more likely to be complied with by other institutions and the public (Peterson 1981; Naurin and Stiansen 2020). Further, greater numbers of certain types of judges on a case may render their arguments more persuasive.

Judges that disagree with the probable decision of a court must weigh whether revealing that disagreement will weaken the decision of the case and limit a judge's ability to mold the majority and whether the benefits to their reputation for dissenting overcome the benefit of a strong court decision. As a result, due to both the desire of courts as institutions to have decisions to strike down laws supported by as large a number of judges as possible and due to presence effects based on individual judges' institutional selector, it follows that the propensity of courts as a whole to issue judicial vetoes should vary with fluctuations in the presence of judges with certain selectors on each case. Based on these arguments:

H2.8: *Changing the composition of judges on a particular case defined by their selecting branch will result in different propensities of the court to strike down laws.*

H2.9: *Changing the composition of judges on a particular case defined by their selecting branch will have a larger effect on the court's overall decision to strike down laws than changes in the court's composition defined by party associations.*

The hypotheses above refer to movements in the proportion of judges sitting together on a particular case and do not provide information about which specific compositions would lead to higher instances of the court striking down laws. Considering the actual combinations of judges appearing on cases is more closely aligned to the realities of judging in the two exemplar courts. Certain combinations of judges are more likely to lead to the court striking down laws than other combinations due to majority decision-making rules, which are used by the two courts in their abstract review decisions analyzed here. In other words, a *critical mass* of judges of similar types and adjudication styles on a case should, on average, influence the courts' propensities to strike down laws. In some circumstances, however, the composition may not be determinative, such as when a judge's individual goals or beliefs on a particular issue conflict with the court's desire to reach unanimity.[22]

In choosing the mixed selection method, policymakers intended to have a particular balance of judges chosen by different institutions. However, because of

[22] The above theory is general and applies to most cases on average, but there may still be some cases in which the court's overall political party orientation may still be at work.

quorum rules, court compositions on these courts vary by case, such that some cases have a critical mass of activist-type judges, and some have a critical mass of deferential-type judges. The above arguments lead to the following:

H2.10: A critical mass of judges of a similar type will influence constitutional courts' propensities to strike down or uphold laws.

While judges' party associations for their individual choice have been downplayed, the party orientation of the full court may prove more influential at the court level in certain instances. Scholars studying judicial vetoes have insisted that party may be an important determinant of a court issuing a judicial veto when the court's collective political party orientation is outside that of the elected legislature (see Rogers 2001; Brouard and Hönnige 2017). On mixed selection courts in which judges are associated with more than two parties or in which there are non-partisan judges, courts will infrequently have a majority (i.e., >50 percent) of judges with party associations that differ from the legislature. However, on courts in which judges are associated with only two main parties, the court composition on many cases will allow judges representing just one party to hold the majority. In these situations, which are country specific, the party orientation of the court will become more important. If a court has a majority of judges from one party that is in line with those approving the legislation, then we would expect the court to defer to the legislature and infrequently strike down its laws. If on the other hand, the court has a majority of judges of one party on any given case that is in opposition to the legislators who drafted and approved the reviewed legislation then judicial vetoes are more likely. Based on the foregoing argument:

H2.11: The Court's propensity to strike down laws will be influenced by the Court's overall party orientation, but only if judges with a single party association make up more than 50 percent of the Court.

2.6 EVIDENCE TO SUPPORT THE THEORY

I have outlined a general theory of judicial decision-making on mixed selection courts that considers the goals of both individuals and collective institutions. The theory presented here is general, because mixed selection courts vary as to which institutions select judges and how many. In the empirical chapters, I will provide more specific hypotheses that focus on the Chilean and Colombian constitutional courts. My arguments are supported by a variety of evidence some of which is described in the country specific historical chapters and some in the empirical chapters.

First, policy debates and legislative histories of reforms support my predictions that judges with different institutional selectors decide cases differently. General arguments by policymakers regarding mixed selection courts and their purposes indicate that judges with different selectors under this method are expected to have unique voices and approach decision-making differently. In the case of the Chilean and Colombian constitutional courts, the legislative histories provide evidence that policymakers specifically chose mixed selection to provide balance in the decision-making forum among the different powers of government. These specific legislative histories support my argument that institutional selectors using mixed selection conceive that judges chosen by different institutions represent different styles of constitutional adjudication. Information from interviews also supports this claim.

Second, an analysis of individual data is needed to understand whether the *mechanism* I describe in the theory is present. Only analyzing aggregated data would mask the mechanism driving the court's overall choice. In other words, aggregate data may mask panel effects – the idea that judges with certain selectors appear to vote with those of different selectors when their presence predominates in a case. Third and in contrast, an analysis of aggregated data is needed to show that mixed selection, coupled with quorum rules, meaningfully influences case outcomes as suggested by the theory. It is possible that what we observe in the individual data, is quantitatively so insubstantial as to have little effect on the case outcome. In other words, the theory on individual choice on mixed selection courts is meaningless if compositional changes of the court fail to shift majority outcomes. Additionally, the aggregated data allows me to analyze whether shifting court compositions on any particular case away from either a balance of judges of any type or away from that intended by constitutional drafters alters the propensity of judicial vetoes. Prior to turning to the empirical analyses, the next chapters describe the prevalence and variation of mixed selection (Chapter 3) and the political and institutional context needed for a closer study of the two exemplar courts (Chapters 4 and 5).

3

Mixed Judicial Selection

Prevalence and Variation

3.1 INTRODUCTION

The selection of judges to high courts is politically impactful. Judicial selection is controversial because those choosing judges have implicit biases about who they believe will serve as the best judge. Political actors who select judges often assume that they can predict the behavior of their appointees and that judges will uphold their selectors' own policy preferences. Even institutional designers who support an independent judiciary create and amend the procedures for selecting judges and other bureaucrats precisely because they believe that they can control ex ante the outcomes of decisions that are delegated to these non-elected actors (Kiewiet and McCubbins 1991). While courts, especially high courts, are supposed to provide a powerful check on the other branches of government, the strength of the check depends on the type of judges chosen to serve on these high courts.

Despite much debate, there may be no ideal type of judicial selection. Rather, each method has its own costs and benefits, such as allowing political actors to influence appointments or striving for diversity, and each method depends on a country's history, political system, and legal culture. Many countries reform their judicial selection processes to expand or curtail the power of judges as well as to alter expectations regarding the competency of judges. For example, in 2010, the Turkish government amended its constitution, increasing the total number of judges on the Turkish Constitutional Court and also increasing the number of judges nominated by the elected branches as opposed to the non-elected judiciary (Varol et al. 2017). Similar examples of strong executives trying to gain control of judicial appointments have been seen in Hungary in 2011 and Poland in 2017 (BBC 2017). Argentina altered the selection method for its Supreme Court many times in the 1990s (see Finkel 2004) and most recently in 2013. Bolivia moved to electing constitutional court judges, although later President Evo Morales acknowledged that it was difficult to choose judges through elections (Driscoll and Nelson 2015). Likewise, policymakers in the US states have changed selection methods hundreds of times since the 1800s.[1] Historic judicial selection reforms in the US state supreme courts were due to concerns that some branches of government (the executive or legislature) had too much influence over appointments, although often new selection methods did not deliver on their expectations for ensuring judicial independence (Hanssen 2004). Even the longstanding method of selecting US Supreme Court justices has come under scrutiny in the wake of the Senate's refusal to confirm President Obama's appointment of Merrick Garland after the death of Justice Antonin Scalia in 2016 and President Trump's selection of one third of the Court's judges during his one-term presidency.

In reviewing judicial selection methods worldwide, more veto players in the selection process may ensure the selection of judges who are not hesitant to question or confront elected actors (Moreno et al. 2003). Those chosen by just one actor may decide cases in a more deferential manner. For example, unilateral appointment by a president rather than presidential appointment with senate confirmation may make judges more beholden to a singular political actor. Mixed appointment methods, the main focus of this book, are thought to make courts more independent in comparison to methods that require only one or two branches to select all judges. However, this expectation may be frustrated in situations in which those involved in selecting judges, despite belonging to different branches, share the same preferences or party (Kelemen 2013).[2] More veto points may not necessarily enhance or encourage judges to check other more powerful political actors if all the veto players involved belong to the same party or are in practice strongly controlled by one political actor, such as the president.

Legislative supermajority confirmation rules also may lead to judges who are more moderate, not beholden to a single political interest and thus able to act more assertively and impartially. This can happen in two ways. First, legislatures may be required to confirm presidential appointees by supermajority vote. It is thought that the supermajority rule would lead to the appointment of more moderate judges even under circumstances of unified government as it is unlikely that all legislators within a supermajority share the same political preferences or party as the president. In other countries, supermajority rules also may lead to more moderate judges in situations where the legislature chooses all judges (which occurs in some Latin

[1] The National Center for State Courts provides information for every state's judicial selection method and reforms to those methods from the 1800s to 2000s. The "History of Reform Efforts" is available from this organization at the following web site: www.judicialselection.com/judicial_selection/reform_efforts/formal_changes_since_inception.cfm?state=.

[2] Keleman notes how "[t]he appointment procedure is the point where constitutional justice and party politics intertwine in the most evident and manifest way." She notes that appointment methods do not lead to the selection of individuals with "unknown political beliefs" as most judges are appointed with some kind of party support. Rather, the appointment method along with other institutional guarantees helps to isolate judges from undue external political pressure.

American and European countries and two US states). For example, referring to the legislative appointment of Peruvian Constitutional Tribunal judges under a two-thirds supermajority rule since 1993, Dargent (2009) argues that "political negotiation was required to reach an agreement, making it more likely that the candidates elected would be independent ones." Supermajority legislative rules for appointment are likely to lead to more moderate judges in multiparty or highly fragmented party systems as well but not when the president has a strong hold over congress. However, Cameron (2002) warns that "explicit structural protections" may be only "parchment barriers to an aggressive executive or legislature unconstrained by voters who value judicial independence."

Another method used to select judges involves the use of judicial commissions or merit commissions to select judges. In general terms, a commission of individuals reviews the credentials of candidates and suggests a list of potential and qualified individuals to another veto player or political actor (such as a president or governor) vested with appointment authority. Several countries have adopted judicial commissions to review judges' credentials prior to appointment by other political branches (usually the president or prime minister) (Hammergren 2002). In Latin America, a wave of reforms led to many countries creating judicial commissions for selecting judges to high courts and other courts. However, Hammergren warns that "[a]s judicial selection bodies, they have made some advances over the prior arrangements, but still have a long way to go in defining what they are looking for in judicial candidates and how they will measure its existence" (Hammergren 2007: 117–118). Some commissions include judges and lawyers, while others include members of civil society.

While all kinds of selection methods have important implications for judicial behavior and the influence of high courts in policy making, in this book I have chosen to focus on courts that select judges through a mixed selection method due to the prevalence of this method of selection and its justifications by institutional designers. As will be seen, mixed selection is chosen for several key reasons – to increase diversity on the court, to allow for an equilibrium of different voices on the court (which in theory may make a court independent of any one political actor), and to improve decision-making. As a result, this method, as opposed to the other methods mentioned above, appears to seek diversification on the court in acknowledgment that representation of different powers of government and society on the court will enhance decision-making.

3.2 MIXED JUDICIAL SELECTION COMPARATIVELY

Mixed judicial selection allows specific branches of government, institutions, or sometimes other actors or nongovernmental groups to choose *different portions* of the court. For example, the Bulgarian Constitutional Court is illustrative of a mixed selection system because the president appoints four judges, the National Assembly four judges and the two high courts (i.e., the Supreme and Administrative High Courts) select four members. As will be discussed below, there is great variation in mixed selection systems as to both the number and kinds of branches that can unilaterally nominate or appoint judges and as to whether another political body must confirm these appointments.

The implications of mixed selection systems on decision-making have been rigorously debated. Governments that adopt mixed selection systems do so in recognition of the fact that courts, with broad powers to strike down laws with *erga omnes* effects and often a priori, should reflect both the pluralism of society and the different interests of elected and non-elected branches (see Sadurski 2008). Even Kelsen's much studied 1920 Austrian Constitutional Court was designed to allow each of the two houses of parliament to choose half of the sitting judges in acknowledgment that this court would serve as a negative legislature (Kelsen 1942; Stone Sweet 2011). In support of more modern-day mixed selection systems, the Venice Commission, a leading authority on constitutional law, has succinctly stated the various arguments in favor of this method. First, the Commission suggests in its Vedemecum[3] that mixed selection allows societal pluralism to be represented on high courts as follows:

> Society is necessarily pluralist – a field for the expression of various trends, be they philosophical, ethical, social, political, religious or legal. Constitutional justice must, by its composition, guarantee independence with regard to different interest groups and contribute towards the establishment of a body of jurisprudence which is mindful of this pluralism. The legitimacy of a constitutional jurisdiction and society's acceptance of its decisions may depend very heavily on the extent of the court's consideration of the different social values at stake, even though such values are generally superseded in favor of common values. To this end, a balance which ensures respect for different sensibilities must be entrenched in the rules of composition of these jurisdictions. (Venice Commission 2007)[4]

Second, the Commission suggests that because constitutional courts are empowered to decide important separation of powers issues, mixed judicial selection provides courts with judges who espouse or represent different views of key actors regarding issues related to separation of powers. In this regard the Venice Commission stressed:

3 The Venice Commission's Vademecum is a compilation of "opinions adopted by the Venice Commission" on constitutional justice and is "a source of reference for drafters of constitutions and of legislation on constitutional courts, researchers as well as the Venice Commission's members, who are requested to prepare comments or expertise" (p. 4). It is not a static document and thus is updated.

4 This quotation was repeated from a 1997 report citing CDL-STD(1997)020 entitled "The Composition of Constitutional Courts – Science and Technique of Democracy," no. 20 (1997).

> Constitutional jurisdictions may, by some of their decisions, appear to curb the actions of a particular authority within a State. The Constitution will often confer to the constitutional court the power to deliver its opinion on issues concerning the separation of powers or the relationships between the organs of the State. Even though constitutional courts largely ensure the regulation of these relationships, it may well be appropriate to ensure in their composition a balanced consideration of each of these authorities or organs. (Venice Commission 2007: 21)

This particular benefit has been echoed by national policymakers who have chosen to select judges in this manner including in Chile and Colombia, countries with mixed selection constitutional courts that are the focus of the historical and empirical analyses presented in this book. As noted by Driscoll and Nelson (2015), judicial selection methods, which have over time come to include more participants in the selection process, may "lessen the grip of the legislative and executive branches on the process, perhaps emboldening judges to participate more actively in the policy-making process" (p. 12) and altering what types of judges are selected in the first place (see Ríos-Figueroa 2011). By including judges chosen by diverse selecting institutions on constitutional courts, policymakers also hope to enhance the quality of deliberation and ultimately decisions. Finally, society may be more willing to accept constitutional decisions the more they appear "mindful" of different viewpoints or perspectives (Venice Commission 2007, 2015).

While accolades for mixed selection systems focus on how the involvement of more institutions in the selection process improves representation of different interests, enhances deliberation and decision-making, and helps society embrace decisions issued by constitutional courts, critics argue that in practice mixed selection cannot achieve these goals and this selection method may undermine the ability of a court to check the very branches involved in selecting judges. First, mixed selection may result in judges serving the interest of their appointers so closely that they do not exercise the necessary independence and impartiality to determine if a law is constitutional or not. For example, Sadurski (2008) claims that "[W]hen the appointment process is managed by different bodies acting separately from one another, one danger is that each of the bodies will elect their own judges who will then be held under obligation to be loyal to the appointing body" (p. 17). The concern of overt loyalty by judges to the institutions that select them is seemingly brushed aside by the Venice Commission, which suggests that the collegial nature of constitutional courts as well as their responsibility to uphold the constitution will safeguard against this (Venice Commission 2015: 8). In any event, if judges' votes are divided by the political branch that selects them, this may provide certain branches with additional veto powers, not provided to them within the normal legislative process.

A related criticism of mixed selection systems is that they may cause internal fragmentation within a court making it difficult to reach decisions. Indeed Ginsburg

(2003: 45) suggests that if separate bodies select their own judges, the court itself will become fragmented internally. However, the extent of this fragmentation depends "not only on the institutional interest, but also on the party allegiances and ideological orientations of the appointing bodies" (International IDEA 2017: 11). Disagreements on the court due to overt political differences of judges also may weaken a court's decisions or its reputation (MacGregor Burns 2010; Couso 2004; Kelemen 2013).

For the two constitutional courts analyzed in this book, lawmakers intended to have different branches of government choose a certain number of judges so that the courts themselves would be more representative bodies and independent from any one branch of government or institution. Mixed selection systems are a rarely studied theme despite their prevalence, variation, and implications for judicial behavior. Indeed, many judicial reforms have involved adopting, amending, or retreating from this selection method. For example, the first Chilean Constitutional Tribunal created under Allende in 1970 used a mixed selection system. The second Tribunal created under the Pinochet dictatorship in 1980 also employed a mixed selection method, which was amended to another mixed selection configuration after the country's return to democracy and then to yet another variation under constitutional reforms in 2005. Turkey also changed its mixed selection system in 2010 and again in 2017.[5]

In most cases, at least some of the institutions that choose judges under mixed selection systems also serve as "veto players" in the legislative process.[6] To determine the prevalence of this selection method and its main variants, an analysis of 130[7] constitutional courts or supreme courts with constitutional review powers was undertaken.[8] Of these 130 courts, 68 courts or 52 percent as of 2021 choose their constitutional court judges through some type of mixed selection method. Indeed, this prevalence suggests that this method warrants further specific study. Also a focused analysis of this method may provide insights not

5 See Appendix to the book, Table A1, for these and other changes.

6 Tsebelis (2002) defines veto players as "individual or collective actors whose agreement is necessary for a change of the status quo" (p. 19).

7 The number of courts reviewed has been increased since Tiede (2020) and are listed at the end of Appendix A1.

8 There are several sources for this table. One main source is the Constitute Project website. Elkins, Zachary, Tom Ginsburg, and James Melton. 2021. Constitute: The World's Constitutions to Read, Search, and Compare. Online at constituteproject.org. Additional sources reviewed were the Venice Commission (Council of Europe), which lists website links for constitutional courts at www.venice.coe.int/webforms/courts/; the CIA, World Factbook, which lists the appointment mechanism for all levels of national courts in a given country at www.cia.gov/library/publications/the-world-factbook/fields/2094.html/; Marjan Mavčič (2018); and court specific websites.

only into the behavior of courts but also the behavior of other bureaucracies, even the above described judicial commissions, which often select members using various forms of mixed selection.

While many countries use mixed selection to choose members of their highest courts, there are significant variations among them. Table 3.1 describes these variations for the sixty-eight constitutional courts mentioned above of which there

TABLE 3.1. *Variations in mixed selection of constitutional court judges as of 2022*

Constitutional court[a] in named country allows selection by:				
(1) Two political actors or branch appointers, unilaterally	(2) Three or more political actors or branch appointers, unilaterally		(3) Diverse political actors or branches nominate and others confirm	(4) Appointers include other non-typical actors or consider ethnicity
Andorra	Albania[b,c]	Italy[b]	Austria	Bosnia & Herz.
Armenia	Algeria[b,c]	Kazakhstan[c]	Belgium[d]	Cyprus
Belarus	Angola[b]	Korea[b]	Colombia	Guatemala
Benin	Bulgaria[b,c]	Madagascar[b]	Congo, Dem Rep.[c]	Guinea
Chad	Burkina Faso[c]	Mali[b]	Equatorial Guinea	Greece
Côte d'Ivoire[c]	Cambodia[b,c]	Mauritania[c]	Indonesia	North Macedonia
Ethiopia	Cameroon[b]	Moldova[b]	Latvia	Niger[c]
Germany	Cape Verde	Mozambique[b]	Lithuania[c]	Tanzania
Iran	Central Afr. Rep.	Romania	Luxembourg	
Lebanon	Chile[b,c]	Togo	Mongolia	Not easily classified:
Morocco[c]	Comoros	Tunisia	Montenegro	Ecuador[c]
Portugal	Congo, Rep. of[b]	Ukraine	Myanmar	Mauritius
Timor-Leste	Djibouti[b]		Serbia	Thailand
Turkey	France[c]		Spain	
	Gabon[c]			
	Georgia[b]			
	Haiti[b]			

[a] Constitutional Courts may also be referred to as Constitutional Tribunals or, in the case of Iran, the Guardian Council. They also may be referred to as Supreme Courts such as in Cape Verde, Mauritius and Timor-Leste in which the Supreme Court is the singular high court and has constitutional review powers.

[b] Courts that allow all three branches (executive, legislature, and judicial) to appoint a certain number of judges unilaterally.

[c] Courts in which the constitution calls for replacing a portion of the court after a certain period.

[d] Belgium's constitutional court must include six Dutch- and six French-speaking judges.

Note: See Appendix A1 to this volume for a specific description of the form of mixed selection for each court.

are four main variations, although the majority of these constitutional courts are classified within the first three categories.[9] The first main difference among mixed selection systems divides courts into those that allow diverse political actors to appoint judges *unilaterally* without confirmation or approval by another branch or political actor and those that require one branch to nominate judges and a different branch to confirm. In Table 3.1, most mixed selection systems, found in columns 1 and 2, allow political actors or branches to appoint a certain number of judges or a quota *unilaterally*.

In column 1, fourteen courts use two separate political actors or branches of government to unilaterally appoint judges, and in column 2, twenty-nine courts allow at least three separate political actors or branches to appoint unilaterally. Unilateral appointment allows each appointer to choose judges who best represent their interests, preferences, or ideal type of constitutional adjudicator. Generally, courts with two appointers allow the president and legislature to appoint. However, there are a few courts in this category, such as the German Constitutional Court, that allow each house of the legislature to appoint judges without executive involvement. Courts that allow three appointers, found in column 2 of the Table 3.1, are of two main varieties. Some courts allow all three branches (executive, legislative, and judicial branches) to be involved in appointment. Indeed, allowing all three branches to appoint unilaterally is the most prevalent mixed selection method and includes seventeen of the twenty-nine courts appearing in column 2 and labeled accordingly. The Chilean Constitutional Tribunal is included in this category. Other courts in column 2 allow the president and each house of the legislature (Congress and Senate) to appoint. While there are three separate political bodies that appoint, two of those bodies are separate chambers of the same legislative institution. Further, some countries with unilateral appointment also have other requirements that add to the diversity on the court. For example, the Constitutional Court of the Central African Republic allows each of the three branches to choose one judge unilaterally, but also allows other selectors and mandates that at least four of nine judges are women.

Another main variant of mixed selections allows separate political actors or branches to propose or nominate candidates but requires another branch to either choose from lists or confirm and appoint these nominations (found in column 3). Fourteen countries have constitutional or supreme courts with this type of selection. This method gives actors who nominate a first mover advantage over those who confirm and allows more veto players into the selection process. A variation of this type of method is seen on the Colombian Constitutional Court in which the president, the Supreme Court, and the Consejo de Estado (i.e., the highest

9 Appendix A1 at the end of this book provides more details on these courts' mixed selection methods and provides further information on judicial tenure and rules regarding replenishing portions of these courts.

administrative court) each nominate a third of the Court's judges. By choosing who can appear on a nomination list, nominating branches significantly influence a court's composition. However, the Colombian Senate's ultimate choice ensures that each nominator takes into consideration the preferences of the majority of elected legislators in this chamber. Further, in countries that require senates to confirm judicial candidates by majority and supermajority rules, the ultimate judicial selections may be more moderate and tend to appeal to more interests because a higher level of senate agreement is needed to confirm the nomination (see Dargent 2009). In multiparty democracies, approval by the Senate may result in candidates with a broad range of political interests.

There are eight constitutional courts with mixed selection, which either allow for some accommodation of a country's ethnic make-up or allow non-traditional actors to appoint judges (see column 4). As far as ethnic diversity, courts in this column either allow actors with different ethnicities to appoint judges or require ethnic or national identity quotas for the judges themselves. North Macedonia provides a unique way of ensuring that ethnicity on the constitutional court reflects that within the society. After armed conflict ended between ethnic Albanians and Macedonian security forces in 2001, the government made constitutional changes to several institutions under the Ohrid Agreement. In general, this agreement ensured that members of several institutions, including the country's constitutional court, included individuals who represented ethnic minorities especially Albanians, Macedonia's largest minority group.[10] Similarly, the Constitutional Court of Bosnia and Herzegovina considers the ethnic composition of the country when selecting judges and also allows unusual actors to select some judges (see Schwartz and Murchinson 2016).[11] Additionally, the Supreme Constitutional Court of Cyprus, with three judges, requires that one is a Greek, one a Turk and one a neutral judge and only this neutral judge can serve as the president of this court. Another variation of this type involves the Tanzanian Special Constitutional Court, which requires that half of the judges are appointed by the United Republic of Tanzania and half by

[10] Under this agreement, different majorities of the National Assembly choose different judges to serve on the Constitutional Court, which includes nine judges. The Assembly, by majority vote of all of its representatives, chooses six judges. The Assembly by a majority of "the total number of representatives belonging to minority communities in Macedonia" chooses three judges. In this way, one-third of the Court will represent judges approved by minority representatives in Parliament.

[11] For this Court, the House of Representatives of the Federation chooses four judges and the Assembly of the Republika Srpska chooses two judges. The remaining three judges are chosen by the president of the European Court of Human Rights with consultation with the presidency. The appointment method of this Court seems to reflect a concern for a fair distribution of different ethnic groups on the Court. However, the involvement in appointment of the president of the European Court of Human Rights is highly unusual and appears to reflect the volatility of this country's fragmented society as well as a lack of trust in political actors choosing judges to this important court.

the Revolutionary Government of Zanzibar to reflect these two entities historic separation and reunification.

Finally, several courts in column 4 allow some nongovernmental actors to appoint different numbers of judges. As mentioned by Moreno, Crisp, and Shugart (2003), courts may be more likely to check other powerful branches when judges chosen by civil society serve on the court. It is thought that nongovernmental appointees may represent important interests that diverge from the government. Further, because nongovernmental actors lack powers to remove disloyal agents who they choose, their appointees may be more impartial. In Guatemala, Guinea, and Niger, political actors or branches of government choose some constitutional court judges, but these countries also allow universities, attorneys' associations and in the case of Guinea and Niger human rights' organizations to choose judges. These three courts also impose professional requirements, such that some of the judges are professors, teachers, or representatives of human rights' organizations themselves. In this way, the mixed selection mechanism assures that some judges represent important interests in society. In an interesting variation on the inclusion of law professors, the Supreme Special Court in Greece requires two law professors to sit on the court when they are deciding issues of constitutionality or conflicts among courts, and these two professors are chosen by lots.

Column 4 of the table also includes three courts, the Mauritius Supreme Court, the Constitutional Court of Thailand, and the Ecuadoran Constitutional Court, which are not easily classified into one of the four categories. The Mauritius Supreme Court only allows the president to appoint the judges, but with whom he must consult varies by each appointment. In one instance, he must consult the prime minister, in another the chief justice, and finally in his third appointment the judicial and legal service commission. Similarly, in Thailand the king appoints all judges to the country's Constitutional Court, but the judges themselves come from distinct institutions, such as the Supreme Court and the Supreme Administrative Court as well as from a university's political science or public administration departments or from the director-general. In this case, while the king has full control over the appointments, the institutions from which specific judges originate vary by type. The Ecuadoran Constitutional Court allows a qualifications commission composed of members chosen by the legislature, the executive, and the transparency social monitoring institution to each pick three judges for the Court, who are then subject to a public exam and citizen oversight, and the Court must seek "parity" in the sex of the judges serving on this Court (Constitution of Ecuador, Article 434).

An important feature of constitutional courts with mixed selections, which distinguishes them from the extensively studied US Supreme Court, is that generally judges employed in these courts do not have life tenure. Of the sixty-eight mixed selection constitutional courts reviewed here, only the Austrian, Belgium, and Luxembourg Constitutional Courts provide judges with the safeguard of life tenure. Another group of courts allows judges to serve lengthy terms but requires that they resign at a certain age as in the case of the Armenian Court that limits judicial service to age sixty-five and the Indonesian Constitutional Court, which limits service to age seventy. Of the remaining mixed selection courts, judges have limited terms, ranging from five years on several courts to twelve on the German and Turkish Constitutional Courts. Thirteen of these courts allow their judges to renew their term one or two times, although the Ecuadoran Constitutional Court does not allow for immediate re-election. The remaining courts do not allow judges to be re-appointed at all. Several of these courts that disallow re-appointment also require judges to terminate their service at a certain required age. Judges' relatively short terms provide them with incentives to use their decisions to solidify their reputations ultimately used for further career advancement once off the bench (see Garoupa and Ginsburg 2015: 153).

Another institution that works in association with mixed selection systems involves rules for some courts that require that a portion of a court, usually one-third, be replenished every few years. This rule is used in conjunction with term limits and ensures that judges selected in a prior period serve with more recent appointees. In practice this means that at no time is the court ever reconstituted in its entirety and ensures that judges chosen by different politicians from different time periods decide cases together. Of the sixty-eight constitutional courts with mixed selection, sixteen have this partial replenishment rule mentioned in their constitutions. It should be noted that even if the constitution does not require partial replenishment at regular intervals, in practice this may occur informally on many constitutional courts when judges' appointments are staggered and they have fixed tenure without re-election, such as in the case of the Colombian Constitutional Court. As discussed in this book, the fluctuating composition of courts has consequential behavioral implications.

3.3 LATIN AMERICAN COURTS AS A FOCAL POINT

In order to illustrate the theoretical arguments presented in Chapter 2 about what determines judges' and courts' decisions to strike down laws within the mixed selection context, the book focuses on two mixed selection courts, the Chilean CT and the Colombian CC. As of 2021, only five constitutional courts in Latin America use mixed selection: Chile, Colombia, Guatemala, Ecuador,[12] and Haiti. The prevalence of this method in Latin America indicates the influence of the Kelsian or European model of constitutional justice in this region. However, this model has not been fully embraced by designers of constitutional courts within Latin America due to the prevalence of other models, some which mirror selection

[12] Ecuador is not a clear case of a mixed selection court as its judicial commission, which chooses the judges, is chosen through a mixed selection method but not the judges directly by different branches.

used by the US Supreme Court – such as in Argentina and some borrowing from the American states allowing for nonpartisan elections as in the case of Bolivia's Constitutional Court. Legislative appointments in Costa Rica, El Salvador, and Peru mirror two American states, and the use of judicial commissions in Panama and Paraguay for at least nominating or suggesting judges is somewhat similar to the US state merit selection procedures. While mixed selection of constitutional court judges is not dominant within Latin America, it is quite prevalent throughout the world and Latin America's rich history of frenetic judicial reforms makes the mixed selection method a possible candidate for future reforms for constitutional and other courts.

The two exemplar courts in Chile and Colombia that are the focus of the historical and empirical analyses in the remaining chapters allow me to test the theories about mixed selection courts in countries whose courts share a similar structure and are embedded in a similar legal culture within Latin American. Further, the region provides a dynamic arena for studying judicial vetoes within the context of democratization and constitutional reform. Historically, Latin American countries have experienced "cycles of democracy" (Smith 2012: 19). From a comparative perspective, the road to democratic consolidation in Latin America has moved with fits and starts with some countries experiencing democratic backsliding and leaving others with competitive authoritarian regimes (Levitsky and Way 2010) or "disjunctive democracies" in which new democracies make great strides in establishing free and fair elections, but fewer steps toward guaranteeing rights (Caldeira and Holston 1999). Still other countries in the region have been more successful in consolidating democracy despite significant challenges.

Although not always concurrent with democratic transitions, Latin America has witnessed cycles of constitutional reform intended to define the democratic order. A significant component of democratic consolidation and constitutionalism in Latin America has involved legal and judicial reforms,[13] used to address deficiencies in governance. Many reforms sought to empower courts specifically so that they may provide a counterbalance to the use and abuse of power by the elected branches. Policymakers also empowered courts to protect individual rights, due to their past abuse by authoritarian or weak governments and due to the regions' drafting of new laws and constitutions that often increased the breadth of rights needing protection. At the same time, courts in the region also have played an important role in both democratization and constitutional reform, often strengthening the rule of law and trust in institutions. Legal and judicial reforms in the region were also galvanized by foreign donors that were intent on democracy promotion in the 1990s, mirroring similar but less expansive efforts, undertaken during the law and development movement of the 1960s (see Merryman 2007). Oftentimes constitutional courts were asked to review the reforms themselves and their decisions were quite instrumental as will be described in subsequent chapters.

[13] Hammergren (2007) refers to judicial reform in Latin America as a "growth industry" (p. 1).

Reforms following democratization in the late 1980s and early 1990s in Latin America as well as those seen in Eastern Europe from the 1990s onward included "top down" and "bottom up" reforms (Carothers 1999). The former emphasized reforms to state institutions including constitutions, judiciaries, legislatures, local government, and civil–military relations (p. 158). As far as judicial and legal top-down reforms, these focused on rewriting codes, creating new or reinvigorating existing institutions, such as courts and prosecutors; improving professionalization of legal practitioners and increasing individual access to justice. "Bottom up" reforms emphasized civil society and the use of nongovernmental organizations, which often lobbied for specific legal changes. In Latin America, judicial and legal reforms were both top down and bottom up and according to Hammergren (2007) tended to focus on criminal law reforms, court modernization, professionalization and independence of the judiciary, access to justice, and finally improving the ability of courts to check other branches of government, the main focus of this book. The success of institutional reforms, and specifically those dealing with law and courts, varied widely although the reasons for unsuccessful reforms are largely acknowledged as due to a lack of knowledge about the place of courts in society (Hammergren 2007: 3) or an understanding of a country's legal and political culture, as well as a lack of resources and political will. Despite the dynamic nature of judicial reforms in the region, their impact on case decisions has been largely understudied.

3.4 WHY FOCUS ON THE CONSTITUTIONAL COURTS OF CHILE AND COLOMBIA?

Both Chile and Colombia have extensively reformed their courts and judiciaries from the top down and bottom up since the early 1990s. Change also continues, and both countries have recently experienced democratic successes and setbacks. For example, in 2019, Chile experienced large protests and violence providing the impetus for the convocation of a constituent assembly, approved by a referendum supported by 78 percent of those voting in October 2020. It is likely that reforms to the CT and its selection method will be contemplated by this assembly, although several commentators are concerned about the requirement that every article of a new constitution be approved by a 2/3 vote perhaps leading to horse-trading or a minimalist constitution (Bello 2021). In Colombia, the country passed a historic peace accord in 2017, ending fifty years of civil conflict, but the country's stability is still in question as many have contested the prosecution or lack thereof of former members of the Revolutionary Armed Forces of Colombia (FARC) and other guerilla groups in a newly created court and fighting seems to have continued (Turkewitz and Villamil 2021). Further, protests from 2019 through 2021 underscore citizens' discontentment on socioeconomic issues, similar to Chile. To fully understand the role of constitutional courts in dynamic democratization and constitution building contexts as well as their ability to check the elected branches, the historical and empirical analyses in this book focus on two decades of decision-making by the Chilean and Colombian constitutional courts starting from the early 1990s. Reforms in the 1990s to the Chilean Constitution of 1980 and reforms in 2006 significantly impacted the selection of judges to the Chilean CT and its powers. Colombia's Constituent Assembly drafted the 1991 Constitution, which created the current CC and justified both its powers and method of selecting constitutional court judges.

The two courts were chosen as they have similar institutional rules but operate within somewhat different political and social contexts. Both courts analyzed are highly regarded constitutional courts with vast constitutional review powers arising from the same legal tradition and similar colonial history. While sharing remarkably similar institutional rules regarding selecting judges and court powers, these two courts have had different influences on policy due to their different paths to democratic development as well as the issues that their respective governments faced over time. Chile and Colombia both experienced transitions in their governance in the late 1980s and early 1990s. While Chile transitioned from authoritarian rule to the provision of democratic elections in 1989 with some amendments to its authoritarian-born constitution, Colombia experienced an abrupt change in its governance, not due to regime change but rather due to the convening of a Constituent Assembly and its drafting of a new constitution in reaction to a perceived constitutional crisis. As a result of these two different historical constitutional drafting experiences,[14] Chile's Constitutional Tribunal (created under the military junta) emerged from authoritarian rule virtually unchanged, while Colombia's Constitutional Court was created as a new institution under a new constitution. As will be mentioned in the later chapters focusing on judges' and courts' decisions, the countries' varied democratic paths have at various times affected the ability of the two courts to invalidate laws.

While the exact origins of the two courts are significantly different, the conception, role, and rules governing the courts' powers and selection of judges are remarkably similar. Both courts are modeled after the Kelsian prototype created outside the judicial branch tasked with constitutional review (Kelsen 1928, 1942; Verdugo 2017). For these countries, Kelsian-type constitutional courts were created to serve as either the singular (the Chilean CT) or final (the Colombian CC) institution for determining the constitutionality of laws passed by the elected branches. According to Stone Sweet, Kelsian constitutional review was more

[14] Linz and Stepan (1996) note that a little-studied area related to democratic transitions and consolidations involves the constitution-making environment that may suggest when countries may falter in consolidation. Interestingly, of the six different constitutional drafting environments provided by these authors, Chile's in the 1980s under authoritarian rule and amendments later under a pacted transition represents the most constrained because it retained "a constitution created by a nondemocratic regime with reserved domains and difficult amendment procedures" (p. 82), while Colombia's was the most "free and consensual" because it involved a constituent assembly with the participation of democratically elected representatives (pp. 82–83).

appropriate for countries that were founded on principles of parliamentary sovereignty, which Kelsen viewed as "[l]ogically incomplete, and indeed unstable" (Stone Sweet 2011: 81). For Kelsen, the solution to such political systems rested in guaranteeing "the normativity of the constitution ... through the delegation of constitutional powers to constitutional judges" (p. 81). Kelsian courts, with their own unique variants, also have been adopted by American presidential regimes that were heavily influenced by European civil law and have been adopted by Eastern European countries as well prior to and after the fall of communism (Hanretty 2014; Stone Sweet 2000).[15]

Both the Chilean and Colombian constitutional courts have similar powers, which are extensions from the Kelsian model, allowing for abstract review of laws, although additional powers of a priori abstract review were provided to the Chilean Constitutional Court and less extensively to the Colombian Constitutional Court. Both courts also share mixed judicial selection methods. Due to the role of Kelsian constitutional courts in the legislative process, the selection of judges who will act as good policymakers was paramount. For some, the mixed selection system offered the perfect solution by allowing judges who represent different branches or institutions of government into the policy-making realm. Similar to a legislative body in which individual legislators represent different geographic areas, a court composed of judges chosen by the different branches of government or other groups is thought to allow judges to represent the diverse interests of government branches or society. As will be seen in the rest of the book, much of the justification for the mixed selection systems used by these two courts was in acknowledgment that these courts had pseudo-legislative features and thus required judges who represented different branches of government. Finally, both the Chilean CT and the Colombian CC are similar in that they are highly regarded both within and outside of the region, but both countries, like many others, are facing challenges to their democracies in the twenty-first century.

The empirical analyses in subsequent chapters are based on originally collected data of decisions of judges and courts on abstract constitutional review of laws enacted by the government still in power at the time of the decision. The book also is based on archival research of legislative histories regarding the courts' mixed selection method and powers, a review of the courts' decisions, and interviews of judges and court personnel in Santiago and Bogotá in 2016. The analysis of the two courts seeks to show how judicial selection and political and legal contexts affect the behavior of judges individually and collectively.

One advantage of studying two courts is that it allows for a careful and detailed analysis of a range of evidence in support of the arguments in this book. By only focusing on two courts, I am able to analyze high-quality individual and case-level

[15] Finally, some countries with unicameral parliaments, such as Bulgaria, created constitutional courts to serve as alternative legislative chambers.

data while at the same time being able to control for a myriad of other factors that would be difficult to hold constant in a comparative study involving many courts. The rest of the study focuses on these two courts by providing a historical analysis of the countries' legal and political context and the creation of the two courts as well as empirics to support the theoretical arguments presented in Chapter 2. The obvious tradeoff of studying these two courts in detail involves whether the empirics can be generalized beyond these two courts – a theme touched on in Chapter 9.

4

The Chilean Constitutional Tribunal in Political Context

4.1 INTRODUCTION

The arguments presented in this book suggest that decisions made by judges and courts in constitutional review cases depend both on the rules that govern the courts' composition and powers as well as the political institutions and context in which they work, all conditioned on the type of constitutional review and subject area of the law. This political context is especially important for understanding the work of the Chilean Constitutional Tribunal (CT) as this court was created under Pinochet's military dictatorship but has continued to operate to this day, through the country's transition to democracy, several changes of elected governments, and several constitutional reforms.

Chile's military coup of 1973 and the constitutional order established by the junta under its 1980 Constitution, as well as the way in which the country in 1989 negotiated a transition back to democracy, allowed initially for significant military oversight of the government. The 1980 Constitution and its amendments greatly constrained the Tribunal and the country's three branches of government allowing for "vestiges of authoritarianism" within political institutions, such as non-elected senators, and stifling the hopes of Chile's democratic transition. Not until constitutional reforms enacted in 2005, which came into force in 2006 (hereinafter the 2005 constitutional reforms or 2005 reforms) did Chile eliminate most of the nondemocratic elements that constrained the government. One controversial issue after the 2005 reforms is the continued requirement that legislatures must pass certain important but unusual laws, such as organic laws, legal precepts and treaties, under strict supermajority rules requiring 3/5 or 4/7 of the legislature to agree and thus providing significant veto powers to minority or opposition interests (see Sierra 2011).[1] Such rules will be

[1] Constitutional reforms also must be passed under supermajority rules, but this category of laws is not as unusual an area for supermajority legislative voting rules from a comparative perspective.

considered by Chile's Constituent Assembly, whose delegates were elected in 2021 after violent demonstrations in November 2019 forced president Piñera's government to commit to considering the drafting of a new constitution. Citizens voted to reform the constitution in a referendum with 78 percent approval in 2020.

Throughout the democratic era, both before and after the 2005 reforms, Chile's Constitutional Tribunal has worked to determine whether laws violate the constitution and to resolve several conflicts that divided parties, branches of government, and society itself. As discussed below in more detail, despite its origins during the authoritarian period and the presumably tight control by the junta over the Tribunal, during the span of the military dictatorship, the Tribunal found significant opportunities to positively influence the country's transition to democracy (Barros 2002). The Tribunal, which emerged in the first years of the democratic era, was composed of some judges who had been appointed by the outgoing junta. Later, the Tribunal consisted of fewer judges appointed by the junta, and more selected by the Supreme Court, arguably itself a deferential institution (Hilbink 2007). After the 2005 constitutional reforms, the Tribunal's selection mechanism allowed more constitutional judges to be selected by elected institutions and more of the judges appear to have party associations. Legislation reviewed by the Tribunal after the 2005 reforms was approved by politicians all of whom were elected. The first Bachelet and Piñera presidencies operated under divided government and the second Bachelet presidency under unified government. However, these three presidencies that followed the 2005 reforms never had the required supermajority of seats required to pass legislation, which the Tribunal is obligated to review. Since 2005, debate has continued about the Tribunal's powers and even its existence in Chilean democracy. And, it will certainly be taken up as a subject of debate of Chile's Constitutional Assembly at work at the printing of this book.

To understand the work of the Tribunal within Chile's societal and political context, this chapter briefly reviews the Chilean political and economic history prior to the coup. The chapter then reviews institutions and legal and political developments under the junta as well as developments leading to Chile's transition to democracy. The chapter follows with an analysis of the elected branches in the democratic era prior to and after the 2005 reforms. The final part of the chapter provides a rich description of the Tribunal itself.

4.2 BRIEF HISTORY OF POLITICAL AND ECONOMIC DEVELOPMENTS PRIOR TO THE MILITARY COUP

Chile is often characterized as a country with relative political stability from independence in 1818 until Pinochet's coup in 1973. This political stability, however, was punctuated with civil war and strong presidencies as well as fluctuations between a presidential system, a short-lived parliamentary system (from 1891 to 1925), and back again to a presidential regime (Oppenheim 2007). The country also experienced conflicts among political parties, class struggles, and contestation over economic policy. Prior to the coup, Chile was characterized as having one of Latin America's "most durable and progressive democracies" (Drake and Jaksić 1995: 1). The political landscape included a multiparty system with "three poles," which included a Right composed of conservative economic elites, a Center that was "reformist," and "a Marxist Left anchored in the working class" (Drake and Jaksić 1995: 2).

Prior to the installation of the military government under General Augusto Pinochet, the country was governed by the 1925 Constitution, which created a legislature with a Chamber of Deputies and Senate as well as a strong presidency and a Supreme Court with limited powers to find laws inapplicable in a given case rather than unconstitutional. Under this constitution, presidents had the ability to exclusively introduce legislation to increase expenditures in the general budget law, to change political or administrative divisions of the country, to tax, and to create public services (Mainwaring and Shugart 1997: 444–445). Under the 1925 Constitution, the president also had veto powers that could only be overturned by votes supported by two-thirds of each house of Congress.

The inability to resolve conflicts over the relative powers of the executive and legislative branches and the lack of an institution with constitutional review powers were problems that existed throughout Chile's history. The chronic conflicts between the executive and Congress were due to the manner in which the 1925 Constitution "had allocated the legislative and regulatory powers" making it unclear which regulatory powers were the "exclusive province" of the president and leading "Congress to often overstep its powers and to enter areas clearly within the domain of administrative action" (Couso et al. 2011: 122). Such interbranch conflicts increased in the 1950s. President Jorge Alessandri (1958–1964), frustrated with "what he perceived as the unconstitutional intrusion by congress into the regulatory powers of the president" (Couso 2011: 1528), attempted to propose legislation that would create a legal mechanism to resolve such disputes. Due to his lack of support in Congress, his proposal was not approved. However, at the same time and outside of political discourse, several legal organizations and law schools began discussing the creation of a Kelsian constitutional court. After Alessandri's presidency, Eduardo Frei assumed the presidency in 1964. Experiencing conflicts with Congress, similar to those experienced by his predecessor, he proposed reforms in 1965, which called for the creation of a constitutional tribunal. These reforms were approved by Congress, but not the Senate. Not until 1970, with a realignment of parties in Congress, were constitutional reforms approved creating Chile's first Constitutional Tribunal (Ley y Reforma Constitucional No. 17.284 de 23 de Enero de 1970).

This first constitutional court issued decisions from 1970 to 1973 when it was closed by the military regime. A description of this Tribunal's powers and appointment mechanisms is discussed in more detail in this chapter's final section where it is compared to the Tribunal later created in 1980. However, Verdugo (2017) provocatively asks why elected officials in 1970 would create such a constitutional court to check their powers. He suggests that conservative legislators supported the creation of a constitutional tribunal at this time because they assumed that Alessandri would win the 1970 election and a newly created constitutional court would help him to reach his policy objectives without a meddling Congress. According to Verdugo, these legislators failed to foresee the election of Salvador Allende, a Socialist (see also Mac-Clure 2011: 196).[2]

Not only did conflict between the executive and legislative branches make it difficult to secure policy, but as with other countries in the region in the twentieth century, politicians disagreed over how to achieve economic development. Specifically, politicians clashed over whether economic goals should be undertaken under a capitalist system, favored by US President John F. Kennedy's Alliance for Progress and subsequent American administrations, as well as Chilean presidents Alessandri and Frei or under a socialist system championed by Salvador Allende and his Unidad Popular, or UP party. While the Frei administration had "awakened great expectations on the part of the poor – workers, peasants, and the urban poor – who expected the state to enact programs that would help change their life circumstances" (Oppenheim 2007: 26), this group became disillusioned when promised reforms failed to allow for the revolutionary redistribution of wealth.

Such dissatisfaction set the stage for the presidency of Salvador Allende, who advocated structural reforms that would allow the country to transition away from capitalism toward socialism. However, Allende's presidential victory was hard won leaving him with a weak mandate. Allende secured only 36.2 percent of the vote in the first round of voting followed by his rival, Jorge Alessandri, who won 34.9 percent of the vote. At the time of the election, if neither of the two top candidates received an absolute majority of votes, Congress would choose between the two. Legislators from the Right strongly considered choosing Alessandri rather than Allende, who had received more votes, but ultimately confirmed Allende as president. Allende's Popular Unity or Unidad Popular (UP) party initially controlled 42 percent of the seats in Congress and later dipped below this level.

Initially, Allende's campaign strategy of freezing prices and raising wages resulted in a consumer buying boom. Remaining true to his campaign promises, upon assuming office, Allende and his UP party sought at once to structure economic programs that would break Chile's dependence on other countries and create the basis for socialism. The UP relatedly strove to foster employment, welfare, and equality. Despite these lofty goals and after initial successes, such as a unanimous vote in Congress to nationalize the copper companies (Skidmore and Smith 2001: 126), the UP party's internal fragmentation and the government's hold on only a minority of seats in Congress undermined Allende's policy objectives.

2 Mac-Clure (2011) notes the irony of the creation of the CT under Allende as his supporters from the left, under Frei, opposed it (p. 196).

Further, judges on the Supreme Court and lower courts were appointed by previous governments and generally disfavored the UP plan. Finally, the Allende government's main goal of socialism ran counter to the interests of the United States during this Cold War period and many middle-class Chileans feared that the UP plan would hurt their own economic interests. Over the course of Allende's short term in office, both his political rivals and increasingly his allies as well as many other societal actors began to oppose the UP's program. The economy began to falter in 1972. High inflation and a limited supply of goods, including food, further weakened popular support for Allende. At the same time, society and political parties polarized within Chile as it faced destabilizing actions instigated by the United States.

Allende's weak and fragmented political support and opposition from the Right made it difficult for him to gain congressional approval for one of the main parts of his economic program – the creation of the APS or *área de propriedad social* or social property area. The APS provided a blueprint for socialism, including the governmental takeover of certain industries and increased workers' influence within such industries. Allende in 1970 had initially attempted to get the UP to agree to support a constitutional amendment to create the APS, however, the UP did not support this approach. Despite a consensus within the UP about the socialization strategy, internal disagreements as to how to structure the area delayed the presentation of appropriate legislation on the issue. As a result, Allende sought other "legal options" (see Oppenheim 2007: 53) including direct sales with owners of private property and a referendum on the constitutional amendment. Such options had drawbacks, so instead Allende resorted to issuing "intervention and requisition decrees" to attempt to socialize industries, which did not in fact create the desired APS (Oppenheim 2007: 54).

The heavy use of decree powers, even if somewhat ineffectual in furthering Allende's goals, led to more conflicts among political actors, and factions developed within the UP with some favoring gradual socialization of the economy, while others, especially those representing the Partido Demócrata Cristiano (PDC) or Christian Democrats, favoring a slower approach. After much delay, the PDC introduced its own APS bill envisioning a more constrained approach to socialism, which Congress approved. Subsequently, Allende vetoed the bill and Right-wing parties in Congress overrode Allende's veto of the original bill with a majority vote. Allende contested the override opining that 2/3 of Congress must approve the veto override, rather than a simple majority, although constitutional drafters of institutional reforms in 1970 had not been clear on this point (see Verdugo 2017). To resolve the impasse, some wanted to invoke a referendum, which again under the 1970 reforms seemed the appropriate option when the executive and legislature could not agree on policy. However, the constitution also was unclear on this point. Allende supporters argued against the referendum concerned that in the future "[t]he opposition-controlled legislature would be able to rule by constitutional amendment unless the president was willing to call repeated plebiscites" (Oppenheim 2007: 61).

Perhaps in order to avoid these hypothetical repeated referendums and further protests, Allende chose to appeal to the newly created Constitutional Tribunal to resolve the conflict. Those opposing Allende contended that the Tribunal lacked jurisdiction to hear the matter and threatened the court should it rule in favor of Allende (Verdugo 2017: 490, citing Silva 2008).[3] Ultimately, the judges refused to hear the case claiming they had no jurisdiction to do so (Rol #15, 1973). Indeed, "amidst the worst constitutional crisis the country had experienced in a half-century, the Constitutional Court was not even able to fulfill its role of arbiter between the executive and legislative branches, which was precisely the function for which it had been created" (Couso 2011: 1529).

Due to the Tribunal's treatment of the APS case, Allende had only a short time to enact the PDC's version of the law that he had previously vetoed. He attempted to delay its promulgation by diluting the PDC's version and only approving the parts of the law he had not initially vetoed. The Comptroller General rebuked Allende and "the opposition declared that the rule of law was broken" and at this point there existed "no institution capable of arbitrating the conflict" (Verdugo 2017: 491). Congress impeached several secretaries of state and other officials and some members of Congress claimed that the UP government had "committed illegalities," which subsequently led to UP representatives walking out of Congress. Polarization within the political institutions led to further political and social conflicts, civil disorder, and economic distress, eventually allowing for the military junta to take over the government (Faundez 1980).

Valenzuela (1994) attributes the democratic breakdown in part to Chile's presidential system (versus a parliamentary system), which failed to allow for more negotiations and compromises within a polarized party system. Faundez (1997) counters that negotiations failed not due to presidentialism, but rather due to the extremely polarized political context that would have prevented either side from "persuading its supporters" from accepting any agreement with their rivals (p. 319). Further, the Constitutional Tribunal's refusal to provide guidance did not assuage the crisis. The anticipated coup occurred on September 11, 1973, and at first was supported by many as a way of alleviating the economic and political conflicts associated with Allende's presidency.

4.3 CHILE UNDER THE JUNTA (1973–1989)

Upon coming to power in 1973 after a violent *golpe de estado*, the junta dissolved Congress and eliminated the country's first constitutional court. The junta exiled, "disappeared," tortured, and killed thousands of Chileans and others. Torture

[3] Enrique Silva was a constitutional court judge at the time appointed by Allende.

centers were created throughout the country including those with especially notorious reputations located in the National Stadium, on the naval ship *Esmeralda*, and at Villa Grimaldi to name only a few. A "Caravan of Death" led by one of Chile's military generals traveling through northern Chile killed scores of political prisoners.

Despite the junta's suppression of opposition voices and subversion of political institutions, Pinochet and the junta planned to return the country to some type of what they referred to as democratic rule. In 1977, in his infamous *Chacarillas* speech, Pinochet described his vision for the country's political governance, which would take place in three phases from 1977 to 1985. First, the government would get rid of the 1925 Constitution and create a new constitution that would allow for the gradual transfer of power from military to civilian rule. In the second phase, a transition would occur allowing cooperative military and civilian leadership of the government, at least in theory, but with the junta exercising power through the legislature and a newly created Consejo de Seguridad Nacional de Chile, or COSENA. In the third phase, voters would be allowed to choose two-thirds of the legislature, which would in turn choose the president. After 1985, the country would prepare for presidential elections.

After taking power, Pinochet and the junta repeatedly emphasized that all their efforts to recreate institutions were done in the name of democracy and the rule of law.[4] To make good on his purported commitments as well as his time frame, Pinochet created a constitutional drafting commission, the Ortúzar Commission, to oversee the drafting of a new constitution although Pinochet supplied them with an outline of "what he wanted" (Oppenheim 2007: 116). Despite commencing its work in 1973, the Ortúzar Commission did not complete its draft until 1978, at which time it was sent to the Council of State, which made some additional changes. After these revisions, a working group composed of military members chosen by Pinochet added additional changes to the draft more aligned with his original instructions. The resulting constitution of 1980 was approved by a plebiscite, which many voters may have been too scared to oppose.

Chile's 1980 Constitution established a framework for slowly transitioning the country to a democracy, which would allow the military to guide or oversee institutions to varying degrees according to the timetable outlined in Pinochet's speech and later changed slightly. To this end, the 1980 Constitution included two types of articles – transitory and permanent. The transitory articles institutionalized the phases of government outlined in Pinochet's speech until a plebiscite would be held in 1988 to elect a president. The permanent articles established a "protected

[4] In reviewing many of the laws enacted under the junta in Chile's Congressional Library in Santiago in 2016, I noticed the extensive and ironic use of the terms "democracy" and the "rule of law."

democracy" guided by the military. This would occur after the presidential election, which at the time Pinochet assumed he would win.

As to governance under the military junta, the transitory provisions of the 1980 Constitution provided for strong presidential powers and empowered the junta to act as a legislative body (see Couso 2011: 1531; Barros 2002: 49–51). The transitory provisions rendered General Pinochet irremovable as chief of the army – a post he held until 1998. The constitution also restricted many individual and collective rights, such as restrictions on political parties, labor unions, and free press (see Heiss and Navia 2007). The 1980 Constitution created Chile's Constitutional Tribunal, which was the second in the country's history and has existed continuously since that year. The 1980 Constitution also created the aforementioned Consejo de Seguridad Nacional, or COSENA, made up of the president of the nation, the presidents of the Senate and the Supreme Court, the heads of all three branches of the armed forces, and the national police, or *carabineros*. This composition, as originally conceived under the 1980 Constitution, provided the military with the absolute majority needed to "make decisions and adopt agreements" (Siavelis 2000: 38).

The permanent articles of the 1980 Constitution, established a framework for the "protected democracy," which would exist after a president was elected in 1989. Jaime Guzmán, a prominent member of the drafting commission,[5] viewed democracy as an "inevitable, but rather dangerous, regime – one that any modern society should have but that was susceptible to manipulation by demagogues to the detriment of private property rights" (Couso 2011: 1531). As a result, the country needed a "model of constitutionalism" that would "prevent contingent majorities" from fundamentally changing the political system designed under the authoritarian regime (Couso 2011: 1532). In accordance with Guzmán's view, permanent provisions of the constitution allowed the military to intervene in government affairs preventing it from operating in a completely democratic manner. In essence, the provisions ensured that the military had a veto in policy making and that the political and constitutional order could not easily be changed without acquiescence from the military. The provisions also made it quite difficult to reform the constitution, requiring 3/5 approval for such changes (Constitution 1980, Article 116).

Not only did the junta create a blueprint for governance prior to and after democratic elections to be held in 1989, but Pinochet also ushered in extensive neoliberal economic reforms, championed by the "Chicago Boys," which many argued contributed to Chile's short-run economic success in the early 1980s. Guided by Milton Friedman, who visited Chile in 1975 and favored a free market model for the country, Pinochet instituted a program to support economic recovery by tackling extreme inflation occurring under the Allende government. Besides this "Shock

[5] Gúzman worked under the Pinochet administration and was the founder of the Unión Demócrata Independiente (UDI).

Treatment," Pinochet sought to privatize industries that had been taken over by the Allende government. While Pinochet's initial economic programs proved fruitful, by 1982 the country was shaken by an economic crisis due to a deteriorating balance of payments and lower external credit and bank failures, leading the government to devaluations, which caused more banking failures, an increase in unemployment, and a drop in GDP. While economic crises have precipitated democratic transition in many countries, Haggard and Kaufman (1995) classify Chile at this time as an anomaly because the authoritarian regime survived this severe economic crisis. These authors attribute Pinochet's survival in the 1980s to "institutional characteristics that strengthened the hand of the military" as well as the "absence of serious intra-elite divisions" that "provided the political basis for a more coherent response to economic difficulties" (p. 75).

4.4 CHILE'S DEMOCRATIC TRANSITION

Chile's 1980 Constitution provided a blueprint for transitioning the country away from military rule toward a protected democracy, which involved a plebiscite to take place in 1988 to determine whether a candidate proposed by the junta (Pinochet himself) would continue running the country "as an 'elected' president" (Linz and Stepan 1996: 206) for another eight years (i.e., from 1989 to 1997). If citizens voted "no" on the plebiscite, then democratic elections without a junta candidate would take place in 1989. The 1980 Constitution also provided direct guidance for Chile's transition to democracy, by including two types of previously mentioned provisions: permanent and temporary. The permanent provisions would provide structure for the envisioned guided democracy after the plebiscite and the transitional provisions would provide structure to the prior transitional period from March 11, 1981, to 1989. The 1980 Constitution included twenty-nine transitional provisions and transitional Article 21 stated which specific permanent provisions of the Constitution were suspended until the plebiscite was held in 1989.

According to Barros (2002), attempts made by the junta to retain power, despite its promised election, were stymied by disagreements fomenting within the junta itself. These disagreements in turn allowed institutions, such as the Constitutional Tribunal (CT), an opening to issue decisions regarding future elections, which ultimately defenestrated the junta. As regards the 1989 plebiscite and subsequent envisioned elections, the 1980 Constitution again provided some guidance through both permanent and transitory provisions. Permanent provision 18 stated that there "shall be a public electoral system" as provided in the Constitution and an organic law that "shall regulate the manner in which electoral processes and plebiscites will be conducted." Permanent Article 84 of the Constitution required the Tribunal Calificador de Elecciones, or Electoral Qualifying Tribunal, to take "cognizance of the general scrutiny and qualification" of presidential and congressional election results as well as plebiscites and called on the Tribunal to resolve any complaints about the electoral process. While these permanent provisions were to govern the operation of the Electoral Tribunal *after* the plebiscite on Pinochet, the Constitution's transitory Article 11 stated that the Electoral Tribunal should become effective thirty days *prior* to the first election of Senators and Deputies, which was scheduled to take place in 1989.

The Organic Law on the Tribunal Calificador de Elecciones discussed both the powers and rules governing this tribunal and more controversially when it would begin operation. In a mandatory constitutional review case triggered by an organic law, the task of the CT judges was to determine whether the law violated the provisions of the Constitution of 1980. The CT faced an interpretive conundrum because the Constitution's transitory Articles 11 and 21 seemed to contradict one another and some of its permanent articles. Therefore, the Tribunal had to determine whether the date creating the Electoral Tribunal was required by transitory provision 11 or whether instead it violated the Constitution's permanent Articles 18 and 84.

In its decision, the CT declared unconstitutional, by a slim four to three majority, the organic law's own transitory provision and its final article creating the Tribunal Calificador de Elecciones, tasked with supervising the agreed upon elections of December 1989. The CT, in Rol #33 (1985), found the Organic Law (Ley No. 18.460)[6] in violation of the Constitution's Article 84 because it permitted the new electoral court to exist only thirty days prior to the 1989 elections and not prior to the 1988 plebiscite itself (Figueroa 2013: 402; Couso 2011: 1531; Valenzuela Somarriva 2006). Accordingly, the CT stated that the Electoral Tribunal must begin operation prior to the presidential plebiscite to properly oversee it and must promulgate further organic laws to assure the constitutionality of the plebiscite itself (p. 296). As to the contradictory transitional Article 11 of the Constitution, which seemed to require the later start date, the CT found this article inadmissible as it contradicted other transitory and permanent provisions of the Constitution.

The decision pitted the four-justice majority against a minority of three judges on the issue of constitutional interpretation.[7] The majority argued for a "harmonious, systematic interpretation of the constitution" (i.e., both transitory and permanent provisions), which took into account the "letra y espíritu de la Constitución" (i.e., the letter and spirit of the Constitution), while the minority wanted to interpret the provisions literally and "true" to the "original intent" of the framers (see Barros 2002: 296). According to the majority, a contrary interpretation would not only undermine the spirit of the constitution "but also the common meaning that is the bases of all logical interpretation that would expose the referendum itself to an indictment of

6 El Proyecto de Ley Orgánica Constitucional sobre el Tribunal Calificador de Elecciones (1985).

7 Ministers Ortúzar, Aburto, and Urzúa dissented.

legitimacy with grave damage to the normal development of future institutionality"[8] (Rol #33, October 3, 1985).

In response to this decision, the junta's legislative body changed the organic law eliminating the troubling transitory article and published the new law in the official daily on November 15, 1985. The landmark decision provided a layer of important oversight and accountability to the atmosphere surrounding the plebiscite. According to Barros (2002), the Tribunal's ruling

> was not the first to impugn the constitutionality of norms enacted by the Junta and the president. However, it was without doubt the most important, as it compelled the regime to enact further legislation and laid the conceptual foundation for later rulings which assured that the eventual plebiscite on the Junta's candidate for the second presidential term (or any plebiscite to ratify a modification to the constitution) would take place under scrupulous conditions of impartiality. (p. 293)

Without this decision, Pinochet's defeat would have been all but impossible (Couso 2011: 1531; see also, Valenzuela Somarriva 2006, one of the judges in the majority for his and other officials' comments on the importance of the decision).

After this decision, the CT continued to rule on laws that related to political representation and elections, looking toward the 1988 plebiscite and 1989 elections. The CT proved instrumental in upholding rights related to due process and equality before the law as well as free association counter to the desires of the junta. In this regard, in 1986, the CT struck down portions of Ley 18.556 establishing a system of voter registration and electoral services (Rol #38) and in 1987, struck down portions of the much-anticipated Organic Law of Political Parties (Rol #43; Figueroa 2013: 402; Navarro Beltrán 2011).

While the CT helped set the stage for citizens to vote against the military government, Pinochet's defeat also has been attributed to efforts by opposition party members who actively campaigned, registered voters, and enlisted electoral observers to monitor the plebiscite and assuage the fear and apathy of voters. Chile's former president Lagos (2006–2010), in his memoir, indicates that a turning point in citizens' desire to participate in elections and oppose Pinochet occurred during an April 25, 1988, television program in which Lagos himself, representing the center-left Partido por la Democracia (PPD), publicly denounced Pinochet declaring that a "no vote" "would mark the end of the dictatorship" and prevent "another eight years ... with torture, assassinations, with violations of human rights" (Lagos 2012: ix). To the surprise of many, including Pinochet, the plebiscite of 1988 resulted in a "no vote", allowing democratic elections to occur in 1989 without Pinochet as a candidate. In this referendum, Pinochet did not receive the needed 50.1 percent of

[8] The exact wording in the case is "sino, también el sentido común, que es base de toda interpretación lógica, ya que ella podría importar exponer el plebiscite mismo a un enjuiciamiento de legitimidad con grave perjuicio para el desarrollo normal de la futura institucionalidad."

votes required to continue as an elected president, only receiving 44 percent of the votes, which Linz and Stepan (1996) note was disturbing as at that time he had received "one of the highest votes of a nondemocratic incumbent in any transition" (p. 206, fn. 3). As part of the transitional provisions of the constitution, Pinochet remained as commander in chief of the military until 1998, well into the democratic period. He was sworn in as a senator for life in March of 1998.

As a result of this "no vote" and in anticipation of the upcoming democratic elections scheduled for December 1989, the junta, and moderate members of parties from the center left and right, began negotiations to amend the 1980 Constitution. By all accounts, the amendments favored the military at the expense of the opposition parties, who felt they had little room to maneuver in order to ensure that the subsequent democratic election would indeed go forward (see Heiss and Navia 2007: 166). The 1989 constitutional reforms included fifty-four amendments that ensured the continuance of "vestiges of authoritarianism" after the transition but made some changes related to civil rights and the powers and procedures of the elected and non-elected branches.

As to political and individual freedoms, the 1989 reforms eliminated in part the Constitution's controversial Article 8, which allowed the government to find political parties and other groups unconstitutional and criminally punish their members if they threatened or attempted to subvert the Chilean republic (see 1980 Constitution, Article 8). The 1989 reforms also disallowed punishment of legislators who voted for laws that the CT later held were unconstitutional (Heiss and Navia 2007: 174). The amendments of 1989 did, however, list "human rights" as a duty for the state to defend (Article 5); however, states of exception allowed for the suspension of such rights.

As to the elected branches, the 1989 reforms affected both the executive and legislative bodies. As regards the presidency, the amendments prevented the executive from dissolving the lower house of Congress. The amendments placed limitations on the president's ability to declare a state of emergency by requiring agreement by the COSENA. As noted by Siavelis (2000), the amendments also provided Congress with important executive oversight functions, including the ability to create investigatory commissions, make observations, and request information.

Regarding the legislative branch, the 1980 Constitution had envisioned the creation of two houses of congress, which included a Senate with twenty-six elected members and two types of non-elected senators: nine appointed for eight-year terms as well as former presidents, who had previously served six years, for lifetime positions. However, the constitutional reforms, agreed upon prior to the transition, increased the number of elected senators from twenty-six to thirty-eight. For the Senate, the military government negotiated the appointment rather than election of nine senators, including two former justices of the Supreme Court, one former comptroller general, and four former commanders of each branch of the armed services, one university president, and one former cabinet minister. Linz and Stepan

(1996) argue that the non-elected senators created a "key de jure limitation on democratic sovereignty, which in turn limited the democratic government's authority to generate new policies" (p. 207), a constraint that extended until the implementation of Chile's constitutional reforms in 2005.

The 1989 reforms also changed some of the rules for legislative voting. In general, regular legislation only required passage by an absolute majority of both houses in two consecutive sessions. However, the 1989 amendments made it more difficult to amend the constitution in certain specific substantive areas. Constitutional reforms must be approved by 3/5 of each house of Congress, unless they dealt with presidential powers, constitutional rights and obligations, the armed forces, or the CT in which the 2/3 of legislators in both houses must agree (Siavelis 2000: 41; Mainwaring and Shugart 1997: 446). Further the 1989 reforms changed the rules for Congressional passage of legal precepts, organic laws, or Leyes Organicás de la Constitución, and treaties requiring their approval by various supermajority voting rules (i.e., 3/5 and 4/7).

The military government used these organic laws as a vehicle for controlling future democratic governments from changing the junta's policies. For example, three days prior to the democratic transition, the junta placed its education policy into an organic law (Ley Orgánica Constitucional de Enseñaza, or LOCE), which transferred the ownership and administration of schools from the national government to municipalities and favored a voucher system allowing municipal and private schools to compete. By requiring the education policy to be approved through an organic law, these policies became nearly impossible to change especially with the non-elected senators present (Elacqua and González Soto 2014: 282). As will be seen later, problems with the country's approach to education have plagued Chile in the democratic period.

As to the non-elected branches, under the provisions of the 1980 Constitution, the military was to have a strong role in shaping and protecting Chile's nascent democracy. First, Pinochet ensured that he was the commander of the armed forces from 1990 to 1998. Constitutional amendments in 1989 favored a strong military role in the new democracy, but as argued by Heiss and Navia (2007), negotiations led to the junta dropping some of the provisions related to the military's role in the new government in exchange for making the military more autonomous. The reforms changed the composition and the powers of the COSENA. Civilian members were added such that the COSENA was comprised of four military commanders in chief and four civilians, thus requiring the military to have the acquiescence of at least one civilian to support its positions. Through the COSENA, the military exerted influence over the democratic government, allowing it to appoint lifetime senators and choose some members of the Constitutional Tribunal.

The amendments also increased the military's powers in civilian arenas and its autonomy (Heiss and Navia 2007: 167). To add to this autonomy, prior to Aylwin's assumption of the presidency, the junta promulgated a new Organic Law of the

Armed Services (i.e., Ley No. 18.948), of which the CT approved most of its provisions (Rol #98), with one judge dissenting in part. This law prevented democratically elected presidents from forcing military officers, such as Pinochet and others who had committed human rights abuses, into retirement and "made the gate keeping of nominations to major general (from which future commanders in chief could be drawn) the exclusive prerogative of the armed services, thus reinforcing ambitious officers' dependence on Pinochet" (Linz and Stepan 1996: 208). The law also precluded lowering the budget of the Armed Forces below its 1989 level and provided it with 10 percent of foreign exchange from the export of copper.

As to other non-elected political actors, Pinochet attempted to wield his influence when it was clear that he had lost the possibility of being elected as president. Accordingly, he offered Supreme Court judges' financial incentives to retire so that he could appoint younger members who could serve until the mandatory retirement age of seventy-five. As to the Constitutional Tribunal, changes were made as to which authorities could appoint judges under the Tribunal's mixed selection system (which included three appointments by the Supreme Court and two by the COSENA). The referendum on these pre-transitional constitutional amendments passed by 85.7 percent of the votes in July of 1989.

4.5 POLITICAL INSTITUTIONS IN THE DEMOCRATIC PERIOD

To fully understand the behavior of Chile's Constitutional Tribunal after the democratic transition, it must be analyzed under two distinct periods. The first period, spanning from Chile's return to democracy in 1990 until the passage of constitutional reforms in 2005, was constrained by the 1980 Constitution allowing for military oversight. The second period spans from the enactment of the 2005 constitutional reforms in 2006. During this second period, Chile's political institutions were modified by constitutional amendments that eliminated many of the authoritarian aspects of the 1980 Constitution. These major reforms allowed the president to dismiss commanders of the armed forces and police, rendered the COSENA an advisory board to the president rather than an independent agency with veto powers, and eliminated the non-elected senators. The reforms also changed the composition and powers of the Constitutional Tribunal. Some scholars suggest that reforms occurring fifteen years after Chile's democratic transition were only possible after the center right agreed to such reforms perhaps brought on because Chile's center left, or Concertación, acknowledged that it would soon lose power to the opposition for the first time since the country's return to democracy (see Montes and Vial 2005; Heiss and Navia 2007 for an overview).[9]

9 Siavelis (2013) notes that immediately after the transition, parties of the Right were supported by powerful economic interests. Gradually, however, the Right began to have broader appeal, perhaps leading to the election of Piñera.

Arguably a third era, of which the complete effects are beyond the scope of this book, began in 2015 when Chile passed electoral reforms effective in 2017. These reforms most significantly changed the electoral system from a binomial to a more proportional system (see Gamboa and Morales 2018) and introduced gender quotas. Congressional elections in 2017 resulted in an increase in seats for non-traditional parties. At the time of the writing of this book, the supermajority rules for passage of organic laws and legal precepts remain one area of unfinished business in Chile's democratic reform efforts.

To understand the context in which the Chilean CT operates and in which it reacts, it is paramount to understand the lawmaking process and the powers and constraints faced by the elected branches who write the laws reviewed by the Tribunal. The president's strong powers ensure that much of the policymaking process involves negotiations between the president and Congress. However, institutional rules within Congress and negotiations among legislators also influence policy. Chile has a bicameral Congress, which until 2005 allowed for a chamber of deputies with 120 seats and a Senate with 47 seats including those for non-elected senators. Constitutional reforms in 2005 eliminated the non-elected seats, reducing the Senate size to 38 seats. Members of the chamber serve for four years and senators for eight years. Half of the Senate is elected every four years, however. The authoritarian constitution and its amendments created a binomial electoral system, with two seat districts by which coalitions may choose two candidates to present at Congressional elections. This system forced the main parties within each of the two coalitions to negotiate and coalesce around a candidate for the center left Concertación and one for the center right, the Alianza. Due to this unique voting system imposed by the military junta, most elections were a "foregone conclusion" with the Concertación usually winning one seat within a district and the Alianza another. In 2015, further constitutional changes increased the seats in Congress to 155 in the chamber of deputies and 43 in the Senate, introduced gender quotas, and changed the electoral system to one that was more proportional. These changes affected the results of the 2017 congressional elections by increasing the number of legislators who represented non-traditional parties.

Since the return to democracy and even prior to the coup, Chile's many political parties have formed around the two aforementioned coalitions. Although originally consisting of seventeen parties, after the democratic transition, the center left coalition, or Concertación, included the following five parties: the Christian Democratic Party (PDC, or Partido Demócrata Cristiano), the Party for Democracy (PPD, or Partido por la Democracia), the Socialist party (PS, or Partido Socialista), the Radical Party (PR, or Partido Radical), and the Social Democratic Party (PSD, or Partido Social Demócrata). The PR and PSD later merged into the single party known as the Radical Social Democratic Party (PRSD for Partido Radical Social Demócrata). The center right coalition, or Alianza, included the National Renewal Party (RN, or Partido de Renovación Nacional) and the Independent Democratic Union (UDI, or Unión Demócrata Independiente). These two major coalitions have played an integral part in politics since the country's return to democracy.

With both plebiscites behind them, Chilean citizens in 1989 elected President Aylwin of the PDC by 55 percent of all votes. Aylwin was supported by a majority of the Concertación de Partidos por la Democracia, CPD or Concertación,[10] in Congress. As a result of the authoritarian constitution and transition to democracy, the military government had replaced Chile's pre-junta multidistrict proportional representation system with a two-member district electoral system, which obliged the Concertación "to engage in a complex game of deal making and power sharing in order to divide electoral slates" among all of its parties (Siavelis 2013). Indeed, after the election of Aylwin, the new government faced significant constraints imposed by both the 1980 Constitution and the 1989 amendments. Despite the fragility of the transition, however, Chileans' commitment to democracy as well as a rejection of the Pinochet era, resulted in Chileans electing four consecutive presidents from the center left, or Concertación, including Patricio Aylwin (1990–1994, Christian Democrat), Eduardo Frei (1994–2000, Christian Democrat), Ricardo Lagos (2000–2006, Party for Democracy), and Michele Bachelet (2006–2010, Socialist). The Concertación's success resulted from its skilled accommodation of interests of the Alianza, and this post transition period became known as the *democracia de los acuerdos* (democracy by agreements) in which Concertación presidents "consistently engaged in a pattern of informal negotiations" with the opposition especially in the area of budgets (Siavelis 2014: 29). The Concertación's consensus-building tactics eventually led to its defeat allowing for the election of Chile's first center right president since the military junta – Sebastián Piñera of the National Renewal or RN (2010–2014) (Sehnbruch and Siavelis 2014). Piñera's term was followed by the return of Bachelet (2014–2018) and a subsequent re-election of Piñera in 2018. In 2021, Gabriel Boric, a former student leader and member of the left-leaning Social Convergence Party, won the election to serve as Chile's subsequent president beginning in March 2022.

Chilean presidents, like many in Latin America, have been imbued with strong powers to influence policy both under the 1925 and 1980 constitutions. Under the 1980 Constitution and its amendments, presidents hold significant agenda-control powers by providing the president with the "exclusive right to introduce bills that establish or modify taxes, public salaries, public services, administrative functions, collective bargaining, pensions and social security" (Alemán and Navia 2016: 94) and to demand government expenditures. Executives also have power over the

[10] Party sharing within the Concertación on the *cuoteo*, which allowed "careful division of ministerial portfolios among its constituent parties" (Siavelis 2013: 209). According to Siavelis, the *cuoteo* was one of the "keys to success" of the Concertación after the democratic transition (p. 209). Eventually, however, this system was viewed negatively by the Chilean public, who viewed it "as a form of *politiquería* (crass politicking) and as a way to ensure political positions for politicians" some of who could not win at the ballot boxes (p. 210).

amendment procedure and the scheduling of bills for debate. Members of the executive branch often negotiate directly with congressional committee members or participate in debates on the floor (p. 95). Executives also may assert influence over the legislature by declaring an executive urgency, which according to Siavelis (1997) is "one of its most important prerogatives" (p. 325).

While the president wields much power in the legislative process, legislators also have agenda-setting powers through the "directorate (lower chamber Mesa and Senate president), the leadership committee made up of party bloc chiefs as well as permanent conference committees" (Alemán and Navia 2016: 99). Control of these different institutions allows legislators to control the timing of voting on legislative proposals and amendments although assistance from the executive on these matters is required. Party leaders in turn determine the composition of these agenda-setting institutions.

The two main party coalitions of center left and center right were the dominant competitors in all elections from the democratic transition until the elections in 2017, which were conducted under new rules. Through almost the entire post transition period, Chile has functioned under divided government necessitating the need for compromises between branches of government and opposing party coalitions. Table 4.1 shows the initial elected compositions of the Chamber of Deputies and Senate under each president from 1990 to 2022. Prior to the 2005 constitutional reforms, the Senate's inclusion of lifetime senators made it difficult for the Concertación to ever have the required supermajorities to pass constitutional reforms and organic laws without some agreement from legislators of the center right. Immediately following the democratic transition, these non-elected senators were often aligned with the junta or at least the center right. As these first non-elected senators completed their eight-year terms, they were replaced by others who were not selected by the prior military government. As to the lifetime senators who gained their seats due to their prior status as presidents who had served six years, Pinochet was appointed to the Senate in 1998 after leaving his position as head of the armed forces. Although he was officially a lifetime senator, his legal difficulties in the United Kingdom led to his immunity being stripped in 2002. President Frei also served as a lifetime senator from 2000 to 2006. After the reforms, Frei was subsequently popularly elected as a senator.[11] As discussed more below, after the 2005 constitutional reforms, the first presidency of Bachelet operated initially under a unified government, but subsequently some legislators changed parties depriving her of this unified support. Piñera's coalition during his first presidency had one more seat in the House but fewer in the Senate compared to parties of the Concertación. Not until Bachelet's second term did she have the support of a unified government as her governing coalition had a majority of seats in both the chamber and the Senate.

[11] President Aylwin did not qualify for one of these lifetime Senate seats as he had only held the presidency for four years, not the required six.

TABLE 4.1. *Chile political context, 1990–2022*

	Concertación or center left Seats (%)	Alianza or center right Seats (%)	Coalition with most seats in full legislature	President's party
		Aylwin 1990–1994[a,d]		
H/120	Concertación, 72 seats (60%)[b]	Alianza, 48 seats (40%)	Concertación	PDC (part of the Concertación)
S/47	Concertación, 22 seats (47%)	Alianza, 25 seats (53%) (of which 9 non-elected)		
		Frei 1994–1998[a,d]		
H/120	Concertación, 70 seats (58%)	Alianza, 50 seats (42%)	Concertación	PDC (part of the Concertación)
S/47	Concertación, 21 seats (45%)	Alianza, 26 seats (55%) (of which 9 non-elected)		
		Frei 1998–2000[a,d]		
H/120	Concertación, 70 seats (58%)	Alianza, 47 seats (39%)	Concertación	PDC (part of the Concertación)
S/48	Concertación, 20 seats (42%)	Alianza, 27 seats (56%)[c] (of which 10 non-elected)		
		Lagos 2000–2002[d]		
H/120	Coalition for Democracy, 70 seats (58%)	Alianza, 47 seats (39%)	Concertación	PPD (part of the Concertación)
S/48	Coalition for Democracy, 24 seats (50%) (of which 4 non-elected)	Alianza, 24 seats (50%) (of which 4 non-elected)		
		Lagos 2002–2006[d]		
H/120	Coalition for Democracy, 62 seats (52%)	Alianza, 57 seats (48%)	Concertación	PPD (part of the Concertación)
S/48	Coalition for Democracy, 24 seats (50%) (of which 4 non-elected)	Alianza, 24 seats (50%) (of which 6 non-elected)		

(continued)

TABLE 4.1 (*continued*)

	Concertación or center left Seats (%)	Alianza or center right Seats (%)	Coalition with most seats in full legislature	President's party
		Bachelet 2006–2010[d,e,f]		
H/120	Coalition for Democracy, 65 seats[d] (54.20%)	Alianza, 54 seats (45.8%)	Concertación	Socialist Party of Chile (part of Concertación)
S/38	Coalition for Democracy, 20 seats (52.63%)	Alianza, 17 seats (44.73%)		
		Piñera 2010–2014[d,f]		
H/120	Coalition for Democracy, 57 seats (48%)	Coalition for Change, 58 seats (48%)	Concertación	RN (part of Alianza)
S/38	Concertación and Juntos Podemos, 19 seats (50%) CPD[c]	Coalition for Change, 16 seats (45%)[c]		
		Bachelet 2014–2018[d,f]		
H/120	New Majority, 67 seats (56%)	Alianza, 49 seats (41%)	Concertación	Socialist Party (part of Concertación)
S/38	New Majority, 21 seats (55%)	Alianza, 16 seats (42%)		
		Piñera 2018–2022		
H/155	Chile Vamos, 72 seats (47%)	Force of Majority, 56 seats (36%)	Chile Vamos	RN (part of Alianza)
S/43	New Majority, 17 seats (40%)	Chile Vamos, 19 Seats (44%)		

[a] Siavelis (1999) for all numbers house and Senate for Aylwin and Frei. Siavelis notes that the designated senators were under no obligation to support the right, but they assured the right of an effective veto especially on legislation with many conflicts (pp. 229–231).

[b] Carey (2002) states that the Concertación had seventy seats in Congress at this time.

[c] Siavelis (2002) updated the Senate numbers for the election in 1997 (p. 91).

[d] Parliamentary Union; Siavelis (2013).

[e] Alemán and Navia (2016) note that although Bachelet's coalition originally resulted in unified government, subsequent defections from the House and Senate resulted in her coalition losing the majority.

[f] Fuentes (2014: 92) had slightly different percentages. For Congress, from 1998 to 2000, he calculates that the Alianza had 41.7% of the seats in Congress and this same percentage from 2000 to 2002. For the Senate, from 1998 to 2002, Fuentes (2014) states that the Senate was evenly split for each coalition with the Concertación holding 50% of the seats and the Alianza the other 50%. Also, for the Senate from 2010 to 2014, he states that the Concertación had 52.6% of the seats and the Alianza 44.7%.

Note. Percent of seats needed to pass in both houses of Congress is as follows: Ordinary laws: 51%; Organic laws: 4/7ths or 57.14%; Precepts or treaties: 3/5 or 60%; certain constitutional reforms: 3/5 or 60%; other constitutional reforms: 2/3 or 66%.

It is worth noting, however, that no government at any time since the return to democracy has ever had a supermajority of seats required for passage of constitutional reforms (60 or 67 percent), organic laws or treaties (4/7 or 57.14 percent) or legal precepts (3/5 or 60 percent). Thus, these laws require agreement by some members of the opposition and many compromises. As argued in this book, these legislative supermajority voting rules also make it difficult for the full CT to congeal on a decision that is outside the preferences of legislators voting under such rules.

Chile's post transition governments all had distinct policy agendas although their implementation was affected by the political context in which they served. The Constitutional Tribunal was required to review the constitutionality of many important policy changes instigated by these various governments. The Aylwin presidency, under a government constrained by the military and also divided between the major coalitions, dealt with both the democratization of political institutions and the immediate aftermath of the authoritarian government (Siavelis 2014: 37). In the area of reforming political institutions, Aylwin was careful to avoid changes that would "provoke a strong military reaction" because the executive had already determined that the political opposition in the form of the center right "would strongly support any military demands" (Fuentes 2014: 76–77).[12] As part of the tacit agreements under the packed transition, Aylwin's government as well as successive Concertación presidents accepted and did little to change the neoliberal economic model established under Pinochet (Fuentes 2014: 76–77).

Instead, of committing to a "comprehensive agenda for social democratization," Aylwin was instead guided by "a case-by-case strategy of trying to obtain circumstantial majorities in Congress to pass some legislation" (Fuentes 2014: 77 referencing Garretón 1993). Aylwin's main initiatives included a significant tax reform to ease the "social debt ... inherited from the military dictatorship" (see López 2014) and measures to alleviate poverty including the creation of the Solidarity and Social Investment Fund to directly aid poor communities.

Additionally, one of Aylwin's first actions as president was to establish the Commission for Truth and Reconciliation (the Rettig Commission) to investigate and report human rights abuses under the Pinochet regime. In February 1991, the Rettig Commission issued its report, which included among many other criticisms of the junta, a full chapter criticizing the courts during the dictatorship (*Report of the Chilean National Commission on Truth and Reconciliation* 1991). The report stated that judges on the Chilean Supreme Court had failed to protect human rights by upholding a 1978 amnesty decree.[13] Besides suggesting that courts and legal procedures related to human rights be changed, the Commission called on the

[12] Pinochet did on occasion use the show of the military to assert his power.

[13] Chile's Supreme Court, under both authoritarian rule and its immediate post transition past was criticized for insufficiently constraining the executive (Correa Sutil 1993; Hilbink 2007; Couso and Hilbink 2011).

government to specifically change the constitution as well as criminal law and procedure to ensure the protection of human rights. Following the Rettig Commission's lead and criticizing judges for their lack of "moral courage" under the Pinochet regime, President Aylwin proposed a number of substantive changes to the legal system, which included reforms to the structure of the judiciary, the criminal justice system, and to deal with past human rights atrocities. Of these reforms, only a few were enacted under Aylwin.

As with his predecessor, Chile's second president post transition, Eduardo Frei, was careful in attempting reforms that would have freed Chile from the bonds of the former military regime. Frei did attempt to initiate constitutional reforms (i.e., removing appointed senators, modifying the CT, reducing the COSENA's powers and allowing the president to remove army officers) (Fuentes 2014). When no agreement could be reached in Congress about such far reaching reforms, they were withdrawn. Frei's government, however, was able to alter the process for appointing Supreme Court judges. Immediately after the democratic transition, Chilean Supreme Court judges were largely selected by the Court itself, which prepared a list of five candidates from which the president nominated one. This self-selection or preparation of the list of the candidates by the Supreme Court was thought to reinforce its insulation from politics (Hilbink 2007: 213). This appointment procedure remained intact until a 1997 reform that required the Senate to confirm the appointments by a two-thirds vote. One lingering criticism of the Supreme Court, which has resurfaced in recent years, involves its influence over lower court judges that it ranks, disciplines, and promotes every year.[14]

Frei's economic policies focused on opening Chile to free trade and international markets and dealing with the fallout of the Asian currency crisis. Frei also shifted his focus from antipoverty programs to educational reform, increasing the value of vouchers, lengthening the school day, and updating curriculums. However, as to vouchers, the "education committees in both chambers of congress were concerned that the voucher system was exacerbating school segregation" (Elacqua and González Soto 2014: 290), an issue that plagued subsequent presidents.

Frei presided over several reforms to the judicial system. One such change focused on replacing Pinochet-era judges on the Supreme Court. The other change involved a complete overhaul of the criminal justice procedure, which came to be referred to as the country's "reforms of the century" (Mohor and Covarrubias 2007:

[14] While a court's power to discipline and remove its own judges may enhance the judicial branch's independence, the Chilean Supreme Court's ability to discipline and promote lower court judges is thought to thwart the independence of these individual judges. In 2017, the Inter-American Commission on Human Rights took up this matter after the National Association of Magistrates of Chile complained about this situation, which many lower court judges feel violates their due process rights and is unfair (González Schmessane 2017). The Chilean Supreme Court does not rank or discipline Constitutional Tribunal judges, who are considered outside the judicial branch.

75). These reforms, enacted between 1995 and 2000, moved Chile's criminal law system closer to that existing in Western democracies in Europe and the United States, and Chile's efforts were similar to those occurring throughout the region (see Tiede 2012). The CT upheld these reforms, many enacted through organic laws, although there was some public backlash against their emphasis on defendants' rights (Duce and Riego 2009). Little action on prosecuting human rights abuses or responding to victims' demands occurred until late in Frei's presidency when Pinochet was arrested in the United Kingdom in 1998 and subsequently indicted following his return to Chile in 2000.

Under the presidency of Ricardo Lagos of the PPD (2000–2006), "Chile witnessed a more proactive executive branch" and one that was decidedly different from those of the 1990–1999 period (Fuentes 2014: 79). This classification of the Lagos' years is influenced by the successful implementation of further judicial reforms and the previously discussed 2005 constitutional reforms, which removed many of the authoritarian enclaves originally agreed to around the time of the democratic transition. Specifically, the constitutional reforms rid the country of non-elected senators, changed the influence of the COSENA, and changed the selection of CT judges. Despite these constitutional reforms, some criticize Lagos as making only limited advances related to reducing inequality and poverty. Lagos made some changes to the education system by increasing funding for poor students (Oppenheim 2007: 199) and lengthening the school day, but these changes were not substantial enough to satisfy students who held massive protests under subsequent presidents.

Concurrent with Lagos' policy gains, many feared that once back in Chile, Pinochet's case would be dismissed as he was a lifetime member of the Senate. However, in August of 2000, the Chilean Supreme Court confirmed that Pinochet could be stripped of his parliamentary immunity. Following the lifting of immunity, in the most well-known case against Pinochet – the Caravan of Death – Supreme Court judge Juan Guzmán indicted Pinochet on fifty-seven counts of homicide and eighteen counts of kidnapping. In July 2001, the criminal chamber of the Supreme Court ruled that Pinochet was not competent to stand trial and Pinochet died in December 2006 avoiding conviction. The sequence of events leading to his arrest and return to Chile added new life into cases dealing with the military era human rights violations. Following the passage of the 2005 constitutional reforms, Michele Bachelet (a Socialist) was elected as the country's first woman president. After Bachelet's election victory, small-scale student protests in 2006 exploded into large-scale protests of about a half million college and high school students, their parents, and unions over increases in student fees and other dissatisfactions with the educational system (Siavelis 2014: 38). Despite these early protests, Bachelet's government oversaw several important and, at times, controversial policies. In response to student protests, Bachelet's government did manage to overturn the junta's education policies enshrined in the Ley Orgánica Constitucional de Enseñanza

(LOCE) by enacting the General Law of Education, which attempted to reduce discrimination, improve education, and provide more accountability. Under her administration, she also reformed Chile's transportation system in the form of the controversial Transantiago program. She introduced measures to improve women's rights and specifically health rights (including public access to the morning-after pill), public administration, and regional government decentralization, allowing the country to get through the financial crisis of 2008.

The Constitution's limit on presidents' service to two non-concurrent terms resulted in Bachelet leaving office in 2010 with the highest approval rating of any Chilean president (around 80 percent), while at the same time allowing Sebastián Piñera, a candidate from the opposition coalition, to subsequently win the presidency – the first center right president since the country's return to democracy.[15] Several commentators suggest his win was due to his campaign's commitment to establishing a "New Right" with wider social appeal than that embraced by the Alianza previously.[16] Piñera's rise and the end of the Concertación's hold on the presidency for twenty years may also be due to a popular rejection of the consensus-building model that the Concertación had followed for so long (Sehnbruch and Siavelis 2014: 3) and of which the population became tired as they saw elite politicians relying on "a process of government by negotiation and horse-trading rather than true representative democracy" in which citizens matter (p. 3).

Days prior to Piñera's assumption of the presidency, Chile experienced a catastrophic earthquake requiring Piñera to rely on key personnel in Bachelet's government to help deal with the crisis as well as to find ways to finance reconstruction efforts. Piñera's government held neither a majority in the house nor Senate (although it had more seats than won by the Concertación in the House) and his form of leadership was characterized as *presidencialismo plebiscitario*, a system which reinforced presidential powers by appointing technocrats to government positions, many of whom had financial conflicts of interest (Varas 2014). Piñera's first term also experienced student protests in 2011 demanding "structural reforms from elementary to higher education" and constituting "one of the most massive and original social movements Latin America has seen in the last decade" (Salinas and Fraser 2012). Piñera did not commit to student demands to reduce for-profit means of education.

In 2014, Bachelet regained the presidency, and her coalition had a majority in both houses. However, while the governing coalition's majority allowed it to pass laws under simple majority rules, the percentage of seats won by her coalition did not provide the needed majorities to pass treaties, legal precepts, or organic laws,

[15] Rules preventing non-concurrent presidential terms may reduce the sitting president's incentives to support their party in a subsequent election in hopes to regain the presidency later.

[16] There are many reasons for Piñera's first presidential victory (see Varas 2014 for an overview).

many of which the Tribunal reviews, without some agreement by opposition members. Bachelet's campaign promises included tax reforms to lower inequality and initiatives dealing with health. She also campaigned on education reform, and her government, reacting to severe student protests, passed reforms to end subsidies to schools making a profit and improve their entrance requirements. However, students decried the law as not going far enough or forcing parents to send their students to poorer public schools or private schools that they could not afford. Subsequently the Constitutional Tribunal struck down many of the law's provisions claiming that they discriminated against poor students who were not receiving assistance (Rol #2787). Bachelet's second term also attempted to make good on her campaign promises to reform the constitution further, which many said still had not freed the country completely from its authoritarian past. Despite attempts to reform the constitution, it was only sent to Congress in the remaining days of her presidency (see Verdugo and Contesse 2018).

Piñera regained the presidency in 2018. In October of 2019, large-scale protests, seemingly over fare hikes on public transportation, erupted and focused on economic inequality, perpetuated by a weak pension scheme and problems with the education and health systems. In response, Piñera issued a state of emergency, a curfew and allowed military tanks in the street, which raised citizens' concerns due to Chile's brutal military legacy. Congress rejected a motion to impeach Piñera for his failure to protect citizens against police tactics purportedly used to quell the violent protests. Piñera suggested that the government would put forward proposals for constitutional reform and citizens overwhelmingly approved drafting a new constitution by a constituent assembly.

4.6 THE CHILEAN CONSTITUTIONAL TRIBUNAL

Although Chile's current CT was created by Pinochet's military junta, it has emerged as a formidable institution within the constraints of the 1980 Constitution and reforms in 2005. The CT played a particularly important role in Chile's democratic transition by ensuring that procedures for elections remained fair and transparent such that citizens could oust Pinochet in elections held in 1989. Since that time, the CT has provided opinions in cases under its automatic review mechanism or referrals from politicians predominantly representing the coalition out of power. Many of the rulings have involved significant laws that have allowed Chile to consolidate its democracy and proceed with the difficult task of providing for its citizens.

The current Chilean Constitutional Tribunal, created in 1980 under the military junta, has functioned continuously from its creation until the present day. However, it is worth noting that prior to this time, Chile provided a limited form of judicial review, created in its 1925 Constitution, allowing Chile's Supreme Court to hear *recursos de inaplicabilidad por inconstitutionalidad*, which allowed individuals to claim that particular pieces of legislation were unconstitutional as applied only to the party bringing the case. As noted by Couso (2011), because the *recurso* "could only affect the particular case at hand, even a ruling accepting that a given piece of legislation was in fact unconstitutional left the challenged law intact" (p. 1525).

As previously discussed, beginning under the Alessandri government (1958–1964), legal scholars and politicians began discussing the possibility of creating a constitutional court for Chile. This very first Constitutional Court, created during the presidency of Frei but beginning work under Allende,[17] was modeled after France's Kelsian-inspired Constitutional Council, which Charles de Gaulle introduced to the French Constitution of 1958. Like in France, the Tribunal "operated in fact as a 'third legislative chamber' preventing the approval of bills deemed unconstitutional" (Couso et al. 2011: 123, citing Stone Sweet 1992). This first Chilean constitutional court was provided with four distinct powers. It could rule on the constitutionality of diverse legal instruments such as projects of law, international treaties, decrees, and referendums. It could resolve issues regarding the ineligibility of government ministers and conflicts between the executive and legislature. It could also resolve complaints against states for failing to promulgate laws or promulgating unconstitutional laws (Vial Correa 2006: 34). Despite these four powers, the main emphasis of the Tribunal's work focused on deciding cases involving jurisdictional conflicts between Congress and the president (see Couso 2011: 1529) and did not focus on the Tribunal's role of defending the Constitution, which is the main purpose of most Kelsian-styled constitutional courts. Further, Frei, whose constitutional reform included the creation of the Tribunal, was intent on reinforcing the powers of the president in lawmaking through the support of the Tribunal (see Mac-Clure 2011: 195) perhaps a reason for the Tribunal's later ineffectualness.

In this first Constitutional Court, judges were also selected through a mixed system in which the president appointed three of the justices with Senate confirmation and the Supreme Court chose two of its own members to serve on the Court all with four-year terms. During its short existence, the Tribunal heard seventeen cases of which many favored the Allende government (see Verdugo 2017 for an overview). However, its refusal to decide the *Áreas de la propriedad social* case mentioned previously, seriously hurt this court's reputation and may have inevitably led to the military coup. The court functioning from 1970 to 1973, was disbanded by the military government.

4.6.1 *CT Origins, Powers, and Selection of Judges, 1980–2005*

In an unusual move for an authoritarian government, the military junta created the current Constitutional Tribunal under the 1980 Constitution, and it began work on

[17] Ley 17.283 de 23 de enero de 1970 que Modifica la Constitución Política del Estado.

March 11, 1981. The creation of the Tribunal was justified as "an essential support of the integrity of a fundamental system of law" (CT website). In response to an ongoing scholarly debate regarding why authoritarian regimes may empower constitutional courts, some scholars see it as evidence of the "insurance theory" in which authoritarian politicians empower independent courts and banks to protect their interests when they are no longer in power (see Ginsburg 2003).

When the Tribunal was first created, it was provided with a multitude of specific powers, listed in the Constitution of 1980, Article 82.[18] The 1980 Constitution provided the Tribunal with relatively broad powers of abstract constitutional review, in which the Tribunal may find parts of proposed legislation unconstitutional and require the legislature to abandon the law or make modifications prior to its final enactment. The Tribunal contemplated under the military regime was "new" and "more powerful" than the first court that operated under Allende and had its origins in the Spanish Constitutional Court of 1978, the German Constitutional Court of 1940 and the French Constitutional Council of 1958 (Couso et al. 2011: 124). Under the 1980 Constitution until the present time, the Tribunal's abstract review of the constitutionality of laws has taken two forms. First, the Tribunal has obligatory or automatic constitutional review of all laws that involve a precept of the constitution, organic law, or treaty norms. This means these laws must be reviewed by the Tribunal after the legislature approves them, but prior to their enactment. Indeed, the Tribunal was required to review the Organic Law for the Constitutional Tribunal prior to beginning its operations. To handle what Barros describes as a "Gordian knot," the Ministry of Justice recommended that the CT "review its own organic law as its first act" (Barros 2002: 271), and the junta approved this idea and forwarded the organic law to the Tribunal. In a secret communique, the Tribunal informed the minister of justice, who in turn notified the junta that the CT had unanimously questioned the constitutionality of one provision, which would require that if the Tribunal needed documents that the junta had declared as "secret" it would have to maintain their secret status. The CT objected asserting that this violated the Constitution's Article 19(3) regarding individuals' rights to equal protection and legal defense without restriction. According to Barros, the CT made a further "political argument" that the Tribunal's guarding of secret evidence would have "highly detrimental consequences for Chile" because it would violate one of the most fundamental human rights requiring defendants to answer charges based on revealed rather than secret evidence (Barros 2002: 272–273).[19]

During the drafting of the 1980 Constitution, a working group modified prior drafts regarding the legislative voting requirements of the laws that the Tribunal was

[18] See Table 4.2, comparing powers under the 1980 Constitution to those under the 2005 reforms, renumbered as Article 93.

[19] The Tribunal's guarding of secret information would mean keeping informants and their information secret to convict individuals under the notorious Article 8, which allowed parties to be found unconstitutional and their members criminally punished.

obliged to review (i.e., obligatory review). The working group required 3/5 of the legislature to approve legal precepts, organic laws, and treaties prior to being reviewed by the Tribunal. This requirement for organic laws was later changed in 1989 to 4/7 as part of the agreements reached to facilitate the democratic transition (see Sierra 2011). As a result, when the Tribunal's obligatory review is triggered, it must review laws that are passed by the above supermajority rules, which, given Chile's political make-up, require approval from some opposition legislators.

Second, the Tribunal also was empowered to review abstractly other laws that the president or either chamber (in its entirety or one-fourth of its members) refers for its review, known as *requerimientos de inconstitucionalidad presentado por senadores o diputados*. Under the military government, the junta as a legislative body could bring such cases to the Tribunal's attention. While most of Chile's abstract review cases involve policy changes that must be reviewed by the Tribunal due to their nature as an organic law, treaty, or legal precept, these *requerimientos* are initiated by politicians at any stage of the legislative process and do not necessarily involve these types of laws. In practice, this process primarily has allowed the opposition in Congress to submit legislation or executive decrees for constitutional review on controversial issues, which in the democratic period have included disputes over distribution of the morning-after pill or financing the controversial Transantiago project, improving Chile's public transportation system.[20]

As with the first constitutional court, the Tribunal created in 1980 selected judges through a mixed appointment system. The Ortúzar Commission[21] set up by Pinochet in 1973 debated this selection mechanism. Commission member Gustavo Lorca suggested that the president, Congress, and the Supreme Court each choose three judges to maintain the equilibrium of the distinct parts of government (Vial Correa 2006: 68). Alternatively, Commission member Enrique Ortúzar wanted a Tribunal composed of three judges with one selected by the president, one the Senate, and one by the Supreme Court (p. 68). Commission member Jaime Guzmán, who as previously mentioned was adamant about the Constitution's protected democracy provisions, advocated that the president should choose five judges with agreement by the Senate, the Supreme Court should choose three judges, and the Court of Appeals of Santiago two judges (Vial Correa 2006: 68). Ultimately, the Ortúzar Commission decided that the Tribunal should be composed of seven judges of whom one was chosen by the president and one by the Senate. The remaining five members would be chosen by the Supreme Court by an absolute majority of which three came from the Supreme Court itself and two were

[20] My review of legislators bringing *requerimientos* showed that they were predominantly filed by legislators from the minority coalition parties.

[21] In its final version, the Ortúzar Commission members included Enrique Ortúzar, Jamie Guzmán, Alicia Romo, ex deputy Gustavo Lorca, ex-Senator Sergio Diaz, and ex-Senator Juan de Dios Carmona, Raúl Bertelsen and Luz Bulnes (see Vial Correa 2006 for this list). The latter two were subsequently members of the CT.

outside attorneys. As originally constituted, judges' tenure was limited to six years, but they were required to retire at the age of seventy-five. The Consejo approved the Ortúzar draft in this regard.

Ultimately, however, the junta made a drastic change to the selection process, dropping "una verdadera bomba" (Vial Correa 2006: 74), allowing the COSENA, made up of a majority of individuals from the military, to choose two attorneys to serve on the Tribunal. As a result, under the final draft of the 1980 Constitution and prior to the democratic transition, the Supreme Court chose three of its own judges or ministers, the COSENA[22] two, the government junta one and the president one.

While, retaining seven members on the Tribunal, after the democratic transition in 1990, the mixed selection system was amended slightly in 1989 such that the president nominated one, the Senate (by absolute majority) selected one, and the military dominated COSENA selected two, and the Supreme Court selected three of the Tribunal's ministers from among judges of the Supreme Court, who split their time between the Supreme Court and the Tribunal. The judges were to serve eight-year terms and a quorum was reached with five judges. Couso (2004) points out that judges selected by the Supreme Court from its ranks tended to be particularly apolitical "bring[ing] to the court the deferential habits of the regular judiciary" (p. 87). The Tribunal prior to the 2005 constitutional reforms largely consisted of judges who were associated in some way with the Supreme Court and generally non-partisan as well as several judges who were appointed under the junta and thus representative of those era's preferences. Under this pre-reform selection method, only about 30 percent of Tribunal judges were appointed by elected politicians. Candidates for the CT at this time also were required to have a "professional degree for at least fifteen years" and to "have had an outstanding performance in professional, university or public activities" without any impediments or incapacities (Constitution, Art icle 81).

4.6.2 *CT Powers and Selection of Judges after Constitutional Reforms of 2005*

The impetus for reforms to the CT as part of the broader 2005 reforms was due to the fact that the potentially expansive powers of the CT in conjunction with the political detachment of its authoritarian origins led to questions about the Tribunal's legitimacy after the transition (Heiss and Navia 2007) and about the pattern of judicial restraint it exhibited.[23] The constitutional reforms of 2005 (effective in February 2006) were designed to remake the Tribunal as an institution of the democratic period, although occurring sixteen years after the country's return to democracy.

[22] The COSENA created under the 1980 Constitution was composed of the President of the Republic, the president of the Supreme Court, presidents of the Senate and Chamber of Deputies, heads of the armed forces and the Controller General.

[23] Couso (2004) has interpreted this restraint at this time as necessary to protect the Tribunal's autonomy.

While the Tribunal maintained its powers of mandatory abstract review of organic laws, precepts of law, and treaties as well as abstract review of legislation or presidential decrees initiated by a certain number of legislatures or the president, the reforms added other powers in a "dramatic way" including "concrete and a posteriori control of the constitutionality of legislation" (Couso 2011: 1534). As seen in Table 4.2, the constitutional reforms provided the CT with additional types of constitutional review under Articles 93.6 and 93.7 of the Constitution. Under Article 93.6, the CT hears cases referred to as *requerimientos de inaplicabilidad por inconstitucionalidad.* These were cases that were originally heard by the Chilean Supreme Court as concrete review cases, which were called *recursos de inaplicabilidad.* Although in theory these cases are similar to those heard by the Supreme Court, the Constitutional Tribunal has a slightly different understanding about how these cases should be decided. Legislators moved these cases to the Tribunal for two reasons. The first was that increasingly the Supreme Court was seen as unwilling to confront the state on important issues. Second, by transferring these cases to the CT, it was thought to make constitutional interpretation more uniform (Pfeffer 2005; Couso and Coddou 2010: 394–395, fn. 22). This particular shift centralized constitutional review in one court in Chile, which is done by some but not all legal systems throughout Latin America (see Ríos-Figueroa 2011) and is in line with the Kelsian conception of the role of a constitutional court (Kelsen 1942).

These new concrete cases transferred to the CT are not heard by the full court but rather by five judge panels whose membership is fixed by the president of the court each year. For these types of cases, judges' decisions are based on a majority voting rule. For concrete cases, the Constitutional Tribunal decides whether the application of legislation to a particular case is contrary to the Constitution or not (see Couso and Coddou 2010). According to legal scholars, the post-reform concrete cases required an actual case and controversy. These concrete cases may now be brought by ordinary citizens. "This increased accessibility and visibility strengthened the link between the citizenry and the Court while at the same time lowering the political cost of decision-making for the justices" (Couso et al. 2011: 126). More generally, in concrete cases, the Tribunal is often reviewing the applicability of legislation of prior governments to a given case and controversy.

Additionally, concrete cases have inter partes effects and not *erga omnes* effects, which means the decision is "valid only for participants in the case" (Ríos-Figueroa 2011: 41). In other words, in these concrete review cases the Tribunal does not have the ability to render a law or part of a law unconstitutional.

The reform also allowed for an additional new type of abstract review allowing judges to find unconstitutional statutes already passed by the legislature or a posteriori. These cases are heard by the full court and require 4/5 of the judges to agree. Under Article 93.7, the Constitutional Tribunal can provide that a concrete case has *erga omnes* effects if the law's inapplicability has been established in prior concrete cases under Constitution, Article 93.6, described above. Although this is a

TABLE 4.2. *The CT's powers and underlying legislative voting rules under the 1980 Constitution and 2005 reforms*

CT Powers Article 82 of the 1980 Constitution with 1989 amendments Renumbered Article 93 under the 2005 reform	Rules regarding review • Standing to initiate review • Legislative voting rules to pass law reviewed, • Tribunal voting rule is by majority of those present, unless otherwise indicated with a *
1. Exercise control of constitutionality of organic laws, treaties and precepts of law. (Article 82(1)/Article 93(1))	1. Automatic review Legislature passes organic laws by 4/7 and treaties and legal precepts by 3/5 prior to enactment
2. Resolve questions of constitutionality of auto accords (agreed orders) dictated by Supreme Court, Appellate courts, and Election Tribunal courts. (Article 93.2)	2. Brought by president, either house of Congress or 10 of its members
3. Resolve questions of constitutionality arising in processing of bills, treaties or constitutional reform. (Article 83.2/Article 93.3) (*Requerimientos de inconstitucionalidad presentado por senadores o diputados*)	3. Brought by president, either house of Congress or ¼ of its members prior to enactment of the law
4. Resolve questions of constitutionality of a decree with the force of law. (Article 82.3/Article 93.4)	4. Brought by president after Comptroller General finds law unconstitutional
5. Resolve questions of constitutionality of the convocation of plebiscite. (Article 82.4/Article 93.5)	5. Brought by Congress or Senate
6. Resolve inapplicability of legal precept before ordinary court or contrary to the constitution. (Article 93.6) (*Requerimientos de inaplicabilidad por inconstitucionalidad*)	6. Brought by litigants of a concrete lawsuit or judge from court familiar with case. (*Decided by 5 judge panel with majority voting rule.)
7. Resolve unconstitutionality of legal precept declared inapplicable under prior paragraph (ie. Article 93.6 above). (Article 93.7)	7. Brought by public action after the law found inapplicable based on prior paragraph. (Decided by full court 4/5 of judges need to agree.)
8. Resolve complaints when President does not promulgate a law when required or promulgates a different text than constitutionally required. (Article 82.5/Article 93.8)	8. Brought by either house of Congress or ¼ of its members

(*continued*)

TABLE 4.2 (*continued*)

CT Powers Article 82 of the 1980 Constitution with 1989 amendments Renumbered Article 93 under the 2005 reform	Rules regarding review • Standing to initiate review • Legislative voting rules to pass law reviewed, • Tribunal voting rule is by majority of those present, unless otherwise indicated with a *
9. Resolve constitutionality of a presidential decree which the Office of the Comptroller General has objected to as unconstitutional. (Article 82.6/Article 93.9)	9. Silent
10. Declare unconstitutionality of organizations and movements or political parties involved in events that led to declaration of unconstitutionality under Constitution Article 19(15). (Article 82.7/93.10)	10. Public action unless affected individual was president or president elect and then request by Chamber of deputies or ¼ of its members
11. Inform the Senate about cases referred to it under Constitution Article 53.7 (declaring incapacity of the president or president elect due to mental or physical impediments to perform duties. (Article 93.9)	11. *Requerimiento* by Senate
12. Resolve conflicts of competence (ie. jurisdictional conflicts) which arise between the political or administrative authorities and the courts of justice. (Article 93.12)	12. Brought by those in conflict
13. Resolve constitutional or legal issues regarding the inabilities that affect the appointment or remaining in office of a minister of state. (Article 83.10/ Article 93.13)	13. Brought by public action
14. Resolve inabilities or incompatibilities and ground for removal from office of parliamentarians. (Article 83.11/Article 93.14)	14. Brought by president or at least 10 parliamentarians
15. Qualify the inability invoked by a parliamentarian in terms of the final paragraph of Constitution Article 60 and decide concerning the renunciation of responsibilities. (Article 93.15)	15. Silent
16. Decide the constitutionality of supreme decrees, regardless of alleged defect and including those issued under president's independent regulatory authority when they refer to matters that may be reserved by law under Constitution Article 63. (Article 83.12/Article 93.16)	16. Brought by either houses of Congress. If decree involves presidential powers, must be brought by 1/4 of members of Congress

new and potentially important power of the CT, it has been used sparingly. As of February 2022, the Tribunal has heard only fifteen of these cases. The Tribunal also chose to announce that one case under article 93.7 (Rol #681) was Chile's first precedent-setting case, a surprise for a country based on a civil law system without the practice of stare decisis.

At first glance, it appears in Table 4.2 that the Tribunal has expansive powers. However, a closer look at the actual distribution of cases by review type found in Table 4.3 shows that the number of powers is not instructive. Despite the listing of sixteen specific powers, the Tribunal's docket is mostly filled with cases of concrete review, which the Tribunal has heard since the 2005 reforms as well as cases of obligatory abstract review (93.1) and *requerimientos* brought by senators or deputies (93.3).

The empirical analysis that follows in subsequent chapters is limited to analyzing cases under 93.1 and 93.3 between 1990 and 2016, all with a priori review and passed by the legislature in power at the time of the review. The 93.6 cases are not reviewed in this book as they are not comparable, arising from a case and controversy and decided by just half the Tribunal.

Figure 4.1 indicates trends in the Tribunal's caseload for the most prevalent case types. As seen from this figure, the Tribunal hears about 20 to 30 abstract review cases under 93.1 per year and has done so consistently since 1990. The depiction, however, masks the increasing complexity of these obligatory review cases. While cases in the early 1990s through 2006 had very few decisional paragraphs, cases since the reform have had many more decisional paragraphs reflecting the complexity of the laws themselves. Some believe that the obligatory review of the CT of organic laws should be completely removed and instead that the CT's review should be limited to *requerimientos* and other types of review. The criticism of the cases under 93.1 is due to the supermajority rules to pass organic laws reviewed under this section, which greatly constrain elected officials and judges.[24] The figure also shows that the number of *requerimientos* has remained fairly consistent over time and there are fewer of these types of cases than those of obligatory review, although they may represent some of the most contentious laws faced by the Tribunal or at least ones that legislators are willing to publicly contest. Finally, the figure shows that the concrete cases (decided under Article 93.6), with the numerical numbers on the right axis, now make up a large portion of the Tribunal's work. The addition of concrete review has added hundreds of cases to the Tribunal's annual docket. This increase may show the popularity of this new legal tool, which allows citizens to directly approach the Tribunal. While the numbers are nowhere near those of the Colombian Constitutional Court or other prominent courts in Latin America, such as the Peruvian and Costa Rican constitutional courts, the trends may be worrisome if court resources are not commensurate with the growing caseloads.

[24] Author interview held at the CT, January 23, 2016, Santiago.

TABLE 4.3. *Distribution of cases before the Chilean CT, 1990–2022*

Constitutional provision	Number of cases 1990–2005 (pre-reform)	Number of cases 2006–2022 (post-reform)
93.1	299	295
93.2	0	33
93.3	41	66
93.4	4	0
93.5	0	0
93.6	–	2,418
93.7	–	15
93.8	0	1
93.9	0	1
93.10	0	0
93.11	0	0
93.12	–	92
93.13	0	2
93.14	3	3
93.15	0	0
93.16	20	0

Source. Based on a review of cases listed on the Tribunal's website by constitutional provision at www .tribunalconstitucional.cl, last reviewed February 9, 2022..

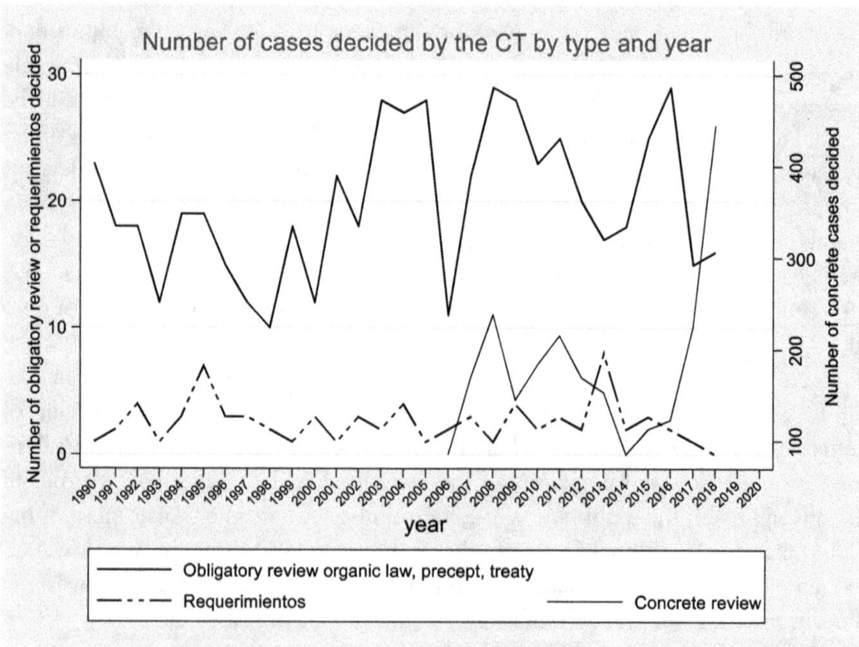

FIGURE 4.1 Caseloads of the Chilean CT from 1990 to 2020

As to judicial selection, the reforms of 2005 eliminated judges chosen by the Consejo de Seguridad Nacional (COSENA) and allowed more elected actors to be involved in the selection process. The debates found in the reform's legislative history in general revolve around the idea of finding an equilibrium of different types of judges within the Tribunal itself. In Chile, there were several possibilities for the configuration of mixed selection of judges to the Chilean CT under the junta and after the country's return to democracy. Debates concerning the mixed selection of judges and composition of the CT in the 2005 constitutional reforms were part of a larger debate about the constitution and democratic governance regarding the removal of authoritarian features from the 1980 Constitution, such as changing the composition of Congress, decreasing the role of the COSENA in appointments, and increasing the powers of the CT. In drafting the constitutional reforms pertaining to the CT, there was a considerable debate within the commission of *Constitución, Legislación, Justicia y Reglamento* and within both houses of Congress about which institutions would select judges to the CT and how many under the amended constitution. The emphasis placed on creating an equilibrium of powers on the Tribunal through selection is revealed in a review of the Legislative History of Chile's 2005 reform in which the word "equilibrio" or "equilibrium" appears 136 times in this almost 3,000 page document.[25] Interestingly, legislators and invited commentators during the debates included some former CT judges, such as Aburto Ochoa and Enrique Valenzuela, as well as those serving as legislators or members of the government who would later be selected to serve on the CT, such as José Viera-Gallo, Jorge Correa-Sutil, and Gonzalo García Pino.

The legislative debates regarding mixed selection and the composition of the Chilean Constitutional Tribunal revolved around several key themes, independent from removing the COSENA as a selector. In early debates in 2000, the two main party coalitions presented distinct ways to select CT judges. The Alianza's position was that the Tribunal membership should be increased from seven to nine judges in which the Supreme Court would choose three of its own judges to serve on the Tribunal, the president would choose four judges with agreement by 2/3 of the Senate, and the Tribunal itself would choose two attorneys (Historia de la Ley, No. 20.050: 15). At this early point in the debate, the Concertación recommended that the Tribunal continue to have seven judges with two chosen by the Supreme Court, one by the president and two each by the Senate and Congress (p. 22). The Concertación generally argued that judges selected by the Supreme Court should not come from the Court, but be attorneys working outside the judicial branch (Historia de la Ley No. 20.050: 542). Other influential speakers further debated whether the Supreme Court nominees should be judges or attorneys. Eugenia

[25] See Historia de la Ley No. 20.050 Modifica la Composición y Atribuciones del Congreso Nacional, la Aprobación de los Tratados Internacionales, la Integración y Funciones del Tribunal Constitucional y Otras Materias que Indica, 26 de agosto, 2005.

Valenzuela Somarriva, a former CT judge, preferred that the nominees had served as judges and were not just attorneys and deputy José Viera-Gallo of the Socialist Party and later a CT judge asserted that the Supreme Court nominees could be judges from courts other than the Supreme Court, such as the court of appeals, which had many distinguished and well-prepared judges (p. 541).

During later discussions in March of 2005,[26] issues were raised about how many judges each political actor, including the Supreme Court, the president, and Congress, should choose and whether these selections should be unilateral or not. Both major political coalitions changed their proposals from those of 2000 and a fierce debate among legislators and others ensued. For example, Sr. Gonzalo Uriarte of the UDI, a party of the center right, suggested rather than having the CT choose some its own judges, an original position of the Alianza, the Tribunal would have nine ministers or judges of which two were chosen by the president, three by the Supreme Court who were attorneys, and two each by the Senate and Congress. He added that the "goal" of his party was to have the legislature choose four judges in order to "weaken the preponderance of the president in nominations." His suggestion implied that presidential nominees had previously afforded the Concertación with too much power on the Tribunal.

Designated Senator Enrique Silva Cimma, who had been a member of the Radical Party of Chile and president of the precursor to the Concertación during the junta and later a minister of exterior relations under President Aylwin, discussed the nomination of Tribunal members in reference to the aspirations of constitutional drafters to have an "equilibrium" of powers in government institutions. Silva Cimma indicated that it was indeed desirable to have an equilibrium of powers, but such an equilibrium could not succeed under the current system of electing legislators, which favored two large coalitions. Others advocated increasing the number of judges selected by Congress, either by the Senate alone or by the Senate and the House. While originally the Senate was to choose three judges, this proposal was conceived when the total number of judges was to include nine. To weaken the president's influence on the Tribunal, a concern of the right, Senators decided after much debate that Congress should choose four judges, increasing the size of the CT to ten and eventually deciding that the Senate and the House could each choose two.

Discussion in the Cámara de Diputados also focused on whether the mixed selection system would lead to politicizing the Tribunal. Guzmán, a deputy of the center right RN party, suggested that although some may argue that the inclusion of judges selected by Congress would lead to politicization of the Tribunal, the opposite would occur due to other constitutional safeguards put in place to constrain judges. These included the fact that judges did not come from the ranks of the selecting institution and could not be removed or re-elected and thus could not

[26] The legislative history spanned five years.

lobby the Senate, House of Deputies, or Supreme Court. She concluded that the mixed system would provide a true equilibrium, "protected and free that will assure us of preventative constitutional control and ex post [control] which is quite necessary in all for the rule of law."[27] Bustos, a Socialist deputy, also suggested that requiring judges to work exclusively for the Tribunal, not holding other offices or working in the private sector as done previously, would make their work more transparent, a goal of the Concertación (see discussion of Juan Bustos, deputy of the PS (Historia Legislativa, 20.050: 2473–2474).

Figure 4.2 provides a comparison of the selection process under the 1980 Constitution after the democratic transition and under the 2005 reforms. Under the reforms in 2005, the legislature eventually agreed that the Supreme Court would continue to select three individuals for membership, but these judges are now required to be from outside the judicial branch and primarily have academic or professional backgrounds (see Pardow and Verdugo 2015). Also, under the reforms, the president now chooses three members, the Senate chooses two members (by a two-thirds majority), and the Chamber of Deputies with Senate approval chooses two members (Publication of Ley No. 20.050, August 26, 2005 in Diario Official). According to the reform's legislative history, Congress was concerned with ensuring that the three branches of government have representatives on the Tribunal in a manner that creates a "real equilibrium" within the Tribunal and among the branches of government.[28] With the reform, the Tribunal's size increased from seven to ten members, and each judge now serves for a nine year non-renewable term. After the reform, 70 percent of the Tribunal is appointed by elected politicians rather than 30 percent prior to the reform. The requirements for holding the office of Constitutional Tribunal minister remained virtually unchanged from the 1980 Constitution. Judges still must have a degree as a lawyer for at least fifteen years. The language as to qualifications of the judges is slightly different from the 1980 Constitution. Under the new Constitution, judges "must have excelled in professional, academic or public activity" (Article 92). Judges are generally irremovable unless they become incapacitated or commit serious crimes and cannot be re-elected after serving a complete term. Judges are required to retire at the age of seventy-five.

The Tribunal's composition since the time of the transition has been influenced by the pre- and post-reform rules that determine who appoints certain judges. The composition also has been determined by tenure rules as well as rules that require that 1/3 of the court is replenished every three years under the 2005 reform and that judges retire at a required age. As will be argued in empirical Chapters 6 and 7, the

[27] In Spanish, Guzmán stated: "verdaderamente equilibrada, protegida y libre, que nos asegurará ese control de constitucionalidad preventivo y ex post tan necesario en todo estado de derecho" (Historia Legislativa, 20.050: 2471).

[28] Historia de la Ley No. 20.050, Moción Parlamentaria, page 9.

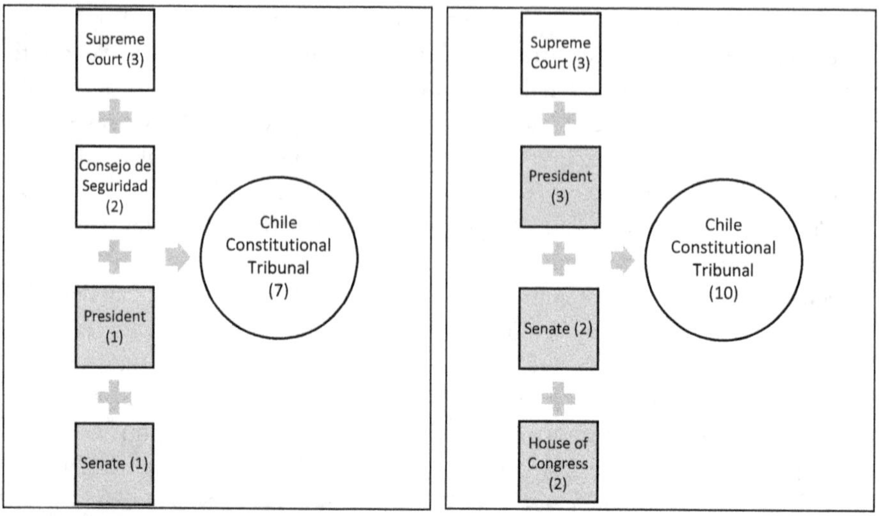

Pre-reform Tribunal (1990 to February 2006) **Post-reform Tribunal (February 11, 2006–)**

FIGURE 4.2 Mixed selection of Chile's CT under the 1980 Constitution and 2005 reforms
Note: Shaded boxes represent nominators who are elected by voters, and white boxes represent appointers who are not elected. Numbers in parentheses indicate the number of judges chosen by each institution and included in the Tribunal.

exact composition of the court at any given time, as well as the composition on specific cases, determines both how individual judges and the court as a whole make decisions. Trends in the composition are discussed more in detail in Chapter 6. However, it is worth noting that immediately after the democratic transition in 1990 and as part of the agreements reached with the junta, several judges who had been appointed by the junta remained on the Tribunal and one (Valenzuela) was selected by the Senate after the transition.[29]

Following the democratic transition, the CT had a composition that included a majority of judges who were selected by and were judges of the Supreme Court, considered a deferential institution (Hilbink 2007). The CT also had some members selected by the COSENA, two of whom remained on the Tribunal until 2010. After

29 Valenzuela was instrumental in the decisions that limited the junta's ability to control the election process in a manner favorable to its interests. However, other judges, who had served during the military regime and after the democratic transition had dissented on some of the most important and democratically transforming decisions of the CT under the junta. For example, in the case dealing with the Tribunal Calificador de Elecciones (Rol #33), judges Aburto and Urzúa voted against the finding of unconstitutionality along with Ortúzar, the drafter of the Constitution. In Rol #43, regarding political parties, Aburto wanted to restrict the findings of unconstitutionality. Finally, in the CT's transformative decision about popular voting (Rol #53), Jiménez and Ortúzar dissented. These judges, with the exception of Valenzuela, began to retire between 1991 and 1997.

the 2005 reforms, some of the judges appointed by the House or Senate were selected as a result of horse-trading agreements between the two political coalitions allowing them to alternate their favored appointments. For example, the paired selections of Hernán Vodanovic (Concertación) and Raúl Bertelsen (Alianza) and the later selections of Cristian Letelier (UDI) and Nelson Pozo (PC) were due to political accords between the main coalitions, which has drawn some criticism even from the CT's past president, Marisol Peña.[30] In a counter argument, Supreme Court justice, Milton Juica, has pointed out that despite political party attitudes influencing legislators' selections of judges, each institution that appoints judges is still responsible for conducting a public competition for the candidates (El Mercurio).

In Chile, for constitutional review decisions prior to the reform, five of seven judges make a quorum for deciding these types of cases. After the reform, ten judges serve on the court and a quorum is reached if at least eight of ten judges are present.[31] When the CT's obligatory jurisdiction is invoked for organic laws, the CT may find those laws constitutional or unconstitutional or may not decide if it determines the law is not an organic law.[32] For constitutional review cases, judges vote in reverse order of seniority.[33] In the event of an even number of judges and a tie, the president of the court makes the decisive vote (*voto dirimente*), which occurred infrequently until about 2014. According to interviews with judges and court personnel, generally judges on the CT tend not to deliberate extensively during closed discussion on the merits, although judges seem well aware of how others will vote prior to the discussion.[34] Once a decision is made, it is published in

30 In an interview with Marisol Peña in the newspaper *el Mercurio*, she said "la autonomía de un tribunal se basa en la independencia de cada ministro; cada uno de nosotros sabe que cuando es designado opera el deber de ingratitud, y uno se olvida de quién lo designó y es completamente independiente. Los jueces constitucionales que acaban de jurar tienen el desafío de demostrar que son profundamente independientes de las causas que van a fallar." An informal translation is as follows: The autonomy of a tribunal is based on the independence of each minister; each one of us knows that when designated one operates under the duty of ingratitude and forgets who designated them and is completely independent. The constitutional judges after taking their oath have a goal of demonstrating that they are profoundly independent of the cases they will rule on. See "El Mercurio 13 de Enero de 2015." "Cristián Letelier y Nelson Pozo jurarán como nuevos integrantes del TC").

31 Ley No. 17.997 Orgánica Constitucional del Tribunal Constitucional Artículo 30.

32 When the CT is reviewing organic laws, which are automatically submitted for review, it does have the option of saying that the laws or parts of laws are not organic laws and thus inadmissible for the CT to review. When the CT makes this decision, then it does not decide the law's constitutionality formally and thus defers to the legislature.

33 Ley 17.997. Article 20. Author interview of Tribunal staff, January 13, 2016, Santiago, Chile.

34 Based on author interviews with judges and court personnel of the Chilean CT held in Santiago in January 2016. Some interviewees raised concern that the Tribunal does not take enough time to debate and that under Chief Justice Carmona judges were given a short time to present their viewpoints.

el Diario Oficial. The Court's website provides the majority opinion and reasoning as well as the identity of judges who cast votes in each case. The cases also indicate if anyone was absent from the vote. Judges' separate or joint dissents, concurrences, and the reasons for the dissents, appear after the majority opinion.

It should be noted that constitutional reform efforts under Michele Bachelet in 2018 resulted in a draft constitution in which the proposed selection mechanism diverged from the mixed selection system under the 2005 reforms and seems to provide the president with significantly more powers in selection and allows all three branches to be involved in the process.[35] The new Constitutional Assembly constituted in 2021 with a diverse membership will take up issues related to the CT in the future, but are beyond the scope of this book.

4.7 CHAPTER SUMMARY

Chile's Constitutional Tribunal has emerged from a political context with historical contestation between the executive and legislative branches and parties from the center right and left. Further, it was created under an authoritarian government, but still was instrumental in Chile's transition to democracy. Until the reforms of 2005, the CT was influenced by authoritarian vestiges present in the 1980 Constitution, which affected both the selection of some of the judges and the laws reviewed. After the reforms it emerged as a powerful political institution with a revised mixed selection method allowing more judges to be chosen by elected branches.

Policymakers in Chile from the 1960s onward, however, seemed committed to establishing a constitutional court that embodied the ideals of Hans Kelsen and the French Constitutional Court. Besides having broad powers, democratic and authoritarian policymakers were intent on using a mixed selection method to choose judges. The first Tribunal under Allende as well as the Tribunal created in 1980 all allowed for a mixed selection court. This commitment to mixed selections was reinforced by the 2005 reforms, which allowed elected branches to choose more of the judges. Some scholars have argued that the 2005 reforms have led to a more activist Tribunal (Couso 2011: 1535). However, this remains an empirical question. As will be argued in later chapters, as to the constitutional

[35] The draft provision related to the selection method is as follows:

The Constitutional Tribunal will be composed of ten members, designated according to the following procedure: (a) The Supreme Court convenes a public contest to form a three candidate list that will be sent to the president of the republic (b) The president of the republic proposes one of the nominees from said three candidate list to the two houses of the National Congress (c) Each of the houses, with an affirmative vote of at least two-thirds of their members in office, give their approval to the candidate, (d) The president of the republic designates his or her selection naming them as a minister of the Constitutional Tribunal (The Constitute Project, Chilean Draft Constitution 2018).

review of laws put in place by legislators still in power at the time of review (to which the empirical analysis of this study is limited), the reforms seem to have introduced more diverse interests in the Tribunal, leading perhaps to some surprising consequences as to the direction and quality of the Tribunal's decisions evaluated on two metrics discussed in Chapter 8.

5

The Colombian Constitutional Court in Political Context

5.1 INTRODUCTION

As with Chile's Constitutional Tribunal, understanding Colombia's institutions and historical context are paramount for understanding the work of its Constitutional Court (CC). Throughout much of its history, Colombia, like Chile, experienced conflicts among political parties and conflicts regarding the delineation of power between the executive and legislative branches, making political reforms difficult. Unlike Chile, however, Colombia experienced conflicts arising from divisions between rural and the increasingly urbanized populations as well as between national and subregional governments. These conflicts were exacerbated by the country's electoral system, which rewarded patronage.

Also, distinct from the Chilean context, high levels of violence due to the rise of leftist insurgents and paramilitary groups as well as narco-traffickers plagued the country from the 1960s onward leading to a constitutional crisis in the late 1980s. The Colombian government attempted to address this crisis by convening a Constituent Assembly and drafting a new Constitution in 1991, which created Colombia's existing Constitutional Court, providing a clear contrast to Chile's CT created by a military junta. While the new constitution eased some problems with governance, violence with insurgent groups continued and culminated in the extended presidency of Alvaro Uribe. Ushering in a new era of peace in the country, President Juan Manuel Santos' presidency oversaw Congress' passage of a historic peace accord in 2016 allowing members of militant groups, such as the Fuerzas Armadas Revolucionarias de Colombia (FARC), to set aside arms for representation in Congress for the first time in fifty years. Subsequent to Santos' presidency, citizens elected Iván Duque with a decided turn toward more conservative policies and skepticism about the historic peace accord. As with Chile, Colombia has experienced protests related to socioeconomic discontent and inequality since 2019.

This chapter provides the context for understanding Colombia's Constitutional Court as a political actor, which often is called upon to mediate important disputes related to the separation of powers, the definition and protection of rights, as well as other disputes that divide society and its elected officials. The 1991 Constitution created Colombia's Constitutional Court (CC) and provided it with a broad mandate and significant powers. The new constitutional order protected by the CC placed rights and their protection as a significant goal of Colombian society. However, the work of the CC cannot be completely understood unless fluctuations in presidential and legislative leadership and institutional and constitutional changes are taken into account. Further, under the mixed judicial selection system, the CC has had several distinct compositions, which also have affected its role in policy-making. In the early years of the CC, judges were overwhelmingly associated with the Liberal Party, perhaps because the presidency and a majority in Congress during this period were from the Liberal Party. Beginning in 2002 with the election of President Uribe, the CC's composition began to change and lean in a more conservative direction as Uribe ultimately nominated three judges to the CC and two Supreme Court nominees were supported by his party or coalition. Additionally, political parties have become increasingly fragmented influencing Senate confirmation.

To understand these different contexts, similar to the description on Chile, this chapter reviews the country's political and economic history and several crises that led to the convening of a Constituent Assembly in 1991. The chapter reviews the legal and political basis for the Constituent Assembly. The chapter then analyzes the elected branches created by the 1991 Constitution. As with the prior chapter, this chapter provides a description of the Colombian Constitutional Court and legislative debates related to its creation, powers, and mixed selection method.

5.2 BRIEF HISTORY OF POLITICAL AND ECONOMIC DEVELOPMENTS PRIOR TO THE CONSTITUENT ASSEMBLY

Colombia's history has been marked by political and territorial conflicts, violence, and constitutionalism. Colombia's state building also has required the representation of diverse peoples and interests.[1] In 1819, the state of Gran Colombia, which included modern Ecuador, Panama, Venezuela, and Colombia emerged after Simon Bolivar defeated the Spanish at Boyaca. Subsequently, between 1829 and 1830, Gran Colombia dissolved when Ecuador and Venezuela refused to participate in the Ocaña Convention to unify these regions under one constitution and one government with its seat in Bogotá. Civil war ensued, leading ultimately to a

1 Besides historical borders, Colombia is marked by many distinct ethnic populations including those that are indigenous as well as those with heritages deriving from European colonialism, as well as the influx of peoples from the slave trade.

new constitution and the election of Paul Santander to head the new region of Nueva Granada (1830–1849), which now included Colombia and Panama. Nueva Granada's first constitution of 1832, resembling that of the 1811 Constitution of Cundinamerica, established a republican form of government, albeit with strong executive powers, a system of separation of powers, and the listing of individual rights.

Colombia's history is further characterized by violent discord between two dominant political parties,[2] the Liberals and Conservatives, which erupted in the nineteenth and twentieth centuries and informed many of the country's most significant constitutional debates. These political debates focused on the state's organization as a centrist or a federal system and resulted in the enactment of subsequent constitutions and civil war. For example, a constitution in 1863 favored federalism and "followed the North American model of 1787," taking "cues from positions elaborated by George Washington, John Adams and the Federalist party" (LaRosa and Mejía 2017: 56). However, this constitution failed due to divisions among the different party interests, resulting in civil war.

Finally, in 1886, a more durable constitution was enacted, which favored a centralized or unitary government as opposed to a federal system, "once again causing an unequal distribution of power among branches of government in favor of the president, his ministers, the governors and the mayors" (LaRosa and Mejía 2017: 60). This constitution, lasting for 106 years, was considered "the oldest continuously functioning constitution of Latin America" (Archer and Shugart 1997: 110). On its face, the 1886 Constitution seemed to provide presidents with the expansive powers they needed to steer Colombia through the myriad of conflicts it encountered and to enact policy reforms. Under this constitution, the president had the exclusive right to introduce legislation including "organic rules for the national budget; public works; the structure of the executive ministries; salaries for public employees; general norms for foreign exchange, external trade, the national debt, and tariffs; laws decreeing public or private investment or creating new services" (Mainwaring and Shugart 1997: 447). This Constitution provided the president with a veto that could only be overturned by two-thirds of the legislators voting in both chambers if the law was of a certain form or involved certain issue areas. Congress could also imbue the president with extraordinary powers as needed or for the public good. With the consent of his cabinet, the president also had broad decree powers to declare a state of siege and suspend existing law. The Constitution provided the president with broad appointment and removal powers although appointments required an equitable share to the second largest party.

[2] Writing in 1987, Dix claims "Colombia has historically been … one of the most violent societies in the world in its internal politics" (p. 7).

The 1886 Constitution defined the powers of the judiciary and other non-elected bodies. The Constitution allowed for a Supreme Court, a Consejo de Estado,[3] and Superior Tribunals for each judicial district as well as inferior courts. Under the 1886 Constitution, Colombia's Supreme Court was eventually endowed with many powers including the ability to strike down laws and some presidential decrees (see 1886 Constitution, Article 90; Cepeda Espinosa 2004: 537). Indeed, the Supreme Court also had the power to act more like a constitutional court than a high appellate court as contrasted to the Chilean Supreme Court. In the area of decrees, the Supreme Court could resolve conflicts between the president who had vetoed a bill he believed was unconstitutional, and the Congress that overrode the veto (Cepeda Espinosa 2004: 538). In 1910, Legislative Act No. 3 broadened the powers of the Supreme Court, allowing for an *action popularis*, in which public citizens could directly file a case with the Supreme Court claiming the unconstitutionality of both national laws in the abstract as well as presidential decrees issued when Congress had expressly delegated its powers to the president (*Decreto con fuerza de ley*). This may have been the first time that such an action was allowed in the world (Cepeda Espinosa 2004: 538). The Legislative Act also allowed an "unconstitutionality exception" in which judges or other political actors could decide not to apply laws to specific concrete cases if they were unconstitutional and the effect of the decisions was limited to the parties of the case.

Despite the longevity of the 1886 centrist Constitution, Colombian society was fragmented along many dimensions.[4] LaRosa and Mejía (2013) note that "[t]he lesson of Colombia's nineteenth century was clear: presidentialism/centralism created fertile ground whereby party-led management of the state became the factor that contributed most directly to chronic violence" (p. 49). Deep historic divides between Colombia's rural and increasingly urban populations further permeated society.[5] Fragmented interests, however, did not end there. Especially violent periods and civil war due to political party conflicts over whether Colombia should take a centrist or federalist form of government occurred during the War of the Thousand Days (1899–1902), resulting in hundreds of thousands of deaths. In 1902 a treaty ended the Thousand Day War. In 1903 Panama separated from Colombia with support from the United States.

Colombia's "nation building" was intrinsically tied to political partisanship and conflict between the two main parties. Citizens' party affiliations with the Liberals or Conservatives "formed an essential part of what it meant to be Colombian" (LaRosa and Mejía 2017: 69). The two national parties were maintained due to their control over the "electoral machinery" and their ability to name governmental functionaries

3 The Consejo de Estado served as the country's highest administrative law tribunal.

4 Some historians debate the fragmented nature of Colombian society (Safford and Palacios 2002), while others, LaRosa and Mejía (2013), focus on the endurance of Colombian institutions.

5 By 2005, around 74 percent of the population lived in cities (LaRosa and Mejía 2013: 37).

in the regions, allowing people to receive state benefits through their connections with a well-recognized political party (LaRosa and Mejía 2017: 69). However, despite the strength of the two parties, intraparty tensions arose resulting in factions within single parties that would negotiate or merge with factions of the opposing party.

In 1910, reforms to the Constitution of 1886 somewhat weakened the centrist tendencies in government, which had disfavored state and local governments. The reforms attempted to end one-party dominance in government by ensuring seats for the minority in any "electoral jurisdiction" (Dix 1987: 26) and reduce the presidential term from six to four years. For some, "[c]onstitutionalism could function as a means of legitimation as long as the elites of the two parties could agree on basic rules of coexistence" (Safford and Palacios 2002: 316). Through the 1930s, political violence seemed to be contained despite continued party polarization.

This apparent containment, however, began to unravel in the 1940s when the Liberal Party, after holding power for sixteen years, failed to win the presidential election of 1946. This election pitted two liberal candidates against each other: Gabriel Turbay, the party nominee and Jorge Eliécer Gaitán, who was considered by some a populist because of his attempts to deal with inequality brought on by citizen migration to urban centers and the growing middle class, which accentuated disparities in wealth. The divide between these two Liberal candidates provided room for the election of Conservative party challenger, Mariano Ospina Pérez. The elections led to significant amounts of local partisan violence as well as counter protests thus beginning the period known as "*La Violencia*," which would last from 1946 to 1957 and result in the deaths of a quarter million civilians. In April 1948, Gaitán, who still had significant mass support, was assassinated in Bogotá. The strife that immediately followed was classified as the "closest Colombia had come to overt class warfare" since the mid-1800s. While at first parties united against the violence, subsequently Gaitán's martyrdom destroyed both "constitutionalism and party coexistence" (Safford and Palacios 2002: 319). Driven by party polarization and violence, President Ospina declared a state of siege, and in November of 1949 he closed the Liberal Party-dominated Congress. The Liberals then refused to take part in the presidential race scheduled for that month.

Violence continued with the election of Conservative Laureano Gómez and a subsequent *golpe de estado* by General Gustavo Rojas Pinilla in 1953, whose rule became increasingly oppressive and corrupt. However, Rojas Pinilla's reign ended after he attempted to be named president for an additional four years and the army forced him out of office in 1957. The military junta issued Decree 247 in 1957 asking for reforms and ending their own dictatorship. Citizens approved this decree, which included Article 13 stating that only Congress could amend the Constitution (see Cepeda Espinosa 2019).

By 1960, *La Violencia* was regarded as one of the "greatest armed mobilization of peasants" in the western hemisphere's recent history with the possible exception of the Mexican Revolution (Dix 1987: 37). There were many causes for *La*

Violencia, and it emerged from different motivations and interests at different times. However, its duration is attributed to a weak state that "lacked legitimacy ... in an era when government had taken on more functions and greater importance that ever before" making it impossible to act as "a neutral arbiter or enforcer of the public peace." Additionally, "the court system was generally held to be partisan and ineffective in bringing culprits to justice or holding them in prison once convicted" (Dix 1987: 39).

To resolve the partisan conflicts, quell the violence, and return Colombia to civilian rule, the political parties ultimately agreed to establish a sixteen-year power-sharing arrangement referred to as the Frente Nacional or National Front, officially lasting from 1958 to 1974. This arrangement allowed alternations in Liberal and Conservative Party control over the presidency and an equal balance of Liberal and Conservative Party representation in all national and subnational legislatures, bureaucracies, and courts. The National Front arrangement also required that 2/3 of Congress approve legislation. The National Front's power sharing was incorporated into the constitution by referendum in December 1957 and has been classified as a "form of constrained democracy, whereby a variety of antimajoritarian devices assured that neither party could win an election, or lose one" (Dix 1987: 42), but also restricted "democratic politics" (Bushnell 1993: 224). One extraordinary feature of the National Front was that it "followed a set of mathematical guidelines written into the constitution itself" (Bushnell 1993: 224).

In 1968, constitutional reforms allowed for the *Desmonte* or dismantling of the National Front and ended the 2/3 supermajority rules for passage of legislation and in 1970 abolished the party seat requirements at the municipal and departmental levels. The 1968 Constitutional reforms also strengthened the president's preexisting powers under the 1886 Constitution related to declaring a state of siege or an economic emergency (Constitution of 1886, Article 121). The president's "right to declare an economic emergency, and to do so without a convincing reason" gave the president "a tool" that some claim allowed him to "circumvent Congress to implement policy" (Archer and Shugart 1997: 129; see also Cepeda Espinosa 1985).

A 1968 amendment also allowed ex officio review by the Supreme Court of the above-described decrees issued by the president during an economic emergency or state of siege. The Supreme Court on its own "expanded the scope of its own constitutional review functions through a number of landmark decisions" such as using its action *popularis* jurisdiction to review constitutional amendments passed by Congress and international treaties (Cepeda Espinosa 2004: 538–539). The Consejo de Estado, the highest administrative court, also had such powers. The *Desmonte* allowed for the restoration of electoral competition in 1978 and ended alterations of president by party. However, it did allow for the "'equitable' representation of the two parties in the cabinet" to continue (Safford and Palacios 2002: 324). Although officially ending earlier, the National Front was thought to last until 1986, when President Virgilion Barco, a Liberal, returned the country to "one-party rule, which represented the apex of presidentialism in the country" (LaRosa and Mejía 2017: 57).

While the National Front may have helped end political violence and sideline the military, which had strongholds in other Latin American countries, it also weakened party ideology, allowing parties to gain loyalty through clientelistic networks and patronage (LaRosa and Mejía 2013: 50). The National Front's allowance for alteration of power by only two powers also prevented political participation by other parties and interests and may have resulted in high rates of absenteeism for elections (Dix 1987: 42; Bushnell 1993: 224). It also led to the rise of significant opposition movements, such as the National Popular Alliance, or ANAPO.[6]

From 1974 to 1990, Colombia's democratically elected presidents attempted government reforms to address a myriad of problems associated with the legacy of the National Front government, impotent Congresses, inequality (especially the growth of the poor as a result of the country's increased urbanization), and new violent actors who had entered the scene. In the 1960s, several left-wing guerilla organizations were created in the countryside adding to increased violence and ungovernability in the country. These groups included the Revolutionary Armed Forces of Colombia (Fuerzas Armadas Revolucionarias de Colombia – FARC), the National Liberation Army (Ejército de Liberación Nacional – ELN), and the Popular Liberation Army (Ejército Popular de Liberación – EPL), and several other smaller groups. In 1970, a fourth large group, the 19th of April Movement (Movimiento 19 de Abril or M-19), began operations in urban areas.

For years, Colombia's elected presidents had used strong proactive and reactive powers to rule the country, and the political system was set up in such a way as to reward legislators who were more interested in local politics than national policy. Despite the presidents' seemingly strong executive powers under the 1886 Constitution, from the 1970s onward, presidents' powers had decreased leading to the impotence of executives in enacting policy reforms. Presidential action also was stymied by "intraparty competition," which exacerbated conflicts between those living in urban and rural areas. This intraparty competition, attributed to electoral laws, which favored legislators who built their reputations on "narrow clientele networks," also led legislators to focus their interests and incentives away from creating national policy supported by party coalitions (Archer and Shugart 1997: 117).[7] Further, legislators' disinterest in national policy, except when it helped their own personal goals led

[6] Former general and coup leader Rojas Pinilla formed a new political movement, the Alianza Nacional Popular, or ANAPO, and Rojas himself, running as a Conservative candidate, almost won the presidency in 1970. In any event, those in the lower- and lower-middle classes, who were more weakly tied to the two main political parties, often favored ANAPO, which provided an alternative to the National Front government.

[7] Despite these powers, Colombia's Congress still had a significant role in governing because it determined "the allocation of powers under the constitution," which required that for "most reforms to stick over the long term, they must be converted into regular law" (Archer and Shugart 1997: 131).

executives to use their strong powers, rather than the regular legislative process, to enact some of their policy goals. Conflicts among parties, urban and rural politicians, citizens, and the president and Congress continued to foment in the context of violence and corruption exacerbated by paramilitary forces, guerrillas, and narco-traffickers. Further, the National Front power sharing, which was extended to some extent through 1986 and limited to two parties, had resulted in "the absence of a real opposition and alternative mechanisms for participation" (Rampf and Chavarro 2014: 5) resulting in social protests appearing in many forms.

Economic and social problems could not be addressed as the institutional structure and constraints mentioned above made it increasingly difficult for the government to pass reforms. Further, even when the government and Congress were able to pass reforms, the Supreme Court struck them down for largely procedural reasons. For instance, in 1977, President Alfonso López Michelsen (Liberal) attempted to convene a Constitutional Assembly to amend the 1886 Constitution to alleviate the institutional barriers for enacting much needed policy reforms. The Supreme Court ruled this unconstitutional in May 1978 stating that Congress had the exclusive power to amend the constitution and the president could not delegate this to another body. In 1979, President Julio César Turbay Ayala (Liberal) also supported constitutional reforms that would substantially change the administration of justice as well as the country's economic and banking institutions. The Supreme Court in 1981 struck down this entire reform project as unconstitutional due to defects in the constitutional process. As mentioned later in the section on the Constitutional Court, members of the Fourth Commission within Colombia's subsequently convened Constitutional Assembly in 1991 cited these two cases as signs of the Supreme Court's ineffectualness at a time of crisis and in support of the creation of a new constitutional court. As recalled from Chapter 4, Chilean policy-makers in the 1960s and early 1970s similarly justified the creation of Constitutional Tribunal due to the ineffectualness of the Supreme Court during a time of constitutional crisis.

5.3 THE MOUNTING CRISIS

The diverging interests of Congress and the executive on national policy made it difficult for politicians to provide the country with the security and decisiveness that were needed to deal with a myriad of challenges that had emerged in preceding decades. Further, the institutional structure described above continued to make it difficult for the government to pass constitutional reforms although the necessity of reforms had become even more urgent.

For example, subsequent to reform attempts by presidents López Michelsen and Turbay, President Belisario Betancur (Conservative, 1982–1986) won the presidency and attempted many initiatives and reforms to deal with government weaknesses and the country's violence. In most cases, like his predecessors,

Betancur was unsuccessful. In addition to the balance of powers' problems discussed above, presidents also faced increasing violence and lawlessness presented by drug cartels and guerilla movements. As to narco-traffickers, Betancur, who initially wanted to deal with such groups internally, changed course and allowed some extraditions to the United States after the assassination of Justice Minister Rodrigo Lara Bonilla. As to guerrilla groups, Betancur's approach was to deal with the crisis through a broad agenda of social and political reforms. He created a peace commission in 1982 and ceasefires and truces were reached with M-19, ELN, the FARC and some parts of ELN in 1984, although they did not last (Rampf and Chavarro 2014: 6). One consequence of these agreements was that the FARC and the Colombian Communist Party created the Unión Patriótica (UP), which would allow the FARC in theory to participate in the political arena. In 1984, Betancur issued a decree (Decreto 1038 de 1984) declaring that the country was in a state of siege because the public order had been disturbed within the country. Such a declaration is a requirement for the president to later suspend some Congressional acts and issue his own decrees with the force of law although Banks and Alvarez (1991) claim that sidestepping Congress to issue such decrees is not expressly allowed in Colombia, but understood in Colombian constitutional law (p. 56, fn. 77).

Despite concessions under the peace agreements, some groups later claimed that Betancur had violated provisions of these accords. In 1985, members of M-19 stormed the Palace of Justice and took Supreme Court justices and court personnel hostage with the intent of putting the president himself on trial for violations of the peace accord. Subsequently, the military responded in what many thought was inappropriate force. The M-19 attack and military response resulted in the killing of guerilla members, twenty-five Supreme Court justices and many others.[8]

Despite Betancur's failure to reform many aspects of government in 1986, he succeeded with a constitutional reform that allowed for the direct popular election of governors and mayors, which occurred for the first time in 1988. However, although this reform weakened the parties' control over elections, it did not reduce clientelism and allowed other actors to influence the political process.[9] Furthermore, the changes did not make regions more autonomous and strong executives often still controlled what happened at the local level. Further, these reforms were not extensive enough to respond to "challenges posed by the radical

[8] In 2014, after years of litigation, the Inter-American Court of Human Rights found that the Colombian government was responsible for some murders and disappearances related to the Palace of Justice siege. Case of *Rodríguez Vera et al. (The Disappeared from the Palace of Justice)* v. *Colombia*. Judgment of November 14, 2014, available at www.corteidh.or.cr/docs/casos/articulos/seriec_287_ing.pdf.

[9] Some political elites, threatened by Betancur's opening of mayoral elections to the popular vote, allied themselves with paramilitary groups to attack left wing movements, including the UP party, which had emerged during peace talks with the FARC (Rampf and Chavarro 2014: 5).

transformations of Colombian society and culture" nor did they "expand the bases of political participation within the state" (LaRosa and Mejía 2013: 50).

Following the Betancur presidency, Virgilio Barco (Liberal, 1986–1990) became president, winning by a large margin of votes. However, the problems of violence associated with drug cartels and guerrilla groups continued.[10] His presidency was plagued by a public order crisis and many assassinations escalating during the presidential campaign of 1989 when presidential candidate, Luis Carlos Galán Sarmiento, supported by the Liberal power, was assassinated, signaling for many the "ultimate decomposition of Colombia as a functioning, civilized polity" (Safford and Palacios 2002: 336). This also led to the creation of a more organized social movement demanding reforms to open the political process to more actors in the hope of ending the political violence (Rampf and Chavarro 2014: 5; Villarraga 2009).

Negotiations between the government and guerrilla groups focused on the ability of these groups to have meaningful access to political participation, and most of these groups suggested the creation of a constituent assembly. Barco reached a historic peace agreement with M-19 and later agreements were signed with other groups. Despite these groups' demands for a constituent assembly, the Political Pact for Peace and Democracy, signed in November 1989 did not "explicitly mention" the creation of an assembly, and its subsequent creation was instead "a product of a conjunction of different reformist groups within civil society and traditional political parties seeking a modernization and re-legitimation of the political settlement" (Rampf and Chavarro 2014: 7). Indeed, the mounting public disorder and constitutional crisis resulted in many political elites themselves suggesting that the only solution was a new constitution that would "legitimate the state through a system that was more participative and decentralized, more oriented to social justice, more transparent, and less corrupt" (Safford and Palacios 2002: 336).

President Barco's more direct response to the social unrest and political violence involved an attempt to enact constitutional reforms himself to counter Colombia's growing governance and violence problems, although these were unsuccessful leading him to eventually support the creation of a Constituent Assembly. As with his predecessors, Barco first sought approval from parties for his large reform package based on reforms attempted by the three prior presidents with the goal of opening the country's democracy after the National Front era. While initially Barco seemed to have Congressional support for his reforms, the original agreement among parties failed and many blamed the legislature for this (Rampf and Chavarro 2014: 5). In response to this failure, a large student movement called for "an unofficial plebiscite" to be held during the local and congressional elections of March 1990.

[10] In two rulings in 1987, however, the Colombian Supreme Court invalidated extradition treaties, which deprived Barco of a valuable and much feared tool by traffickers.

Although the referendum was not legitimate, students called on citizens to register their assent to convoking a constituent assembly by attaching a "seventh-ballot," which over 3 million Colombians did.

Subsequent to this unofficial show of support, President Barco introduced a referendum on the Constituent Assembly through a decree of martial law (Decreto 927 de 3 mayo de 1990) in which he ordered electoral authorities to count the votes in support of the convening of a constitutional assembly. This decree also led to presidential candidates for that year's election to support the creation of an Assembly. Barco's decree included the following justifications:

> – That the action of groups that promote various forms of violence has intensified, which has aggravated disturbances related to the public order and created a popular clamor for institutions to be strengthened;
> – That urgent institutional strengthening is necessary to return to normality and to overcome the permanent situation of public order disturbances. . . .
> – That the popular mandate must be recognized not only in order to contribute to normalize the situation of disturbance of public order that the country is going through, but to obtain new alternatives of political participation that lead to the achievement of the restoration of public order;
> – That frustrating the popular movement in favor of institutional change would weaken the institutions that have the responsibility to achieve peace and would generate discontent in the population;
> – That such strengthening is possible with the broad and active participation of the citizenship that is necessary for the institutions to regain their full effectiveness. (Decreto 927, 1990)

The Public Ministry opposed Barco's decree opining that a public siege order is used to "maintain" public order rather than change it through a referendum. Further, the Ministry declared that the decree did not contain any mandatory obligation but was used to produce a "political" effect (see Gaceta Especial Sala Constitucional 1993: 13).

Despite the Public Ministry's opinion and the Supreme Court's prior decisions opposing reforms using this procedure, the Supreme Court held that the presidential decree was constitutional (see Supreme Court Sentence 59 of 1990 in Corte Suprema De Justicia, Gaceta Especial Sala Constitucional, Tomo 1 1993). Although previously failing to allow presidential attempts to side step Congress, the Supreme Court this time affirmed Barco's decree claiming that it was constitutional on the grounds that the state of public disturbance had increased since Betancur's declared state of siege (Decree 1038) in 1984 and cited such instances as the Palace of Justice Siege in 1985, the assassination of three presidential candidates, and multiple other violent instances (see Supreme Court sentence 59 (1990)). The Supreme Court also justified its decision by claiming that the decree was neither a reform to the Constitution nor a referendum but rather should be simply treated as providing a legal possibility for counting votes about the public will for creating a Constituent

Assembly to reform the Constitution (see Supreme Court Sentence 59 (1990) in Gaceta Especial Sala Constitucional 1993: 17).

On the same day as he was elected, President César Gaviria issued a Siege Decree (No. 1926 of 1990) defining the "legal framework" for the Assembly. In the decree, the president claimed that government institutions were "'not sufficient to confront the diverse forms of violence'" and a constituent assembly was billed as "a peace pact that would [m]ake the incorporation of armed groups into civil life possible" (Rampf and Chavarro 2014: 6). The decree envisioned a seat on the new Assembly for every armed group that was already in an "advanced stage" of negotiation with the government, which necessarily excluded the FARC. The decree set out the mandate for the Assembly and allowed for the election of seventy delegates and a duration of 150 days spanning from February 4 to July 5, 1991. The decree also listed the topics to be discussed by the Assembly.

The Supreme Court, in what many consider one of its most controversial decisions (Sentencia No. 138 of October 9, 1990), narrowly ruled that this decree was constitutional (Sentence No. 138, 1990) (see Gaceta Especial Sala Constitucional 1993: 37). As with the martial law decree under Barco, the Supreme Court justified Gaviria's decree through a careful analysis of nine points related to its constitutionality. Some of these points included the connection between the Supreme Court's decision to uphold Barco's prior Decree 927 due to the exigent circumstances faced by Colombia. The Court in its opinion stated that the "duty to guard the integrity of the constitution," included preserving the values of the political organization and avoiding a rupture in the constitutional order (p. 62). The Court also upheld Gaviria's decree because it was self-limiting – it was only to exist for a certain time and only for the purpose of strengthening Colombia's system of participatory democracy (p. 66). While upholding the decree in general, a few provisions were found unconstitutional and the Supreme Court's vote was not unanimous.

For some scholars, the decree convoked "an essentially unconstitutional constituent assembly" because Congress was the only institution with the power to amend the constitution (Archer and Shugart 1997: 115, 147; see also Safford and Palacios 2002: 336; Shor 2009). However, this interpretation has come under scrutiny by Manuel J. Cepeda Espinosa (2019), an advisor to Presidents Barco and Gaviria concerning the Assembly and CC constitutional justice from 2001 to 2009. Using the lens of "responsive constitutionalism," Cepeda Espinosa argues that opponents of the Supreme Courts' decisions supporting the Constituent Assembly were based on legal formalism. However, the Supreme Court took a more flexible approach supporting its decisions with ideas of "responsive law and the principle of the sovereignty of the people in democracy" (p. 26) (see also Selznick 1994). Further, Cepeda asserts that "the generation that voted in 1957 could not after 30 years, tie the hands of the 1990 generation" (Cepeda Espinosa 2019: 26.). His reference to 1957 is to the previously mentioned referendum in which Colombians had voted to end a military dictatorship and in the same document required that amending the

Constitution could only be done by Congress (Article 13 of that referendum). Regardless of the legal debate, the legitimacy of the Constituent Assembly was compromised by the low voter turnout, in which 74 percent of individuals failed to vote for delegates (Safford and Palacios 2002: 336; Rampf and Chavarro 2014: 9) and several major players, such as the FARC, its political party the UP, and some other traditional political elites did not participate in the process. The creation of a Constituent Assembly itself was also ironic because it was largely driven by presidential decree with the purpose of undermining executive powers (Archer and Shugart 1997).

5.4 TRANSITION THROUGH THE CONSTITUENT ASSEMBLY AND THE NEW CONSTITUTION OF 1991

Under Gaviria's decree the Constituent Assembly, composed of seventy seats, was chosen through a nationwide district election, and members of Congress were prohibited from running, unless they resigned those seats. Ultimately, the Assembly "mainly represented urban-based reformist sectors of the traditional parties at the expense of regional elites" (Rampf and Chavarro 2014: 10; Dargent and Muñoz 2011: 52) and demobilized guerrillas such as M-19. Prior to and during the work of the Assembly, widespread citizen participation occurred in the form of computerized input given to Assembly delegates from *mesas de trabajo*, or citizen workshops set up across the country (Cepeda Espinosa 2019: 26). The delegates agreed that the Assembly would have a joint presidency among M-19, Movimiento de Salvación Nacional (MSN), and the Liberal Party. All other parties were assured at least one presidency or vice presidency of a substantive commission. The purpose of the Assembly was to restore democracy and peace to Colombia generally by allowing for participation of more parties in the political process and a "more equitable balance of power among the three branches by trimming certain powers from the formerly dominant executive branch in favor of vesting the legislative and judicial branches with greater authority" (Fox and Stetson 1992: 139). The Assembly sought to integrate more rights into a new constitution with more institutions to support their protection. President Gaviria largely took control of the Assembly's specific agenda and the government itself was indirectly represented by the Liberal Party with its own right to present initiatives.

The Constituent Assembly began its work in February 1991 and consisted of five commissions dealing with the following subjects: (1) Principles and rights, (2) Territorial planning, regional and local autonomy, (3) Government and Congress, (4) Justice administration and public ministry, and (5) Economic, social, and ecological affairs. Each commission considered and deliberated on various proposals in these areas for the new constitution. While working on a myriad of issues, one important issue was the reorganization of the judicial system and the creation of a new constitutional court, which President Gaviria greatly supported and of which there was significant debate among delegates over its creation, powers, and selection mechanism, discussed below. The Constitutional Assembly passed a far reaching and rights-based constitution on July 4, 1991.

Ultimately, the Assembly delegates decided on a resolution to dissolve parliament and hold early elections and accepted that they would be barred from running as members of the Senate or the House in the 1991 elections.[11] As these delegates were important members or leaders of their parties or movements, being barred from participating in the newly elected Congress had a "far-reaching impact on the implementation of the new charter" (Ramf and Chavarro 2014: 15) and resulted in at least eight constitutional counterreforms between 1993 and 1998. Further, the constitution did not constitute "a viable political pact" for ending violence because the FARC and ELN were not involved in the new constitution's drafting (Vanden and Prevost 2015: 447).

5.5 POLITICAL INSTITUTIONS UNDER THE 1991 CONSTITUTION

The 1991 Constitution constrained some of the powers of the executive. For example, under this Constitution, the president could no longer appoint governors as these positions became elective. This change resulted in the president losing "an enormous patronage resource" (Archer and Shugart 1997: 119). Additionally, the president's reactive and proactive powers were reduced with the new constitution. Under the 1991 Constitution, it is easier for Congress to overcome a presidential veto and while the president is allowed to veto part of a law, he does not have the concurrent power to partially promulgate legislation (p. 120). As far as proactive or decree powers, some important limits were placed on the president's use of decrees as well as their duration depending on the type of decree. For example, the Constitution of 1991 allowed Congress to amend or appeal presidential decrees dealing with economic emergencies. Such reforms sought to cut back on the president's excessive reliance and use of decree powers (LaRosa and Mejía 2013: 63). The president also can issue decrees if requested by the government and Congress agrees by an absolute majority, although each approved decree is valid only for six months. The president's emergency powers such as declaring a state of siege remained quite expansive under the new Constitution, although there were new limitations as to their duration. A subsequent 1994 law stated that the Constitutional Court could overturn emergency decrees if they "usurp constitutional guarantees; and the Congress may revoke or amend any emergency decree at any time" (Archer and Shugart 1997: 128; see also Carroll and Pachón 2016: 125).

[11] See Ramf and Chavarro (2014: 14–15) for a detailed discussion of the complicated negotiations related to dissolving the existing Congress and barring delegates from elections for a new Congress.

Under the 1991 Constitution, presidents are elected through majority run-off elections and may serve one four-year term. Under a 2005, constitutional amendment, presidents could be reelected to a consecutive second term. Presidents have partial and total veto powers that can be overridden by an absolute majority of both Congressional chambers. Further, presidents have the exclusive power to introduce certain important bills related to the structure of executive ministries, public employees' salaries, and general norms relating to trade, foreign exchange and the national debt to name a few (see Mainwaring and Shugart 1997: 448–449 for an extensive list). The president can also call a referendum. Based on the president's dependence on Congress for the use of many of his powers, the president is incentivized to "form stable relationships" with Congressional deputies in his coalition (p. 127).

As mentioned above the 1991 Constitution attempted to strengthen Congress in relation to the president with some, but not overwhelming success. The electoral system was based on proportional representation, but constitutional reforms ensured that Senate elections would be conducted by a single national district to cut down on clientelism. After the constitutional reforms, some positive trends appeared to have weakened the "old clientele networks" (Archer and Shugart 1997: 116). However, parties within Colombia were increasingly fragmented, and the president needed to rely on such parties to conduct his business (Pachón and Shugart 2010) and "[w]ithout unilateral avenues or strong congressional party support, the president faced constant legislative resistance" (Carroll and Pachón 2016: 122). In 2003, reforms to the electoral system allowed for an open list system rather than "a multimember plurality system preventing cohesive majorities."

As shown in Table 5.1 the orientation of political parties in Colombia is distinct from Chile, especially as time has progressed. The first two presidencies after the Constitutional Assembly, those of César Gaviria and Andrés Pastrana, were held by presidents associated with the Liberal Party and supported by a majority of representatives also associated with the Liberal Party in both houses. However, subsequent to these two presidents, Pastrana, Uribe, Santos, and Duque, all considered more conservative, were elected and governed with the support of very diverse coalitions, some containing factions from both the Conservative and Liberal Parties. Unlike Chile, in which coalitions of parties are similarly oriented along a more traditional left/right spectrum, in Colombia, beginning with Uribe, president's coalitions are made up of diverse parties, such that although the president's full coalition held the majority in both houses in almost the entirety of these presidencies, no single party held a majority. As a result, for both comparison purposes and future coding of judges' orientation (which is only related to the Conservative and Liberal Parties) in relation to the identity of the legislature passing bills that the Court reviews, I list all parties in the Senate and House, the president's party, and whether the president's coalition held a majority in Congress. Additionally, I list which parties hold the *most* seats in Congress for these three presidencies.

TABLE 5.1 *Colombian political context, 1991–2022*

House size	Parties in respective houses, Number of seats	Party with most seats in Congress	President's party	President's coalition has majority
	Gaviria (1991–1994)[a]			
H 161	Liberal Party (PL), 86 Social Conservative Party (PSC), 15 Democratic Alliance (ADM-19), 15 New Democratic Force (NFD), 12 National Salvation Movement (MSN), 12 Seats held by other parties, 21	Liberal	Liberal	Yes
S 102	Liberal Party (PL), 58 Social Conservative Party (PSC), 10 Democratic Alliance (ADM-19), 9 New Democratic Force (NFD), 9 National Salvation Movement (MSN), 5 Seats held by other parties, 11			
	Samper (1994–1998)[a]			
H 161	Liberal, 94 Conservative, 56 Independent, 13	Liberal	Liberal	Yes
S 102	Liberal Party (PL), 59 Social Conservative Party (PSC), 27 New Democratic Force, 5 Seats held by other parties, 9			

(*continued*)

TABLE 5.1 (*continued*)

House size	Parties in respective houses, Number of seats	Party with most seats in Congress	President's party	President's coalition has majority
	Pastrana (1998–2002)[a,b]			
H 161	Liberal Party (PL), 98 Social Conservative Party (PSC), 52 Seats held by other parties, 11	Liberal	Independent backed by conservative party	Yes[b]
S 102	Liberal Party, 58 Conservative Party, 28 Seats held by other parties, 16			
	Uribe I (2002–2006)[a]			
H 166	Liberal Party (PL), 54 Social Conservative Party (PSC), 21 Coalition, 11 Radical Change, 7 Liberal Opening, 5 Seats held by other parties, 68	Liberal	Independent	Yes
S 102	Liberal Party, 50 Conservative Party, 30 Independent, 10 Seats held by other parties, 12			
	Uribe II (2006–2010)[a]			
H 166	Liberal Party (PL), 36 Conservative Party, 30 Social Party of National Unity (Partido de la U), 29	Liberal	P de U, with the Liberal party in the opposition.	Yes

	Radical Change, 20 Alternative Democratic Pole, 9 Popular Civic Convergence (CPC), 8 Team Colombia, 7 Liberal Opening (Apertura Liberal), 5 Seats held by other parties, 19			
S 102	Social Party of National Unity (Partido de la U), 20 Conservative Party, 18 Liberal Party (PL), 17 Radical Change, 15 Alternative Democratic Pole, 11 Popular Civic Convergence (CPC), 7 Team Colombia, 5 Seats held by other parties, 9			
Santos (2010–2014)[a]				
H 166	Partido de la U, 47 Conservative Party (CP), 38 Liberal Party (PL), 37 Radical Change (RC), 15 National Integration Party (PIN), 12 Seats held by other parties, 15	Party de U with Liberal support	P de U	Yes
S 102	Partido de la U, 28 Conservative Party (CP), 22 Liberal Party (PL), 17 National Integration Party (PIN), 9			

(*continued*)

TABLE 5.1 (*continued*)

House size	Parties in respective houses, Number of seats	Party with most seats in Congress	President's party	President's coalition has majority
	Radical Change (RC), 8 Alternative Democratic Pole (ADP), 8 Green Party, 5 Seats held by other parties, 5			
	Santos (2014–2018)[a]			
H 166	Liberal Party (PL), 39 Partido de la U, 37 Conservative Party (PC), 27 Democratic Center, 19 Radical Change (RC), 16 Green Party, 6 Citizens' Option Party (POC), 6 Seats held by other parties, 14	Liberal	P de U	Yes
S 102	Social Party of National Unity (Partido de la U), 21 Democratic Center, 20 Conservative Party (PC), 18 Liberal Party (PL), 17 Radical Change (RC), 9 Citizens' Option Party (POC), 5 Green Party, 5 Alternative Democratic Pole, 5 Seats held by other parties, 2	P de U		

Duque (2018–2022)[a]				
H 172	Liberal Party (PL), 35 Democratic Center (CD), 32 Radical Change (CR), 30 Partido de la U, 25 Conservative Party (CP), 21 Green Alliance, 9 Seats held by other parties, 13	Liberal	Democratic Center	Yes
S 108	Democratic Center (CD), 19 Radical Change (CR), 16 Conservative Party (CP), 15 Liberal Party (PL), 14 Partido de la U, 14 Green Alliance, 10 Alternative Democratic Pole (POLO), 5 Seats held by other parties, 9	Democratic Center		

[a] Information from the Interparliamentary Union http://archive.ipu.org/parline-e/reports/2067_A.htm was the source for this table.

Other sources vary slightly as follows:

Archer and Shugart (1997) indicate that in 1991, the Liberal Party held 87 seats in the House and 56 in the Senate and the Conservative Party held 56 in the House and 9 in the Senate. In 1994, this source indicates that the Liberal Party had 88 seats in the House and 56 in the Senate and the Conservative party had 56 in the House and 20 in the Senate.

Posada-Carbó (2013: 243) indicates that in 2006 in the House, the Party of the U held 29 seats, the Conservative Party 29 and the Liberal Party 37 and in the Senate, the Party of the U had 20 seats, the Conservative Party 18 and the Liberal Party 18. In 2010, in the House, the Party of the U held 47 seats, the Conservative Party 37 and the Liberal Party 35 and in the Senate, the Party of the U had 28 seats, the Conservative Party 22 and the Liberal Party 17.

[b] See Carroll and Pachón (2016: 128) showing that President Pastrana's coalition held the majority of seats in both houses from 1998–2000 and 2001–2002, but not 2000 to 2001.

Colombia's presidents have all had distinct policy agendas and faced particular challenges implementing them. The Constitutional Court was often required to review the constitutionality of important policy changes instigated by these various governments. The Gaviria presidency (1991–1994) under the new Constitution focused on ending drug cartel violence by offering traffickers reduced sentences and the avoidance of extradition.[12] Gaviria attempted to crack down on drug crimes, especially in reaction to a Constitutional Court decision that allowed for the personal use of drugs but supported penalties for drug sales and distribution (C-221/1994). Gaviria's administration also attempted peace negotiations with the FARC and ELN, which were unsuccessful.

Following Gaviria, Ernesto Samper Pizano of the Liberal Party was elected as president (1994–1998), but his presidency was marred by accusations that he had received millions of dollars from the Cali cartel for this election campaign. Congress attempted to impeach him twice, and the Clinton administration "decertified" Colombia in its review of country cooperation with the American War on Drugs. The corruption scandal and focus on drug cartels allowed left-wing guerrilla and right-wing paramilitary groups to expand their reach during his presidency (Vanden and Prevost 2015: 448). Following Samper, Ernesto Pastrano, a conservative, won the presidency (1998–2002). He instituted Plan Colombia, designed to eradicate illegal groups, support settlement with guerrilla groups such as the FARC and ELN, and strengthen the economy, human rights, and judicial institutions. In practical terms, Plan Colombia became a "conduit for U.S. military and police assistance" (Vanden and Prevost 2015: 449).

Subsequently, Alvaro Uribe, a Conservative and formerly associated with the Liberal Party, was elected. His presidency is marked by two distinct periods, the first spanning from 2002 to 2006, the normal four-year term for a Colombian president who at that time was prohibited from reelection and a second term from 2006 to 2010 subsequently allowed by a constitutional amendment and confirmed as constitutional by the CC on substantive and procedural grounds (C-1040/2005), although an attempt to allow a third term also through constitutional amendment was not allowed by the CC (C-141/2010).

The Court's two decisions to allow Uribe's second term but disallow a third term rested on a controversial doctrine established by the Court itself known as the substitution of constitution doctrine, established in a prior case (C-501/2003). Article 374 of the Colombian Constitution allows the Constitution to be amended in only three ways: (1) by approving votes of two consecutive sessions of both houses – the first by simple majority and the second by absolute majority, (2) by a Constituent Assembly, and (3) by a popular referendum (introduced by a specific percent of

[12] Under one such deal, Pablo Escobar surrendered to the authorities but subsequently escaped and was shot in 1993 leading to the dismantling of the Medellín cartel, and the Cali cartel soon after took control.

voters and passed by Congress or introduced by the Colombian government) (see Cepeda Espinosa and Landau 2017 for this explanation: 327–328). In 2003, the Constitutional Court established the "substitution of constitution" doctrine in a case involving constitutional amendments through referendum (C-551/2003; Cepeda Espinosa and Landau 2017: 341). This doctrine asserted that if changes of the constitution are so broad and sweeping as to provide for a new or substitute constitution then they are not allowed without convening a constitutional assembly (see Bernal 2013 for more on this doctrine). In establishing the doctrine, the Court in this case stated that "[t]he power of reform, a constituted power, has material limits, because the power to reform the Constitution does not include the possibility of derogating it, subverting it or substituting it in its integrity" (excerpted by Cepeda Espinosa and Landau 2017: 341).

This substitution of constitution doctrine was at issue in Uribe's quest for a second term and supported by a relatively new party, the National Social Unity Party (Partido Social de Unidad Nacional commonly referred to as Partido de la U), made up of some former liberals and conservatives who broke from traditional parties to support Uribe. In 2004, Uribe's coalition enacted Legislative Act No. 2, which would amend the Constitution to allow a president to be reelected for an additional consecutive or nonconsecutive term. The CC reviewed the constitutionality of this law in C-1040/2005.[13] Those bringing the case to the CC argued that there were ten procedural flaws in the legislative act. The Court disregarded these flaws in a 6 to 3 vote. Additionally, those bringing the case asked the CC to decide if the law constituted an improper substitution of constitution. The Court found that the law did not constitute such a substitution in a 7 to 2 vote. The Court carefully analyzed the legislative act and asked whether it replaced a "core element" of the 1991 Constitution with a completely different text. According to the majority, the amendment did not constitute a substitution because it did not replace "essential elements that define our democratic and social state, founded on human dignity." The Court reasoned that the people still were allowed to choose their presidents and that institutions and checks and balances would remain in place. Further, the Court reasoned that the president would not be vested with new powers (see Cepeda Espinosa and Landau 2017: 345). In dissent, Judge Jaime Araújo Rentaría argued that the legislation was a substitution of the constitution as it "changed the form of government" (p. 350) and Judge Alfred Beltran Sierra also argued that the

[13] In this decision favoring the reelection of Uribe, the Court's members included three appointees of President Pastrana (Cepeda, Monroy Cabra, and Tafur Galvis, all associated with the Conservative Party), three selected by the Supreme Court (Vargas Hernández, Cordoba and Beltrán, all associated with the Liberal Party), and three selected by the Consejo (Sierra Porto and Araujo Rentaría, linked to the Liberal Party, and Escobar Gil associated with the Conservative Party). On the procedural issues and favoring unconstitutionality of the additional term, Rentaría, Beltrán and Cordoba dissented and on the substantive issues in which the majority favored constitutionality, Rentaría and Beltrán dissented.

amendment constituted a substitution because it violated "norms of equality," which petitioners bringing the case had argued placed the incumbent president on unequal footing with any other presidential candidate.

President Uribe's popularity and authoritarian tendencies led him to seek a third term in 2010. His supporters gathered signatures to hold a referendum on this third term and the CC was asked to determine its constitutionality in C-141/2010. At this time, some thought that judges appointed by Uribe as well as three other conservatives sitting on the Court would allow the third term and the decision would be similar to the one in 2005.[14] Despite this, the Court defied expectations finding that the law allowing a third term by Uribe was unconstitutional on procedural grounds by a 7 to 2 vote and on substantive grounds, for unlawfully substituting the constitution with a new law, by a vote of 5 to 4. One of three judges chosen by Uribe, María Victoria Calle Correa, voted with the majority finding the law unconstitutional.[15] Again, the Court's decision is not easily explained by partisanship or even the Court's concern that the decision would be overridden by the increasingly authoritarian standing president. Other factors relating to making the correct constitutional decision and upholding the legitimacy of the Court seem to be at play.

The Court's decision regarding the status of the referendum for a third term as a substitution of constitution required it to carefully distinguish its prior decision, which allowed the second election and claimed that this was not an improper substitution. Much of the Court's reasoning turned on the prior decision's own distinctions, which supported the idea that a one-time change in the number of terms was not in and of itself a problem. However, in the 2010 case, the Court became concerned with the total length of time that Uribe would serve as president if the referendum approved this third election. The Court stated that approval of the referendum would extend the duration of Uribe's presidency to twelve years in total and this not only violated Colombia's "institutional history" but also would affect the "institutional equilibrium" (see Cepeda Espinosa and Landau 2017: 354). The two opposing case outcomes suggest that the Court was uncomfortable with too much executive reach and invoked the argument of institutional equilibrium to justify its decision. As will be seen in the next section on the CC, institutional equilibrium

[14] The Court in this case was composed of six judges associated with the Conservative Party (Gonzalez Cuervo (President Uribe), Calle Correa (President Uribe), Mendoza Martelo (*Consejo*), Palacio (Supreme Court), Pretelt (President Uribe), and Pinilla (Supreme Court) and three associated with the Liberal Party, Henao (Consejo), Sierra Porto (Consejo), and Vargas Silva (Supreme Court)). However, two conservative judges (Calle selected by Uribe and Mendoza selected by the Consejo) sided with the majority finding that the law allowing a third term was unconstitutional.

[15] In an interview of with María Victoria Calle Correa on May 2, 2016, when she was president of the Court, I asked her questions about whether she thought judges voted based on loyalty to their appointer, she responded no and used her vote in this case as an example as she was selected by President Uribe, but voted against his third-term election and against the positions of the two other Uribe nominees, Pretelt and Pinilla.

arguments also justified the mixed selection method that the Constituent Assembly ultimately approved for selecting CC judges.

During his presidency, Uribe, who had been critical of Pastrana's peace negotiations, instead strengthened state security forces against insurgents. His policies were thought to have reduced violence but veered away from establishing any meaningful peace and gave rise to new paramilitary forces and extrajudicial killings, which led to criticisms from human rights groups. Uribe also made progress on the Colombian economy by implementing his own variety of neoliberal economic programs, which were disfavored by labor groups.

Following Uribe, Juan Manuel Santos, Uribe's former defense minister, was elected president in 2010 and served two consecutive terms allowed under the aforementioned constitutional amendment. While formerly aligned with Uribe and in agreement with his stance on peace negotiations, Santos changed his position and publicly declared in 2012 that his government would enter into peace negotiations with the FARC, which initially took place in Havana. By 2013, agreement had been reached on political participation of guerrillas and agrarian reforms. However, a final agreement was not reached or signed until September 2016, and Santos, who was committed to having such a historic peace accord approved by the population, called a referendum in which the accord was rejected by 50.2 percent of those who voted. Subsequently, the agreement was revised in the form of legislation made to appease those who had voted against it during the referendum, and Santos met with Uribe to consider his objections. The Colombian Congress voted overwhelmingly for the revised peace accord ending fifty-two years of civil conflict. Among other novel items, the peace agreement allowed for the establishment of the Jurisdicción Especial para la Paz (JEP), a court of eighteen justices divided into three chambers to hear some of the most egregious cases during Colombia's civil conflict with the participation of victims. Also, under Santos, Congress adopted a reform for the balance of powers and institutional adjustment (Acto Legislativo 2 de 2015, D.O. No. 49.560, 1 de julio 2015). Iván Duque was elected in 2018 campaigning on the need to rewrite the peace accord. Protests in 2019 on economic and social reforms as well as other issues were on a "scale not seen since the assassination of Jorge Eliécer Gaitán" (Franz and Gómez Suárez 2019). Colombia is set to elect a new president in May 2022.

5.6 THE COLOMBIAN CONSTITUTIONAL COURT

5.6.1 *Creation and Powers of the Constitutional Court*

Unlike Chile's CT, created under the military regime, the Colombian Constitutional Court was created by the Constituent Assembly as part of a new constitution intended in part to bolster an ineffectual Congress and curb executive powers as well as to provide an institution of constitutional review that would have more power than the preexisting Supreme Court. Additionally, the Court was put in place to protect new rights that were found in the new Constitution.[16]

To consider constitutional changes, the Fourth Commission of the Constituent Assembly dealt exclusively with issues related to the administration of justice, which included all levels of courts and other legal actors. The Fourth Commission included its president, Fernando Carrillo from the Liberal Party, and its vice president, Jaime Fajardo Landaeta of EPL. The commission had a total of nine members. Among many issues, this Commission and the full Assembly vigorously debated whether the country should create a constitutional court to replace the Supreme Court as the chief institution dealing with the constitutionality of laws and how to select judges if such a court was created. Their discussions highlighted the creation and powers of other constitutional courts worldwide. President Gaviria, on February 5, 1991 appeared before the Constituent Assembly to support the creation of a new constitutional court (see Diario de la Asamblea Nacional Constituyente, martes 5 de febrero de 1991: 3–4).

In meetings as early as April 8, 1991, conflicting proposals and justifications were heard about the viability of creating a constitutional court separate from the existing Supreme Court and Consejo de Estado. Some argued that a new court was needed because the existing Supreme Court had historically been ineffectual citing decisions in 1977 and 1978 in which the Court had stricken down needed constitutional reforms (discussed above). Others such as José María Velasco Guerrro, a conservative party member chosen by M-19 and a former Supreme Court magistrate, argued that a new court was unnecessary because the Supreme Court had previously preserved the constitution and the Colombian legal method used by this court was revered in other countries. The conservative party was generally against the creation of a new court and thought a constitutional chamber within the Supreme Court was sufficient.

Although changes were accepted by the Commission on issues regarding the Supreme Court and the Consejo de Estado, additional discussion was needed regarding the creation of the CC (see Comisión Cuarta, Informe de Minoría sobre la Creación de una Corte Constitucional, 22 mayo, 1991). Commission members Teresa Garcés Lloreda, associated with the conservative party and chosen by M-19 to serve on the Constituent Assembly, and Velasco Guerrero presented arguments on May 22 regarding the creation of the CC. Garcés Lloreda presented arguments in favor of creating a CC, again referring to faulty decisions of the Supreme Court of 1977 and 1979, which had rejected reforms that may have prevented the problems the country faced subsequently. She also suggested that it was necessary to have a separate

[16] Author interview with José Gregario Hernández Galindo in Bogotá on April 29, 2016, who emphasized the need of a constitutional court in Colombia and other democracies to defend the constitution and protect fundamental political, social, and collective rights. He emphasized the need for the court to protect the "integridad y supremacia" of the constitution.

court of judges who were public law specialists and who could unify constitutional jurisprudence, which was decentralized in Colombia. Additionally, she argued that a constitutional court would provide the country with a political mechanism of control ("*un mecanismo de control politico*" (Comisión Cuarta, Informe de Minoría sobre la Creación de una Corte Constitucional, 22 mayo, 1991: 6)

According to Cepeda Espinosa (2004), one of the arguments in favor of creating the Constitutional Court was the perception that the Supreme Court, under the 1886 Constitution and other laws was seen as insufficient for providing a real check on other political actors and was politicized. The Supreme Court chose its own justices and "required respect for political parity" between the two main parties (p. 540). Second, the Supreme Court at that time was seen as out of touch with citizens and unable to adequately protect rights due to its "organic-formalist interpretive approach," which widened the gap between the court and "everyday socio-political life." (p. 543) In his analysis of some prior Supreme Court decisions, Cepeda Espinosa (2004) noted that the Supreme Court tended to focus on procedural and jurisdictional issues rather than substantive rights.

Ultimately after considering the costs and benefits of the creation of the new court, the Commission voted on a constitutional article making the CC the guardian of the integrity and supremacy of the constitution. This was approved by a majority of Commission members (six) including Garcés Lloreda, Salgado Vásquez, Gómez Hurtado, Carrillo Flores, Holguín Sarria, and Abello Roca. Three judges voted against the creation of the CC including Velasco Guerrero, Londoño Jiménez, and Fajardo Landaeta. Like Chile's CT, the CC ultimately was provided with vast review powers allowing it to review, abstractly and with *erga omnes* effects, the constitutionality of laws[17] and executive decrees as well as individual rights cases in the form of *tutelas*.

The CC's docket includes cases that require both mandatory and a priori review of international treaties and statutory law. Unlike the CT, citizens may bring certain types of abstract constitutional review cases before the CC, which also has heavy caseloads hearing thousands of *tutelas*. Table 5.2 describes the court's powers and whether citizens can trigger the Court's review powers and includes amendments of 2015. Writing in 2019, Cepeda Espinosa (2019) notes that "[a]ll the presidents and parliamentary majorities have found in the Constitutional Court a limit to their most important policies" (p. 31).

As shown in Figure 5.1, in Colombia, the Court has a considerably larger yearly caseload than the Chilean Tribunal (see Figure 4.1 in Chapter 4 for a comparison). Besides reviewing thousands of *tutelas* and presidential decrees, the CC has heard on average hundreds of abstract review cases per year. Of these, about seventy-three a year are for the review of legislation passed by the government in power at the time

[17] Colombia does not have as expansive supermajority requirements as Chile but does require the legislature to pass amendments and constitutional reforms under these rules.

TABLE 5.2. *The CC's powers under the 1991 Constitution and 2015 reforms*

Powers of Colombia's Constitutional Court under the 1991 Constitution, Article 241
1. Decide petitions of unconstitutionality against measures amending the Constitution, no matter the origin, exclusively for errors of procedure in their formation (Article 241(1)). Citizens can initiate.
2. Decide, prior to a popular expression of opinion, on the constitutionality of the call for a referendum or a constituent assembly to amend the Constitution, for errors of procedure in their formation (Article 241(2)).
3. Decide on the constitutionality of referendums about laws and popular consultations and plebiscites of a national scope, in case of the latter exclusively for errors of procedure in their convocation and implementation (Article 241(3)).
4. Decide on the petitions of unconstitutionality against statutes, both for their substantive content as well as for errors of procedure in their formation (Article 241(4)). Citizens can initiate.
5. Decide on the petitions of unconstitutionality against decrees with the force of law issued by the government on the basis of Article 150, paragraph 10, and Article 341 of the Constitution for their substantive content as well as for errors of procedure in their formation (Article 241(5)). Citizens can initiate.
6. Decide on the exceptions provided for in Article 137 of the Constitution (Article 241(6)).
7. Decide definitively on the constitutionality of the legislative decrees by the government on the basis of Articles 212, 213, and 215 of the Constitution (Article 241(7)).
8. Decide definitively on the constitutionality of the bills or proyectos de ley opposed by the government as unconstitutional and of proposed statutory bills, both on account of their substantive content as well as for errors of procedure in their formation (Article 241(8)).
9. Revise, in the form determined by law, the judicial decisions connected with the protection of constitutional rights (Article 241(9)).
10. Decide definitively on the constitutionality of international treaties and the laws approving them. With such a purpose, the government will submit the treaties to the Court within six (6) days following the their approval. Citizens can initiate.
11. Settle conflicts that occur between distinct jurisdictions (Article 241(11) was modified as a result of Article 14 acto legislative 2 de 2015).
12. Adopt its own regulations (Article 241(12) added as a result of the acto legislativo 2 de 2015).

of review. The Court also has used its powers to develop Colombia's constitutional jurisprudence. For example, the CC includes international law as part of its domestic constitutional jurisprudence, known as the "constitutional block" (see Cepeda Espinosa and Landau 2017: 7). Furthermore, many of the important cases for which the CC has forged its reputation are not only in the form of decisions of abstract review, but also include tutelas or other types of review. In 2016, when asked about the most important cases that the CC had decided, the president of the Tribunal then, Calle Correa, listed ten of which four involved abstract review.[18]

[18] During an author interview in April of 2016 in Bogotá with Calle Correa, she indicated that in the Court's twenty-four years of existence it had made decisions on about 23,500 cases. The ten cases she listed as the most important included (1) C-221/1994 (authorizing personal use of

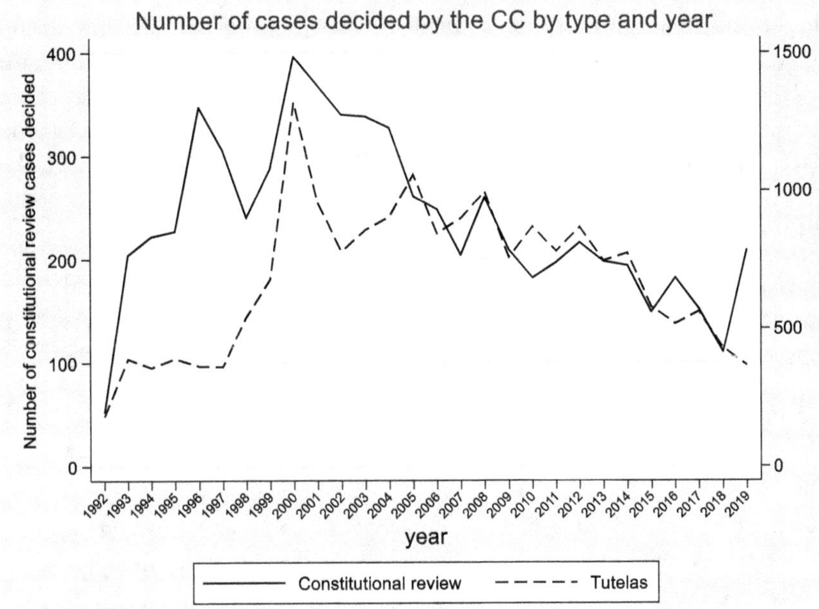

FIGURE 5.1 Caseloads of the Colombian CC, 1992–2019

5.6.2 *Selection of the Constitutional Court*

Debates about the selection of judges for Colombia's CC occurred within Colombia's Fourth Commission of the Constituent Assembly and the Assembly as a whole, which was tasked with drafting a new constitution. As with the Chilean legislature, members of the Colombian Constituent Assembly were concerned

drugs, but allowing the state to regulate some use based on certain age and location conditions); (2) SU-047/1999 (regarding parliamentary inviolability and closing the investigation of the Supreme Court against some members of Congress); (3) T-025/2004 (recognizing many rights for those internally displaced under Colombia's international obligations); (4) T-760/2008 (recognizing a fundamental right to health); (5) SU-039/1997 (the first time the CC spoke about the right to consult with indigenous communities on legislation that affected them directly); (6) T-523/1997 (discussing the constitutional limits related to indigenous justice and recognizing that western traditions of punishment and sanctions are incompatible with ethnic diversity); (7) C-004/1992 (recognizing that the Court has the competence to control declarations of a state of exception and describing criteria for analyzing their appropriateness), (8) T-881/2002 (related to the suspension of electricity to prisons for failure to pay and discussing human dignity); (9) C-141/2010: (relating to convoking a referendum for a third consecutive re-election for a president); and (10) C-577/2011 (recognizing the rights of same sex couples to form a family). Additionally, the CC's website provides what it considers the CC's "main decisions," which it provides in English, available at www.corteconstitucional.gov.co/english/#MainDecisions.

about establishing a more plural society and one in which there was also an equilibrium of powers within government institutions. The Fourth Commission voted on several proposals regarding the selection of judges if the Court was ultimately created. The first proposal concerning whether the CC should have nine judges was approved by seven commission members with two dissents by Fajardo Landaeta and Londoño Jiménez. For the selection of judges on a future CC, the Commission could not reach consensus, but it considered the following proposals listed with their votes.

- Garcés Lloreda and Velasco Guerrero proposed that magistrates would be named from lists sent by the Consejo Superior de la Judicatura.[19] This proposal was approved by only the two who proposed it with 7 votes against.
- Carlos Daniel Abello Roca, selected to the Assembly by the Movimiento de Salvación Nacional or MSN, proposed that judges would be selected by the Senate with a third nominated by the president and 2/3 by the Consejo Superior de la Judicature. Four commission members voted for this proposal with 5 against (i.e., Salgado Vásquez, Londoño Jiménez, Velasco Guerrero, Fajardo Landaeta y Garcés Lloreda).
- Holguín Sarria of the Liberal Party proposed that two judges would be chosen by the Supreme Court, two by the Consejo, two by the president, two by the Defensoría del Pueblo and one by the Colombian Academy of Jurisprudence. This method was not submitted for vote.
- Londoño Jiménez suggested that the first CC would be chosen by the president for four years and subsequent courts would allow the Supreme Court to choose three, the Consejo de Estado three and the Consejo Superior de la Judicature three judges (see Informe de Minoría of May 22, 1991: 22–23). Ultimately, the Commission could not agree on any of these proposals but did suggest two for the Assembly's plenary to consider – the proposal by Abello Roca and that of Holguín Sarria (Gaceta Constitucional, May 29, 1991: 12).

In the plenary session, in one of the few speeches made before the Constituent Assembly, President Gaviria adamantly supported the creation of the CC and advocated the selection of its judges by the Senate from separate lists of three nominees proposed by the president, the Supreme Court, and the Consejo, with these institutions proposing judges for three of nine seats on the CC (see Landau 2015). He was supported by Jaime Castro, who gave a speech before the Assembly in June 1991. Conservative party member Hernando Yepes Arcila counter-argued that

[19] The Consejo Superior de la Judicatura is a judicial council tasked with administration, planning, and the discipline of judges within the regular judicial branch. Judicial councils are a common feature of many countries (see Garoupa and Ginsburg 2015).

the president's proposal was a "power grab." Ultimately, Gaviria's proposal was adopted, and this method of selection is still used to select judges.

However, where Chile's CT allows three branches of government to unilaterally choose judges, Colombia's CC requires branch (i.e., executive and two high courts) nominees to be confirmed by the Senate. As suggested by Moreno et al. (2003) and Dargent (2009), allowing additional veto points into the appointment process raises the likelihood of judicial candidates who are more moderate since agreeing on candidates should require compromises by different partisan interests. However, this of course depends on whether branch appointers are in fact controlled by different interests.[20]

Like the Chilean CT, the CC selects judges under a mixed appointment method, which allows different political actors to select a certain number of judges. On both courts, judges serve only one full term and cannot be reappointed. Figure 5.2 describes how different judges are chosen on the CC from 1993 to the present.[21] Since 1993, three branches of government have been involved in appointing CC judges in a two-step process. First, the president, the Supreme Court, and the Consejo de Estado (i.e., the highest administrative court) each draft a list of three candidates for each of these institution's three designated seats on the Court as they become vacant. Second, the Senate chooses and confirms one individual from each list of three.[22] Shor (2009) emphasizes that this appointment mechanism found in the 1991 Constitution dramatically differed from the appointment of Supreme Court judges who internally chose their own judges, similar to Chile's Supreme Court and "created an appointment mechanism that made the Constitutional Court broadly representative of the political forces of the nation" (p. 15) [23]

Colombia's particular mixed selection system may allow for the selection of a full court that is not too heavily influenced by any one political force. Cepeda Espinosa (2019: 31) suggests that for presidential appointees, "few elected justices have been close to the actual president of the Republic" and for the Supreme Court appointees, these are nominated by an independent court. Further, the Senate confirmation makes it hard for the Court to be dominated by politics

[20] Stone Sweet (2012) suggests that "[r]equiring compromise among political elites is less likely to produce a polarized court" (p. 824).

[21] When the Court was first created, it had a slightly different selection mechanism in which two judges were chosen by the president, one judge was chosen by the chief prosecutor, one by the Supreme Court, and one by the Consejo de Estado. The five judges then chose the other two judges. This selection method was only used for the initial Court and Congress did not have any influence over it. The Court also employs different types of auxiliary judges to sit on cases when a quorum is not possible.

[22] In theory, the Senate could reject the branch nominators' lists in their entirety. However, the Constitution and court rules do not specifically state this and it does not appear to have occurred in the history of the Court.

[23] Further, a large number of judges at least in the initial court were academics which "[a] number of important politicians believed . . . were more likely to have attitudes 'in accord with a progressive, new-constitutional political agenda'" (Shor 2009: 17, citing Landau 2005).

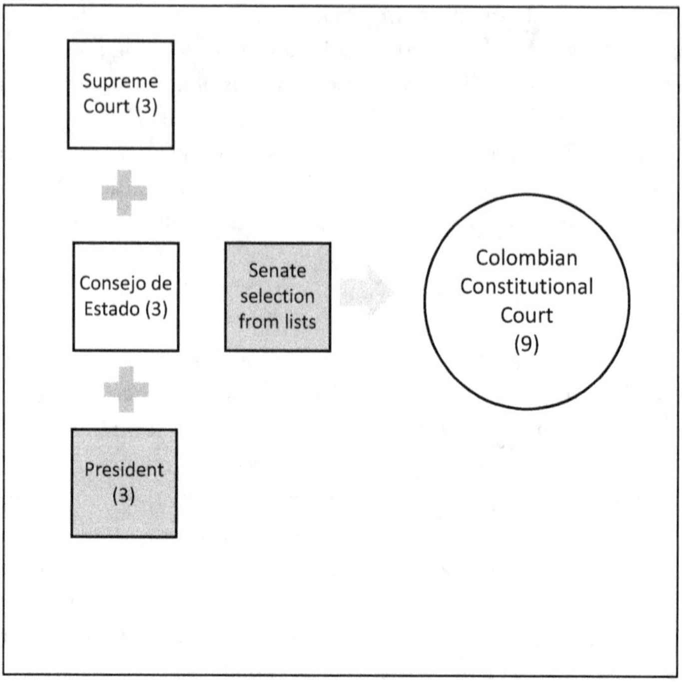

FIGURE 5.2 Mixed selection on Colombia's CC, 1993–present
Note: In the first row, shaded boxes represent nominators who are elected by voters and white boxes represent appointers who are not elected.

because the Senate "rarely has an absolute majority" held by one party and "is bound to select candidates" from the lists prepared by the institutional nominators. However, Montoya Garcia (2013) claims that the Senate considers judges' political ideology in its confirmation decisions and that judges must lobby Senators for support, which is crucial for their approval. Lamprea (2010) argues that the Consejo de Estado chooses judges based on their perception of judges' political preferences based on a liberal and conservative "dichotomy," while the Supreme Court chooses judges based on their assessments of judges' "loyalty towards the Supreme Court" once nominated (p. 16). Despite, these anecdotal accounts, ultimately the politicization of CC judges is an empirical question.

Besides voting on the creation of the CC, its powers and selection method, the Fourth Commission and ultimately the Constituent Assembly voted on additional items related to judges' qualifications, disciplinary measures, and judges' term length. The commission voted that judges would remain on the Court for their term length as long as they exercised good conduct. Additionally, the Commission approved nine-year terms for constitutional court judges as well as the judges of the other high courts. This was affirmed by a majority with three dissents (Londoño Jiménez, Velasco Guerrero y Fajardo Landaeta). The current term for CC judges is now eight years. In general constitutional judges must be attorneys who are Colombian citizens by birth with no criminal record and have worked within the judicial branch, the public ministry or as an attorney or academic for fifteen years. Judges can be investigated and accused by a commission of immunity (Article 178-A and removed by the Senate (Article 175).

In Colombia, since 1993, the CC has included nine judges. Decisions are reached by a majority voting rule (Decreto Ley 2067 de 1991, D.O. No. 40.012 del 4 de septiembre 1991). If a judge recuses himself, then they are replaced with an ad hoc judge or *conjuece*.[24] According to the Court's rules, seven of nine judges constitute a quorum.[25] In abstract review, the focus of this book, the CC considers amicus curiae briefs, and the influential procurator-general offers an opinion on every case that the Court hears. As with Chile, the CC is quite transparent posting all of its majority decisions as well as dissents and concurrences on its website. Judges on the CC often deliberate quite a bit on cases of constitutional review and other important cases.[26] After the chief judge determines that all deliberation has been exhausted, judges raise their hands to signal their positions about the laws and the chief judge counts the votes that constitute a majority position.[27]

5.7 CHAPTER SUMMARY

Colombia's Constitutional Court emerged from a political context with historical contestation between the executive and legislative branches as well as between the two main political parties, the Liberal Party and the Conservative party, who were the only parties represented in the power-sharing government of the National Front. Unlike the emergence of the CT, the CC was not created under a dictatorship, but instead resulted from at times heated political negotiations during a Constituent Assembly, which was demanded by political leaders and citizens to deal with the ineffectualness of government during this time.

Despite much debate, President Gaviria, some members of the Fourth Commission, and ultimately the Constituent Assembly supported the CC's creation, which like Chile's was based on the Kelsian constitutional court model seen in

[24] An analysis of over 89,000 judges' votes on the CC from 1992 to 2014, including review of executive decrees, shows that votes of these auxiliary judges account for 2 percent of the data.

[25] Ley 270 de 1996, Marzo 7 Estatutaria de la Administración de Justicia, Artículo 54.

[26] Based on author interviews with judges and court personnel of the Colombian CC held in April and May of 2016 in Bogotá.

[27] Author interview of Calle Correa, the president of the Court at the time of the interview (May 2, 2016, Bogotá). Another CC judge interviewed suggested that often time there is extensive debate ("debate, debate, y debate") (April 29, 2016, Bogotá). Additionally, former justice José Gregorio Hernández Galindo explained that it was up to the president of the Court to determine when there had been sufficient debate prior to a vote (April 29, 2016, Bogotá).

Europe. In fact, arguments behind the creation of these European courts were discussed during the debates surrounding the creation of the CC. Further, debate ultimately resulted in the CC's mixed selection mechanism, which has not varied since 1993. Unlike Chile, the Colombian Constitutional reformers were intent on a break from the past and the creation of the new Court and a new Constitution replete with rights for the Court to protect.

6

Determinants of Legal Invalidation by Constitutional Judges

6.1 INTRODUCTION

As suggested in Chapters 4 and 5, both Chile and Colombia's current constitutional orders emerged from conflict. Chile retained much of its 1980 Constitution with some changes for the pacted transition, and Colombia's arose from a Constitutional Assembly that was convened due to ongoing violence in the country. In both cases, it was understood that constitutional reforms to institutions were much needed to usher in new eras of government. While Chile ultimately kept its Constitutional Tribunal established under the military junta intact with some significant reforms in 2005, Colombia's constitutional court was created under the 1991 Constitution. In both instances the powers of these courts and the type of mixed selection chosen were carefully considered.

Whether the constitutional courts in these countries are able to constrain elected politicians as intended and under what conditions requires an understanding of what drives individual and collective choice and by what manner individual choices are aggregated (see Coleman 1990: 769). Judges may have their own individual goals and opinions, but they must weigh these against other considerations imposed upon them by the collegial forum within which they work. This chapter thus explores individual choice, while Chapter 7 investigates the determinates of the decisions of the two constitutional courts acting collectively. Understanding both provides information about when these two mixed selection constitutional courts are most likely to veto laws.

Policymakers choose mixed selection and other appointment methods to control the choices that judges make singularly and collectively. Over half of the constitutional courts worldwide currently choose their judges through a mixed selection method that allows *different* political actors to nominate or appoint a specific number of judges or a portion of the court. Most mixed selection courts are modeled after Hans Kelsen's constitutional court prototype, which emphasizes the "duty" of constitutional court judges to "control the exercise of legislative authority" (Stone Sweet 2012: 89). In other words, the role of constitutional judges on these courts is conceived as both legislative and judicial. By design, judges on mixed selection constitutional courts may be thought of as serving as agents or representatives of the institutions that select them calling into question their impartiality in constitutional review decisions. However, because judges on these courts have limited tenure and do not always serve concurrently with their selectors, judges on mixed selection courts are more likely to be representatives of each selection branch's ideal of a constitutional adjudicator rather than as direct representatives of their political preferences. While the goal of mixed selection is to have a court filled with judges selected by different governmental institutions, judges on these courts may also have party affiliations, which judicial scholars traditionally have claimed also influence their decisions (Sadurski 2008: 17; International IDEA 2017: 11).

As discussed in Chapter 3, significant debates surround the use of mixed selection methods. These debates are found at the international level in reports from organizations such as the Venice Commission (2007) and at the domestic level found within legislative histories of constitutional reforms. Politicians choose mixed selection generally because such systems allow government actors and sometimes other organizations to have a voice on a constitutional court and to diversify the deliberative process. In Chile (in several different eras) and in Colombia (during the Constituent Assembly), policymakers chose mixed selection methods generally to allow for an "equilibrium" of different types of judges' voices on their country's constitutional courts and to provide the entire political system with more balance within and between institutions. Through mixed selection, a country's own separation of powers system can be mirrored within the court itself.

As demonstrated by the legislative histories, presented in the respective country chapters, policymakers in both countries rigorously debated which form of mixed selection to implement. The debates in Chile and Colombia demonstrate that constitutional designers were concerned about who would serve on their respective constitutional courts and how governmental institutions would be represented within them. Despite the stated goal of creating constitutional courts with an equilibrium among judges selected by different political actors, the debates reveal a concern that certain selectors would be afforded too much influence on these courts. Implicit in these concerns is that judges' behavior on constitutional courts is tied to the institution that selects them and that judges represent the different selecting institutions' ideal type of constitutional adjudicator who affords appropriate weight to political and legal factors in their decisions. As revealed in the respective countries' legislative debates, the mixed selection system was chosen to balance powers within the courts themselves in the least partisan way possible. However, in practice, as seen below, judges do have party associations and some parties have input in selection. The empirical question, however, is whether the mixed selection method reduces the influence of partisan voting.

To more fully understand the extent that the debates about selection are reflected in behavior, this chapter focuses on how mixed selection methods operate in practice to influence judges' individual decisions to veto or strike down laws as unconstitutional. In doing so, the analysis also ascertains the extent to which supporters' and critics' arguments about mixed selection, found in Chapter 3, are well founded by determining whether judges' votes to strike down laws are correlated to differences in their selecting institution and whether a judge's nominating or appointing branch has a greater influence on their individual decisions than their party affiliations, which scholars indicate is an important determinant of judges' decisions on many high courts (Segal and Spaeth 2002). To analyze these debates, the chapter first provides a description of the judges on the court and then provides a summary of the compositions of the Chilean Constitutional Tribunal (CT) and the Colombian Constitutional Court (CC), based on judges' voting records over time. The chapter provides specific hypotheses pertaining to the Chilean CT and Colombian CC that were introduced more generally in Chapter 2. The analysis uses originally collected data on judges' *votes* on the two exemplar mixed selection courts.

The empirical analysis in the latter part of this chapter shows that judges' behavior varies with the institutions that select them and is a more significant factor than judges' party affiliations. On the Chilean CT, presidential and legislative appointees are more likely to strike down laws than those appointed by the Supreme Court. In Colombia, judges nominated by the president and Supreme Court are less likely to veto laws than those selected by the Consejo de Estado. Besides the direct influence of judges' selecting institution on their own votes, the results indicate that the composition of the court made up of judges selected by different institutions, which fluctuates over time (as judges exit and enter the court) and by case (due to quorum rules), influences individual judge's decisions and provides some evidence that judges' viewpoints can be changed by the presence of judges with different selectors.

6.2 JUDGES ON THE CHILEAN AND COLOMBIAN CONSTITUTIONAL COURTS

Analyzing individual choice and its relationship to judges' selectors require an understanding of judges' characteristics, training, and background. Judges on constitutional courts serve on the highest court in their respective countries and most often have held prestigious positions prior to serving on constitutional courts as well as after their terms end. Judges are selected due to their prior experience, legal acumen, and the type of constitutional adjudicator they are perceived to be by their selecting institution. This book argues that judges' own individual characteristics, defined by their selecting institution, as well as the characteristics of other judges on collegial constitutional courts drive their decisions.

6.2.1 *The Chilean Constitutional Tribunal Judges*

Under the Chilean Constitution, ministers or judges to the Tribunal must have been attorneys with impeccable credentials. Further, they may serve for a limited period of eight years prior to the 2005 reforms and nine years after these reforms. While reelection is not possible, a judge who completes a term for another judge who was compelled to retire due to a mandatory retirement age or some other reason may be re-appointed. Table 6.1 shows judges on the Chilean CT by their selector and party associations from the return to democracy until 2016. More details about the judges' background since the 2005 reform and sources for this information are found in the book's Appendix Table A.2.

Figures 6.1 and 6.2 provide a bird's eye view of the Chilean Tribunal's composition based on the distribution of votes of judges appearing on constitutional review cases of legislation authored by the presiding Congress by both selecting institution and party. The CT's composition has changed over time and most notably after 2006. Figure 6.1 shows a snapshot of the distribution of Chilean judges' institutional selectors based on judges' votes. There are five types of institutional selectors for the entire time span (1990–2016), including judges chosen by the outgoing junta, the Supreme Court, the president, and the legislature. A fifth category, referred to as "auxiliary" judges, refers to certain individuals appointed as auxiliary members of the Court who sit on a case if a quorum of judges is unavailable. Several justices on the Tribunal previously served as auxiliary judges. Prior to the reform, the Tribunal had seven judges and quorum rules allowed as few as five judges to make decisions. After the reform, the Tribunal had ten judges and quorum rules allow as few as eight judges to make decisions.

In order to compare the composition over time, despite the fluctuating number of judges, the bars of the diagram depict the average percent of votes of judges selected by different institutions by year on abstract review cases of laws drafted by the government in power. As shown in Figure 6.1, from 1990 to 1996, the Tribunal consisted of over 50 percent of junta appointees. From 1996 through the Constitutional reforms of 2005, most of the Tribunal was made up of judges who were appointed by non-elected actors (the COSENA or the Supreme Court) as well as some auxiliary judges. After the reforms of 2006, judges were more evenly divided among appointees of the three main branches of government, although two of the judges appointed by the pre-reform system's COSENA remained on the court until 2010. After the reform, average statistics show that no one branch's appointees ever hold a majority on the Tribunal.

Figure 6.2 depicts the Chilean Tribunal's composition based on party affiliation. Like Figure 6.1, through about 1996, the Tribunal contained members selected by the junta who are not ascribed a political association separate from that with the military government that selected them. Through 2005, the Tribunal had many nonpartisan judges due largely to the fact that it consisted of many Supreme Court

TABLE 6.1. *Chilean Constitutional Tribunal judges and coding (1990–2016)*

Minister name	Institutional appointer	Party association
Luis Maldonado Boggiano (1985–1991)	Pinochet/under junta	Chosen under junta
Eduardo Urzúa Merino (1985–1991)	Pinochet/under junta	Chosen under junta
Marcos Aburto Ochoa (1985–1997)	Supreme Court/under junta	Non-partisan
Manuel Jiménez Bulnes (1988–1997)	Pinochet/under junta	Chosen under junta
Hernán Cereceda Bravo (1989–1993)	Supreme Court	Non-partisan
Ricardo García Rodríguez (1989–1997)	Pinochet/under junta	Chosen under junta
Luz Bulnes Aldunate (1989–2002)	COSENA/under junta	Chosen under junta
Eugenio Velasco Letelier (1991–1993)	President Aylwin	Concertación
Osvaldo Faúndez Vallejos (1991–2001)	Supreme Court	Non-partisan
Servando Jordán López (1993–2002)	Supreme Court	Non-partisan
Mario Verdugo Marinkovic (1997–2001)	COSENA	Non-partisan
Eugenio Valenzuela Somarriva (1981–1989, 1997–2006)	Senate (Right majority)	Right
Hernán Alvarez García (1997–2005)	Supreme Court	Non-partisan
Juan Agustín Figueroa Yávar (2001–2006)	President Lagos	Concertación
Marcos Libedinsky Tschorne (2001–2006)	Supreme Court	Non-partisan
Eleodoro Ortíz Sepúlveda (2002–2006)	Supreme Court	Non-partisan
Urbano Marín Vallejo (2005–2006)	Supreme Court	Non-partisan
Juan Colombo Campbell (2002–2010)	COSENA	Concertación
José Luis Cea Egaña (2002–2010)	COSENA	Non-partisan
Jorge Correa Sutil (2006–2009)	President Lagos	Concertación
Raúl Bertelsen Repetto (2006–2015)[a]	Senate	Right
Hernán Vodanovic Schnake (2006–2015)[a]	Senate	Concertación
Mario Fernández Baeza (2006–2011)	Camera/Senate	Concertación
Marcelo Venegas Palacios (2006–2013)	Camera/Senate	Right

(continued)

TABLE 6.1 (*continued*)

Minister name	Institutional appointer	Party association
Marisol Peña Torres (2006–2009, 2009–2018)	Supreme Court	Non-partisan
Enrique Navarro Beltrán (2006–2012)	Supreme Court	Non-partisan
Francisco Fernández Fredes (2006–2015)	Supreme Court	Concertación
Carlos Carmona Santander (2009–2018)	President Bachelet	Concertación
José Antonio Viera Gallo Quesnay (2010–2013)	President Bachelet	Concertación
Iván Aróstica Maldonado (2010–2013, 2013–2022)	President Piñera	Right
Domingo Hernández Emparanza (2012–2020)	Supreme Court	Nonpartisan
Gonzalo García Pino (2013–2022)	Camera/Senate	Concertación
Juan José Romero Guzmán (2013–2022)	Camera/Senate	Right
María Luisa Brahm Barril (2013–2022)	President Piñera	Right
Cristián Letelier Aguilar (2015–)[a]	Senate	Right
Nelson Pozo Silva (2015–)[a]	Senate	Concertación
José Vásquez Márquez (2015–)	Supreme Court	Non-partisan

Notes. Below the thick dark-black horizontal line are all judges that appeared on the Tribunal after the 2005 reforms. The judges appearing between the dark-black horizontal line and the thinner dark line are two judges, Colombo and Cea, who were chosen by the COSENA prior to the reform but remained on the Tribunal until 2010.

[a] Vodanovic and Bertelsen were both chosen by the Senate at the same time. Their nominations were part of a "horse-trading" deal in which the two main coalitions (the Right and Center Left) were able to each choose a candidate. Under similar agreements, parties from the Right chose Letelier and those of the Concertación chose Pozo.

Sources: See book's Appendix, Table A.2, for additional information about judges' backgrounds and the sources for this coding.

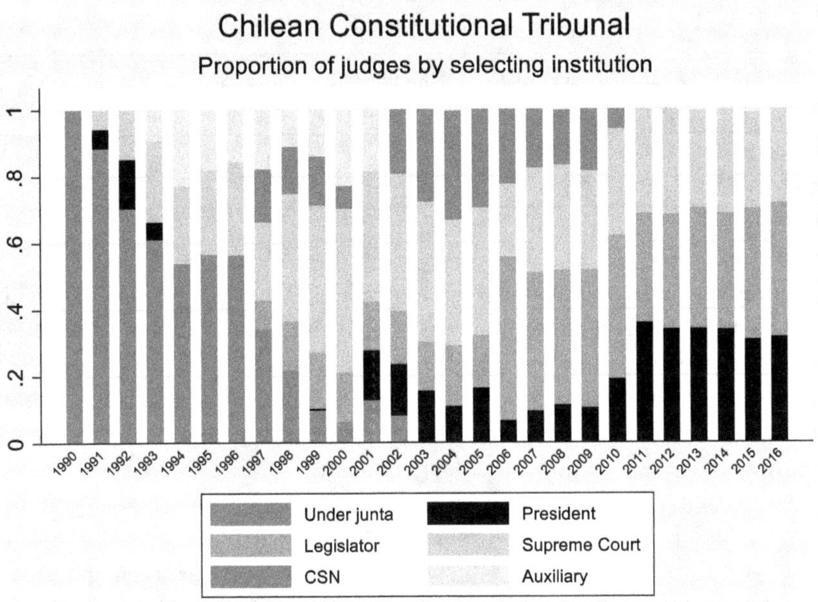

FIGURE 6.1 CT composition by selecting institution

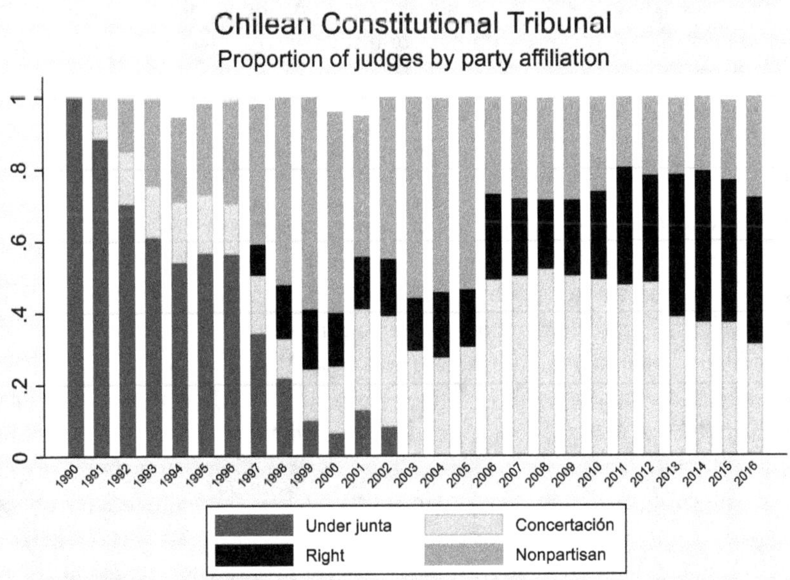

FIGURE 6.2 CT composition by party association

TABLE 6.2. *Percentage of unconstitutional votes by selector and party post reform, Chilean CT*

	Presidential appointer	Legislative appointer	Non-elected appointer	Concertación associated	Right associated	Non-partisan
% unconst	26	24	19	24	24	19
No. of votes	927	1,502	1,431	1,705	1,182	973

appointees who were, prior to the reform, members of the Supreme Court itself and mostly non-partisan. After the reform was implemented in 2006, more elected actors were involved in the selection process and, as a result, more judges have party associations. Within this period, from 2006 to 2012, those affiliated with the Concertación represented at or near 50 percent of the Court. By 2013, however, there is a more even distribution among appointees affiliated with both the Right and Left coalitions and those who were nonpartisan. By 2013, no singular party interest holds a majority on the Tribunal on average.

Table 6.2 shows the percent of unconstitutional votes of legislation approved by the government in power at the time of review by CT judges' institutional appointer and party association for the post-reform period up until 2016. These summary statistics indicate that judges appointed by the elected president and legislature have higher rates of striking down laws as unconstitutional than those appointed by the non-elected Supreme Court and COSENA. Likewise, judges associated with the two political coalitions also strike down laws more frequently than non-partisan judges. The statistics, however, do not control for panel effects, changes in overall composition of the Tribunal, type of review, or the laws' subject area.

6.2.2 *Colombian Constitutional Court Judges*

When the Colombian CC was first constituted, under a transitional article, seven judges were appointed to the Court for one year. Of these judges, the president chose two, the Supreme Court one, the Consejo de Estado one, and the prosecutor general one, and these judges chose the remaining two from lists that the president proposed (see Colombian Constitution, Transitory Article 22). Some of these initial judges were renominated to serve longer terms. Under the Constitution after this initial year, the size of the Court reverted to nine, allowing only three institutions to nominate the judges (i.e., the president, the Supreme Court, and the Consejo de Estado) with confirmation by a Senate majority (see Ley 5 de 1992, Articles 317–319). Judges serve eight-year terms and cannot be reelected. Table 6.3 lists the judges by their institutional nominator, confirming Senate, and party associations. There were six different confirming Senates, referred to as S1 to S6 and explained in the note below the table. A description as to the specific party seat share for both houses of

TABLE 6.3. *Colombian Constitutional Court judges and coding (1991–2014)*

Magistrate	Institutional nominator	Confirming Senate[c]	Party association
Ciro Angarita Barón (1991–1993)	President Gaviria	S1	Liberal
Eduardo Cifuentes Muñoz (1991–2000)	PG[a]/President Gaviria	S1	Liberal
José Gregorio Hernández Galindo (1991–2001)	President Gaviria[b]/SC	S1	Conservative
Simón Rodríguez (1991–1993)	Consejo de Estado	S1	Liberal
Alejandro Martinez Caballero (1992–2001)	President Gaviria	S1	Liberal
Fabio Morón Díaz (1992–1993)	President Gaviria[b]/SC	S1	Liberal
Jaime Sanin Greiffenstein (1991–1993)	Supreme Court	S1	Liberal
Carlos Gaviria Díaz (1991–2001)	Consejo de Estado	S1	Liberal
Jorge Arango Mejía (1991–1998)	Supreme Court	S1	Liberal
Antonio Barrera Carbonell (1993–2000)	Consejo de Estado	S1	Liberal
Hernando Herrera Vergara (1993–1999)	President Gaviria	S1	Liberal
Vladimiro Naranjo Mesa (1993–2000)	Consejo de Estado	S1	Conservative
Alfredo Beltrán Sierra (1998–2006)	Supreme Court	S2	Liberal
Jaime Araújo Rentería (2001–2009)	Consejo de Estado	S3	Liberal
Manuel José Cepeda Espinosa (2001–2009)	President Pastrana	S3	Conservative
Jaime Córdoba Triviño (2001–2009)	Supreme Court	S3	Liberal
Rodrigo Escobar Gil (2001–2009)	Consejo de Estado	S3	Conservative
Marco Gerardo Monroy Cabra (2001–2009)	President Pastrana	S3	Conservative
Luis Eduardo Montealegre (2001–2004)	Consejo de Estado	S3	Liberal
Alvaro Tafur Galvis (1999–2007)	President Pastrana	S3	Conservative
Clara Inés Vargas Hernández (2001–2009)	Supreme Court	S3	Liberal
Humberto Sierra Porto (2004–2012)	Consejo de Estado	S4	Liberal
Nilson Elías Pinilla (2006–2014)	Supreme Court	S4	Conservative

(continued)

TABLE 6.3 (*continued*)

Magistrate	Institutional nominator	Confirming Senate[c]	Party association
Mauricio González Cuervo (2007–2017)	President Uribe	S4	Conservative
María Victoria Calle Correa (2009–2017)	President Uribe	S5	Conservative
Juan Carlos Henao Pérez (2009–2012)	Consejo de Estado	S5	Liberal
Gabriel E. Mendoza Martelo (2009–2017)	Consejo de Estado	S5	Conservative
Jorge Iván Palacio (2009–2017)	Supreme Court	S5	Conservative
Jorge Ignacio Pretelt Chaljub (2009–2017)	President Uribe	S5	Conservative
Luis Ernesto Vargas Silva (2009–2017)	Supreme Court	S5	Liberal
Luis Guillermo Guerrero Pérez (2012–)	Consejo de Estado	S6	Conservative
Alberto Rojas Ríos (2012–)	Consejo de Estado	S6	Conservative
Gloria Stella Ortiz Delgado (2014–)	Supreme Court	S6	Conservative

[a] This judge was chosen by the Office of the Prosecutor General.
[b] These judges were chosen by President Gaviria according to the transitional mechanism of the 1991 Constitution.
[c] The confirming Senates are referred to as S1 to S6 as follows: S1 (1991 to July 1994), S2 (July 20, 1994 to July 1998), S3 (July 20, 1998 to July 2002), S4 (July 20, 2002 to July 2006), S5 (July 20, 2006 to July 2010), and S6 (July 20, 2010 to July 2014).
Sources: See book's Appendix, Table A.3, for additional information about judges' backgrounds and sources for coding.

Congress was discussed in Chapter 5. However, it is worth noting that between 1991 and 1998, the Senate was dominated by the two traditional main parties in which the Liberals held the majority of Senate seats from 1991 to 1998. After 1998, no party held a majority of seats because the Senates after this year included many fragmented parties. In these later years, however, legislators affiliated with the Liberal Party hold more seats than legislators of any other parties until 2010 and after 2010 legislators with the Party de la U have the most seats. More details about the judges' backgrounds are found in the book's Appendix Table A.3.

For comparison with the Chilean Tribunal, Figures 6.3 and 6.4 show the Colombian Constitutional Court's composition by institutional selector and party association by judges' votes when voting on legislation approved by the Congress in power at the time of review. Figure 6.3 depicts CC judges by their institutional selectors. There are four types of institutional nominators for the entire time span, including judges chosen by the Supreme Court, the president, and the Consejo del Estado. A fourth category of judges, referred to as "auxiliary" allowed either ad hoc judges or *conjueces* to vote on a case if a quorum of judges was unavailable. To compare more easily, for the initial years when the Court contained only seven judges and allowed different institutions to select, judges are coded by their selector as of 1993. As shown in Figure 6.3, until about 2000, a majority of judges were nominated by the president and the rest by the two courts or were auxiliary judges. From 2001 to

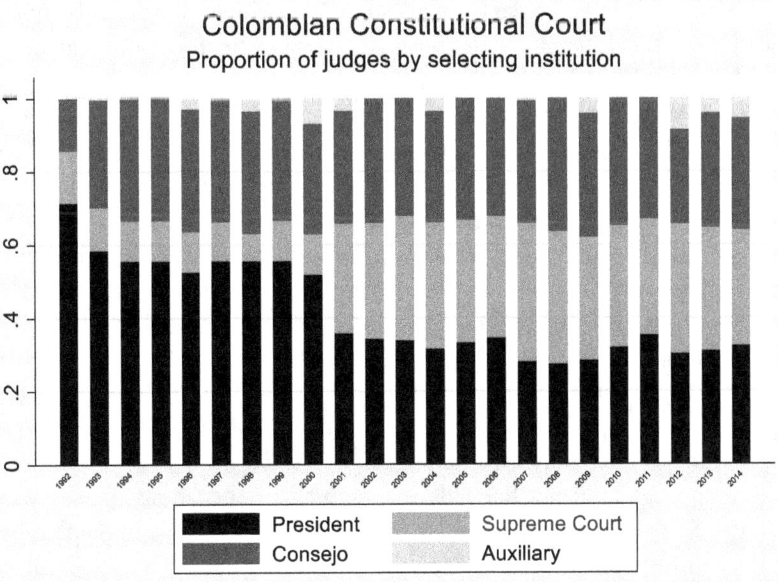

FIGURE 6.3 CC composition by selecting institution

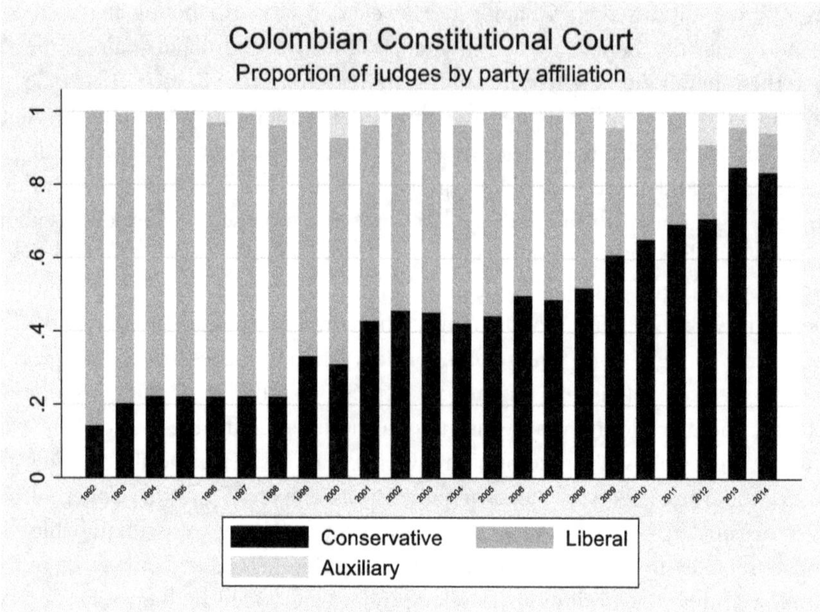

FIGURE 6.4 CC composition by party association

2014, the CC is more evenly divided among judges nominated by the three institutions with no one nominating institution holding a majority on the Court.

In Colombia all judges have been classified by multiple sources as being either affiliated with the Liberal or Conservative Parties, the two historical divisions within the country. Although Colombia has evolved into a multiparty polity and some of the historical distinctions between the Liberals and Conservatives have faded especially since the presidency of Alvaro Uribe (see Carroll and Pachón 2016), judges are still associated with these two parties in the popular media, and there are no judges without party associations. As shown in Figure 6.4, judges associated with the Liberal Party make up about 50 percent of the court through 2006. Then starting in 2009, judges associated with the Conservative Party take over the majority. Taken together, these two figures show that the CC's composition based on party association has changed more over time than its composition based on institutional selector.

Table 6.4 shows the percent of unconstitutional votes by CC judges' institutional nominator and party association for the period from 1996 onward. These summary statistics indicate that judges appointed by the president have slightly lower rates of striking down laws as unconstitutional than those appointed by the two high courts. Judges associated with the Liberal Party are slightly more likely to opine unconstitutionality than those associated with the Conservative Party. The percentages for these categories are very similar and do not factor in other control

TABLE 6.4. *Percentage of unconstitutional votes by selector and party, Colombian CC*

	Presidential nominee	Supreme Court nominee	Consejo nominee	Liberal Party associated	Conservative Party associated
% unconst	28	31	31	31	28
No. of votes	6,391	4,663	5,439	8,266	8,227

variables. However, the similarity of unconstitutional votes by selector and party may in part be due to the Senate confirmation requirement, which may allow for compromises among many political interests especially after Colombia's drift toward multiparty politics.

6.3 PREDICTIONS RELATED TO INDIVIDUAL CHOICE FOR THE CHILEAN AND COLOMBIAN CONSTITUTIONAL COURTS

The hypotheses regarding individual choice based on court composition build on those generally developed in Chapter 2 but pertain to the Chilean and Colombian courts. The hypotheses regarding the importance of case context – type of review and subject area – are explored more fully in the subsequent chapter regarding collective choice but are used in this analysis as important control variables as mentioned in the data and analysis section.

6.3.1 *Hypotheses Based on Judges' Individual Characteristics*

Summarizing the theory in Chapter 2, I argue that different institutions select different types of judges that reflect each institution's ideal approach to constitutional decision-making and an understanding of the role that such institutions should play in the policy-making process. As stated in the legislative histories of the two courts, policymakers wanted to create an equilibrium of judges on the courts by having different branch selectors choose different judges. It is inferred from these legislative histories, as well as interviews, that judges with different selectors have different constitutional adjudication styles driving them to weigh judicial and political concerns that arise from the legislation reviewed differently. In other words, judges' votes should be correlated with their institutional branch selector. Judges live up to the expectations of their selectors in deciding the constitutionality of laws due to an understanding of the selecting institution's mission and role in government and to build their own reputations for future careers after relatively short terms on the court.

H6.1. *Judges' selecting institutions should have more of an influence on their individual decisions to strike down laws than their party associations.*

H6.1a. *Chilean CT judges' propensities to strike down laws will be based more on the judges' selecting institutions (president or Congress/Senate or Supreme Court and COSENA) than their party associations (Concertación, right, or nonpartisan).*

H6.1b. *Colombian CC judges' propensities to strike down laws will be based more on the judges' selecting institutions (president or Supreme Court or Consejo de Estado) than their party associations (Liberal Party or Conservative Party).*

H6.2. *On constitutional review cases, fragmentation will be based more on differences among judges' selecting institutions than differences due to their party associations.*

These hypotheses may be conditioned on differences between the Chilean CT's unilateral appointees and the Colombian CC's requirement of Senate confirmation. Judges should diverge more in relation to their institutional selector in Chile than in Colombia. Senate confirmation in Colombia may also make judges' party associations more relevant to their decision-making than in Chile (see Montoya 2013 claiming that the Colombian Senate considers judges' political ideology in its confirmation decisions).

6.3.2 *Hypotheses Based on Presence or Panel Effects*

Judges may be influenced by their own selectors or parties or may be highly influenced by the presence of *other* judges with different selectors or party associations with whom they decide cases. As argued in Chapter 2, an individual judge may be influenced by the mere presence of judges with different characteristics on the court (i.e., contextual, presence or panel effects). Individual judges will assess the characteristics of judges who are present on any case to determine strategically how best to use their vote. In court compositions in which judges with certain selectors are highly present on a case, a judge with a different selector may go along for a variety of reasons including influencing the majority opinion, increasing a court's stature by issuing stronger opinions defined by those with little dissent, and through deliberation by which the most prevalent voices are the most persuasive. Based on these arguments, the following predictions pertain to the two courts.

H6.3. *Presence or panel effects have an indirect and independent influence on CT and CC judges' individual decisions to strike down laws as unconstitutional.*

H6.4. *Presence or panel effects based on institutional selector have a larger effect on CT and CC judges' individual decisions to strike down laws than panel effects based on party associations.*

In Chile and Colombia, the overall composition of the court is changed every three years. Staggering of constitutional terms at set intervals changes the overall court composition with whom judges vote and should have an independent influence on their voting.

H6.5. Overall changes in court composition on the CT and CC should have an independent effect on judges' decisions to strike down laws.

6.4 DESCRIPTION OF DATA AND ANALYSIS

To explore the specific predictions regarding judges' characteristics and court composition, the votes of judges on the Chilean CT and the Colombian CC are analyzed separately. The analysis focuses only on the abstract constitutional review of laws *approved by the legislature serving at the time of review.* Focusing on only these cases allows predictions regarding judges' party associations to be explored in relation to the parties in the legislature that approved the law under review, rather than parties of past legislatures, which Dahl (1957) and Shapiro (2004) indicate are less costly for judges to strike down. The data is constrained as to this type of legislation and to abstract review in order to control for a wide range of case-level factors that influence judges' decisions and to more easily compare the two high courts.[1] The unit of observation is each judge's individual vote. Three general regression equations are analyzed, which focus on the influence of institutional selectors, their party affiliations, and both as follows:

$$\Pr(y_{ij} = 1) = \alpha + \beta_1 \textit{Institutional selector}_{ij} + \beta_2 \textit{Tenure}_{ij} + \gamma \textit{Case context}_j + \varepsilon_{ij} \quad (6.1)$$

$$\Pr(y_{ij} = 1) = \alpha + \beta_1 \textit{Party association}_{ij} + \beta_2 \textit{Tenure}_{ij} + \gamma \textit{Case context}_j + \varepsilon_{ij} \quad (6.2)$$

$$\begin{aligned}\Pr(y_{ij} = 1) = \alpha &+ \beta_1 \textit{Institutional selector}_{ij} + \beta_2 \textit{Party association}_{ij} \\ &+ \beta_3 \textit{Tenure}_{ij} + \gamma \textit{Case context}_j + \varepsilon_{ij}\end{aligned} \quad (6.3)$$

The main dependent variable is y_{ij}, which is an individual vote of unconstitutionality for a decisional paragraph in each case for judge i in case j or a judge's opinion that a law should be vetoed or stricken down as unconstitutional. The individual votes are coded to account for the courts' majority and whether a judge agreed with it or not. This manner of coding was used to make the two courts as comparable as possible.

Both the Chilean and Colombian Constitutional Courts review laws passed by Congress in the context of a unique case. Within a case, reviewing a particular law, the courts decide about the constitutionality of an entire law or, more frequently, there are separate decisional paragraphs about the constitutionality of distinct parts of the law. Generally, the separate decisional paragraphs mirror the separate votes undertaken by Congress on distinct parts of the law. Judges' majority and dissent coalitions, and thus their individual voting, often vary depending on what part of the

[1] While most of the CT's abstract cases involve a priori review, Colombia's CC reviews both types and thus reviews a larger share of laws enacted by prior governments than in Chile. Constraining the analysis to the review of legislation by the Congress in power at the time of review makes the decision-making on the two courts more comparable.

law or decisional paragraphs that the courts are reviewing. Therefore, in the empirical analysis in this chapter, judges' votes are recorded for each separate decision within a case. Some cases have multiple decisional paragraphs while others (especially in the early years of these two courts) have fewer paragraphs.

In the case of the Chilean CT, judges' individual votes were coded for abstract review cases of laws enacted by the Congress in power at the time of constitutional review. For Chile, these cases were those before the Tribunal under Constitution Articles 93.1 (i.e., a priori review of organic laws, legal precepts, or treaties) and 93.3 (i.e., *requerimientos* or a priori review of laws at any stage of the legislative process prior to enactment brought to the Tribunal's attention by politicians). Judges' individual votes were determined by the outcome of the decisional paragraph (which represents the Tribunal's majority opinion) as well as whether the judge voted with the majority, concurred (preventiva), or dissented. Specifically, the outcome or majority vote on a decisional paragraph indicating "constitucional," or constitutional, is coded as zero and the outcome on a decisional paragraph indicating "inconstitucional," or unconstitutional, was coded as 1. For individual judge-level coding, if a judge voted with the majority or concurred on a constitutional outcome or dissented from the majority's unconstitutional decision, the judge's vote is considered constitutional and coded as a 0. If a judge voted with the majority's unconstitutional outcome or dissented from the majority's constitutional decision, the judge's vote was considered for unconstitutionality and coded as 1. Decisional paragraphs in which the majority opined that the case was inadmissible for various reasons, such as it was not an organic law, were removed from the analysis as the Tribunal did not consider the constitutionality of the law.

Figure 6.5 is an example of individual decisional paragraphs nested within a case in which the Chilean Constitutional Tribunal reviewed the General Education Law (Rol #1363). In the first paragraph, the Court declares that it will not pronounce (*no se pronuncia*) a decision on this paragraph because it does not include norms that are part of the organic law. As decisions of inadmissibility are not included in this analysis, this particular paragraph is not in the data set. In the second paragraph, the Tribunal declares that the articles referred to within the paragraph are constitutional (*son constitucionales*), and in the third paragraph the Tribunal deems the article as unconstitutional (*es inconstitucional*) and must be eliminated prior to enactment of this law. Judges' individual votes were found after the majority decision.

In the case of the Colombian CC, judges' individual votes were coded for abstract review cases of laws enacted by the Congress in power at the time of enactment. These cases were either a priori or a posteriori review. In Colombia, decisional paragraphs were broken down within a case similar to the Chilean decisions. The judges' votes were oriented by looking at the outcome of the decisional paragraph and the judges' position in relation to that outcome. Colombia's CC has more options for majority outcomes and choices for judges' individual votes than Chile.

Decision of the Chilean TC concerning the General Education Law

Case or Rol #1363

SE DECLARA:

1. QUE ESTE TRIBUNAL NO SE PRONUNCIA SOBRE LA SIGUIENTES DISPOSICIONES DEL PROYECTO DE LEY REMITIDO A CONTROL, POR NO CONTENER NORMAS PROPIAS DE LEY ORGÁNICA CONSTITUCIONAL: artículos 11, incisos segundos y siguientes, 12 y 16.

2. QUE SON CONSTITUCIONALES LAS SIGUIENTES DISPOSICIONES DEL PROYECTO DE LEY REMITIDO:

Artículos 1°, 2°, 3°, 4°, 5°, 6°, 7°, 8°, 11, inciso primero, 13, 14, 17, 18, 19, 20, 21, 22, 23, 24, 25, inciso primero, 26, 27, 28, 29, 30, 1, 32,33, 34, 35, 37, a excepción de la oración final de su inciso tercero que se declarará inconstitucional, 38, 39, 40, 42, 43, 44, 45, 46 –con las precisiones que se indican en los considerandos Decimosegundo a vigesimoquinto, respecto de la letra a)-, 47, 48, 49, 50, 51, 52,53, 54, 56 -sin perjuicio del entendimiento que el Tribunal le atribuye a su inciso sexto-, 57, 58, 59, incisos primero y tercero, 60, 61, 62, 63, 64,65, 66, 67, 68 y 70 permanentes y 1°, 2°, 3°, 4°,5°, 7°, 8°, 9° y 10 transitorios.

3. QUE ES INCONSTITUCIONAL la oración *"sin perjuicio de las excepciones que establezca el reglamento"* contenida en el inciso tercero del artículo 37 del proyecto de ley remitido y, en consecuencia, debe eliminarse de su texto.

FIGURE 6.5 Example of structure of constitutional review decision from the Chilean CT.
Source: CT decisional paragraphs in Rol #1363 (2009): Proyecto de ley, aprobado por el Congreso Nacional, que establece la Ley General de Educación (Case no. 1363: Project of law approved by the National Congress that establishes the General Education Law). Emphasis by author.

A decisional paragraph was considered constitutional and coded as zero if the majority of the court decided the case was constitutional (*exequible*), conditionally constitutional (*exequibilidad condicionada*), or it did not grant a presidential objection (*infundadas-exequible*). A decisional paragraph was considered unconstitutional if the Court declared the law unconstitutional (*inexequible*), partially unconstitutional or constitutional (*parcialmente exequible* or *parcialmente inexequible*), or the court granted a presidential objection in whole or in part (*fundadas-inexequible*).

For the individual CC judges, a judge's vote was coded as zero and voting for constitutionality if the Court found the law constitutional as defined above and the judge agreed with the majority, concurred (or issued an *aclaración*) or if the majority found the law was unconstitutional and the judge disagreed. Judges have several ways of stating disagreement with the majority including declaring a dissent (*salvamento*) or a partial dissent (*salvamento parcial*). A judge's individual vote was coded as 1 or unconstitutional if the majority voted for unconstitutionality and the judge agreed in the various ways stated above or the majority was for constitutional, and the judge disagreed in full or in part. Similar to the inadmissible cases for Chile, which were removed from the data, for Colombia, cases in which the court was reluctant to rule (*inhibida*) or voted for res judicata (*estarse a lo resuelto*) were

Decision of the Colombian CC concerning *Ley 1448 de 2011* on the assistance and reparations for victims of internal armed conflict.

Case #C253A/2012

VII. DECISION

En mérito de lo expuesto, la Corte Constitucional de la República de Colombia, administrando justicia en nombre del pueblo y por mandato de la Constitución,

RESUELVE

Primero.- ESTARSE A LO RESUELTO en la sentencia C-250 de 2012, que declaró la EXEQUIBILIDAD de la expresión *"a partir del 1° de enero de 1985"* contenida en el inciso primero del artículo 3° de la Ley 1448 de 2011.

Segundo.- Declarar la EXEQUIBILIDAD de las expresiones *"por hechos ocurridos"* contenida en el inciso primero del artículo 3° de la Ley 1448 de 2011, *"simbólica"* y *"como parte del conglomerado social y sin necesidad de que sean individualizados"*, contenidas en el parágrafo 4° del mismo artículo.

Tercero.- ESTARSE A LO RESUELTO en la sentencia C-250 de 2012, que declaró la EXEQUIBILIDAD de la expresión *"entre el 1° de enero de 1991 y el término de vigencia de la ley"* contenida en el artículo 75 de la Ley 1448 de 2011.

Cuarto.- Declarar la EXEQUIBILIDAD del primer inciso del parágrafo segundo del artículo 3° de la Ley 1448 de 2011.

Quinto.- INHIBIRSE de hacer un pronunciamiento de fondo en relación con las expresiones demandadas del segundo inciso del parágrafo 2° del artículo 3° de la Ley 1448 de 2011.

Sexto.-Declarar la EXEQUIBILIDAD del parágrafo 3° del artículo 3°de la Ley 1448 de 2011.

FIGURE 6.6 Example of structure of constitutional review decision from the Colombian CC.
Source: CC decisional paragraphs in case #C235A (2012) concerning *Ley 1448 de 2011* on assistance and reparations for victims of internal armed conflict. Emphasis by author.

similarly removed as there was no decision on the constitutionality of the substance of the law.[2]

Figure 6.6 shows a case in which the Colombian CC is deciding the constitutionality of several parts of a law dealing with reparations for victims of internal armed conflict (C235A/2012). In paragraphs 2 (*segundo*), 4 (*cuarto*), and 6 (*sexto*), the majority held that the provisions of the law referred to in these three decisional

[2] The decision to remove cases due to findings of inadmissibility or *res judicata* was not taken lightly and I am not implying that such decisions are not substantively meaningful, political or influential. Rather, the decision was made to remove them to make the analysis more comparable between the two countries as the reasons for inadmissibility are quite different for the two courts. For Chile, refusing to find a law organic under obligatory review is quite different than a finding in Colombia that the case was already decided. Further, including such decisions may result in double counting of cases.

paragraphs were constitutional (*exequibilidad*). In the first (*primero*) and third (*tercero*) paragraphs, the majority ruled that these provisions could not be decided due to res judicata or *estarse a lo resuelto* as they had been previously held constitutional in another case. In the fifth paragraph, the Court indicated that it was inhibited from making a decision (*inhibirse*). For purposes of coding, paragraphs 2, 4, and 6 were included in the data base with each of the judges' individual decisions because these paragraphs made a pronouncement regarding the constitutionality of the law. The decisions for the remaining paragraphs were not included in the data base as the Court did not decide on the substantive issue of constitutionality in these cases.

With this judge-level dependent variable for unconstitutionality, a determination can be made whether judges with different selecting institutions, which themselves represent branches of government have different propensities to strike down laws passed by the current legislature. As one of the purposes of adopting a mixed selection system for the Chilean and Colombian constitutional courts was to provide a balance of powers within these courts hearing cases of abstract constitutional review, the dependent variable is oriented to determine whether judges with certain selecting institutions are more likely to strike down legislation or opine a legislative veto than others. The dependent variable has the added advantage of concurrently allowing an analysis of the effect of judges' party associations on decisions to strike down laws in a meaningful way. In Chile, parties associated with the Center Left held the majority or the most seats in the bicameral legislatures for the entire period as described by an analysis of congressional seat shares (see Chapter 4, Table 4.1). Similarly, for Colombia, the Liberal Party held a majority of seats in the bicameral Congress until 1998 and then held the most seats until 2010. From 2010 to 2014, the most seats were held by the Partido de la U as indicated by an analysis of Congressional seat shares (Chapter 5, Table 5.1). For all years, the presidents' governing coalition held a majority of seats. In essence, the orientation of the legislation reviewed is controlled for to ascertain the influence of judges' party associations on their decisions without accounting for seat shares of an enacting legislature no longer in power.

The main explanatory variables are judges' political characteristics (i.e., institutional selector and party association). Other independent variables include each judge's years on the court at the time of the decision and a vector of case-specific attributes (γ) related to the political and legal context, such as type of review and subject matter of the law. The term ε_{ij} represents the error term. A random intercept probit model is used to address the hierarchical nature of the data in which judges' votes are nested within the courts' cases (in which membership varies). Failure to address the multilevel nature of the data leads to inaccurate standard errors and spurious significant results (Hox 2018). An analysis of the data reveals that the within-judge dependence is weak (intra-class correlation of 0.01 for the two courts), while the within-case dependency is fairly significant (intra-class correlation is 0.21 for

Chile and 0.48 for Colombia). As a result, a random-intercept model is used with justices' votes nested inside cases to account for the case-level variation and its influence on interdependent judge-level observations (see Barcikowski 1981; Blair et al. 1983).

The analysis for Chile spans from after the enactment of the 2005 reforms in 2006, which ushered in a reformed mixed selection system, and for Colombia from 1997 onward. In both countries, the full court must review these laws. The analysis for the Chilean CT focuses on the post-reform court as the pre-reform court had different rules regarding selection and included some judges selected by the junta.[3] The post-reform analysis for this court involves 3,860 judges' votes on 247 separate cases, which included 431 separate decisional paragraphs from 2006 to 2016. The analysis for Colombia focuses on the period from 1997 as the rules as to selectors and number of judges changed in 1993, and until 1997 there was insufficient variation in judges' political associations to conduct the analysis. For this period, the analysis of the Colombian CC involves 16,493 judges' votes on 1,332 cases, which include 1,963 separate decisional paragraphs spanning from 1997 to 2014.

The main explanatory variables refer to judges' institutional selectors and their party associations (see Tables A.2 and A.3 in the book's Appendix for further information on judges' backgrounds, coding, and sources). For Chile, the analysis includes two binary variables for branch appointers, *Presidential appointee* and *Legislative appointee*. Appointees of the Supreme Court and the COSENA, or Consejo Nacional de Seguridad, constitute the base group.[4] The Colombian CC judges are similarly coded by institutional nominator: *Presidential nominee* indicates whether the president nominated the judge or not, and *Supreme Court nominee* indicates whether the judge was nominated by the Supreme Court. Nominees of the Consejo de Estado constitute the base group.

Judges for both courts have been coded for their underlying party associations. Such party associations are based on judges' associations or work for a party or particular government or appointment by a president of a specific party or in the case of the legislature by agreement to alternate judges preferred by opposing parties. For Chile, judges are coded as *Concertación* or *Right* to indicate judges' party associations with the Center Left Concertación or Center Right Alianza respectively. Judges not affiliated with parties constitute the base group, and the majority of these judges are chosen by non-elected actors (i.e., the Supreme Court or COSENA). Couso (2004) points out that judges chosen by the Supreme Court in Chile tended to be particularly apolitical "bring[ing] to the court the deferential habits of the regular judiciary" (p. 87) (see Couso and Hilbink 2011). Judges were

[3] See Carroll and Tiede (2011) comparing the pre- and post-reform Tribunal through 2010 using institutional selector and some different covariates, but not testing judges' party and institutional selector together.

[4] While the reform excluded the COSENA as a selector, two judges, Cea and Colombo, chosen by this institution prior to the reform remained on the court until 2010.

coded as having no party associations when there was no mention of the judge having any party association or work for or appointment by any elected actor. Judges' party affiliations should be interpreted in relation to legislation that was passed when the Concertación had a majority of seats in Congress under both Bachelet's presidencies and a slim majority under the center right presidency of Piñera[5] (see Chapter 4, Table 4.1). While the Concertación held a majority of seats in Congress for the entire period under study, it never held the required supermajority of seats (60 or 67 percent) to approve obligatory laws, which the Tribunal reviews abstractly.

In Colombia, the variable *Liberal Party* refers to judges associated with the Liberal Party and its associates and judges associated with the Conservative Party constitute the base group. Again, these are based on judges' party associations or work for a party or government or selection by a president with certain party affiliations. As with Chile, Colombian judges' party associations are oriented to a legislature in which the majority or the greatest number of seats were held by the Liberal Party or their affiliates until 2010 and the greatest number of seats were held by the Party de la U from 2010 to 2014 (see Chapter 5, Table 5.1 describing the coding of seats held by the legislature and revealing the complexity of Colombia's highly fragmented party system). Further, in Colombia, the presidents' party coalition (made up of many diverse parties in the later presidencies) held the most seats for almost the entire period under study.[6] During the second Uribe and Santos presidencies, factions of the Liberal and Conservative Parties were both part of the president's coalitions (see Carroll and Pachón 2016).

Tenure was created by subtracting each judge's appointment year from the year of the constitutional review decision. Judges who have been on the courts only a short time are more likely to have been chosen by selectors who are still in office at the time of their decisions. Judges early in the tenure also may exhibit a "freshman effect" (see Hettinger et al. 2003; Bowen and Scheb 1993). Further, judges who are nearing the end of their term on the bench (with no possibility of reelection) may be quite intent on building a legacy through their decisions to secure future jobs (Magaloni 2003). Finally, judges who have been on the bench longer have more experience as constitutional adjudicators.

To analyze general presence or panel effects, the court composition variables are created in a manner similar to that of Fischman (2015), who replicated eleven prominent studies. In Chile, four composition variables are created including *Average number of other presidential appointees*, *Average number of other legislative appointees*, *Average number of other Concertación judges*, and *Average number of other Right judges*. In Colombia, three composition variables were created including

[5] Piñera's center right coalition won one more seat than the Center Left coalition in the chamber of deputies, but the Center Left had the majority of seats in the Senate.

[6] See Chapter 5, Table 5.1, note b showing that Pastrana's coalition did not hold a majority from 2000 to 2001.

Average number of other presidential nominees, *Average number of other Supreme Court nominees*, and *Average number of other Liberal judges*. Each of these variables was created by the following equation:

$$\text{Other judges' institutional selector or party attribute} = \frac{(\text{No. of judges with attribute}-\text{attribute of judge voting})}{(\text{total number of judges}-1)}$$

So as not to inflate the presence of judges with certain party or institutional selectors, the total number of judges in the denominator includes supplementary or auxiliary judges who occasionally appeared on the cases. The composition variables refer to the composition of the court faced by a particular judge in each decision and therefore, excludes the influence of the judge's own selecting institution or party on their vote. These composition variables vary by case and are what Grossman et al. (2016) calls "plausibly random" due to judges' personal schedules and quorum rules. Judges' presence on a case is due to days of vacation and sick leave, which are orthogonal to case characteristics such as type of review or subject matter.

Another related variable to court composition is an indicator for when a portion of the court's personnel is changed as required by law in Chile and which occurs due to staggered terms in Colombia at regular intervals. As noted by Brouard and Hönnige (2017), overall changes in composition brought on by turnover of judges on a court may influence whether judges or the court as a whole are willing to strike down laws. To reflect these compositional changes *Composition change 1* and *Composition change 2* are two binary variables that indicate when the two courts changed composition during the period analyzed. The base category for these two variables is the court composition that existed at the starting point of the analysis. In Chile, the Tribunal changed composition after the reforms in 2009 and 2012.[7] In Colombia, court composition changed in 2001 and 2009.

While judges' selecting branch is an important influence on their individual decisions, case context cannot be overlooked (see Amaral-Garcia et al. 2009; Scherer 2004). Judges should be influenced by the type of constitutional review and the subject matter or area of the law being evaluated. For type of constitutional review in Chile, the cases analyzed involve two types of a priori review. First, cases coded as *requerimientos* are referred to the Tribunal predominantly by opposition legislators. Second, laws that the Tribunal must review involving legal precepts, organic laws, or treaties, which are all constrained by arduous supermajority legislative voting rules, constitute the base group. Colombia's cases are divided by whether they require a priori review (only referred to the court by political actors) or a posteriori review (referred to the CC by citizens). Case control variables include the two types of cases of a priori review, *Treaties* and *Statutory law*, both binary variables. Cases brought by citizens for a posteriori review constitute the base group.

7 The change in 2015 is too close to the end date of the data analyzed to include in the regression.

As to subject matter, Shapiro (2004) argues that high courts' constitutional review functions should be evaluated over three broad issue areas including separation of powers, federalism, and rights. First, cases involving separation of powers' issues may be especially controversial or salient as they highlight conflict among the branches. Second, cases involving individual and minority rights implicate the role of courts as protectors of minority interests and often involve issues that deeply divide societies. Third, judges may vote differently on issues related to the nation as opposed to regional or subnational issues (see Pellegrina and Garoupa 2013). Chile and Colombia do not have federal systems, but the government legislates in the area of subnational governments. To capture these case types, the analysis includes the following three variables: *Separation of powers*, *Rights*, and *Subnational*. These subject areas are coded based on the constitutional provisions referenced in each case. Appendix Table A6.1 to this chapter provides specifics on case subject coding, and Tables A6.2 and A6.3 provide summary statistics for both courts. The statistical analysis allows for causal inference due to the "plausibly random" and fluctuating nature of which judges appear on which cases. Further proof and testing of the "exogeneity of justices' absences" (see Holden et al. 2021) is explored in Chapter 7.

6.5 RESULTS

The results are found in Table 6.5 for the Chilean CT and Table 6.6 for the Colombian CC. There are three columns in each of these tables representing the various models. The first column analyzes the influence of institutional selector on judges' decisions, the second column, the influence of party associations, and the third column, both institutional selector and party associations. In general, the results support the hypotheses regarding institutional selector and panel effects.

6.5.1 *The Chilean CT*

The results for the Chilean CT indicate that judges' institutional selector is an important determinant of decisions to strike down laws and judges' propensity to strike down laws diverges by selecting institution. For Chile, the regression in column 1 (analyzing institution alone) is compared to the regressions in columns 2 and 3. On the CT, when analyzed separately (Table 6.5, column 1) individual judges selected by the elected president are 10 percent more likely to strike down laws, and judges appointed by Congress or the Senate are 12 percent more likely than those selected by nonelected institutions. When party is tested alone (column 2), it appears to influence judges on the Tribunal and may explain the results of similar attitudinal studies of mixed selection courts that focused on party alone rather than institutional selector (see Tiede 2016). Judges associated with the Concertación are 5 percent and judges associated with the Right are 7 percent more

TABLE 6.5. *Determinants of judges' unconstitutional votes on the Chilean CT*

Variables	Institutional Selector	Party Association	Institutional Selector & Party
Judge level variables			
Presidential appointee	0.49***		0.63***
	(0.10)		(0.20)
Legislative appointee	0.56***		0.72***
	(0.14)		(0.21)
Concertación associated judge		0.25	−0.16
		(0.17)	(0.19)
Right associated judge		0.36**	−0.28
		(0.15)	(0.25)
Tenure	0.01	0.00	0.01
	(0.01)	(0.01)	(0.01)
Case level variables			
Requerimiento	0.91***	0.89***	0.96***
	(0.23)	(0.23)	(0.23)
Separation of powers	0.50***	0.51***	0.45**
	(0.17)	(0.18)	(0.18)
Rights	0.45***	0.52***	0.42***
	(0.16)	(0.16)	(0.16)
Subnational	0.48***	0.48***	0.48***
	(0.16)	(0.16)	(0.16)
Avg. other presidential appointees	1.42*		2.46
	(0.74)		(1.52)
Avg. other legislative appointees	2.52**		3.68**
	(1.10)		(1.60)
Avg. other Concertación assoc. judges		0.02	−1.54
		(1.20)	(1.33)
Avg. other Right associated judges		1.03	−1.94
		(1.04)	(1.78)
Composition change 1	0.10	0.07	0.11
	(0.31)	(0.31)	(0.31)
Composition change 2	0.51**	0.57**	0.50*
	(0.24)	(0.23)	(0.27)
Level 2 variance	−0.28	−0.26	−0.29
	(0.19)	(0.19)	(0.19)
Constant	−3.34***	−2.24**	−2.71***
	(0.60)	(0.90)	(0.88)
Number of judge level observations	3,860	3,860	3,860
Number of cases	247	247	247
Number of decisional paragraphs	431	431	431
AIC	3,529	3,543	3,534
BIC	3,610	3,624	3,640

Robust standard errors in parentheses; *** $p < 0.01$, ** $p < 0.05$, * $p < 0.10$.

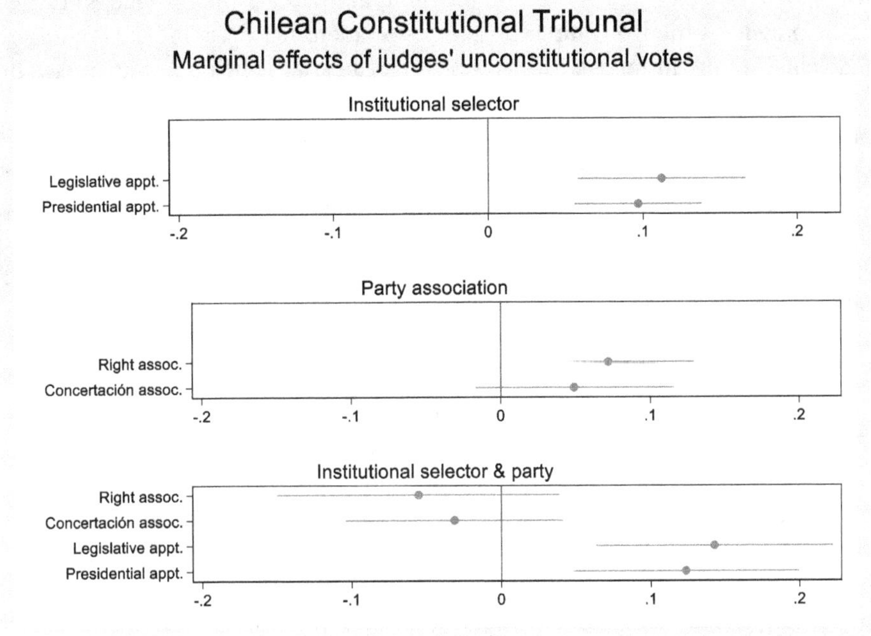

FIGURE 6.7 Marginal effects of judges' unconstitutional votes on the Chilean CT

likely to strike down laws compared to nonpartisan judges in this regression. However, the coefficient for Concertación is not statistically significant.

When institutional appointers are analyzed with party (column 3), institutional selectors are the predominant individual characteristic that drive decision-making on the Chilean Tribunal, with presidential appointees 13 percent more likely to strike down laws and legislative appointees 15 percent more likely when compared to Supreme Court or COSENA appointees. In this final regression, party has no individual influence on judges' decisions. Figure 6.7 represents the influence of institutional selector and party for each of the three different regressions. A comparison of the fit for the three models indicates that for Chile's CT, the model in column 1 with only variables for institutional appointers is a better fit than the other two models as evidenced by a lower Akaike Information Criteria (AIC) and Bayesian Information Criteria (BIC).

Regarding panel effects, the presence of judges with other institutional selectors has an independent influence on individual judges' decisions (H6.3) and this influence is greater than the presence of judges with other party affiliations (H6.4). For Chile, when institutional selector is tested alone, the best fitting model, an increase in the average of other presidential appointees leads judges without this selector to increase their propensity to strike down laws by 11 percent and an increase in other legislative appointees leads judges to strike down laws 19 percent more often when these variables are moved from their minimum to maximum value. In model 2, the presence of judges with other party associations has no influence on judges' individual voting. In model, 3 when tested together, an increase in the average of other presidential appointees again increases judges' propensity to strike down laws, but this coefficient is not significant. However, an increase in average other legislative appointees leads to a 26 percent increase in judges' propensity to strike down laws. As regards compositional changes in personnel on the court, the variable for the change in 2009 was not statistically significant, but the one for 2012 was compared to the base group of the court composition after the constitutional reforms. This may be due to the fact that by 2012, the Tribunal also had judges selected by a center right president populating the court for the first time since the democratic transition.

Case types are also influential to individual voting. In Chile, as shown in Table 6.5, judges are 18–20 percent more likely to strike down *requerimientos*, which represent especially important societal issues and can be brought at any stage of the legislative process, usually by legislators in the opposition. The subject area variables all have a positive and significant effect on judges' propensity to strike down laws. Judges are 9–10 percent more likely to strike down separation of powers cases, 9–11 percent more likely to strike down a law involving rights, and 10 percent more likely for laws involving subnational issues.

6.5.2 *The Colombian CC*

On the Colombian Court, when institutional selectors are analyzed alone (Table 6.6, column 1), judges nominated by presidents are 7 percent less likely and those selected by the Supreme Court are 2 percent less likely to strike down laws than those nominated by the Consejo de Estado; however, the coefficient for Supreme Court nominees is not significant. The difference in propensity (but not significance) to strike down laws by the two high courts may be due to their different roles in government. The Supreme Court serves as an appellate court, while the Consejo serves a more political role as advisor to the government on administrative matters and has the power to find presidential decrees unconstitutional in some circumstances.

When party is tested alone (column 2), judges affiliated with the liberal party are only 1 percent more likely to strike down laws, which is substantively quite small. When institutional appointers are tested with party (Table 6.6, column 3), presidential nominees are 6 percent less likely and Supreme Court nominees 3 percent less likely to strike down laws than Consejo nominees. Unlike Chile, in this third model, however, the party variable reaches statistical significance at the 0.05 level such that judges associated with the Liberal Party are 1 percent more likely to strike down laws than those affiliated with the Conservative Party. Figure 6.8 provides a visual representation of the marginal effects for institutional selector and party across the

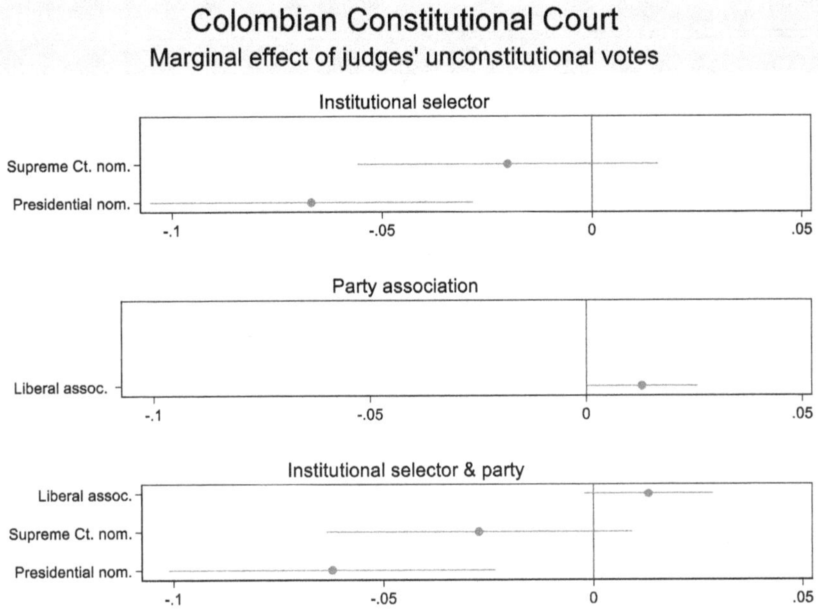

FIGURE 6.8 Marginal effects of judges' unconstitutional votes on the Colombian CC

three regressions. Model fit for Colombia does not as clearly suggest preference for one model over another.

On the Colombian CC, panel effects attributed to increases in presidential nominees are significant in models 1 and 3. Increasing the number of judges selected by the president leads judges without this nominator to decrease their propensity to strike down laws by 19–21 percent compared to Consejo nominees. Increasing the number of Supreme Court nominees leads other judges to decrease their opinions to strike down laws by 6–7 percent but these coefficients are not statistically significant. Regarding the presence of Liberal Party–associated judges, an increase in this variable leads judges without this party association to decrease striking down laws by 7 percent, but this variable is only significant in model 2. Compositional changes of the entire court also matter. The CC's second compositional change in 2012 was statistically significant, leading judges to strike down laws 9–11 percent less often.

As to the influence of type of constitutional review on judges' decisions in Colombia across the regressions, judges are 11–12 percent more likely to strike down statutory laws and 18 percent less likely to strike down international treaties compared to laws brought to the court's attention by citizens. Judges might be less likely to strike down treaties as these involve foreign affairs, an area traditionally reserved to the elected branches. As to the other subject areas, judges are 4 percent more likely

TABLE 6.6. *Determinants of judges' unconstitutional votes on the Colombian CC*

Variables	Institutional Selector	Party Association	Institutional Selector & Party
Judge-level variables			
Presidential nominee	−0.56***		−0.53***
	(0.16)		(0.17)
Supreme Court nominee	−0.17		−0.23
	(0.15)		(0.16)
Liberal Party associated judge		0.11**	0.11*
		(0.05)	(0.07)
Judges' tenure	0.03***	0.02**	0.03***
	(0.01)	(0.01)	(0.01)
Case-level variables			
Statutory law	0.93**	0.99***	0.93**
	(0.36)	(0.38)	(0.37)
International treaty	−1.51***	−1.52***	−1.51***
	(0.16)	(0.16)	(0.16)
Separation of powers	0.31**	0.31**	0.31**
	(0.13)	(0.13)	(0.13)
Rights	−0.05	−0.06	−0.05
	(0.11)	(0.11)	(0.11)
Subnational	0.08	0.08	0.08
	(0.15)	(0.15)	(0.15)
Avg. other presidential nominees	−2.52**		−2.66**
	(1.19)		(1.23)
Avg. other Supreme Court nominees	−0.98		−1.17
	(1.11)		(1.12)
Avg. other Liberal Party associated		−0.73**	−0.23
		(0.30)	(0.36)
Composition change 1	−0.02	0.00	−0.02
	(0.23)	(0.23)	(0.24)
Composition change 2	−0.87**	−0.76**	−0.89**
	(0.38)	(0.37)	(0.38)
Level 2 variance	1.83***	1.84***	1.84***
	(0.15)	(0.15)	(0.15)
Constant	−0.46	−1.58***	−0.27
	(0.85)	(0.26)	(0.86)
Number of judge level observations	16,493	16,493	16,493
Number of cases	1,332	1,332	1,332
Number of decisional paragraphs	1,963	1,963	1,963
AIC	13,408	13,418	13,398
BIC	13,516	13,511	13,521

Robust standard errors in parentheses; *** $p < 0.01$, ** $p < 0.05$, * $p < 0.10$

to strike down laws involving separation of powers. The coefficients for rights and subnational laws are not significant and substantively small and, except for separation of powers cases, stand in contrast to the Chilean CT in which all three case areas were significant.

6.5.3 *Robustness Checks*

Additional robustness checks are described in detail and presented in the Appendix to this chapter, Tables A6.4 and A6.5. Although the Colombian data, provides counterfactuals for all combinations of institutional selector and party such that there were liberal and conservative associated judges for each of the institutional selectors, this was not the case with Chile. The data for Chile lacked a counterfactual for judges selected by the Supreme Court or COSENA who were associated with parties from the Right. To further test the strength of the main results for Chile, two additional tests were run. First, regression results after removing all nonpartisan judges were consistent with the main models (see Table A6.4). Second, a regression was run with variables that combined judges' selection with their party (see Table A6.5). If judges with elected appointers but with opposing party associations are all more likely to strike down laws than the nonelected appointees, then this is additional evidence that institutional selector is a more important determinant of judges' votes than party. The results of this second regression provide this additional confirmation.

6.6 CHAPTER SUMMARY: DISCUSSION AND IMPLICATIONS

The chapter began with an inquiry about the extent to which mixed systems reflect arguments put forth by proponents and opponents of this selection method. The legislative histories in both Chile and Colombia indicated that policymakers in these countries strove for a balance of judges selected by different branches of government on the two respective courts but were concerned that some institutional selectors would be afforded more powers than others. The results showing that judges' decisions divide depending on their institutional selector suggest that judges with different selectors have distinct voices. However, the results also call into question whether judges are impartially checking the power of powerful branches of government and upholding the constitution. For example, in Chile, the higher likelihood that presidential and legislative appointees strike down laws passed by the legislature calls into question whether judges chosen by the Supreme Court are able to check the powers of either the elected or nonelected branches in a meaningful way. In Colombia, the results suggest that Colombia's Consejo de Estado, an administrative high court with some significant political powers, has a perhaps unintentionally stronger voice in vetoing legislation than afforded it in the regular legislative process. Further, there is some evidence that there are more distinct and larger divisions between the influence of institutional selectors on judges' individual voting in Chile than in Colombia where Senate confirmation may somewhat mute the apparent differences in judges based on institutional selector.

A comparative analysis of the results for the two courts raises the issue of why presidential appointees on the Chilean CT are more likely to strike down laws and presidential nominees on the Colombian CC act more deferentially. As noted in the introductory chapters, judges' voting should be related to their institutional selector, but no universal statement can be made that appointees or nominees of one branch are universally more deferential or more willing to strike down laws. This depends on the exact mixed selection method used in a country as well as which selecting institutions are being compared to one another. Further, the history and context of the selecting institutions determines what particularly they value in their choices of constitutional judges. For instance, Lamprea (2010) suggests that the two high courts selecting judges to the CC were looking for very different types of judges. In Colombia, deference by presidential and Supreme Court nominees is relative to those of the Consejo nominees. Additionally, President Uribe has the longest presidency of the data period analyzed, and his increasingly authoritarian tendencies during his presidential terms may have made judges weary of defying his policies and created some deference by those chosen by him. Finally, as shown in Chapter 5, despite the many parties, the president's party coalitions held the majority of seats in Congress for almost the entire period under study, which may have been a factor in the CC's presidential nominees display of deference.[8]

Despite its many advantages, critics of mixed selection warn that it may lead to a court that is fragmented and unable to make decisive policy (Ginsburg 2003) or one in which institutional selectors have "co-opted" portions of the court that they have selected (Sadurski 2008). The results add some support to the co-option argument as judges' votes seem to divide by their distinct selection origins. Additionally, scholars critiquing this selection method have voiced concern that a mixed selection court may be internally fragmented due to judges' party associations. The results, however, show that judges' preferences based on party loyalties, tested often on many high court studies but recently called into question by Voeten (2008) and Epstein and Knight (2013), are not the most important determinant of individual votes to strike down laws. The addition of the Senate as a confirming institution introduces party into Colombian judges' decision-making considerations, but the concern by Ginsburg (2003) that judges' votes would fragment a court along party divisions seems minimal at least in the case of

[8] Presidential nominees are the most deferential of all judges, confirming in part Rodríguez-Raga's (2011) results on a sample of cases, which included presidential decrees for a different time period.

Chile and Colombia's constitutional courts. While party association does not seem to influence judges as much as the character of their selecting institution, this is not to deny the fact that some cases are more politically divisive than others, an issue that is taken up in Chapter 8

The results regarding panel effects support arguments that mixed selection courts may lead to better decision-making that reflects different institutional viewpoints. The results provide some evidence that judges may be deliberating and changing their decisions due to the presence of judges with other institutional selectors. However, it is difficult to interpret to what extent panel effects are based on judges' characteristics, their votes, or both. The results highlight, however, that individual judges are collegial, influenced by others, and have strategic reasons to vote with the dominant type of judge present on the court on any given case. This chapter has focused exclusively on judge-level data. In Chapter 7, an analysis of the decision-making by the full courts is undertaken. It analyzes whether the panel effects observed at the individual level make a difference in the aggregate.

APPENDIX

TABLE A6.1. *Coding of case subject areas based on constitutional provisions referenced*

Subject areas found in constitutions	Constitutional provisions		Coding of variables for case types
	Chile 2006–	Colombia	
Bases for unconstitutionality	1–9		
Nationality & citizenship	10–18	96–102	
Political parties		103–112	
Rights and Duties	19–23	11–95	Rights
Government	24–45	188–227	
President and ministers	24–37	188–227	Separation of powers
State administration	38	113–131	
States of exception	39–45	212–215	
Congress	46–75	132–187	Separation of powers
Judicial power	76–82	228–245	Separation of powers
Public ministry	83–91	275–284	
Constitutional Court	92–94	239–245	
Electoral justice	95–97		
Comptroller general	98–100	267–274	
Armed forces & security	101–105	216–223	
Consejo Nacional de Estado	106–107		
Economic		332–370	
Central Bank	108–109	371–373	
Subnational government	110–126	285–331	Subnational
Constitutional reform	127–129	374–380	

TABLE A6.2. *Summary statistics of judge-level data for the Chilean CT (2006–2016)*

Variable	Mean	Std. Dev.	Min	Max
Judges' unconstitutional vote	0.23	0.42	0	1
Presidential appointee	0.24	0.43	0	1
Legislative appointee	0.39	0.49	0	1
Concertación associated judge	0.44	0.50	0	1
Right associated judge	0.31	0.46	0	1
Judge tenure	3.61	2.55	0	11
Requerimiento	0.09	0.29	0	1
Separation of powers	0.24	0.43	0	1
Rights	0.30	0.46	0	1
Subnational	0.23	0.42	0	1
Avg. other presidential appointees	0.24	0.12	0	0.43
Avg. other legislative appointees	0.39	0.09	0.14	0.57
Avg. other Concertación assoc. judges	0.44	0.11	0.13	0.71
Avg. other Right assoc. judges	0.31	0.11	0	0.57
Composition change 1	0.12	0.32	0	1
Composition change 2	0.08	0.28	0	1

TABLE A6.3. *Summary statistics of judge-level data for the Colombian CC (1997–2014)*

Variable	Mean	Std. Dev.	Min	Max
Judges' unconstitutional vote	0.30	0.46	0	1
Presidential nominee	0.39	0.49	0	1
Supreme Court nominee	0.28	0.45	0	1
Liberal Party associated judge	0.50	0.50	0	1
Tenure	3.80	2.50	0	9
Statutory law	0.08	0.27	0	1
International treaty	0.15	0.36	0	1
Separation of powers	0.67	0.47	0	1
Rights	0.73	0.44	0	1
Subnational	0.16	0.36	0	1
Separation of powers	0.67	0.47	0	1
Avg. other presidential nominees	0.38	0.12	0	0.63
Avg. other Supreme Court nominees	0.28	0.12	0	0.50
Avg. other Liberal Party associated judges	0.49	0.21	0	0.88
Composition change 1	0.12	0.32	0	1
Composition change 2	0.02	0.15	0	1

EXPLANATION OF ROBUSTNESS CHECKS TO ACCOMPANY TABLES A6.4 AND A6.5

In Table A6.4, the Chilean CT results appearing in Table 6.5 were rerun with the removal of judges not associated with any parties. Column 1 of this table represents

TABLE A6.4. *The Chilean CT main results replicated with nonpartisan judges removed*

Variables	(1)	(2)
Presidential appointee	0.58***	0.52***
	(0.16)	(0.12)
Legislative appointee	0.60***	0.56***
	(0.17)	(0.15)
Right associated judge	−0.14	
	(0.18)	
Concertación associated judge		0.08
		(0.15)
Tenure	0.00	0.00
	(0.01)	(0.01)
Requerimiento	0.82***	0.81***
	(0.20)	(0.20)
Separation of powers	0.50***	0.50***
	(0.15)	(0.15)
Rights	0.45***	0.46***
	(0.15)	(0.15)
Subnational	0.43***	0.43***
	(0.15)	(0.15)
Avg. other presidential appointees	2.19*	1.67**
	(1.17)	(0.78)
Avg. other legislative appointees	2.82**	2.45**
	(1.23)	(1.03)
Avg. other Right associated judges	−0.61	
	(1.00)	
Avg. other Concertación associated judges		0.06
		(0.77)
Composition change 1	0.17	0.17
	(0.28)	(0.29)
Composition change 2	0.44*	0.48*
	(0.25)	(0.25)
Level 2 variance	−0.55***	−0.54***
	(0.20)	(0.20)
Constant	−3.34***	−3.35***
	(0.59)	(0.77)
Judge level observations	2,887	2,887
Number of cases	247	247

Robust standard errors in parentheses; *** $p < 0.01$, ** $p < 0.05$, * $p < 0.1$.

TABLE A6.5. *The Chilean CT main results replicated with variables for appointer and party association combined*

Variables	(1)
Presidential appointees associated with Concertación	0.40*
	(0.22)
Presidential appointees associated with the Right	0.43**
	(0.18)
Legislative appointees associated with Concertación	0.61***
	(0.20)
Legislative appointees associated with the Right	0.40**
	(0.17)
Supreme Court or CSN associated with the Concertación	−0.16
	(0.19)
Tenure	0.01
	(0.01)
Requerimiento	0.96***
	(0.23)
Separation of powers	0.44**
	(0.18)
Rights	0.42**
	(0.16)
Subnational	0.48***
	(0.16)
Avg. other Concertación associated judges	−1.48
	(1.33)
Avg. other Right associated judges	−1.88
	(1.78)
Avg. other presidential appointees	2.35
	(1.53)
Avg. other legislative appointees	3.62**
	(1.60)
Composition change 1	0.11
	(0.31)
Composition change 2	0.51*
	(0.27)
Level 2 variance	−0.29
	(0.19)
Constant	−2.71***
	(0.88)
Judge level observations	3,860
Number of cases	247

Robust standard errors in parentheses; *** $p < 0.01$, ** $p < 0.05$, * $p < 0.1$.

the results when judges affiliated with the Right are included in the regression and those affiliated with the Concertación constitute the base group. Column 2 represents the results when judges affiliated with the Concertación are included in the regression and those affiliated with the Right constitute the base group. The results in these columns are consistent with the main results.

In Table A6.5, a further regression using the Chilean CT data was analyzed as the Chilean data does not contain the counterfactual of judges selected by the Supreme Court or COSENA, who are affiliated with parties of the Right. Therefore, creating variables which represent the appointer with the judges' party provides a robustness check to the main results. If judges selected by the president or the legislature (regardless of party affiliation) are more likely to strike down laws than those appointed by the Supreme Court or COSENA, then this is additional evidence that appointing institution and not party is a viable determinant of judges' decisions to strike down laws. This regression includes the following variables:

Presidential appointees associated with the Concertación
Presidential appointees associated with the Right
Legislative appointees associated with the Concertación
Legislative appointees associated with the Right
Supreme Court or COSENA appointees associated with the Concertación

The base group is judges appointed by the Supreme Court or COSENA who are not associated with parties. The results in Table A6.5 show that judges associated with both parties selected by the president or the legislature are more likely to strike down laws than those selected by the Supreme Court and the COSENA, all consistent with the main results.

7

Determinants of Legal Invalidation by Constitutional Courts

7.1 INTRODUCTION

The prior chapter's focus on individual judge's preferences and decisions is informative but still leaves unanswered which factors guide an entire court's constitutional decisions. It is possible that despite the influence of the mixed selection system on *individual choice*, changes of judges' votes are too subtle to have any real impact on the outcome of a case decided by the full court. As a result, this chapter analyzes how mixed selection and quorum rules influence the full court's majority opinion given the panel effects found in Chapter 6. The chapter is informed by observations that courts often uphold or strike down laws in unanticipated ways – not easily explained by traditional explanations based on the partisan orientation of a court.

For example, alterations in the staffing of the US Supreme Court, due to retirements and the selection of John Roberts by President George W. Bush in 2005, led to predictions that the Court would strike down the Affordable Health Care Act, enacted under President Obama's administration and providing broader healthcare to Americans, and that the Court would favor Arizona's state rights to enact local immigration policy. However, despite the Court's conservative majority, the Court voted contrary to partisan predictions, upholding most of Obama's health care plan and striking down Arizona's local immigration laws. More recently in 2020, Roberts has voted with liberal judges to expand LGBTQ rights, protect young immigrant dreamers from deportation, and strike down a restrictive abortion law in Louisiana. Commentators suggested that these somewhat surprising cases were due to Chief Justice Roberts' concern that the legitimacy of the Court would be undermined if decisions appeared to be overtly partisan (Liptak 2020). Indeed, judges' decisions did not divide strictly along party lines on these important cases suggesting the need for alternative explanations to this Court's decision-making.

Similarly, the Chilean Constitutional Tribunal in 2017 was asked to vote on a controversial law that would allow abortion under three circumstances: risk of life to the mother, viability of the fetus, and rape. The case was brought to the Tribunal through the *requerimiento* procedure by legislators associated with *Chile Vamos*, the Center Right coalition. Prior to the decision, many feared that the Tribunal would strike down the law due to the Tribunal's composition of some judges who were associated with the Right or who favored anti-abortion policies for religious or other reasons.[1] Despite this popular wisdom, the Tribunal voted to uphold the law, a most progressive decision in a country that had prevented legal abortion under any circumstances. The decision was decided by a slim majority of six to four. Although three of the judges in the majority were associated with the Concertación, the majority also contained a minister associated with the Right and chosen by Sebastian Piñera and one chosen by the Supreme Court, the latter considered nonpartisan. These two judges sided with the majority indicating that a more flexible approach to constitutional adjudication, rather than "originalism," was needed for interpreting the right to life.[2]

Additionally, the Colombian Constitutional Court's decision relating to legislation allowing President Uribe to seek a third term, discussed in Chapter 5, defied a purely partisan explanation. Justice Calle Correa, herself selected by President Uribe, voted against this additional term and against some judges on the Court associated with the Conservative Party. Justice Mendoza, associated with the Conservative Party, also voted against the third term. The above examples show the limitations of purely partisan explanations for majority opinion formation found in some of the literature referenced in Chapter 2. To analyze whether individual choice is transformed into collective choice in the manner described in Chapter 6, which supports a theory based on judges' selector and presence or panel effects, this chapter evaluates fluctuations in court composition on decision-making while controlling for other legal and political contextual features.

This book has argued that case contextual features and the configuration of mixed selection courts as well as quorum rules, which allow court composition to fluctuate, are important factors driving decision-making. The empirical results found in this chapter show that the manner in which a case arrives at a

[1] The Tribunal consisted of all ten members of which three were presidential appointees (Aróstica and Brahm chosen by President Piñera and Carmona chosen by Bachelet), four were legislative appointees (Romero Guzmán and Letelier for the Right and García Pino and Pozo for the Concertación), and three were nonpartisan Supreme Court appointees (Peña, Vásquez Márquez and Hernández Emparanza) (see Peña 2017 and El Mercurio 2017 for additional information).

[2] Concurring with the majority, Brahm and Vásquez Márquez stated that "the appropriateness of originalism as the only interpretive criterion of the Constitution, is insufficient and lacks flexibility, in general, so it will always be necessary to use other criteria of hermeneutics to resolve a constitutional conflict with the greatest certainty and adequate reasonableness and weighting" (unofficial English translation of Rol #3729 sponsored by the International Reproductive and Sexual Health Law Program, Faculty of Law, University of Toronto, Canada. Available at www.law.utoronto.ca/utfl_file/count/documents/reprohealth/chile-2017-english.pdf, last accessed February 2022).

constitutional court as well as the reviewed law's subject matter are important determinants of judicial vetoes. While contextual factors inform courts' decisions, court composition, determined through mixed selection, is a significant driver of decision-making. Although the goals for the mixed selection method stated by legislative drafters in Chile and Colombia were about providing a balance of judges selected by different institutional actors or creating an equilibrium on each constitutional court, choices about judicial selection are often about how to control judges and their decisions ex ante (Brinks and Blass 2018; Driscoll and Nelson 2015; Kiewiet and McCubbins 1991). Despite the two countries' intent to balance their courts with certain actors, they may not have anticipated how fluctuations, which alter judges' appearances on certain cases due to quorum rules, influence decision-making in unintended ways.

Because three political institutions choose judges on the two exemplar courts, those selected by any one institution almost never hold a majority on the two courts analyzed. This chapter shows that propensities to veto a law depend on changes in the percentage of judges with certain selectors. Further, the two courts' overall decisions depend on whether a case has a critical mass of certain similar types of judges. As regards to court composition defined by judges' party associations, changes in the percentage of judges associated with certain parties does not seem to independently influence the decisions of Chile's CT because judges associated with one party rarely hold a majority on this Tribunal. The party orientation of the CC, however, is influential, but only when this CC has more than 50 percent or more of its judges associated with one party appearing on a case.

The chapter opens with a summary of trends in the abstract review decisions of the Chilean and Colombian constitutional courts over time and provides summary statistics of the propensity of these courts' striking down laws based on the legal context and the number of judges appearing on cases resulting from quorum rules. The chapter then refers back to the discussion in Chapter 2 on what drives collective choice on mixed selection courts and provides specific explanations and predictions for judicial vetoes by the Chilean and Colombian constitutional courts. After the hypotheses and their justifications, the chapter provides a description of the case-level data and analysis as well as the results previewed above. The chapter ends with case examples.

7.2 CASE-LEVEL TRENDS

7.2.1 *By Legal and Political Context*

The legal and political context (i.e., the type of constitutional review triggered and the subject matter) are important determinants of judicial vetoes that should not be discounted. It should be noted that for both courts the rate of striking down laws ranges from about 18 percent to 30 percent over the history of these courts. In the

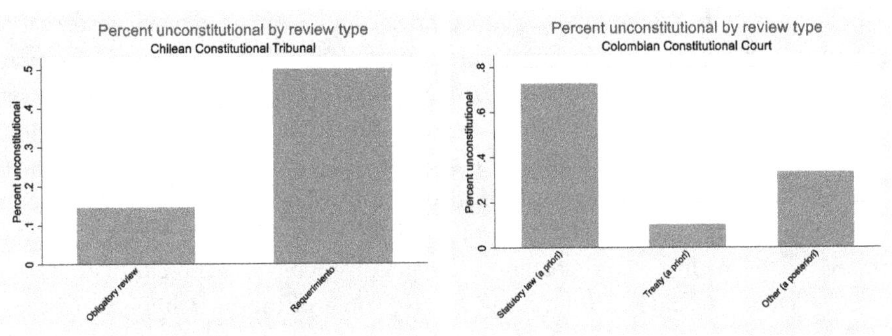

FIGURE 7.1 Percentage of cases striking down laws by type of review and court

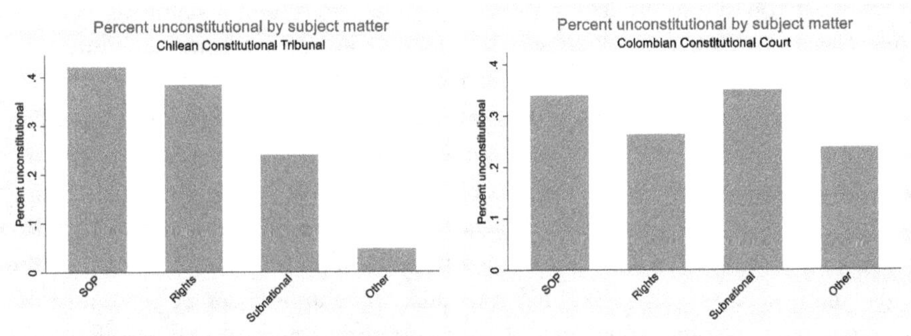

FIGURE 7.2 Percentage of cases striking down laws by subject matter of the law and court

case of the Chilean CT, the Tribunal struck down parts of the reviewed laws in 31 percent of the cases prior to the reform and in 18 percent of the cases after the reform. For Colombia, the Court struck down parts of laws in 29 percent of the cases analyzed for the period 1997 to 2014. These rates indicate that the two courts do not hesitate to strike down laws but are fairly deferential to the legislative bodies.

The manner in which cases reach the courts (i.e., type of abstract constitutional review) as well as the subject manner are significant factors driving judicial vetoes and providing important context for action by the two courts. Figures 7.1 and 7.2 provide a comparison of the rates of striking down laws for the two courts depending on these features. As seen in Figure 7.1, in the panel on the left, the Chilean CT is more likely to find laws scrutinized by the *requerimiento* procedure unconstitutional, which it does 50 percent of the time compared to 15 percent of the time for obligatory review cases, which involve Organic Laws in certain policy areas.[3]

3 According to Sierra (2012) organic laws cover the following twenty-one areas: the Central Bank, bases of state administration, police forces, mining concessions, the National Congress, regional development councils, the Comptroller General, the court statutory code, education,

In the case of the Colombian CC, the propensities for striking down laws also vary by type of review. As shown in Figure 7.1 in the panel on the right, the CC is much more likely to strike down statutory laws and does so 73 percent of the time. As recalled from the data description in Chapter 5, statutory laws were a creation of the 1991 Constitution and are considered of particular importance (see Colombian Constitution, Article 152). These laws involve fundamental rights and duties, the administration of justice, political parties and the state's electoral functions, institutions related to citizen participation, and states of emergency. Therefore, similar to *requerimientos* in Chile, statutory laws involve some of the most important issues facing society. In comparison, the Colombian CC vetoes treaties 10 percent of the time, and all other laws (i.e., reviewed a posteriori and referred to the court by citizens) are stricken down 33 percent of the time. The lower rate of invalidation for treaties may be due to the fact that these laws require more legislators to agree on their passage. Alternatively, treaties involve foreign affairs, an area where courts tend to be especially deferential to the elected branches.

Figure 7.2 compares the two courts' propensities for striking down laws based on the subject matter of the case. The Chilean CT struck down cases involving the separation of powers (SOP) 42 percent of the time, rights 35 percent of the time, and subnational cases 28 percent of the time, all at higher rates than cases involving other issues. The Colombian CC struck down separation of powers cases 34 percent of the time, rights cases 26 percent of the time, and subnational cases 35 percent of the time compared to other subject areas vetoed around 24 percent of the time.

7.2.2 *By Composition*

Besides looking at overall trends in case decisions, this book's focus on court compositions warrants an examination of how often the courts decide cases in the configuration envisioned by political actors who enacted laws defining the selection method and their relation to the frequency of striking down laws. Because this book is concerned with abstract review of laws, the full court is generally supposed to hear such cases and not smaller panels of half the court or less, which hear other types of cases, such as those involving concrete review in Chile or *tutelas* in Colombia. However, institutional design and quorum rules allow fluctuations in the full court size hearing abstract review cases to accommodate situations when all the judges are unable to appear. Tables 7.1 and 7.2, compare the rates of striking down laws by the full court or smaller quorums. Post reform the Chilean CT heard 244 cases between 2006 and 2016. Of these, only thirty-four involved the configuration mentioned in

constitutional states of exception, the armed forces, government and regional administration, electoral registrations and the electoral service, staffing of the electoral service, the public ministry, municipalities, political parties, electoral courts, the Constitutional Tribunal, and popular elections and vote count.

TABLE 7.1. *Chilean CT compositions by cases and rates of unconstitutionality*

Court size	Composition 3 Pres, 4 Leg, 3 SC	Number (%) of cases Out of 244	% cases unconstitutionality for each court size
10 (full court)	Yes	34 (14%)	27
10 (full court)	No	36 (14%)	19
9	No	85 (35%)	17
8	No	89 (37%)	16

Note. For the total post-reform period, parts of laws were stricken down in 18% of the abstract review cases reviewing the work of the legislature in power at the time of review.

TABLE 7.2. *Colombian CC compositions by cases and rates of unconstitutionality*

Court size	Intended composition 3 Pres, 3 SC, 3 Consejo	Number (%) of cases out of 1,333	% cases unconstitutionality for each court size
9 (full court)	Yes	518 (39%)	30
9 (full court)	No	419 (31%)	30
8	No	269 (20%)	24
7	No	127 (10%)	32

Note. For the period 1997 to 2014, parts of laws were stricken down in 29% of the abstract review cases reviewing the work of the legislature in power at the time of review.

the amended Constitution and the legislative history. In other instances when the Tribunal met with the required ten judges, it included one or more of the two judges chosen by the COSENA allowed prior to the reform or during periods in which the Tribunal was transitioning personnel or included auxiliary judges. Taken together for the post-reform period, ten judges met on about 28 percent of the cases or slightly less than a third of the cases heard in abstract review. The rate of striking down laws is higher for cases with the number and type of judges intended by the reform (see Table 7.1, row 1).

In contrast, the Colombian CC decides the vast majority of its abstract review cases with the Court's full membership or nine judges present on the case. As shown in Table 7.2, the CC heard 70 percent of the cases in this analysis with nine judges present. Of those cases, since 1997, about half had the configuration of judges envisioned by the Constituent Assembly and written into the Constitution, evenly split among judges with the three nominating institutions and half had other configurations due to transition periods or inclusion of auxiliary judges. For both categories, the full court struck down laws about 30 percent of the time. This strike-down rate was mirrored for cases that had seven judges present but is lower for those in which eight judges appeared.

7.3 PREDICTIONS RELATED TO COLLECTIVE CHOICE FOR THE CHILEAN AND COLOMBIAN CONSTITUTIONAL COURTS

Case contextual features as well as the composition of the courts should influence the likelihood of the courts issuing judicial vetoes. While these determinants were mentioned in a general way in Chapter 2, here, I provide the specifics of these hypotheses as they pertain to the Chilean and Colombian constitutional courts.

7.3.1 *Legal and Political Context*

There are several different types of abstract review that provide different contexts in which courts can make more precise calculations as to whether striking down a law will carry a risk of punishment or harm the courts' institutional legitimacy. Thus, courts, like individual judges, use the type of review and subject matter to inform them about the costs and benefits of upholding or striking down particular laws. For the Chilean CT, there should be different propensities of striking down laws depending on whether abstract review is triggered by mandatory review or triggered by politicians, usually in the minority, in the form of *requerimientos*. In the case of Organic Laws, treaties, and legal precepts, the mandatory nature of their review requires legislators to work hard to craft laws that are constitutional in anticipation that they will certainly be scrutinized by the Tribunal after legislative approval but prior to enactment. As noted by Langer and Brace (2005), anticipating the nature of the court that is required to review a law, makes legislators more cautious about the legislation they draft. Because the legislature knows that the CT *must* review organic laws, treaties, and legal precepts, they will be especially careful to craft laws that are unlikely to draw objection from the Tribunal. Further, the requirement that organic laws must be approved by 4/7 of legislators of both chambers of Congress and legal precepts and treaties by 3/5 also makes it more likely that these types of laws themselves represent compromises between the two main party coalitions and are more palatable to a court that may represent many diverse interests. As recalled from Chapter 2, Figure 2.1, courts will have a difficult time forming a majority opinion that falls outside the preferences of a supermajority of legislators. Striking down organic laws may involve a higher risk to the CT's reputation because the laws are carefully crafted and require a supermajority of legislators to agree on their passage.

Besides obligatory jurisdiction, the Tribunal also hears *requerimientos* that are brought to the Tribunal's attention by politicians, almost always members of the minority party coalition, at any stage in the legislative process. These cases often involve divisive societal issues and rights, such as those dealing with abortion or other areas of societal conflict. The names of the legislators who bring *requerimientos*, but are not parties to the case, are listed in the case itself and thus politicians may use this type of review to forge their own reputations regardless of how the Tribunal decides. Further, because these cases can be brought at any stage of the legislative process, they are not all passed under legislative supermajority rules as is the case of obligatory review. Although *requerimientos* may involve divisive and salient issues and are used by politicians instrumentally to forge their reputations, the Chilean Tribunal may be more inclined to strike down laws brought to its attention in this way compared to those reviewed mandatorily because they do not always involve the end of the legislative process or the anticipation of constitutional review. Further, because they involve divisive issues, striking down laws may help forge the Tribunal's reputation as an active participant in the legislative process and one that is willing to serve its counter majoritarian role by supporting the viewpoints of politicians in the minority.

Similarly, in Colombia, it is predicted that the CC will have different propensities of striking down laws based on cases that arrive to the Court under different types of review mechanisms.[4] As with Chile, abstract review types encountered by the Colombian CC differ on more than one dimension making it difficult to pinpoint or test the exact reason why different types of constitutional review mechanisms influence the Court's decisions. As recalled from Chapter 5, Colombia's abstract review of legislation includes a priori and a posteriori review. However, a priori cases are confined to the review of treaties, statutory law, and can only be referred to the Court by elected politicians. The a posteriori review cases involve a broad range of laws that citizens are allowed to challenge before the CC.[5] Therefore, when the CC is weighing the costs and benefits of striking down laws across abstract review types, it will assess the risks to its reputation for striking down laws in cases brought by citizens rather than politicians and whether deciding a case a priori has benefits and costs for the Court when acting as a pseudo-legislature. Further, the CC has two types of a priori cases involving statutory laws and treaties. The CC may be more likely to strike down statutory laws brought to it by elected politicians and decided a priori because such laws are especially salient and important and doing so may enhance the CC's reputation as an institution unafraid to use its powers.[6] In contrast

4 Although not tested here, there should be a difference between the Court's propensities to strike down abstract review cases versus *tutelas*, which flood the court in the thousands.

5 Citizens may bring cases to the CC to review some types of laws but not others. Specifically, citizens can challenge regular laws, which consist of Organic Laws (i.e., Regulations of the Congress and of each of the chambers, rules on the preparation, approval and implementation of the budget revenues and appropriations bill, the general development plan, and rules relating to the allocation of regulatory powers to local authorities), Framework laws/Ley Marco (involving public credit, foreign trade and foreign exchange regime, financial activities, securities and insurance, salary and benefit scheme for public servants), Ley de Facultades (granting the president extraordinary powers), and Ordinary laws/Leyes Ordinarias (issued by Congress in exercising its legislative power to regulate correspond to those issued under their regular duties) (see Constitution Article 150).

6 Colombia's 1991 Constitution created statutory laws to regulate specific issues considered particularly important (see Colombian Constitution, Article 152). The issues included under this category involve the following subjects: (1) Fundamental rights and duties and mechanisms for their protection; (2) Administration of Justice; (3) Organization and regime of political

the CC will be less likely to strike down treaties compared to statutory and other laws because these involve foreign policy issues, which courts generally avoid. Again, these different types of review should result in different propensities of striking down laws, although the exact reasons for these propensities, as in the case of Chile's obligatory review laws, are difficult to predict due to their many overlapping features. Based on the above arguments, these predictions follow:

H7.1. Courts' propensities to strike down laws vary with the type of constitutional review.

H7.1a. The Chilean CT is more likely to strike down laws that reach the Tribunal through the requerimiento *process than through obligatory review.*

H7.1b. The Colombian CC is more likely to strike down statutory laws compared to other laws.

H7.1c. The Colombian CC is less likely to strike down treaties compared to other laws.

Similar to abstract review type, the law's subject matter provides the two courts with different contexts for determining the costs and benefits of vetoing a law. Following Shapiro (2004) (discussed in Chapter 2), who looks at the US Supreme Court's various rates of "success,"[7] I analyze the two courts' decisions related to separation of powers and rights. Additionally, although both Chile and Colombia have unitary types of government as opposed to a federal structure, there are many laws that involve subnational regions and their governance, which the courts review and thus provide an important subject area to analyze that is similar to Shapiro's federalism category.

There are significant reputational benefits and costs to constitutional courts for striking down laws involving separation of powers. Legislation related to the separation of powers may involve some of the most important and contentious cases that the court reviews.[8] Most separation of powers cases heard by constitutional courts in electoral democracies involve confrontations between the two elected branches – the presidency and the legislature and "[i]n a polity that is democratic and election based, constitutional courts may well shy away from such conflicts no matter what the constitution says" (Shapiro 2004: 10). However, there may be reputational benefits for constitutional courts in striking down such laws. Because legislation concerning separation of powers' issues is likely to pit the interest of one branch against another or provide broad oversight to bureaucratic agencies, these cases

parties, status of the opposition and electoral functions; (4) Institutions and mechanisms for citizen participation; and, (5) States of emergency.

7 Shapiro tries to quantify when constitutional courts have succeeded in constitutional review defining success "narrowly and positivistically" as occurring "when an exercise of constitutional judicial review has changed public policy in the direction the court wants public policy to go" (2004: 7).

8 Shapiro states that there may be few real separation of powers cases involving "head-on-head confrontations between the branches of government in the hands of political parties" (2004: 11).

provide constitutional courts with the broadest and most visible forum for exercising its legislative role, checking the powers of powerful elected officials. Further, as judges on mixed selection courts represent two or more branches of government, it is unlikely that a majority of judges on these courts will uphold legislation in instances in which it specifically favors one branch over the others.

As with cases involving separation of powers, it is likely that constitutional courts' decisions to strike down laws may depend on whether these laws involve rights that "almost by definition, pit legislative majorities representing electoral majorities against some interest that has lost in the majoritarian arena" (Shapiro 2004: 18). As a consequence, this may lead non-majoritarian courts to favor minority rights. Because individual rights are substantively important and politically contentious, constitutional courts may consider a myriad of costs and benefits relating to how their decisions on individual rights may forge their reputations or legitimacy (see Shapiro 2004: 13). The Colombian Constitutional Court, for example, is often noted for its liberal positions on rights favoring those of the LGBT community or the poor. It is also possible that favoring rights may enhance courts' reputations as a powerful institution, willing to defy majoritarian legislation in favor of individual rights protection. However, such assertions depend much on the politics underlying the legislation to be reviewed, especially when laws are passed by more liberal legislatures or in fact favor minority rights.

Scholars also have theorized whether courts are more likely to strike down laws related to federalism or subnational governments in countries with unitary government. For example, constitutional courts should be most likely to enjoy success on federalism cases as they have the "political support not only of the federal government, but all of the states except the offending one" (Shapiro 2004: 8) and such cases may "bring the states into line with the nationally dominant constitutional vision" (Whittington 2005: 587). Similarly, courts outside of the United States have been found to strike down subnational laws more frequently than national laws (see Pellegrina and Garoupa 2013 for Italy; Tiede and Ponce 2014 for Peru). In Chile and Colombia, which have a unitary rather than a federal form of government, their constitutional courts do not review laws from the regions but rather federal laws dealing with the administration of the regions. Thus, the constitutional courts in these countries may be less likely to strike down federal laws dealing with subnational issues because the administration of regions may be thought of as more bureaucratic and less politically divisive and the Courts may favor the federal government over regional governments. From the above discussion, the following predictions can be formed:

H7.2. *The CT's and CC's propensities to strike down laws vary with the reviewed laws subject matter as follows:*

H7.2a. *The CT and CC are more likely to strike down laws related to the separation of powers than other issues.*

H7.2b. *The CT and CC are more likely to strike down laws related to rights than other issues.*

H7.2c. *The CT and CC are less likely to strike down laws related to subnational government than other issues.*

7.3.2 *By Court Composition*

As discussed in Chapters 2 and 6, there are several reasons why judges may agree with other judges of a different type or with different preferences. Judges who disagree with the probable decision emanating from the court majority must weigh whether disagreeing with judges on the court will limit a judge's ability to influence the majority (Cameron and Kornhauser 2017b). Additionally, judges must weigh whether dissent on a case weakens the decision's influence as argued by several scholars (Eskridge 1991a; O'Brien 2011; Pritchett 1948; Jaros and Canon 1971; Naurin and Stiansen 2020). These individual motivations help explain the presence or panel effects revealed in Chapter 6. In the case of Chilean constitutional judges, an increase in judges selected by the president or the legislature leads to individual judges selected by other nonelected appointers to strike down laws more. In Colombia, the increase in the presence of judges nominated by the president and Supreme Court leads other judges nominated by the Consejo to strike down laws less. In these prior judge-level analyses, contextual or panel effects related to party associations on both courts had no independent influence on judges' decisions and thus subtle changes in the party composition of the full court on any case should have a smaller influence on collective choice than changes in composition based on judges' institutional selector. As a result, due to both the desire of courts and judges to have decisions to strike down laws supported by as large a number of judges as possible and the presence effects based on individual judges' institutional selector, it follows that the propensity of courts as a whole to issue judicial vetoes should vary with fluctuations in the presence of judges of a certain type based on their selectors. Based on these arguments, the following predictions arise:

H7.3. *Courts' propensities to strike down laws vary with court compositions defined by judge types as follows:*

H7.3a. *As the proportion of judges selected by the legislature and/or the president increases on a case, the Chilean CT collectively will be more likely to strike down laws.*

H7.3b. *As the proportion of judges selected by the legislature and/or the president decreases on a case, the Chilean CT collectively will be less likely to strike down laws.*

H7.3c. *As the proportion of judges selected by the president and/or the Supreme Court increases on a case, the Colombian CC will be less likely to strike down laws.*

H7.3d. As the proportion of judges selected by the president and/or Supreme Court decreases on a case, the Colombian CC will be more likely to strike down laws.

H7.4. Court compositional changes on the CT and CC defined by judges' selecting branch will have a larger effect on the courts' overall decisions to strike down laws than changes in the courts' composition defined by judges' party associations.

While judges' party associations revealed little influence on their propensity to strike down laws in the individual-level analysis, they may be more important at the court level. Scholars studying judicial vetoes have insisted that party may be an important determinant of a court issuing a judicial veto when the court's collective political party orientation opposes that of the enacting legislature (see Rogers 2001; Brouard and Hönnige 2017). Judges' voting strategies also may be influenced by opportunities to issue some decisions driven by their partisan associations. However, in certain countries with mixed selection, courts will infrequently have a majority (i.e., >50 percent) of judges with party associations that differ from the legislature because judges represent many parties or the court composition does not change concurrently with elected actors. This situation occurs on the Chilean CT after the reforms in which judges are nonpartisan or associated with coalitions from the Concertación or the Right and judges' terms are longer than those of elected actors. In the time frame of the data analysis, 2006–2016, more judges had associations with the Concertación than with the Right. In the post-reform period, in 76 of 244 cases analyzed, the Tribunal had a composition in which exactly 50 percent of the Tribunal was composed of judges associated with the Concertación. In only thirty-seven cases did judges associated with the Concertación hold more than 50 percent of the seats on a particular case. For this same time period, the Right held 50 percent or more of the seats on only ten cases and judges thought of as nonpartisan never held a majority of seats on the Tribunal on any cases in the post-reform period. As it is infrequent that judges of any political affiliation hold a majority of seats on the Tribunal (in just thirty-seven cases), it is quite unlikely that the composition of the Tribunal defined by party affiliations will have much of an impact on the CT's decisions to strike down laws. The party orientation of the Tribunal should be more pertinent in those cases where judges associated with one party hold a majority of the seats.

When judges, however, are associated with only two possible parties, as in the case of judges on the Colombian CC, judges from one party hold a majority (i.e., >50 percent) of the seats much more frequently than in Chile. In Colombia, out of the 1,333 cases analyzed, judges associated with the Liberal Party had more than 50 percent of the seats on 739 cases and those associated with the Conservative Party did so on 456 cases. This does not account for all the cases analyzed because some include auxiliary judges with unknown party affiliations, creating a situation in which no one party holds a majority of seats on the Court. As a result, party orientation of the entire Court should be a more influential factor on the Colombian CC than the Chilean CT. Based on the foregoing argument, the predictions are as follows:

H7.5. *The Courts' propensity to strike down laws will be influenced by the Courts overall party orientation, but only when judges with a single party association make up more than 50 percent of the judges on a case.*

7.4 DESCRIPTION OF DATA AND ANALYSIS

In determining the propensity of courts to strike down laws, it is important to keep the unit of analysis in mind. As previously stated, a single case refers to the review of one particular law brought before each of the two constitutional courts to determine if the law and all its parts comply with the constitution. Within a case, there are specific decisional paragraphs that refer to specific parts of the law and which judges vote on separately. As a result, the individual analysis presented in Chapter 6 looks at judges' vote on every decisional paragraph within a case because judges form different voting coalitions by decisional paragraphs.

In analyzing the determinants of judicial vetoes issued by the full court, the explanatory variables in the empirical analysis instead focus on case-level data for each of the two courts. As with the individual analysis for the Chilean CT, the analysis focuses only on the post-reform data as the reform changed the selection method for judges. For Colombia, cases from 1997 to 2014 are analyzed, as prior to 1996 the Court consisted of some judges originally selected by a slightly different selection method. Using the case as the unit of analysis is appropriate as the main explanatory variables related to court composition and case context only vary by case rather than decisional paragraphs within a case. As such, using decisional paragraphs as the unit of analysis may bias estimates, especially in situations where the law has been divided into many decisional paragraphs. Further, because the two countries may divide their court decisions differently, focusing on the case as the unit of analysis is more appropriate for comparing the two courts' decisions.

The data analysis focuses on how changes in the proportion of judges with different institutional selectors and party associations, which fluctuate by case, influence the propensity of judicial vetoes. The simple probit regression is as follows:

$$\Pr(y=1) = \alpha + B_1\textit{\%Court selected by institutional actor 1} + B_2\textit{\%Court selected by institutional actor 2} + B_3\textit{\%Court associated with party 1 and/or 2} + B_4\textit{Type of review} + B_5\textit{Separation of powers} + B_6\textit{Rights} + B_7\textit{Subnational} + \varepsilon$$

The dependent variable is a binary variable coded 1 if at least one decisional paragraph within a case is found unconstitutional and zero if the entire law was considered constitutional. In the analysis, the independent variables (summarized in Table 7.3) capture the contextual and court composition factors.

As discussed in the prior section, there is good reason to believe that the type of review influences decisions to find laws unconstitutional. In Chile, the main independent variable for type of constitutional review is *Requerimiento*, coded 1 if this is a case brought under this procedure or zero if the law must be reviewed by the

TABLE 7.3. *Summary of independent variables*

	Chilean Constitutional Tribunal	Colombian Constitutional Court
	Court composition	
Case composition based on judges' institutional selectors	*% appointed by president* *% appointed by legislature* (% appointed by Supreme Court or COSENA is the base group)	*% nominated by president* *% nominated by Supreme Court* (% nominated by Consejo is the base group)
Case composition based on judges' party associations	*% associated with the Concertación* *% associated with the Right* (% nonpartisan judges is the base group)	*% associated with the Liberal Party* (% associated with the Conservative Party is the base group)
Case composition based on whether the court has a majority of judges from one party	*Concertación >50%: Concertación-associated judges hold a majority of seats (binary variable)*	*Liberal Party>50%: Liberal Party-associated judges hold a majority of seats (binary variable)*
Periodic changes in court personnel mandated by law or otherwise	*Composition change 1* *Composition change 2*	*Composition change 1* *Composition change 2*
	Case context	
Type of review	*Requerimientos* (Laws requiring mandatory review and passed by 3/5 and 4/7 supermajority voting rules are the base group)	A priori review, treaties A priori review, statutory law (A posteriori review of laws brought by citizens is the base group)
Subject matter	*Separation of powers* *Rights* *Subnational government* *(Other areas are the base group)*	*Separation of powers* *Rights* *Subnational government* *(Other areas are the base group)*

CT (i.e., obligatory review).[9] For Colombia, contextual variables for *statutory review* and *international treaties* are used in the regressions as two types of a priori constitutional review to be contrasted with other types of a posteriori review. These constitutional review types are specifically mentioned in the cases themselves.

[9] It should be noted that the Chilean CT hears another small group of cases, considered a posteriori abstract review cases under Constitutional Article 93.7, which arise from concrete review cases under Constitutional Article 93.6. These cases have been excluded from the analysis because they appear under a new process under the 2006 constitutional reform, but the Tribunal has only decided such cases fifteen times in sixteen years as of February 2022.

Constitutional courts' propensity to strike down laws also should vary by subject area of the law reviewed. Three types of subject area binary variables are used in the regression analyses for both courts: *Separation of powers*, *rights*, and *subnational issues*. Separation of powers cases involve constitutional provisions dealing with the executive, legislative, judicial branches, or the constitutional court itself. Rights cases are those involving rights defined by the constitution, and subnational issues are determined by the courts' reference to constitutional provisions dealing with subnational government. The types were determined by coding the constitutional provisions referenced in the two courts' decisions.[10]

To analyze varying court compositions by case, several independent variables are constructed to analyze how fluctuations in the proportion of judges with specific attributes influence mixed selection courts' propensities to veto laws. For this analysis, court composition variables, defined by percentage of judges selected by certain institutions or associated with certain parties, are constructed by dividing the number of judges with that attribute over the total number of judges appearing on a case.[11] For Chile, institutional attributes are captured by the *Percentage of judges appointed by president* and *Percentage of judges appointed by legislature*. The percentage of judges appointed by the nonelected COSENA and Supreme Court constitutes the base group. For party associations, *Percentage judges associated with the Concertación* and *Percentage of judges associated with the Right* are used with percentage of nonpartisan judges as the base group. The CC's composition variables are similarly coded. *Percentage of judges nominated by the president* and *Percentage of judges nominated by the Supreme Court* are found in the regressions with the percentage of Consejo nominees constituting the base group. For party, *Percentage of judges associated with the Liberal Party* or its affiliates is used with the percentage of judges associated with the Conservative Party or its affiliates as the base group.[12]

As recalled from the description of data in Chapter 6, the empirical analysis considers only laws reviewed by the two courts that were passed by the legislature still in power at the time of review. This allows the analysis of the party orientation of the court to focus on whether the court opposes the current legislature that could punish it for striking down its laws rather than a prior legislature which cannot punish a court for its decisions. For Chile, the Concertación held a majority of seats in the legislature during the period of analysis although not enough seats to pass organic laws, treaties, or precepts requiring 4/7 or 3/5 approval (see Chapter 4, Table 4.1 discussing the composition of Congress). An increase in seats held by

10 See Appendix A6.1 To Chapter 6 for this coding.

11 This measure is distinct from the court composition variable used in the individual judge-level analysis assessing panel effects in Chapter 6. In that chapter, in which the unit of observation was each judge's vote, the percentages were calculated by considering the attributes of "other" judges with whom a particular judge was making a decision, rather than all judges.

12 Summary statistics for the case-level data for Chile and Colombia appear in the Appendix to this chapter at Tables A7.1 and A7.2, respectively.

judges associated with the Concertación would be an increase of judges favoring the majority of legislatures in Congress for the entire time period analyzed. An increase in seats held by judges associated with the Right would be an increase in judges favoring the opposition or the Center Right during the period under analysis. For Colombia, the Liberal Party held a majority of seats in Congress from 1991 to 1998 and the greatest number of seats compared to other parties from 1998 to 2010 when the legislature contained more fragmented parties. From 2010 to 2014, legislators from the Partido de la U held the greatest number of seats compared to other parties (see Chapter 5, Table 5.1 discussing the composition of Congress). For all time periods analyzed, the presidents' governing coalitions held the majority of legislative seats.

As discussed in the beginning of the chapter, scholars have argued that a judicial veto is only possible when a majority of a court's judges have political preferences that are outside the preferences of a majority or supermajority of legislators depending on the type of law being approved. This may be particularly difficult on mixed selection courts that include judges from more than one party or non-partisan judges such as in the case of Chile. It also may be difficult when legislative parties are highly fragmented preventing a majority of judges associated with one party on any case to coalesce on a position opposing such a wide range of interests as in more recent years in Colombia.[13]

Additional analysis of the two courts' party orientations focuses on whether a majority of judges from a certain party appearing on a case influences judicial vetoes. To conduct this analysis, a binary variable is created for each court to indicate whether a case has a composition in which a majority of the judges are associated with a single party. For the Chilean CT, *Concertación >50%* is a binary variable indicating whether 50% or more judges associated with the Concertación appear on a case. For the Colombian CC, *Liberal Party >50%* represents a binary variable indicating whether the case is composed of more than 50% of judges associated with the Liberal Party. These variables are used to test the hypothesis H7.5 that the party orientation of the court matters for the issuance of vetoes but only when there is a majority of judges from one party present on a case. Further analysis of these party variables is also investigated using matching methods. These party binary variables are tested with the above referenced institutional variables capturing compositional movements in the courts' overall party orientation. Additionally, all of the analyses include variables noting periodic changes in the overall composition of the court based on judges

[13] This intuition is a at odds with some of the judicial politics literature on party fragmentation, which claims that courts are more assertive under divided or fragmented government (McCubbins et al. 1995; Gely and Spiller 1990; Iaryczower et al. 2002) although this argument has its critics (see Herron and Randazzo 2003 and Hilbink 2012) and Stone Sweet (2000) claims that constitutional courts may be more likely to defer to legislation passed by multiparty parliaments because this legislation represents compromises among many actors.

exiting or entering the courts every three years as used in the individual analysis – *Change in court composition 1 and 2*.

The analyses using regression and matching attempt to approximate experimental conditions by taking advantage of the fact that the composition of the court on any case is "plausibly random" or "plausibly exogenous" due to quorum rules that allow for less than the full court to reach a decision (see Grossman et al. 2016: 53; see also Holden et al. 2021 claiming that US Supreme Court recusals and absences are a "plausibly exogenous" source of variation in court size by case). Judges' presence on a case is predominantly based on days of vacation and sick leave, which are orthogonal to case characteristics such as type of review or subject matter. Judges infrequently miss a case due to a conflict of interest. The institutional features of quorum rules and the judges' individual schedules create significant, if not random, variation in court compositions on cases in both countries.

Despite this seeming randomness of judges' appearances on particular cases, there may still be concern that the court's composition on any particular case is based on unobserved events, such as judges choosing on which cases to appear, which may be correlated with the case outcome. Therefore, a few preliminary tests are conducted to determine whether the number of judges on a particular case is endogenous or exogenous. First, a simple difference of means test is conducted to determine whether cases with all judges present (i.e., 10 for the CT and 9 for CC) influence the courts' decisions to strike down a law. For both the Chilean and Colombian constitutional courts, there was no significant difference between the case outcomes for the full court compared to less than the full court.[14]

Additionally, the use of extended regression models (ERMs) establishes that judges' appearances on cases are not endogenous or that judges did not choose their presence or non-presence on a case to influence the outcome. In ERMs, whether a case involves all the judges on the court or just a proportion is modeled as an endogenous variable in the regression. If the variable *Full court*, defined as a case in which all judges are present (i.e., 10 on the CT and 9 on the CC), has a significant correlation with decisions to strike down a law, than it is deemed endogenous and would cast doubt on a causal interpretation of the variables related to compositional shifts by case.[15] However, here the results for the ERMs for the

[14] For the Chilean CT, the mean of unconstitutional cases for the full court is 0.21 and the mean for less than the full court is 0.17 (difference in means t-statistic = 0.78; p-value = 0.43). For the Colombian CC, the mean of unconstitutional cases for the full court is 0.30 and for less than the full court is 0.27 (t-statistic = −1.35; p-value = 0.18). For both courts, the p-value was not less than 0.05, signaling no statistically significant difference in outcomes between the full courts and smaller compositions.

[15] In the nested model for the endogenous regressor, the determinants of *Full Court* are modelled with three independent variables including the average tenure of judges on any decision, as well as whether the case involved separation of powers or rights. The average judges' tenure is the average time served on the court by all judges on a particular case at the time of the decision.

Chilean CT and the Colombian CC did not show a significant correlation between the *Full court* variable and the outcome.[16] Based on the above analyses, choices to appear or not appear on cases and thus the presence of all judges on any case do not seem to be correlated with the case outcomes. Despite the findings, additional matching methods are used later in the case-level analyses to further control for any non-random fluctuations related to the number of judges appearing on a case.

7.5 RESULTS

Tables 7.4 and 7.5 show the results for the two courts. Predicted probabilities and standard errors are shown below each coefficient. For each table, column 1, tests the influence of court composition based on institutional selector, column 2 based on party association, and column 3 both. Column 4 provides a regression with the percentage of judges based on institutional selector with the binary variable for cases in which a majority of judges are associated with one party. Column 5 tests the party binary variable with a variable that combines the percentage of judges on a case with institutional selectors who favor a similar type of constitutional adjudicator (those selected by the president and legislature for the CT and those selected by the president and Supreme Court for the CC). All regressions include the turnover and change in court composition and case context variables. For the two courts, composition based on institutional selector and other case contextual variables are significant. The results for the CC also show that party orientation matters, but only when the Court has a majority of judges associated with the Liberal Party.

For the analysis of the Chilean CT, the coefficients for review types and subject areas are all positive and significant leading courts to strike down these types more often as shown by the predicted probabilities displayed in Table 7.4. The Tribunal is more likely to strike down laws brought to its review through the *requerimiento* process (i.e., 19–23 percent more often than obligatory review cases), which may be due to the fact that these are some of the most politically divisive cases before the Tribunal brought to its attention by legislators belonging to the minority. Further, these laws do not all require mandatory review, and many of the laws reviewed do not require supermajority legislative approval, two constraints that may make it difficult for a majority of the Tribunal to form an opinion outside of the legislature's preference range. Some examples of laws the CT struck down as part of the *requerimiento* process included laws related to subcontracting for transit services (Rol #534), the public sector budget (Rol #1867 and Rol #2935), parental leave (Rol #2025), digital television (Rol #2358), and labor relations (Rol #3016).

[16] For the ERM models, for the CT, the correlation coefficient between the full court and the case outcome was 0.82 and was not significant (p = 0.70). For the CC, the correlation coefficient between the full court and the case outcome was 0.39 and was not significant (p = 0.74).

TABLE 7.4. *Determinants of judicial vetoes by the Chilean CT post reform*

	(1)	(2)	(3)	(4)	(5)
% presidential appointees	2.93*		6.91***	2.90*	
	(1.53)		(2.66)	(1.53)	
	25%		**55%**	**24%**	
% legislative appointees	3.37*		7.29**	3.73*	
	(1.93)		(2.93)	(2.00)	
	37%		**80%**	**42%**	
% presidential and leg. appt.					3.10**
					(1.46)
					48%
% Concertación associated		1.27	−3.36		
		(2.05)	(2.67)		
		14%	−33%		
% Right associated		1.28	−6.46*		
		(1.93)	(3.46)		
		16%	**−79%**		
Concertación ≥50%				−0.29	−0.25
				(0.34)	(0.33)
				−5%	−5%
Requerimiento	0.70**	0.66**	0.81**	0.68**	0.68**
	(0.32)	(0.31)	(0.33)	(0.32)	(0.32)
	19%	**19%**	**23%**	**19%**	**19%**
Separation of powers	1.05***	0.98***	1.00***	1.07***	1.09***
	(0.28)	(0.27)	(0.28)	(0.28)	(0.28)
	31%	**29%**	**29%**	**31%**	**32%**
Rights	0.91***	0.96***	0.93***	0.95***	0.95***
	(0.25)	(0.25)	(0.25)	(0.25)	(0.25)
	25%	**27%**	**25%**	**26%**	**26%**
Subnational	0.68***	0.64**	0.67**	0.69***	0.68***
	(0.26)	(0.25)	(0.26)	(0.26)	(0.26)
	18%	**17%**	**17%**	**18%**	**17%**
Composition change 1	−0.13	0.11	−0.07	−0.16	−0.21
	(0.32)	(0.32)	(0.35)	(0.32)	(0.30)
	−3%	2%	−1%	−3%	−4%
Composition change 2	−0.75**	−0.40	−0.78*	−0.83**	−0.86**
	(0.35)	(0.43)	(0.46)	(0.37)	(0.36)
	−12%	−8%	**−12%**	**−13%**	**−13%**
Constant	−3.52***	−2.56*	−2.57*	−3.61***	−3.40***
	(0.99)	(1.37)	(1.41)	(1.01)	(0.90)
Observations	244	244	244	244	244
AIC	195.2	199.3	195.5	196.4	194.7
BIC	226.7	230.7	234	231.4	226.1

Notes. *** $p < 0.01$, ** $p < 0.05$, * $p < 0.10$. The dependent variable is whether the Tribunal strikes down any part of the law reviewed as unconstitutional. Standard errors appear in parentheses. The predicted probabilities in bold show statistically significant percentage changes in the dependent variable when binary variables are shifted from zero to one and continuous variables from their minimum to maximum values.

TABLE 7.5. *Determinants of judicial vetoes by the Colombian CC*

	(1)	(2)	(3)	(4)	(5)
% presidential nominees	−1.70**		−1.60*	−1.71**	
	(0.85)		(0.85)	(0.85)	
	−33%		**−31%**	**−33%**	
% Supreme Court nom.	−2.31**		−2.09**	−2.43***	
	(0.93)		(0.95)	(0.94)	
	−35%		**−31%**	**−36%**	
% presidential and SC					−1.98**
					(0.79)
					−44%
Percent Liberal		−0.73	−0.54		
		(0.45)	(0.46)		
		−20%	−14%		
Liberal >50%				0.20*	0.20*
				(0.11)	(0.11)
				7%	7%
Statutory law	0.93***	0.91***	0.91***	0.91***	0.91***
	(0.29)	(0.29)	(0.29)	(0.30)	(0.30)
	35%	**35%**	**35%**	**35%**	**35%**
International treaty	0.97***	−0.97***	−0.97***	−0.97***	−0.98***
	(0.11)	(0.11)	(0.11)	(0.11)	(0.11)
	−26%	**−26%**	**−26%**	**−26%**	**−26%**
Separation of powers	0.33***	0.33***	0.33***	0.33***	0.33***
	(0.08)	(0.08)	(0.08)	(0.08)	(0.08)
	11%	**11%**	**11%**	**11%**	**11%**
Rights	−0.07	−0.07	−0.07	0.08	−0.07
	(0.08)	(0.08)	(0.08)	(0.08)	(0.08)
	−2%	−2%	−3%	−3%	−3%
Subnational government	0.21*	0.22*	0.22*	0.21*	0.21*
	(0.12)	(0.12)	(0.12)	(0.12)	(0.12)
	7%	8%	8%	7%	7%
Composition change 1	0.14	−0.17	0.01	0.22	0.06
	(0.20)	(0.13)	(0.23)	(0.21)	(0.10)
	5%	−6%	0	7%	2%
Composition change 2	−0.05	−0.57**	−0.35	0.17	0.00
Constant	0.63	0.01	0.95	0.46	0.57
	(0.53)	(0.34)	(0.60)	(0.54)	(0.53)
Observations	1,333	1,333	1,333	1,333	1,333
AIC	1,509	1,511	1,510	1,508	1,507
BIC	1,561	1,558	1,567	1,565	1,559

Notes. *** $p < 0.01$, ** $p < 0.05$, * $p < 0.10$. The dependent variable is whether the Court strikes down any part of the law reviewed as unconstitutional. Standard errors appear in parentheses. The predicted probabilities in bold show statistically significant percentage changes in the dependent variable when binary variables are shifted from zero to one and continuous variables from their minimum to maximum values.

The positive and significant coefficients for separation of powers, rights, and subnational cases, indicate that the benefits to the Tribunal's power and reputation in striking down these types of laws exceed any costs. The CT is 29–32 percent more likely to strike down laws involving the separation of powers compared to other subject areas. Some examples of laws the CT struck down in part classified as separation of powers (which were not part of the *requerimiento* process) involved access to public information (Rol #1051), tax jurisdiction (Rol #1243), the Organic Law of the CT (Rol #1288), and rules regarding the Ministry of Defense (Rol #1587). The Tribunal is also 25–27 percent more likely to strike down laws related to individual rights compared to other subject areas. Some examples of laws involving individual rights struck down by the Tribunal related to workers' rights (Rol #536), education (Rol #1363), and voting (Rol #2981). Finally, the Tribunal was 17–18 percent more likely to strike down national laws dealing with Chile's regions compared to other subjects and some of these related to the creation of new regions (Rol #719) and recreational fishing (Rol #1017).

The results show that the overall composition of the entire court on any given case based on the judges' selectors influences judicial vetoes more than the court's political party orientation. In column 1, increasing the number of judges chosen by the president or legislature leads to a higher rate of striking down laws. In this first regression, changing the number of presidential appointees on the Tribunal from its minimum to maximum value results in the Tribunal striking down laws 25 percent more often, and moving the number of legislative appointees from its minimum to maximum value results in a 37 percent increase in vetoes. When judges' party associations are tested alone (column 2), a change in the percentage of judges belonging to either of the two party coalitions has no statistically significant impact on the Tribunal's overall decision to strike down laws. In the third regression (column 3) in which institutional selectors and party are analyzed together, the variables based on institutional selector are highly significant and positive, but now the percentage of judges associated with the Center Right is also significant at the 0.10 level. In the fourth regression (column 4), percentage increases in the variable combining the percentage of judges appointed by the president and legislature are significant at the 0.10 level, but inclusion of the binary variable describing when a case involves a majority of judges associated with the Concertación is insignificant and substantively small. In the final column, in which the percent of presidential and legislative appointees are considered together, an increase in these judges from their minimum to maximum value leads to a 48 percent increase in striking down laws and is highly significant, while the binary party orientation variable remains insignificant in this regression. Changes in the Tribunal's composition in 2012 decreased the court's propensity to strike down laws by 12–13 percent, but the prior compositional change occurring in 2009 was insignificant.

The results for the Colombian Constitutional Court found in Table 7.5 are similar to those of the Chilean Tribunal. For case context, both types of *a priori review*, statutory laws, and international treaties are significant determinants of the Court's decisions to veto laws. For statutory review cases, the Court is 35 percent more likely to strike down these cases than other types of review. Some examples of statutory laws the CC struck down in part or entirely involved laws on the administration of justice (C-295/2002) and counterintelligence (C540/2012). For international treaties, the CC is 26 percent less likely to strike down these types of laws than others. Some international treaties which the CC upheld involved maritime borders with Honduras (C1022/1999) and a free trade agreement with the United States (C248/2009).

For case subject areas, laws associated with separation of powers or subnational governments lead the CC to strike down these laws more than other laws. For cases involving the separation of powers, the CC strikes down these laws about 11 percent of the time. Some examples of separation of powers cases that the CC struck down included rules regarding different authorities reducing their budgets when the national government did so (C1379/2000) and Congress' violation of principles regarding publicity for amendments of a criminal law (C760/2001). The CC is 7–8 percent more likely to strike down national laws involving subnational governments than other laws. Some examples of these laws that the CC struck down involved striking down portions of the law dealing with contributions from municipalities to the country's health and pension plans (Law 223 of 1995) (C219/1997) and the National Plan of Development (Ley 508 of 1999) (C557/2000). While the hypotheses suggested that high courts would be more likely to strike down subnational laws because they favored the federal government over regional governments, these cases show that the CC is willing to strike down laws that perhaps demand too much of subnational governments in supporting the national government.

The coefficients for cases involving rights are insignificant. Although the CC is known to be quite progressive on rights cases, the statistically insignificant coefficient simply shows that on average across cases and years, the Court is not more or less likely to strike down these laws compared to others. This does not, however, mean that the CC has not been instrumental in its decisions regarding rights' legislation in certain areas, such as laws involving rights for same sex couples (Wilson 2009). Further, it is possible that the CC is more aggressive in striking down rights legislation of prior governments or when rights are contested by *tutelas*, neither analyzed here.

The CC's composition defined by numbers of judges with certain nominators is an important determinant of the Court's deference, rather than its propensity to strike down laws. In the first regression (column 1), increasing judges nominated by the president from its minimum value to maximum value makes the Court as a whole 33 percent less likely to strike down laws. This same increase for Supreme Court nominees leads the Court to defer to Congress 35 percent of the time. In the second regression (column 2), when tested alone, an increase in judges associated with the Liberal Party has no significant influence on striking down laws. In the third regression (column 3), when percentages of judges selected by institutional selectors and Liberal Party–associated judges appear in the same regression, only the composition related to nominators is significant and each leads the Court to defer to the legislature 31 percent of the time compared to changes in Consejo nominees. In the fourth (column 4) and fifth (column 5), the binary variable indicating that the Court is composed of a majority of Liberal Party–associated judges is statistically significant at the 0.10 level. In both regressions, the Court is 7 percent more likely to strike down laws if the court is composed of a majority of these judges on any case.

The party orientation of the Court may be more influential on the Colombian CC compared to the Chilean CT because judges on this Court can only have one of two party associations compared to one in three on the Chilean Tribunal. Further, Liberal judges may have become increasingly opposed to President Uribe's influence on the legislative policy agenda, especially as he became more authoritarian in his second term.[17]

Further analysis regarding the two courts' overall party orientation is warranted due to the prominence of this explanation in the literature and the influence of party orientation for the Colombia CC, but not the CT. Matching methods preprocess data to obtain a sample in which the distribution of variables between treatment and control groups are as close as possible (see Boyd et al. 2010; Kastellec 2007). According to Ho et al. (2007), "preprocessing makes estimates based on the subsequent parametric analyses far less dependent on modeling choices and specifications" (p. 201).[18]

For the matching analysis, I use the main binary party composition variables used in the previous regression as treatment variables to determine whether cases composed of a majority of judges from one party influence the courts' propensity to veto laws.[19] As a result the main party treatment variables are based on whether judges of a single party hold more than 50 percent of the seats on any particular case on the

[17] An interaction of the party variables with the institutional composition variables did not yield significant results for either court.

[18] Matching is used here to preprocess the data to further analyze the political party orientation of the two courts as a binary treatment variable. The analysis employs Coarsened Exact Matching (CEM) (Blackwell et al. 2009) to find a matched set of data for the treatment and then the regressions are re-run using the matched data as advocated by Ho et al. (2007). Additionally, nearest neighbor matching advocated by Abadie (2004) is used after CEM to "improve the quality of inferences drawn from these methods" (Blackwell et al. 2009: 16). All matching methods in Stata use propensity score methods for "restricting the data to common empirical support. CEM, however, restricts the data prior to matching so that inferences are not based on "extrapolation," which is "extremely model dependent" (Blackwell et al. 2009 16).

[19] Because Chilean judges are associated with two-party coalitions and there are nonpartisan judges, the CT has fewer compositions in which the Tribunal has a majority or 51 percent of the seats held by judges associated with any one party. In the data, the Right holds 51 percent or more of the seats on only 10 cases. The Concertación holds 50 percent of the seats on 76 cases

TABLE 7.6. *Treatments for overall party orientation of the Chilean CT*

	Treatment description	N cases	N cases with T	N Matched data (full set 244 cases)	Coeff. Matched ATE
$T1_{party}$	Concertación >50%	244	37	185	−0.26
$T2_{party}$	Concertación ≥50%	244	113	100	0.23

Note. The numbers provided in the two columns on the far right of the table are coefficients for the Treatment variable (T). ATE refers to the average treatment effect.

courts. Alternatively, due to the judges' party associations in Chile, I also analyze the influence of binary variables describing judges holding at least 50 percent of the seats on any case.

As shown in Table 7.6, for Chile, $T1_{party}$ refers to a Tribunal composition in which judges associated with the Concertación held *more than* 50% of the seats on the Tribunal and $T2_{party}$ *held* 50% *or more* of the seats on the Tribunal. Composition based on the percentage of seats held by judges associated with the Center Right or nonpartisan judges is not analyzed as these compositions rarely or never occurred during the time frame of the data analysis. The results from the matching analysis indicate that neither party treatment had a statistically significant influence on the Tribunal striking down laws. The lack of influence of party orientation of the Tribunal on case outcomes is in opposition to much of the extant judicial veto literature mentioned in Chapter 2. However, it is consistent with the judge-level results presented in Chapter 6. These results suggest that mixed selection courts with judges representing many diverse institutions may dampen the influence of party orientation on the courts' propensity to veto laws.[20]

Unlike on the Chilean CT, judges on the Colombian CC were associated with one of two parties, and as stated previously there are no judges without some kind of party association as defined. As a result, treatments are constructed depending on whether judges associated with either of the two main parties hold a majority of the seats on the Court. $T1_{party}$ refers to cases with court compositions in which a majority (i.e., more than 50 percent) of judges were associated with the Liberal Party, and

and greater than 50 percent of the seats on just 37 cases. Together, there are 113 cases in which the Concertación has 50 percent or more of the seats.

The following covariates were used for matching:

For Chile: two binary variables indicating if the Tribunal was composed of at least 33 percent of judges selected by the president and the legislature and variables related to review type and subject matter of the law.

For Colombia: percentage of judges nominated by the president and percent nominated by the Supreme Court and variables related to review type and subject matter of the law. These matching variables provided the most balanced data.

20 The full results for the party matching with covariates for the Chilean CT appear in Table A7.3 for $T1_{party}$ and Table A7.4 for $T2_{party}$.

TABLE 7.7. *Treatments for overall party orientation of the Colombian CC*

	Treatment description	N cases	N cases with T*	N Matched data	Coeff. Matched ATE
$T1_{party}$	Liberal >50%	1,333	739	857	0.28***
$T2_{party}$	Conservative >50%	1,333	456	925	−0.18*

Note. The numbers provided in the two columns on the far right of the table are coefficients for the Treatment variable (T). *The numbers in this column do not add up to the total number of cases (i.e., 1,333) because in some cases the total number of judges included auxiliary judges who did not have known party association precluding the cases from having a majority of judges from either party. ATE refers to average treatment effect.

$T2_{party}$ refers to a court composition that has 50 percent or more of judges associated with the Conservative Party. The results from matching in Table 7.7 indicate that when the CC has a majority of judges associated with the Liberal Party, it is 28 percent more likely to strike down or veto laws. A majority of judges associated with the Conservative Party has an effect opposite in sign to the treatment for a majority of judges with Liberal Party associations, but these results are smaller than T1 and significant at the 0.10 level. The opposite signs of the two variables suggest that judges of these two parties oppose each other as expected.[21]

Party orientation of the Court may be more relevant in Colombia than Chile due to the fact that in Chile, the party association of the full court is split between three possible orientations and in Colombia the orientation is split between just two parties. Further, in light of the fact that the Colombia's president has strong powers and highly influences its weak and increasingly multiparty Congress, the role of party on this Court emerges as an additional important determinant of judicial vetoes.

7.6 CASE EXAMPLES RELATED TO COURT COMPOSITION

The empirical results related to court composition above reveal average treatment effects. Figure 7.3 demonstrates how an increase in judges with similar propensities to strike down or uphold laws on any case (i.e., presidential and legislative appointees on the CT and presidential and Supreme Court nominees on the CC), approaching a critical mass, on the two courts influences the courts' propensity to veto laws or defer to the legislature.[22]

This section provides examples for the type of cases that fit the empirics revealed in this figure. The first set of examples are confirming, while a second set of

[21] The full results for the party matching equations with covariates for the Colombian CC appear in Table A7.5 for $T1_{party}$ and Table A7.6 for $T2_{party}$.

[22] These figures represent the regression results for column 5 of Tables 7.4 and 7.5.

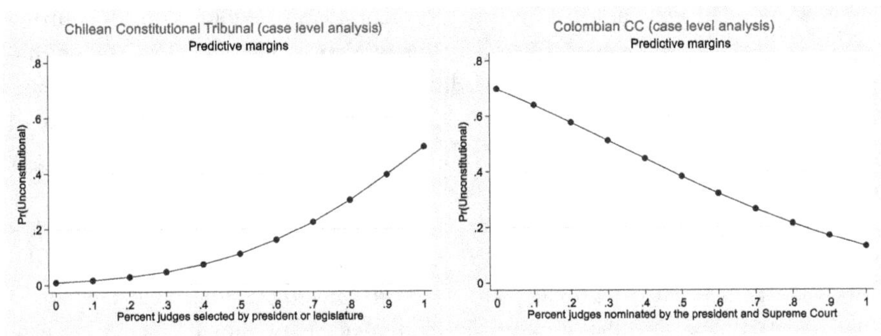

FIGURE 7.3 Predicted probabilities of finding laws unconstitutional based on the composition of the Chilean CT (left panel) and the Colombian CC (right panel)
Note: The vertical axis in each figure represents the probability that the two courts will find laws unconstitutional. The horizontal axis is the percent of judges selected by the listed institutions.

examples indicates cases in which the case outcomes are not well-predicted by the empirics. The examples are illustrative and are not intended to provide an exhaustive list of all cases that fit or diverge from the statistical results.

7.6.1 *Examples Supporting the Critical Mass Approach*

7.6.1.1 The Chilean CT

There are several cases in which the CT found a law unconstitutional when the composition of a case included a significant number of judges (or a supermajority) selected by the president and legislature, which, based on the statistical results, led the Tribunal on average to strike down laws more than other compositions. One such case involves amendments to Chile's Organic Law on Courts making it comply with Chile's obligations under the Organization for Economic Co-operation and Development's (OECD) Convention to Combat Bribery of Foreign Officials in International Business Transactions. In this case, Rol #1316 (2009), the Tribunal was composed of five of nine judges chosen by elected officials. The judges appearing on the case included four legislative appointees (Bertelson and Venegas associated with the Center Right and Vodanovic, and Fernández Baeza associated with the Concertación) one presidential appointee (Correa Sutil associated with the Concertación) and four judges chosen by nonelected actors (Colombo and Cea chosen by the COSENA, the former also associated with the Concertación, and Navarro and Peña chosen by the Supreme Court).

In order to ensure the incorporation of the norms of this Convention into domestic law, Chile needed to modify both its penal code and its Organic Law on Courts, the latter reviewed by the Tribunal in this case. The change to the organic law was intended to establish Chilean jurisdiction over certain crimes occurring outside of the country, namely the bribery of a foreign public official when committed by a Chilean or one habitually residing in Chile. Although the case involved review of an organic law, which the Tribunal was less likely to strike down compared to *requerimientos*, the judges unanimously struck down the modification to the law because it violated a constitutional procedure mandating that modifications related to the organization or attributes of the courts could only be reviewed after the Supreme Court had offered an opinion on the subject. While the majority of the Tribunal was associated with the Concertación, all judges still voted together to strike down the law. Although the decision may be classified as an easy case involving procedure, the composition of the court, which included a majority of judges chosen by elected actors, as well as the infrequency of the CT's judicial vetoes for obligatory review cases provide some evidence of the relationship between case compositions and judicial vetoes.

Another good example of how a critical mass of similar judges operates within a case involves what was considered one of the more important decisions of the CT in 2011 regarding the constitutionality of a private registry of certain users of internet cafes. In this case (Rol #1894(2011)), the CT struck down part of a law (Article 4) establishing a private registry for individuals previously punished for committing sexual harassment of children, child pornography, and possession of pornographic material. The CT found unconstitutional the part of this law that required these individuals to disclose their status as sex offenders to owners of cybercafes prior to accessing the internet in those establishments. The CT reasoned that this restriction violated the Constitution's right to privacy and would disproportionately affect those without access to internet at home. This case supports the proposition that a critical mass of judges selected by elected actors will result in the Tribunal striking down a law because it involves an especially controversial issue of which judges might disagree, balancing protection and safety of children with the privacy rights of those convicted of child pornography. Eight judges were present on this case (Venegas, Bertelsen, Vodanovic, Navarro, Fernández Fredes, Carmona, Viera-Gallo, and Aróstica) of whom six were chosen by the president or the legislature. Four of these judges were associated with the Concertación, three with the Right, and one was considered nonpartisan. While these judges had different political associations, no one party had a majority on the Tribunal. However, the presence of a critical mass of judges chosen by elected actors who have a propensity to strike down laws allowed them to rally around a decision favoring the individual privacy rights of those with prior child pornography convictions, a decision for many in society that would be thought of as unpopular and even against public opinion.[23]

[23] While this case had a dissent even by a judge appointed by the president (i.e., Carmona, associated with the Concertación), this does not undermine the theory, which is about how the presence of certain judges tends to create a context for the court as a whole to strike down

Another good example of a case illustrating the critical mass theory involved legislation that created Chile's system of environmental courts (Rol #2180(2012)). The case came to the Tribunal under its obligatory constitutional review jurisdiction as it involved an organic law. The legislation involved rules regarding the qualifications and selection of judges for these new courts. In this case, the CT struck down as unconstitutional provisions that prevented attorneys previously working for the Supreme Court or Appeals Courts from taking part in the selection of judges for environmental courts. The CT reasoned that such a rule violated the Chilean Constitution's provision regarding equality under the law because it prevented these judges from applying for a public function or job without any justified reason. The CT also struck down as unconstitutional a provision that required the Supreme Court to provide a "motivated resolution" to reject those applicants first proposed by the High Public Management Council, a bureaucratic agency under the Ministry of Finance. According to the CT, such as rule would deny the Supreme Court a role in the selection of environmental judges and leave this role to the Management Council, which would "not ensure the independence and impartiality" required for environmental judges. The CT ruled that the power to propose judicial nominees to these new courts should reside in the Supreme Court.[24] In this case, a critical mass of similar judges, those selected by the legislature and president, appeared on the case. The judges appearing on the case included Bertelsen, Venegas, Vodanovic, Peña, Navarro, Fernández Fredes, Carmona, Viera-Gallo, Aróstica, and García Pino. While this case had dissents and concurrences on various issues even by judges chosen by elected actors, this does not undermine the theory, which is about how the presence of certain judges' types tends to create a context for the court as a whole to strike down controversial laws.

The full court struck down parts of the law creating environmental courts as it did not provide the Supreme Court with a meaningful role in the selection of judges to these two courts but delegated it to a bureaucratic agency.[25] The legislative and presidential appointees support of the Supreme Court's role in the selection may at first seem counterintuitive as the Management Council was a government agency and the decision favored the Supreme Court's role in the selection of environmental judges over that of an executive agency. However, providing the Supreme Court with a clear role in the selection of environmental judges ensures that one of the major branches of government has a role in selecting impartial judges rather than abdicating that role

controversial laws. Recall that presence effects are simply about the characteristics of who is on a collegial body and are not voting effects in which judges change their decisions based on the votes of other judges (see Fischman 2015).

24 The analysis is based on reviewing the CT's original decision in Spanish as well as the Council of Europe's summary in English in its CODICES, identified as CHI-2012-1-002. Quotations in English are based on the Council's version.

25 While striking down major parts of the law, the CT did uphold a norm which defined the profile required for environmental law judges as long as the Supreme Court could name the skills required by such judges.

entirely to an administrative agency albeit of the executive branch. Such a decision enhances both the legislative role of the CT, ensuring that powers are balanced in government, and its judicial role, ensuring that the Constitution is upheld.

Finally, in Rol #2324 (2012), the CT had a critical mass of judges[26] selected by the elected branches and chose to strike down many, but by no means all, provisions of the Primary Election Act, which attempted to establish a framework for nominating candidates for presidential, congressional, and municipal elections. The bill established that political parties as well as independents could conduct primary elections to select candidates and that the results would be binding on all participants, "both parties and individual candidates." The CT struck down part of the law due to vagueness and delegation of important discretionary functions to the Electoral Service, a bureaucratic agency. Specifically, the CT struck down provisions of the bill that allowed the Electoral Service to regulate political propaganda, voting, and counting procedures as so overly vague that it gave the Service "excessive discretion." The CT also struck down a provision that attempted to exclude the established identification procedure for electors for primary elections, although such an identification procedure was used for all public elections. Excluding this section violated citizens' political rights because proper identification of electors is crucial for "exercising those rights." Finally, the CT struck down sanctions against individuals or parties during primary elections because they were defined too broadly and without clarity.[27] Striking down laws that deal with elections relate to the foundation of a country's democracy. A critical mass of similar judges is important in this case to ensure that the legislature that created such a vague and unaccountable primary election service would not be induced to override the CT's decision at a later time and to signal to the public that the unconstitutional ruling was well supported by its judges.

7.6.2 *Colombian Constitutional Court*

In the case of the CC, as shown by the statistical analysis, when there is a critical mass of judges selected by the Supreme Court and the president, then the Court is on average less likely to strike down a law or more likely to defer to the legislature. This finding is reflected in several CC decisions deferring to the legislature. In C-075/2006, the plaintiff claimed that part of Law 812 of 2003, approving the National Plan of Development 2005 to 2006, was unconstitutional because it allowed domiciliary public service companies to compel users to become shareholders. The plaintiff claimed that several rights, including the right of individuals regarding how they choose to invest their money and the right to contract, were violated. The CC disagreed with the plaintiff and upheld the law citing a competing, but vague, right that the state was required to promote access to property and preferential

[26] The judges on the case included Venegas, Vodanovic, Peña, Carmona, Viera Gallo, Aróstica, García Pino, Hernández.

[27] CODICE 2013-1-002.

treatment for workers and solidarity organizations (i.e., Article 60). While the case involves several competing rights, the Court chose to uphold the law based on the vague obligation of the state to promote access to property ownership. The law was held constitutional by the Court here composed of eight members predominantly chosen by the president (Cepeda, Monroy, and Tafur Galvis) and the Supreme Court (Beltrán, Córdoba, and Vargas Hernández) and thus individually less likely to strike down laws. Only two judges on this case were chosen by the Consejo (Rentería and Escobar Gil, the former concurring with the majority's decision). The critical mass of presidential and Supreme Court nominees upheld the law even though interpretations of other rights could have led to a contrary decision. The judges were evenly divided between those associated with the Liberal and Conservative Parties, so the influence of party is not at issue in this example.

In another example, the CC in C577/2014 was asked to determine the constitutionality of amendments to the Legal Framework for Peace arising out of President Santos' historic peace talks. At issue was a provision of the Framework, which allowed demobilized guerrillas convicted of political crimes to participate in politics after serving their punishment, although excluding from participation those who had committed crimes against humanity or genocide. Convictions for regular crimes precluded such participation. In amending the Constitution to allow such political participation, Congress was provided with broad authority to define which crimes were considered political. The petitioner, demanding that the Court strike down the law, argued that Congress' discretion was too broad and violated international law and other parts of the Constitution regarding political participation. The Court in rejecting the petitioner's argument, that the Constitution contained a fundamental principal "requiring political participation be exercised within a context of respect for human dignity and the projection of human rights" (Cepeda Espinosa and Landau 2017: 237), insisted that the case should really be framed around the fundamental principal of political participation and "not its limitation" (p. 237). In summary, the Court held "participation in politics by those selected and condemned ... does not per se affect any of the rights that must be guaranteed to victims of the armed conflict" (p. 237).

The case represents a contentious issue in Colombian society regarding the punishment of former guerillas or alternatively their participation in politics. Comparatively, the "Colombian peace process has been strikingly judicialized at the domestic level" with the CC playing a "pivotal role during its framing and negotiations" (Cepeda Espinosa and Landau 2017: 239). The Court included a critical mass or a supermajority of judges chosen by the president and Supreme Court. In this case of the nine judges present, three were chosen by the president (Calle Correa, González Cuervo, and Pretelt), three by the Supreme Court (Vargas Silva, Ortiz Delgado, Palacio, the latter two dissenting in part), two by the Consejo (Guerrero Pérez and Mendoza, the latter dissenting) and one by the magistrate potencia (Sáchica). The inclusion of the auxiliary judge shifted the composition such that the court included a supermajority of judges who usually voted more deferentially. As regards party, only one of the regular judges was associated with the Liberal Party and the rest were associated with the Conservatives.

The case focuses on how a critical mass of certain types of judges is useful in understanding decision-making over a more attitudinalist approach, which would suggest that a majority of judges aligned with Uribe or the Conservative Party would vote against Congress' wide discretion allowing for broad participation of former guerrillas in the political process. In this decision, a critical mass of more deferential judge types – selected by the president and Supreme Court – was needed to uphold such a controversial law.

Finally, in Case #553/2014, the CC upheld the Ley del Patrimonio Cultural Sumergido or Submerged Cultural Heritage Law, which held that artifacts from shipwrecks or sinkings were considered to belong to the state of Colombia and should be protected, but only if they were found 100 years after the date of the event leading to their submersion. As a result, items found less than 100 years after the event could be sold, transferred, or exchanged. Eight judges were on the case, forming a critical mass of those selected by the Supreme Court and the president, which according to the results in the empirical section tended to result in the Court upholding the law, which it did in this case.[28] Critics of the law claimed that it allowed important cultural artifacts to be sold for profit if they were found before the 100-year period specified by the law. The case also shows the influence of the Court's overall party orientation when judges of one party hold a majority of the seats on a particular case. In this case, seven of the eight judges were associated with the Conservative Party and may have been more favorable to property rights and business interests rather than the preservation of antiquities.

7.6.2.1 Examples Inconsistent with the Critical Mass

The statistical analysis shows general patterns and conditions influencing the two high courts' propensities for striking down laws. However, not every decision is predicted well by a critical mass of judges' types who have similar propensities to strike down or uphold laws appearing on a case defined by their institutional selector.

7.6.2.2 The Chilean Constitutional Tribunal

In some cases, the CT did not strike down a law when it had a critical mass of judges chosen by elected actors. For example, in Rol #1818 (2010), a critical mass of activist judges, six chosen by the president and legislature and two by the Supreme Court, upheld Article 4 of the Framework Agreement of Financial Cooperation between Chile and the European Investment Bank (EIB). In analyzing the constitutionality of

[28] Three of the judges were chosen by President Uribe (Calle Correa, González Cuervo, and Pretelt) and three by the Supreme Court (Vargas Silva, Ortiz Delgado, and Palacio), and two by the Consejo (Mendoza Martela and Guerrero Perez).

this article, the CT found that it did not contradict or limit the functions of Chile's own Central Bank related to foreign exchange reserves and the entry of foreign currency into the country. Further, in its consideration of the constitutionality of this article, the CT suggested that the EIB would be treated similar to other international organizations operating within the country. Despite having a critical mass of activist judges, the CT may have deferred to the legislature because the subject was governed by an organic law requiring a supermajority of legislators to approve the law and also because it involved issues that would benefit Chile's economy.

Similarly, a critical mass of activist judges (again six of eight) also upheld a modification of Law 18.961, an organic law dealing with personnel issues governing the *Carabineros*, the Chilean national police force, specifically requirements for receiving compensation if they are involved in accidents (Rol #3242). In this very short decision, just four pages, the CT cited Article 105 of the Constitution regarding career standards of civil servants and also referred to the fact that the organic law had been approved by both houses of Congress by the supermajorities required under the Constitution. Despite the critical mass of judges with a higher likelihood of vetoing laws, this decision was about a mundane personnel issue that all judges agreed complied with the Constitution. The CT's reference to supermajority legislative approval provides some indication that they were unwilling to decide the issue outside of such a high threshold of legislative preferences.

7.6.2.3 The Colombian Constitutional Court

In Colombia, some cases are not easily explained by the theory I present on Court composition. For example, this occurs when there is a similar type of deferential judges, but the Court as a whole chooses to strike down a law. In C754/2004, involving pension reform, a supermajority of judges or a critical mass of judges were selected by the Supreme Court or president, which should have led to a more deferential decision. This case had eight regular judges including Rentaría, Beltrán, Cepeda, Córdoba, Escobar Gil, Monroy Cabra, Tafur Galvis, Vargas Hernández, and one auxiliary judge, Uprimny Yepes. Further, excluding the auxiliary judge, the regular judges were evenly split as far as associations with the Liberal and Conservative Parties. Despite the critical mass of judges that tended to vote more deferentially, the Court struck down key parts of the pension reform law (Ley 860 de 2003) because it did not allow for real substantive debate in Congress. Commentators suggested that the Court chose to strike down the law in order to make the "congressional procedure more deliberative" (Cepeda Espinosa and Landau 2017: 324). While this decision does not fit the average treatment effects revealed by the statistics, judges may have chosen to strike down the law because it involved a procedural issue regarding Congress' duty to deliberate. For certain issue areas, such as the correct congressional processes, judges with different selectors may more readily unite to veto a law.

In another example, a critical mass of judges who tended to vote more deferentially (i.e., 2/3 chosen by the president and Supreme Court) appeared on C793/2014 and chose to strike down part of Law 1523 dealing with the creation of a national disaster risk management policy. In this case, the plaintiff argued that the law required that public refinancing entities establish rules allowing debtors affected by natural disasters to refinance or suspend their debt but did not include the same relief for debtors of private financial institutions. The CC agreed with the plaintiff indicating that this part of the management policy was unconstitutional because it discriminated against debtors of private financial institutions without sufficient reason. The Court also found that public and private financial institutions have the same obligations to debtors affected by disasters and that the law should be changed to equalize relief for these two groups. The Court's decision was firmly based on the constitutional mandates disallowing discrimination, in this case favoring debtors of public institutions over those of private institutions. As referenced by the Court, Article 13 of the Constitution requires that all individuals are treated equally before the law, and Article 335 renders financial activities and their monitoring a concern of public interest.

7.7 CHAPTER SUMMARY: DISCUSSION AND IMPLICATIONS

Significant prior scholarship has attempted to answer what determines when courts strike down laws. One branch of scholarship focuses on how courts are less likely to strike down laws when facing unified government for fear that elected actors may coordinate some type of retaliatory action against a court that refuses to uphold its legislation (McCubbins et al. 1995; Iaryczower et al. 2002). Increasingly, this literature has been criticized as either only applying to two-party systems or because the measure of political fragmentation is too crude a measurement for assessing reactions by the court (Vanberg 2015; Hilbink 2012). Other scholarship has focused on the idea that striking down laws is more likely when the political preferences of a majority of the court fall outside those of the enacting legislature. Dahl (1957) and Tsebelis (2002) explain courts' modest role in striking down laws as due to the fact that courts rarely are composed of judges with views outside that of the enacting coalition, the former indicating that courts are part of the political elite and the latter noting that judges' selection origins don't allow for them to serve as veto players. In more recent work, Brouard and Hönnige (2017) have countered Tsebelis' assertion.

The prior judge-level analysis showed that judges' constitutional adjudication type varied with the institution that selected them with some types of judges being more likely to strike down laws and others less likely. The individual analysis also showed strong panel effects such that an increase in the presence of judges of one type pulled judges of a different type toward their position. This chapter confirmed that the results from the individual analysis substantively impacted judicial vetoes at the court and case level. In other words, behavior observed at the individual level is substantively significant enough to shift the majority opinion of the two exemplar courts analyzed on average.

The case-level analysis here established that changes in the court's composition by case based on judges' schedules, term limits, and quorum rules influenced the likelihood of the two exemplar courts issuing judicial vetoes. The first analysis for each court indicated that percentage changes of judges selected by different institutions appearing on certain cases was highly correlated with courts' propensities to veto laws. A second analysis using matching determined that the Colombian CC's overall political party orientation also was influential but only when that court consisted of a majority of judges with the same party associations.

While the focus on the composition of the court based on judges' diverse institutional selectors is a main contribution of this study, further analysis focused on the ideological orientation of the Court. Judges on the Chilean Tribunal were either associated with the Concertación, the Right, or were nonpartisan. On some cases, the Tribunal was composed of at least 50 percent of judges associated with the Concertación. At no time did nonpartisan judges hold a majority on the Tribunal. The empirical analysis of party composition of the Tribunal revealed, however, that even when the Tribunal had a majority of judges from one party appearing on a case, it was not a significant determinant of judicial vetoes, providing further evidence that looking at court composition based on judges' selecting origin may provide more purchase in understanding the decision-making of this Tribunal.

Unlike the Chilean CT, the CC has judges associated with only two parties, and the only judges not clearly associated with political parties are auxiliary judges, who do not appear on a large number of cases (see Chapter 6, Figures 6.1 and 6.2). As a result, on certain cases the CC has more than 50 percent of judges associated with the Liberal Party and on others more than 50 percent of the judges were associated with the Conservative Party. The results showed that when the Court was composed of a majority of judges associated with the Liberal Party, it was more likely to veto laws. Cases composed of more than 50 percent of judges who associated with the Conservative Party were less likely to strike down laws. One explanation for the assertiveness of this Court when composed of a majority of Liberal Party judges may be that for most of the time period analyzed, these judges were facing legislation passed under the increasingly authoritarian presidency of Álvaro Uribe. The analysis implies that courts may have a harder time striking down a law when case composition is extremely diverse along both judges' type defined by institutional selector *and* party.

While the results and case examples provide evidence that court composition is a significant determinant of judicial vetoes, the impact of case contextual features should not be minimized. The subject matter of the law and the type of constitutional review matter. While several scholars have theorized that type of constitutional review and the subject of the laws may influence a court's decisions, this analysis provides confirming results. While case subject matter has been well tested in research on other courts, the influence of review type has generally provided theories of its impact with no empirical support. Here, the type of review influences the issuance of judicial vetoes. This finding is especially important as many constitutions and laws establish numerous powers for the courts. For example, Chile's Constitution lists a large number of ways for the court to exercise constitutional review. Previous studies have created typologies of court powers and suggested that courts with certain powers have comparative advantage in checking elected actors (see Shapiro 2004; Brinks and Blass 2017, 2018; Ríos-Figueroa 2011), but these studies, comparative in nature, do not establish how variations in courts' powers influence court decisions. The empirics here connected a variety of constitutional review powers to the courts' ability to strike down laws in practice.

APPENDIX

TABLE A7.1. *Summary statistics for case-level data for the Chilean CT*

Variables	Mean	Std. Dev.	Min	Max
Unconstitutional ruling in case	0.18	0.39	0	1
Percent appointed by president	0.24	0.12	0	0.43
Percent appointed by legislature	0.38	0.07	0.25	0.67
Percent associated with Concertación	0.45	0.10	0.22	0.71
Percent associated with Right	0.30	0.10	0	0.57
Concertación >50% binary ($T1_{party}$)	0.15	0.36	0	1
Concertación ≥50% binary ($T2_{party}$)	0.46	0.50	0	1
Requerimiento	0.10	0.30	0	1
Separation of powers	0.15	0.36	0	1
Rights	0.22	0.41	0	1
Subnational government	0.21	0.40	0	1

TABLE A7.2. *Summary statistics for case-level data for the Colombian CC*

Variables	Mean	Std. Dev.	Min	Max
Unconstitutional ruling in case	0.29	0.45	0	1
Percent nominated by president	0.38	0.11	0	0.56
Percent nominated by Supreme Court	0.28	0.11	0	0.43
Percent associated with Liberal Party	0.48	0.21	0	0.78
Liberal Party >50% binary ($T1_{party}$)	0.55	0.50	0	1
Conserv. Party >50% binary ($T2_{party}$)	0.34	0.48	0	1
Statutory law	0.02	0.13	0	1
International treaty	0.22	0.41	0	1
Separation of powers	0.64	0.49	0	1
Rights	0.69	0.46	0	1
Subnational government	0.12	0.32	0	1

TABLE A7.3. *Chilean CT comparing unmatched and matched data on party binary treatment (>50% judges associated with Concertación)*

Variables	(1) Unmatched	(2) Matched
Concertación >50% binary	−0.09	−0.26
	(0.32)	(0.39)
Percent appointed by president	1.43	2.68*
	(1.18)	(1.57)
Percent appointed by legislature	2.47	4.77*
	(1.88)	(2.65)
Requerimiento	0.75**	0.35
	(0.31)	(0.88)
Separation of powers	0.90***	1.80**
	(0.26)	(0.74)
Rights	0.80***	0.93***
	(0.24)	(0.33)
Subnational	0.63**	1.02**
	(0.25)	(0.41)
Constant	−2.89***	−4.17***
	(0.92)	(1.31)
Observations	244	185

Standard errors in parentheses; *** $p < 0.01$, ** $p < 0.05$, * $p < 0.1$.

TABLE A7.4. *Chilean CT comparing unmatched and matched data on party binary treatment (≥50% judges associated with Concertación)*

Variables	(1) Unmatched	(2) Matched
Concertación ≥50% binary	0.30	0.23
	(0.25)	(0.27)
Percent appointed by president	2.25*	2.24
	(1.31)	(1.45)
Percent appointed by legislature	2.53	2.29
	(1.86)	(2.24)
Requerimiento	0.78**	0.92**
	(0.31)	(0.42)
Separation of powers	0.94***	1.03***
	(0.27)	(0.32)
Rights	0.82***	0.94***
	(0.24)	(0.28)

(continued)

TABLE A7.4 *(continued)*

Variables	(1) Unmatched	(2) Matched
Subnational	0.61**	0.81***
	(0.25)	(0.32)
Constant	−3.29***	−3.18***
	(0.98)	(1.16)
Observations	244	211

Standard errors in parentheses; *** $p < 0.01$, ** $p < 0.05$, * $p < 0.1$.

TABLE A7.5. *Colombian CC comparing unmatched and matched data on party binary treatment (>50% judges associated with the Liberal Party)*

Variables	(1) Unmatched	(2) Matched
Liberal >50% binary	0.21**	0.28***
	(0.08)	(0.10)
Percent nominated by president	−1.88**	−2.12
	(0.82)	(1.36)
Percent nominated by Supreme Ct.	−1.86**	−1.93
	(0.79)	(1.26)
Statutory law	0.91***	1.00**
	(0.29)	(0.41)
International treaties	−0.98***	−1.00***
	(0.11)	(0.16)
Separation of powers	0.33***	0.30***
	(0.08)	(0.11)
Rights	−0.08	−0.15
	(0.08)	(0.10)
Subnational government	0.21*	0.20
	(0.12)	(0.17)
Constant	0.52	0.64
	(0.52)	(0.82)
Observations	1,333	857

Standard errors in parentheses; *** $p < 0.01$, ** $p < 0.05$, * $p < 0.1$.

TABLE A7.6. *Colombian CC comparing unmatched and matched data on party binary treatment (>50% judges associated with the Conservative Party)*

Variables	(1) Unmatched	(2) Matched
Conservative >50% binary	−0.16*	−0.18*
	(0.09)	(0.09)
Percent nominated by president	−1.55*	−1.60
	(0.80)	(1.26)
Percent nominated by Supreme Ct.	−1.69**	−1.50
	(0.79)	(1.59)
Statutory law	0.92***	1.06***
	(0.29)	(0.41)
International treaties	−0.98***	−0.82***
	(0.11)	(0.14)
Separation of powers	0.33***	0.28***
	(0.08)	(0.10)
Rights	−0.07	−0.20**
	(0.08)	(0.10)
Subnational government	0.21*	0.20
	(0.12)	(0.16)
Constant	0.52	0.57
	(0.51)	(0.87)
Observations	1,333	925

Standard errors in parentheses; *** $p < 0.01$, ** $p < 0.05$, * $p < 0.1$.

8

Weak Judicial Vetoes and Contentious Politics

8.1 INTRODUCTION

Certain high court decisions have great impact, while others are less influential. The impact of case decisions may be determined by the salience of the issues adjudicated and whether the decisions call for significant societal changes or reverse the political status quo. The impact of decisions to strike down laws also may be enhanced when they are decided unanimously. For example, the US Supreme Court's unanimous decision in *Brown* v. *Board of Education* in 1954 struck down as unconstitutional state laws that allowed for the segregation of public education. For some, the "[u]namimity appeared necessary if the Court was to preserve its institutional prestige while pursuing revolutionary change in social policy" (O'Brien 2011: 338). In contrast, significant dissensus on a case may undermine the support for momentous decisions as occurred in the US Supreme Court's five to four decision in *Citizens United* v. *Federal Election Commission* in 2009, striking down centuries old election finance restrictions and allowing unlimited spending on elections by corporations and other groups based on first amendment protections of free speech.

Weak judicial vetoes (i.e., those with significant dissent) that reflect deep divides among politicians and within society and undermine the decisions themselves occurred in two Chilean cases dealing with the distribution of the morning-after pill. These cases illustrate how contentious political and societal issues are reflected in court decisions with considerable disagreement as well as how such decisions are of a weaker quality perhaps inviting the executive or legislature to veto a court decision with new legislation. In Rol #591,[1] decided in 2007, the Tribunal was asked to review the constitutionality of a decree by the Minister of Health allowing for the distribution of the morning-after pill in public health centers to women over the age

[1] This particular case does not appear in the dataset as it involved review of a supreme decree by an agency of the executive branch and not legislation.

of fourteen under the National Norms on the Regulation of Fertility (NNRF). This decree built on existing public policy that had previously allowed the distribution of the morning-after pill in private clinics. Deputies of the Right or Alianza (RN/UDI) challenged the decree before the Tribunal using the *requerimiento* process. A deeply divided Tribunal struck down the law as unconstitutional claiming that it had circumvented the legislative process.[2]

In response, President Bachelet, who championed women's reproductive choice and had previously served as the country's Minister of Health, signed Supreme Regulatory Decree No. 48 enacting the same NNRF regulations that the Tribunal had considered before. Again, this decree was challenged before the Tribunal using the *requerimiento* process, and the Tribunal, with almost an identical majority, found the public distribution of the morning-after pill unconstitutional in violation of the "right to life" provision in the Constitution (Rol #740).[3] For some, the case was considered one of the "most controversial rulings of the Chilean Constitutional Tribunal since its reestablishment in 1980" (Muñoz León 2014: 158). The public outrage from segments of the population was swift with large protests "at the doors of the Tribunal" (p. 159). In reaction, Bachelet herself declared that the decision had inflicted "a deep wound to building a more just and equitable society" and that it "affects the poorest women of our country" (p. 159). In a practical solution, the Minister of Health attempted to distribute the morning-after pill through drug stores that had not been mentioned by the CT. However, this prompted a reaction from the Comptroller General claiming that it was illegal for *any* state institution to distribute it.

In seeking a more permanent solution to this controversy, Bachelet submitted legislation to Congress to immediately approve a law that would declare that the public health system could make available all contraceptive methods. This was approved by both houses of Congress with some votes from legislators of the Alianza after the inclusion of the Horvath amendment, introduced by an RN senator of this name and mandating sexual education in high schools. This amendment was then reviewed by the Tribunal under its obligatory review jurisdiction in Rol #1588 (2010) and found constitutional with one concurrence (Peña) and one dissent (Fernández Baeza).[4] The first two CT decisions on the issue illustrate the potential fragility of courts' powers to effectuate policy. The high level of dissent in the first two cases resulted in public outrage, disdain from the president about the decision and a presidential override, and finally new legislation that was then held

[2] The majority consisted of judges Cea, Navarro, Bertelsen, Venegas, Peña, and Fernández Baeza. Appointees associated with the Concertación Fernández Fredes and Correa Sutil dissented together along with Colombo chosen by the COSENA, but associated with the Concertación. See Carroll and Tiede (2012) for a spatial analysis of votes on this case.

[3] Here, Correa Sutil and Fernández Fredes dissented together, while Vodanovic and Colombo individually dissented on separate points.

[4] The nine judges appearing on this case included Venegas, Colombo, Bertelsen, Vodanovic, Fernández Baeza, Peña, Navarro, Fernández Fredes and Carmona. The case fell under the Tribunal's obligatory review because it was related to education policy.

constitutional. While the subject matter and the exact political context may have led to the override, the substantial dissent in the Court decision may have contributed to the ability of the elected branches to ultimately override the CT's decisions.

These Chilean cases also serve as a reminder that Kelsian constitutional courts in their original conception as well as later incarnations were created specifically to check the powers of overzealous executives and legislators. In short, constitutional courts with veto powers have the potential to punish leaders who overstep their powers and issue decisive policy changes. However, this role can be drastically undercut when the decisions themselves reflect substantial dissensus among constitutional court judges, which may allow policymakers, other courts, and society as a whole to potentially disregard such decisions and to seek openings to undermine them at a later date. Beyond analyzing whether the conditions are present for mixed selection constitutional courts to issue vetoes, taken up in Chapter 7, the effectiveness of any veto depends in part on whether the full court agreed to the decision unanimously, signaling a strong legal decision, or whether there was substantial disagreement among judges when vetoing a law.

This book has thus far demonstrated that the Chilean and Colombian constitutional courts' propensities to veto laws were determined in part by the composition of constitutional adjudicator types appearing on a case and influenced by the mixed selection method. While the book has focused on the theoretical benefits of mixed selection systems, which allow for different types of judges with different political ties to offer distinct points of view on the constitutionality of a law before them, another consequence of such a system is that it may introduce fragmentation and disagreement into the decision-making process if judges appear to use votes to demonstrate loyalty to their selector or their constitutional adjudicator type (see Ginsburg 2003; Sadurski 2008) and are not willing to consider other perspectives. In such an eventuality, disagreement may emerge on mixed selection courts and has the potential to erode norms of collegiality and weaken the decisions themselves.

This chapter considers to what extent mixed selection courts may create fragmented voting by examining trends in both the likelihood of vetoing laws and the amount of dissensus that has evolved over time. Trends in dissensus on cases that strike down laws warrant attention as they may undermine the ability of these courts to check elected actors in a meaningful way – one purpose of constitutional courts. I, however, argue that not all judicial vetoes are created equally and those with significant dissent point to deep divisions within society over certain policies and weaken the ability of constitutional courts to check the elected branches in these areas. Further, decisions with considerable dissent reflect areas of contentious political and social debates. Here, substantial dissent is defined as cases in which every judge is considered a pivotal judge such that a change in their vote would change the outcome of the case.

To examine the connection between judicial vetoes and substantial dissent, I suggest that the role that constitutional courts' decisions have on policy making depends on two dimensions: the direction of the decision (deference to the enacting legislature or striking down laws) and the amount of unanimity and dissensus. I then show general trends in the evolution of vetoes and dissensus on the CT and CC over time. While the Chilean CT and CC do not show a large number of cases with significant dissensus, the Chilean CT has inclined toward considerably more dissensus in recent years and an increased resort to the *dirimente* process whereby the chief justice casts the deciding vote when judges' votes are evenly divided and the Tribunal convenes with an even number of judges (i.e., ten when the full court meets or eight as a smaller quorum). Likewise, on the CC, compared to the number of decisions in abstract review that this Court decides, few have significant dissent. However, the emergence of substantial dissent should still be carefully monitored to determine the effectiveness of the CC in areas that divide politicians and society. The chapter concludes with some examples of how decisions with significant areas of dissensus are some of the most contentious socially and politically in the two countries and in some cases divide judges across their political associations, although as shown in prior chapters, on average most decisions are not overtly politicized.

8.2 EVALUATING THE STRENGTH OF SIGNALS EMANATING FROM CONSTITUTIONAL COURTS

Constitutional judges' and courts' decisions to veto a law influence what type of laws a society adopts and to what extent a nonelected court can check the powers of other political actors and protect minority rights. The empirical focus of this chapter moves away from what determines whether judges and courts veto laws on mixed selection courts, established in prior chapters, to an evaluation of the strength of these courts' decisions determined by the amount of dissensus within the decision itself, which could arise due to the heterogeneity of judge types on these courts as well as the underlying controversy enshrined in the law. To evaluate courts' powers to instigate policy change over time, it is necessary to look at two dimensions of courts' decisions: (1) the substantive outcome of the case (i.e., whether the law was upheld as constitutional or not) and (2) the strength of the decision (i.e., was it unanimous or not). The substantive outcome shows whether courts will follow the legislature or subvert it by striking down a law or part of a law as unconstitutional. While tracking the compliance of courts' decisions poses empirical difficulties, alternatively studying the strength of a policy decision provides some indication of whether the decision of the court is more or less likely to be followed by political actors and society as a whole or is likely to be overturned in the future.

8.2.1 *Dimension #1: Case Decision to Defer or Veto the Law*

The first dimension for evaluating constitutional review decisions is to determine whether the law being reviewed is upheld or invalidated. In constitutional review decisions, the court has a choice to either defer to the elected branches' policy preferences or to strike them down as unconstitutional. Many countries that have created constitutional courts outside the judicial branch and coexisting with national supreme courts have done so in order to provide one final arbiter for determining the constitutional validity of laws. In this way, constitutional courts are agents not of one specific political actor, but rather of the constitution itself. When constitutional courts find laws unconstitutional, they are subverting the will or checking the power of the enacting government, which may be the government in power (as in the case of a priori review or the review of recently enacted laws) or a prior government. When courts find laws unconstitutional, they also are acting as veto players. Vetoing laws may result in "divisive" policy change, different from the status quo. When vetoes are not used, policy remains more "resolute" (Haggard and McCubbins 2001). Therefore, one dimension for analyzing the role of constitutional courts in democratic governance is to determine whether the decision upholds or subverts laws approved by elected political actors.

8.2.2 *Dimension #2: Strength of Decision*

A second dimension of a judicial decision goes to the strength of the decision itself. Unanimous decisions are thought to send stronger signals to lower courts and elected officials (Pritchett 1948; Danelski 1986; MacGregor Burns 2010) as well as citizens. By contrast, decisions with significant dissents weaken the decisions themselves. Such decisions invite confusion into the policymaking process (see O'Brien 2011), and they may negatively affect the stature of a court, especially younger courts (Couso 2004; Sadurski 2008; Garoupa and Ginsburg 2015; Kelemen 2013). Decisions with significant dissent also weaken public confidence in courts suggesting that a decision may have been reached on political rather than legal grounds (see Vitale 2014) especially if judges' disagreements are associated with their political associations.[5]

Besides sending a weak and confusing decision to the public and other legal and political actors, decisions with substantial dissent may influence compliance. For example, cases with dissent invite legislative overrides (Eskridge 1991a; O'Brien 2011: 308; Pritchett 1948). Additionally, decisions demonstrating significant dissensus may influence whether lower courts comply or listen to the decision of higher courts (Peterson 1981; but see Jaros and Canon 1971). Naurin and Stiansen (2020) show a strong correlation between state compliance with decisions of the Inter-American and European Courts of Human Rights and dissent on the case. They argue that dissent in a decision undermines the legal authority of the decision, making it easier for countries to avoid implementing decisions.

[5] Not all dissent, however, is negative and may suggest a court that carefully deliberates and includes independent-minded judges.

TABLE 8.1. *Dimensions of constitutional court decisions*

	Constitutional	Unconstitutional
Collegial (unanimous or little dissent)	(1) Strong deference	(2) Strong veto
Substantial dissent (pivotal judge could change outcome)	(3) Cautious deference	(4) **Weak veto**

Further, decisions with substantial numbers of dissenting judges may provide policymakers a foothold and plenty of legal arguments for overturning policy at a later date. As noted by former Chief Justice Hughes of the US Supreme Court, "[a] dissent in a court of last resort is an appeal to the brooding spirit of the law, to the intelligence of a future day, when a later decision may possibly correct the error into which the dissenting judge believes the court to have been betrayed" (Douglas 1948: 153). The need for strong decisions, supported by as many judges as possible is crucial for courts that seek to veto a law. Such decisions and especially those issued by the court in a priori review are counter to legislative drafters who not only will oppose such a court decision but seek ways to undermine it. Indeed, in this book, I argued that judges with different selectors and adjudication styles often went along with other judges in order to bolster the strength of the decision.

To analyze these two dimensions, Table 8.1 describes four combinations for viewing constitutional court decisions. This table provides a useful way of analyzing the quality and strength of courts' decisions across periods of time or subject areas and provides an analytical tool for studying decision-making on any collegial court. In the table's first cell, denoted strong deference, the court agrees with the elected branches and finds the law constitutional. Further, the court decision is reached unanimously or with little dissent. In this case, the court is sending a strong signal of deference or a strong signal that the other branches made the appropriate policy choices. In the second cell, courts instead decide to overturn a law and do so unanimously or with little dissent. In this case, courts are vetoing the elected branches in the strongest form they can – a decision supported by the entire court or close to all the judges in agreement. Thus, in the first two cells, judges are either agreeing with the status quo or overturning it, but they are providing a policy prescription with a strong signal. In the third and fourth cells, courts are determining the constitutionality of laws, but here they send weak signals because the decisions are made with substantial dissent (i.e., in which all judges are pivotal). In the third cell, the court is cautiously deferring to the elected branches. The court decision favors the elected branches, but the signal is weak because it is not unanimous. Such decisions fuel concern by political actors and the public who supported a certain policy because it allows opposition leaders and advocates to seek opportunities to change the policy at a later date. Such opportunities may arise when the legislature has the correct composition to rewrite a law and when the court composition is unlikely to overturn it. However, political actors may seek other opportunities to change weakly supported constitutional decisions through processes that do not require constitutional review. In the fourth cell, the court is exercising its judicial veto but with a weak signal threatening the decisions' longevity. This is worrisome for those who supported the judicial veto and a policy change, and also may provide opportunities for those who opposed the court's action. The case examples at the end of the chapter focus on this cell, which determines the courts' ability to effectively check other government actors or do so in a lasting way.

8.3 CASE-LEVEL TRENDS ACROSS TWO DIMENSIONS

This section describes the trends in the two exemplar courts' constitutional review regarding case decisions to strike or not and whether the case has any dissent. Figures 8.1 and 8.2 show three types of data. One line shows the percentage of cases with unconstitutionality, which occurs if the court found any part of the law unconstitutional. A second line shows the percentage of cases with dissent. However, here dissent simply refers to whether at least one judge dissented on a case. A third line shows the average percentage of judges on any case who dissent.

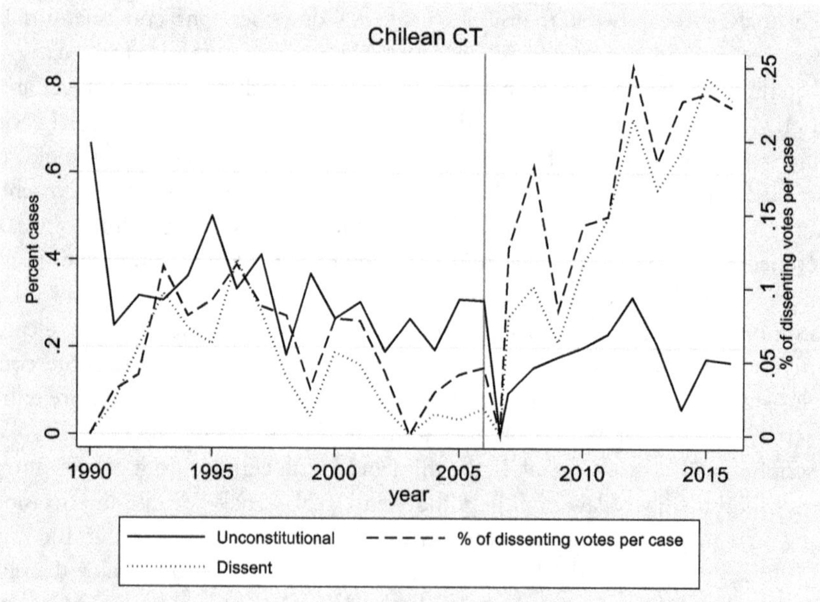

FIGURE 8.1 Percentage of judicial vetoes and dissent on the Chilean CT
Note: A case is considered a judicial veto if at least one decisional paragraph of the case favors unconstitutionality.

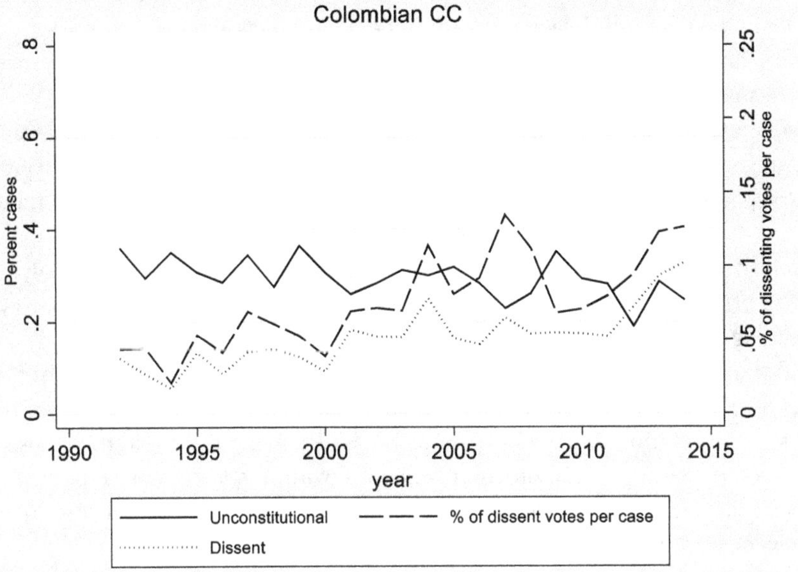

FIGURE 8.2 Percentage of judicial vetoes and dissent on the Colombian CC
Note: A case is considered a judicial veto if at least one decisional paragraph of the case favors unconstitutionality.

Because the cases are divided into paragraphs, some of which have dissent and some that do not, this line represents the average of dissenting votes over all decisional paragraphs within a case. As with the analyses in Chapters 6 and 7, these trends relate to the two courts' abstract constitutional review of legislation that is passed by a legislature still in power at the time of review.

The Chilean CT's case trends, presented in Figure 8.1, range from Chile's return to democracy through 2016. In Chile, the Tribunal has heard on average twenty-one abstract review cases per year, which include cases of obligatory review and *requerimientos*. For the entire post-transition period (1990–2016), the Tribunal on average has found at least one of the paragraphs within a case unconstitutional 26 percent of the time, although this has varied depending on whether the Tribunal heard the cases prior to or after the reform. Prior to the constitutional reforms of 2005, the Tribunal reviewed laws passed by successive Concertación governments, who were operating under a constitution that allowed for authoritarian enclaves, such as lifetime senators and the powerful influence of the COSENA. Figure 8.1 shows that in the early years of the Tribunal the percent of cases with a constitutional violation was higher than in later years, which may be due to the inclusion of judges chosen under the junta prior to the democratic transition who may have opposed some of the laws put forth by the Concertación government. After the constitutional reforms of 2005 (enacted in 2006), indicated by the vertical line, the number of cases in which the Court finds laws unconstitutional plummets and then resumes at a rate lower than that of the pre-reform period. The sudden drop after the reform may be due to a lack of abstract review cases before the Tribunal as it prepared to take cases of concrete review originally heard by the Supreme Court. While the reform, bringing more judges to the Tribunal who are selected by elected actors, seems to have suppressed the number of judicial vetoes issued by the Tribunal, the number of cases with dissent and the average number of judges dissenting seems to have increased. This result was noted in an earlier study, which included data only until 2010 or prior to the first Piñera presidency (see Carroll and Tiede 2012). However, by extending the data through 2016, these two trends seem to be on the rise.

Prior to the reform, the Tribunal found unconstitutionality in 31 percent of the cases it decided. After the reform this was reduced to 18 percent of the time. Prior to the reform, 20 percent of cases had at least one dissent and of those the mean of dissenting votes on all paragraphs within a case was 4 percent. In comparison, after the reform 57 percent of cases had at least one dissent and the average number of dissenting votes over all paragraphs within a case was 13 percent. A regression analysis of the reform on unconstitutionality and these two measures of dissent confirms that the reform significantly decreased unconstitutional cases by 13 percent, increased cases with at least one dissent by 34 percent, and increased the average number of judges dissenting on any case by 10 percent all significant at the 0.01 level (see Appendix to this chapter Table A8.1 for the full regression results).

Figure 8.2 depicts trends in case outcomes and dissensus on the Colombian CC over time since the creation of the Court. Compared to the Chilean Tribunal, the CC has had relatively stable rates of unconstitutionality and cases with dissensus from the period from 1992 to 2014. For this entire period 24 percent of the cases were unconstitutional and 23 percent had at least one dissent. The average of dissenting votes within a case over all paragraphs was about 5 percent. As shown in the figure, after judges chosen by the interim method were no longer on the Court, the rates of unconstitutionality and dissent are somewhat higher. The figure shows that the common perception that the Colombian Court is far more assertive than the Chilean Tribunal may be exaggerated.[6] Although the Chilean Tribunal hears far fewer cases than the Colombian CC, it tends to hear some of the most important cases facing society, and the rate of striking down laws is fairly similar for the two courts[7] given the scope conditions (i.e., 18 percent post reform for the CT and 24 percent for the CC). Furthermore, the CC's reputation may be forged from its

6 Author interview with José Gregario Hernández Galindo. This former justice confirmed that many cases resulted in the Court finding laws constitutional and declarations of unconstitutionality were "abnormal" (May 2016, Bogotá).

7 This perception was provided to me during an interview of a high-level Tribunal official during an interview in Santiago in January 2016.

numerous *tutela* cases or striking down presidential decrees or laws of prior governments rather than abstract review of laws passed by the current legislature, which has been the narrower focus of the empirics presented in this book. For Colombia, upon closer analysis of the figure, the percentage of cases with dissent has increased from 2001 and then again in 2010.

8.4 ANALYZING WEAK JUDICIAL VETOES ON THE CHILEAN AND COLOMBIAN CONSTITUTIONAL COURTS

The figures above show average trends in unconstitutionality and dissent. While dissent may lower the quality or weaken a decision, here I am especially interested in cases in which the judges are significantly divided on a large proportion of decisional paragraphs within a case rather than more modest dissent rates. As such, I selected cases in which the mean of dissenting votes over all decisional paragraphs within a case was around 40 percent of the judges. This necessarily underestimates the cases with substantial dissent. As such cases with very few decisional paragraphs but with significant dissent will be examined further, but those with many decisional paragraphs with little dissent and only a few paragraphs with significant dissent will not appear in this discussion.[8] While choosing cases this way underestimates all cases with meaningful dissent, the number of cases to examine from this method is more manageable, especially given the large number of cases that the CC hears.

Cases with significant dissent may reflect deep divides within the courts that may mirror polarization among politicians and within society. Further, these case decisions may be the most sensitive to a future change in court composition due to tenure and replenishment requirements, changes in the composition of the elected branches (due to elections), and changes in public opinion. Furthermore, cases with such high levels of dissent may indicate politicization of the selection process itself, and high levels of dissent over time may indicate the weakening of norms of collegiality at least on certain issues. For example, over time the US Supreme Court slowly moved away from a long-established norm of collegiality, which weakened under the Roosevelt presidency (see Pritchett 1948). Since that time, the amount of politicization and dissensus has increased as shown by Martin and Quinn Scores.[9] Further, such polarization may result in inquiries as to whether a court should be reformed – a consideration of the Biden presidency, which convened a Presidential Commission on the Supreme Court on April 9, 2021 (Executive Order 14023).

In this section, I explore the two dimensions of judicial decisions and then focus on judicial vetoes with significant dissent (cell #4 in Table 8.1). The purpose of this

8 This was the case of the CT's Rol #1288 dealing with constitutional reforms to the CT itself.

9 See "Measuring the Conservativism of the Roberts' Court," New York Times (July 24, 2010), available at https://mqscores.lsa.umich.edu/media/nyt0710b.pdf (last accessed April 2021).

section is to determine the nature of the courts' decision-making along the two dimensions and to probe one concern raised by the mixed selection system as to the possibility that it leads to fragmented voting. Additionally, this section determines the prevalence of weak judicial vetoes and whether they reflect areas of high political and societal contention as suggested by the literature. For example, are courts divided on cases in which the legislature and society are deeply divided? Do the disagreements reflect political divides among the judges based on differences in judges' institutional selectors? If cases with substantial dissent mirror divisions within politics and society, this may lower the ability of these constitutional courts to effectuate policy in certain areas.

8.4.1 *Weak Vetoes in the Chilean Constitutional Tribunal*

In Table 8.2, I analyze the Chilean CT's cases along the two dimensions – strength and quality of the decision. The CT's decisions are highly collegial with many cases involving little or no dissent regardless of outcome. As regards judicial vetoes, the CT does not veto laws or parts of laws very often, only in 44 of 244 cases analyzed. Of those vetoes, 77 percent are strong vetoes supported by a unanimous court or one with high agreement among its judges (cell 2) and only 10 or 23 percent of these vetoes have substantial dissent as defined (cell 4). As will be seen later, half of these high dissensus vetoes have occurred in 2015 and 2016.

Table 8.3 describes those ten judicial vetoes with large amounts of dissent reflected in cell 4. Of these ten cases, six of them involved the *requerimiento* process by which politicians, usually in the minority, bring a case before the CT at any stage of the legislative process to contest certain provisions. Because the *requerimiento* process is highly political and the cases are brought by legislatures in the minority, it is no surprise that these cases represent some of the most politically and socially fraught policy issues. Additionally, some of the voting divisions on these cases, especially those involving the *requerimiento* process, are among judges with different political associations, but by no means all of the cases. This suggests that when a large amount of disagreement does occur, it divides judges on some issues by their political associations.

Additionally, six of the cases involved an even split of the full court of ten judges (i.e., 5 against 5 or 4 against 4), which is governed by the *dirimente* process, in which the chief justice breaks the tie with his favored position.[10] In four of these cases,

[10] Some other cases involving substantial dissent and the use of the dirimente process upheld the law reviewed as constitutional. Such cases, which would fall in cell #3 in Tables 8.1 and 8.2, are also weak decisions and troubling. The dirimente also was used on decisional paragraphs grappling with whether the part of the law reviewed involved an organic law. *Dirimentes* by the Chief Justice voting in favor of the article reviewed being classified as organic laws occurred in the following Rols: 2036, 2061, 2074, 2557, 2619, 2672. In these cases, the other provisions' decisional paragraphs had a high level of agreement. *Dirimentes* by the Chief Justice voting

TABLE 8.2. *CT cases by strength and quality of decision*

	Constitutional	Unconstitutional
All compositions: 244 cases	No Judicial veto 200 cases	Judicial veto on part of law 44 cases
Collegial **(unanimous or little dissent)**	(1) Strong deference 184 (92%)	(2) Strong veto 34 (77%)
Substantial dissent **(pivotal judge could change outcome)**	(3) Cautious deference 16 (8%)	**(4)** **Weak veto** **10 (23%)**

Justice Carmona (selected by President Bachelet) and associated with the Concertación, broke the tie on the decisional paragraph with the split vote in favor of finding the law unconstitutional. In only two cases were ties broken by a different chief justice – Colombo in Rol #1410, a COSENA appointee and associated with the Concertación, and Raúl Bertelsen in Rol #2446 selected by the Senate and associated with the Right. Finally, four of these cases with substantial dissensus occurred in 2015 and 2016 suggesting that decision-making on the Tribunal has grown more polarized especially in recent years although the number of vetoes with high levels of dissent are still relatively small. Many former judges and other court personnel are not as concerned about high levels of dissent on the Tribunal as the *dirimente* process itself and the power that it affords to chief justices.[11] Correa Sutil, a former justice, and Molina Osorio (2014) raised concerns about the significant use of the *dirimente* process in cases in 2014. Many cases that implicate the *dirimente* process have resulted in the chief justice upholding rather than vetoing the laws, although these cases are also considered weak.

Additionally, the judicial vetoes appearing in Table 8.4 reflect some politicized voting with judges dividing on some paragraphs on a case according to their political associations, although nonpartisan judges were found on both sides. Of the ten cases analyzed, judges divided along partisan lines on seven of these cases for some, but not necessarily all of the paragraphs within the cases, which each had substantial dissent.

The list of cases with substantial dissensus for the most part deal with issues of democracy and social and economic rights. Cases involving democracy dealt with modernizing voting (Rol #2446), increasing integrity in public jobs (Rol #2905), and the strengthening of and transparency of democracy (Rol #2981). Since Chile's

that part of the law was not organic and could not be considered under the Tribunal's obligatory review for that provision occurred in the following Rols: 2730, 2785, 2889, 2899, 2905, 3023, 3081, 3130, 3195, 3279.

[11] Author interviews held in January 2016 in Santiago, Chile.

TABLE 8.3. *Judicial vetoes with substantial dissensus on the Chilean CT (2006–2016)*

Case # (year) CC = constitutional control-obligatory R = Requerimiento	Description of law reviewed	Political split among judges*
1410 (2009) R Voto dirimente[12]	Draft law on Declaration of the Absence of the Forced Disappearance of Persons.	No
2025 (2011) R	Draft law modification of the Labor Code to create parental postnatal leave.	Yes
2358 (2012) R	Bill that allows the introduction of digital terrestrial television.	Yes
2446 (2013) CC Voto dirimente	Draft law that modifies provisions regarding automatic registration and a modernized voting system.	No
2541 (2013) R	Draft law that allows the introduction of digital terrestrial television.	Yes
2787 (2015) R Voto dirimente	Draft law that regulates the admission of students, eliminates shared financing, and prohibits profit in educational establishments that receive contributions from the state.	Yes
2905 (2015) CC Voto dirimente	Draft law on integrity in public functions.	No
2935 (2015) R Voto dirimente	Draft law on the Public Sector Budget bill for 2016.	Yes
2981 (2016) CC Voto dirimente	Draft law on strengthening and transparency of democracy.	Yes
3112 (2016) CC	Draft law that modernizes the labor relations system and introduces modifications to the Labor Code.	Yes

* *Note.* "Yes" indicates that there was split between judges associated with the left and right (with some nonpartisan judges) on at least one of the paragraphs within a case that had substantial dissent overall.

democratic transition, citizens and politicians have held conflicting perspectives regarding Chile's autocratic past and calls to further reform the Constitution, which many see as a legacy of the Pinochet era despite the 2005 reforms. Such divisive issues seem to similarly divide the Tribunal. Divisions over socioeconomic issues are also a theme of many of the Tribunal's vetoes with high dissensus. For example, Rol #2025 involves modification of the Labor Code to create provisions for parental postnatal leave and Rol #3112 attempts to modernize the labor relations system. Rol #2935 deals with reform of the Public Sector Budget.

[12] For a list of cases, in which the *dirimente* process was used, see the following list provided by the CT at www.tribunalconstitucional.cl/wp/wp-content/estadisticas/Voto_dirimente_de_PdteTC.pdf?v=2.

As noted in Chapter 4, access to education has been a contentious issue facing Chileans resulting in the penguin revolution and many subsequent protests. Several cases involving education policy involved significant amounts of judicial dissent both when the majority opinion upheld and struck down laws. Such weak decisions signal that the CT's role in education policy is precarious and its decisions easily subverted. Rol #2731 (2014) exemplifies a case of weak deference in this regard (i.e., finding the law constitutional with substantial dissent). In this case, the CT reviewed a bill that created an interim administrator of closures of institutions of higher education and established regulations on interim administration and educational advocates. The case was brought to the CT through the *requerimiento* process by legislators with the Center Right who opposed the bill arguing that it violated principles of university autonomy. In regards to this specific case, during an interview of CT personnel held January 13, 2016, I was told that this was one of the most important decisions of the CT and many had assumed the CT would strike down the law, which it surprisingly for many, did not. The decision is weak and unstable, however, as several of the decisional paragraphs needed to be decided by the *dirimente* process in which the then Chief Justice Carmona broke the tie in favor of upholding provisions of the law on decisional paragraphs in which judges were evenly divided and some of the disagreements pitted judges associated with one party against those of another. Several other cases since 2006 also upheld certain education policies or were held inadmissible, but again with significant dissent (see Rol #2935, 2889, and 2785).

In Rol #2787 a group of senators from the RN and UDI (parties of the Right) presented a *requerimiento* to the Tribunal requesting it find unconstitutional a draft law modifying the General Law of Education (Bulletin 9366-04) regulating student admissions, eliminating shared financing, and prohibiting profits from educational institutions that received state aid. The lengthy case required CT judges to vote on six separate parts of the law, and five of six of these, ultimately upholding the law, were decided through the *dirimente* process in which Carmona, associated with the Concertación, favored upholding the law with other Concertación-affiliated judges (García Pino, Fernández Fredes, Pozo) and Hernández Emparanza chosen by the Supreme Court and classified as nonpartisan. In opposition, the other five judges were in agreement with the *requerimiento* to strike down the law on these five parts and these judges, except for Peña, were associated with the Right including Aróstica, Romero, Brahm, and Letelier. The case is classified as a judicial veto because despite all this dissent on other provisions, part of the law was struck down by a seven to three vote as violating citizens' fundamental liberties to pursue education. Rol #2787 is a good example of a case that vetoed part of a law and had significant dissent on many provisions and involved a subject area – education policy – that has been politically contentious within Chilean society resulting in several protests. Further, the case also shows that despite much collegiality, certain issues divide judges in a partisan manner.

Additional issues related to governance and socioeconomic equality reviewed in some of the cases involving weak judicial vetoes mirror some of the issues that resulted in social turmoil and violence in October 2019. These cases of weak vetoes signal areas of heightened contention among politicians, society, and the judges themselves. As noted by Luna (2021), the protests in 2019 revealed the harsh divide among citizens and political elites in a country that for the most part had been a "renowned economic success" based mostly on a "consensus oriented political system." The cases with substantial dissensus were in some of the areas in which societal conflict had fomented. The weak vetoes resulting from these cases by no means caused the turmoil, but the weakness of the decisions demonstrated that at least in these areas, the Tribunal was unable to decide issues in a strong and unified voice and as such the Tribunal's role in policymaking in these areas was compromised.

8.4.2 *Weak Judicial Vetoes in Colombia*

As with the Chilean CT, I also analyzed the Colombian CC's cases along the two dimensions of whether a law is vetoed and whether there was a substantial amount of dissent within the decision. As shown in Table 8.4, the Colombia CC's cases follow a similar pattern to those of the CT although this Court not only hears more cases but is arguably even more collegial than the CT. When this Court defers to the legislature, most of the cases (i.e., 70 percent) have a low proportion of dissents over all votes on all decisional paragraphs. This is a somewhat lower level of collegiality for this same category of cases observed for the Chilean CT. However, the real point of divergence between the two courts appears in relation to judicial vetoes. Of the 388 cases in which the CC strikes down part or all of the law, 364 or 93 percent of these are decided with little overall dissensus. Twenty-four or just 7 percent of all judicial vetoes analyzed have substantial dissensus as I have defined it. This is likely driven by a stronger norm of collegiality on the Colombia CC and also due to the fact that there is an odd number of judges and the *dirimente* process is not allowed. Further, the way in which I chose the cases for this table, requiring substantial dissent on a large proportion of decisional paragraphs within a case and does not consider cases in which there may be substantial dissent on one paragraph. For example, C141/2010, finding that Uribe's reelection for a third term was unconstitutional does not appear in this table because only one paragraph of seven involved substantial dissent.

For the Colombian CC, Table 8.5 lists all 24 vetoes that have a high level of dissent across all paragraphs. As with the analysis on Chile, these are cases in which a high proportion of decisional paragraphs within a case had substantial dissent (i.e., all judges were pivotal on those paragraphs). Some of the cases in Table 8.5 involve issues related to the national government's laws related to the

TABLE 8.4. *CC cases by strength and quality of decision*

	Constitutional	Unconstitutional
All compositions: 1,333 cases *Full court: 937 cases*	No Judicial veto 945 cases *654 cases*	Judicial veto on part of law 388 cases *283 cases*
Collegial **(unanimous or little dissent)**	(1) Strong deference 927 (70%)	(2) Strong veto 364 (93%)
Substantial dissent **(pivotal judge could change outcome)**	(3) Cautious deference 18 (2%)	(4) **Weak veto** **24 (7%)**

powers of regional governments. As recalled from Chapter 5, national versus local policy concerns have created many divisions within Colombian society and these seem to be reflected in cases with substantial dissent. For example, C-1098/2001 deals with the reduction of workers' salaries due to territorial entities' loss of autonomy, and C-579/2001 relates to the categorization of territorial budgets. In C-644/2012, the Court dealt with challenges in the national development plan that would allow for the acquisition, contribution, or use of initially designated vacant lands. The law under scrutiny would allow the development of these vacant lands to the detriment of rural populations, which ran counter to restrictions established in 1994 that were used to promote access to property for agricultural workers. In this case, the Court found several of the articles unconstitutional stating that they involved regressive policy, were not justified, and countered achievements previously made by the farming population. Furthermore, these articles did not ensure any balance between the interests of agro-industrial companies and farmers.

A number of cases with substantial dissent involved issues related to the rights and equality of indigenous communities within Colombia. For example, in C-179/2009, the Court found unconstitutional Law 1152 of 2007 establishing the Rural Development Program on the grounds that government failed to consult with indigenous communities and ethnic groups before enacting the law as required by legal obligations under Convention 169 of the International Labor Organization, which is part of Colombia's constitutional block. Additionally, in C948/2014, the CC decided whether to consecrate Mother Laura Montoya Upegui as an "illustrious Colombian saint." The Court struck down part of this law because failing to do so would imply that the state was symbolically supporting this religious representative's specific religion and not respecting the multicultural and pluralistic nature of Colombian society in violation of the rights of indigenous and other people.

TABLE 8.5. *Judicial vetoes with substantial dissensus on the Colombian CC (1997–2014)*

Case # (year) Type of review	Description of law reviewed	Political split among judges*
C-193/1998	Law 393 of 1997 regarding a suitable procedural mechanism or instrument to ensure the material implementation of laws and administrative acts.	No
C-1404/2000	Bill No. 36/99 Senate – 196/99 Chamber regarding presidential power.	No
C-392/2000	Law 504 of 1999 regarding judicial access.	No
C-955/2000	Laws 546 of December 23, 1999, regarding division of power between Congress and the executive as it relates to finances, the stock market, insurance activity, and any other issue related to the management, use, and investment of the resources taken from the public.	No
C-1098/2001	Law 617 of 2000 regarding possible reduction of salary of municipal/territorial workers.	No
C-737/2001	Law 619 of 2000 regarding the process of the formation of laws, and in particular, congressional actions and the "Commission Accidental."	No
C-893/2001	Law 640 of 2001 regarding the right of all persons to obtain effective judicial protection from the judges and courts that make up the administration of justice.	No
C-619/2002	Law 610 of 2000, which establishes fiscal responsibility processes under the jurisdiction of the comptrollers' offices.	No
C-305/2004	Law 812 of 2003, National Development Plan 2003–2006.	No
C-307/2004 Statutory	Bill No. 081/02 Senate and 228/03 House regarding registration and voting mechanisms.	No
C-816/2004	Legislative Act No. 02 of 2003 related to terrorism.	No
C-400/2005 International Treaty	Law 899 of July 21, 2004 approving the Second Protocol of the 1954 Hague Convention for the Protection of Cultural Property in the Event of Armed Conflict.	Yes

C-175/2009	Law 1152 of 2007 related to the rural development statute.	No
C-588/2009	Legislative Act No. 01 of 2008 regarding administrative careers.	No
C-249/2012	Legislative Act No. 04 of 2011 regarding administrative careers.	No
C-331/2012	Law 1450 of 2011 regarding the National Development Plan, 2010–2014.	No
C-540/2012 Statutory	Bill No. 263/11 Senate and 195/11 House regarding the legal framework allowing agencies to carry out intelligence and counterintelligence activities.	No
C-644/2012	Law 1450 of 2011 regarding the national development plan's use of vacant lands.	No
C-740/2013	Legislative Act No. 02 of 2012 regulating military criminal jurisdictions.	No
C-824/2013	Law 1474 of 2011 strengthening the mechanisms of prevention, investigation and punishment of acts of corruption and the effectiveness of the control of public management.	No
C-914/2013	Law 1562 of 2012 modifying the System of Occupational Risks.	No
C-784/2014 Statutory	Draft Statutory Law 063 of 2013 Senate, 073 of 2013 Chamber regarding constitutional referendums on the occasion of a final agreement for the termination of the armed conflict.	No
C-793/2014	Law 1523 of 2012 regarding national policy for disaster risk management.	No
C-948/2014	Law 1710 of 2014 honoring the Holy Mother Laura Montoya Upegui, as an illustrious Colombian saint.	No

* *Note*. "Yes" indicates that there was split between judges associated with the Conservative and Liberal Parties on at least one of the paragraphs within a case that had substantial dissent.

Several of the cases with significant disagreement involve the tricky issue of reforming the Constitution. In C588/2009, the Court reviewed Legislative Act 1 of 2008, which sought to create a civil service system but did not require current government officials to take civil service exams to keep their jobs. In this divided case, the CC held that this change constituted a substitution of the Constitution and thus was improper by regular legislative means. The CC stated that the civil service system related to "meritocracy, equality and other fundamental principles in the constitutional order." Thus, exempting preexisting public employees was such a significant departure from the Constitution that it constituted a replacement (see Cepeda Espinosa and Landau 2017: 368).

Additionally, some cases of judicial vetoes with substantial dissent involve balancing concerns of security and individual rights dealing with legacy of civil war. In C540/2012, which involved substantial and complex dissents, the Court reviewed Statutory Bill 263 (2011 in the Senate) and 195 (2011 in the House), which sought to strengthen the country's legal framework, allowing agencies to carry out intelligence and counterintelligence work while safeguarding citizens' rights. The Court found a number of the bills' articles unconstitutional, such as assigning a legislative competency to the executive. Finally, the Court struck down a provision that allowed the judicial police and the prosecutorial authorities to bring evidence to intelligence agencies without constituting a chain of custody violation. The Court struck this down claiming only the prosecutorial authorities could authorize delivering such documents.

Unlike Chile's CT, as shown in Table 8.5, judicial vetoes with substantial dissent rarely pit judges of one party completely against judges associated with another in Colombia. In reviewing the decisions of all judges on each paragraph within these cases, rarely was the majority or dissent coalition made up of judges exclusively associated with one party, although often, it is a single judge of one party who sides with all judges of another. One case in which there was substantial dissent and judges divided between the two main party affiliations was Case C400/2005, which involved the informal revision of Law 899 of July 21, 2004, to approve the Second Protocol of the 1954 Hague Convention for the Protection of Cultural Property. The case reviewed procedural defects on the part of Congress, such as failing to notify the public about the law in violation of the Constitutions' article 160. In this case, judges associated with the Liberal Party (Rentaría, Beltran, Cordoba, Sierra Porto, and Vargas Hernández) found the law was unconstitutional due to the procedural defects, while judges associated with the Conservatives (Cepeda, Escobar Gil, Monroy Cabra, and Tafur) voted to uphold the law. While the substantive effect of passing the law appears apolitical – i.e., to protect cultural property during armed conflict – the fact that a Congress under Uribe passed the law may have led judges associated with the Liberal parties wanting to punish Uribe for procedural defects and an overreach of his executive powers.

8.5 CHAPTER SUMMARY

This chapter diverged from other arguments in the book which spoke to how mixed selection influences judicial vetoes. The prior findings generally supported the idea that the two courts had well entrenched norms of collegiality. This chapter analyzing a small number of cases with substantial dissent does not undermine this conclusion. While the legislative histories and justification for mixed selection have suggested that this method allows different types of judges to populate a court, share diverging opinions, and ideally come up with better decisions, a concern of this method is that it may lead to fragmentation and disagreement. While disagreement in itself is a healthy sign of deliberation and speaks also to these countries' commitment to transparency in decision-making as the decisions are publicly available and easily accessed, too much disagreement could be worrisome if it undermines the decisions themselves, signals a political court, or diminishes a court's stature.

The results from this chapter have shown that at least for now many of these concerns are unwarranted. In Colombia only a small fraction of the cases involves high levels of dissent in either upholding or striking down the law, although some of the areas where they appear are politically salient. In Chile, the dissensus on the Tribunal warrants more concern because the cases with substantial dissent are on the rise and also seem to be highly correlated to a decrease in judicial vetoes. Further, many of the cases involved 5-5 splits among judges giving the president of the Tribunal arguably too much power in settling such disputes. The results, however, show that while significant dissent occurs on only a small proportion of cases heard by both courts when vetoing laws, many of these laws are politically and socially contentious. Weak vetoes on these laws show the limits of the two constitutional courts' ability to effectuate policy in areas about which citizens are concerned.

APPENDIX

Table A8.1 shows how the 2005 constitutional reforms influenced the number of cases finding at least one paragraph unconstitutional (columns 1 and 2), the number of cases in which at least one judge dissented (columns 3 and 4), and the average number of dissenting votes over all decisional paragraphs within a case (columns 5 and 6).

TABLE A8.1. *Influence of constitutional reforms on judicial vetoes and dissent by the Chilean CT*

Variables	(1) Unconst.	(2) Unconst.	(3) At least one dissent	(4) At least one dissent	(5) Average dissent votes	(6) Average dissent votes
Reform	−0.43***	−0.45***	1.02***	1.09***	0.10***	0.10***
	(0.12)	(0.13)	(0.11)	(0.12)	(0.01)	(0.01)
	13%	−13%	37%	39%	10%	10%
Requerimiento		0.96***		0.32		0.07***
		(0.19)		(0.19)		(0.02)
Separation of powers		0.57***		0.24		0.01
		(0.15)		(0.15)		(0.01)
Rights		0.70***		0.59***		0.05***
		(0.15)		(0.15)		(0.01)
Subnational		0.69***		0.29**		0.02
		(0.15)		(0.15)		(0.01)
Constant	−0.49***	−1.07***	−0.86***	−1.17***	0.04***	0.02*
	(0.07)	(0.10)	(0.08)	(0.10)	(0.01)	(0.01)
Observations	567	567	567	567	566	566

Standard errors in parentheses; *** $p < 0.01$, ** $p < 0.05$, * $p < 0.1$.

9

Conclusion

Judicial Selection and Decision-Making

Constitutional courts, as important political actors, issue decisions reflecting how both mundane and politically contentious laws follow or deviate from a country's constitution. Because of their significant role in the political landscape, politicians have sought to empower these courts to protect democratic ideals and processes as seen in the debates surrounding the reforms to the Chilean CT in 2005 and the creation of the Colombian Constitutional Court in 1991. While these and other constitutional courts have grown in stature over time, they may at times pose a threat to politicians who often seek to have their policy objectives enacted with little scrutiny.

As the importance of these courts in politics and society increases, how judges are selected and their characteristics and roles in a constitutional democracy have been rigorously debated within countries. Policymakers have chosen to select judges through some type of mixed selection method on a substantial number of constitutional courts worldwide. Policymakers and scholars have suggested that this method allows courts and judges to safeguard the constitution because decisions are undertaken by judges with diverse constitutional adjudication styles and cross-cutting associations to different branches of government or other institutions. In countries that adopt a mixed selection method in which all three branches select a different number of judges, policymakers are seeking to create an equilibrium within the court that reflects their own country's separation of powers. As with any judicial selection method, mixed selection incentivizes some judges to consider politics in their decisions, which I have argued is appropriate due to the dual legislative and judicial roles of constitutional courts. This concluding chapter reviews the main findings of the book and then discusses the book's broader comparative implications for judicial selection and other institutional rules, judicial decision-making, and the role of courts in policymaking.

9.1 MAIN FINDINGS

This book has provided an explanation for decision-making on mixed selection high courts that has moved away from attitudinalism based on judges' political party preferences toward focusing on how selecting branches under mixed selection correlate with judges' and courts' abstract review decisions. I focus on the mixed selection method because of its prevalence in 52 percent or 68 of 130 constitutional courts reviewed worldwide as of 2022. The book contributes to our understanding of how mixed selection influences courts' role in striking down laws by examining two constitutional courts. The book relied on evidence from legislative histories and interviews of judges and other court personnel in the two countries. The book also relied on analyses of data of judges' and courts' decisions on abstract review cases from important political junctures in these two countries – the constitutional reforms of 2005 in Chile and the drafting of a new constitution in Colombia – until the mid-2010s.

The data analysis was limited to abstract constitutional review of laws passed by the legislators still in power at the time of review. Thus, the analysis did not include important cases concerning the constitutionality of executive decrees or concrete or other review undertaken by these courts. Further, I did not analyze cases in which the courts reviewed laws by legislatures who were out of power at the time of review. These important scope conditions allow me to focus on the mixed selection method when the courts were required to meet *en plena* (subject to quorum rules) and not in smaller configurations and the scope conditions allow me to control for a wide range of confounding factors that covary with these other types of review such as the effect of a decision, the types of parties to a lawsuit, and the law's influence on current and out-of-office politicians.

Even with these strident scope conditions, there was sufficient variation related to the legal and political context of the laws reviewed to analyze important determinants of decision-making on the two mixed selection courts. The results show, indeed, that the type of laws reviewed and the legal and political processes necessary to approve them as well as the manner in which constitutional review is triggered, influence decision-making. For example, one finding related to the CT was that the Tribunal tended to strike down portions of laws that were brought to its attention by minority politicians through the *requerimiento* process more often than laws that required obligatory review. Similarly, the type of law and the manner in which review is triggered influenced the CC, which tended to strike down statutory laws more often as compared to treaties and other types of laws. The subject matter of the law also influenced the propensity of judicial vetoes.

The main focus of the book, however, is on how mixed selection influences decision-making on abstract review cases. The book not only provides results related to the influence of this selection method on the two courts analyzed but also suggests an approach for analyzing other mixed selection courts. While the specific results as to the Chilean CT and the Colombian CC may not be generalizable to other mixed selection courts with different institutional selectors to compare to one another internally, the way I analyzed the influence of mixed selection on decision-making of judges and courts could easily be applied to analyze other mixed selection courts.

The empirical results for the two courts supported the general theory that judges selected by different branches of government represent different constitutional adjudicator types. Branches choose particular judges for their constitutional adjudicator profile and type and judges live up to these expectations in order to enhance their reputations, which are important assets for judges on these courts who have relatively short terms. While the judges' branch selector is an important characteristic that directly correlates with their own voting, they strategically may agree with other judges with different selector types when the presence of those judges increases on the court. Shifting compositions of judges with different characteristics (which is plausibly random) arise due to quorum rules and periodic replenishment of a portion of the court after a certain amount of time. As the presence of judges of one type increases on the court, this causes judges of other types to agree with them in order to gain some strategic advantage of their vote such as being able to influence the majority opinion or increase the strength of the court's decision and ultimately its stature. The results in Chapter 6 reinforced the theory that an increase in the presence of certain judges with certain selectors influences other types of judges' decisions on average. The analysis of individual vote data confirmed that judges' branch selector origins are significantly more important than their party associations.

Chapter 7, focusing on case-level data, confirmed that the collegial mechanism described above had substantive impact on case decisions. Courts' propensities to strike down laws fluctuated with the proportion of judges on any case defined by their selecting institution and depended on whether there was a critical mass of certain judge types on any given case. In Chile, the Tribunal was more likely to veto laws when the number of judges selected by the elected branches – the executive and legislature increased. In Colombia, the Court was less likely to strike down laws when the number of presidential and Supreme Court nominees increased. The case-level results show that changes in judge types on any case matter, and the individual results showed the mechanism for the court decision by which individual judges' characteristics influenced their votes directly and also indirectly through presence or panel effects. The different influence of presidential nominees or appointees on the two courts was due to the fact that the two courts had different selecting institutions that were not comparable across courts and also perhaps due to the temporal coverage of data in Colombia of which the CC reviewed a substantial number of laws enacted under the increasingly authoritarian presidencies of Uribe.

The results suggest that contextual or presence effects matter but were unable to completely explain why judges of one type agree with judges of another type – was it due simply to the actual presence of judge types populating the court or did the judges actually change their vote due to the votes of others or due to deliberation? As

Fischman (2015) suggests, these different reasons are important for understanding decision-making, but social scientists tend only to model decision-making on characteristics and not votes. Without being present in every single case to hear deliberation or witness the court's dynamics, which change by court composition on each case, these questions do remain unanswered. However, my own interviews with judges in the two countries in 2016 left me with the perception that judges on both courts deliberate about legal issues quite a bit or know the positions of other judges beforehand so they can in turn make strategic use of their own vote. According to information from interviews, the deliberation on the Colombian CC is lengthier than that of the Chilean Tribunal, which may help explain why the CC issues more cases with less dissent than the CT.

The empirical results in Chapters 6 and 7 reveal average treatment effects and are not used to explain anomalies or infrequent types of decisions. As a result, Chapter 8 focused on determining trends in dissent over time and then on cases with substantial dissent, in which all judges are pivotal judges on a substantial proportion of decisional paragraphs within a case. This approach was used to explore two important facets of constitutional court decisions – the direction of the outcome and the quality of the decision. I argued that cases with substantial dissent are weaker decisions, as the policy outcome they support could easily be overridden or changed in a similar case with a different court composition. Additionally, the public and other politicians may not respect or follow such decisions as much as those that are decided unanimously or with little dissent. If a court issues a significant amount of weak judicial vetoes over time or judges' votes seem to be based on their own political party preferences, then a court may in time lose its stature.

The chapter should have allayed concerns that the Chilean CT and Colombian CC are issuing an inordinate number of weak vetoes or weak cases that uphold the legislatures' preferences. At least for abstract review cases with my scope conditions and in the timeframe reviewed, the CC had very few cases with significant dissent compared to the large number of cases it hears. The trends in Chile's cases with substantial dissent (which were only analyzed through 2016) are more worrisome as the percentage of these cases has increased over time and a few of these deeply divided cases also seem to reflect divisions in judges' votes based on their political associations. This situation is exacerbated due to the Chilean CT's particular institutional rules that allow for an *even* number of judges to decide cases when all ten members meet and on the smaller quorum option allowing for eight members *coupled with* a rule that allows the president of the Tribunal to decide the outcome of even splits of votes. These cases with substantial dissent provide the president of the Tribunal with an inordinate amount of power that was probably not intended by constitutional designers and should be taken up in any future constitutional reforms in Chile.

The cases with deep divides also represent many of the issues that have divided society over time and continue to do so. While deeply divided cases provide a metric for gauging divisions within society, they also help measure the strength of court decisions over time and in so doing help to determine whether the court itself effectively checks elected actors on highly divisive political and societal issues. One concern about mixed selection is that it may fragment decision-making (Ginsburg 2003; Sadurski 2008) and thus weaken the power of courts' decisions. In the case of the Chilean CT, the rise of deeply divided cases should be watched carefully over time as it may influence the effectiveness of the Tribunal's cases and eventually its stature, but this is only if the number of these types of cases begins to constitute a major part of the Tribunal's caseload and if the divisions are based on partisanship of the judges themselves.

9.2 GENERALIZABILITY AND BROADER IMPLICATIONS

As indicated in the earlier chapters, the focus on the two constitutional courts allowed me to control for a myriad of factors allowing for more precise empirical results. However, this means that the specific results for each court cannot be generalized to other courts.[1] The study has shown that the connection between judges' selecting branch and voting record have been previously overlooked in the study of judicial politics. Further, how much judges' party associations on mixed selection courts influence their voting will depend on a court's own government make-up and party orientation as well as whether the selecting branches or institution themselves represent a majority or supermajority of members associated with one party and seek judges who are party loyalists (see Garoupa et al. 2021c). In other words, party associations of judges on some mixed selection courts may play a more prominent role.

The results from this two-court study have broader implications for judicial selection, decision making, and policymaking beyond the empirical results. Ultimately, the judges who are chosen to serve on a court determine the role that high courts have in policymaking, subject of course to other constraints discussed in this book. Policymakers must therefore carefully determine what role they envision for a constitutional court in their country's governance and how to best achieve it through judicial selection and other rules that inform how the court makes decisions. Here, I take up the broader interconnections between judicial selection, decision-making, and constitutional courts' role in policymaking.

9.2.1 *Judicial Selection: Direct Control*

Judicial selection is political and has significant implications for policymaking. Politicians attempt to control judicial outcomes through selection processes.

[1] Garoupa et al. (2021b) confirmed for the Spanish Constitutional Court my general findings regarding the influence of mixed selection on individual judges' votes here and in Tiede (2020), but acknowledged that "the patterns are complex" (p. 27).

Judicial selection also involves both a delegation and a countermajoritarian dilemma. As to a delegation dilemma, by empowering constitutional courts, elected officials delegate powers to nonelected officials and provide them with resources to effectuate policy. However, once power has been delegated, judges, especially those within independent courts, may use their powers and resources against those that selected them (see Kiewet and McCubbins 1991). Further, while lip service may be paid to judicial independence, policymakers may rue an overtly independent court especially when it can stymie their policy objectives. As a result, judicial selection and policymakers' conception of the role of constitutional courts are intertwined. Policymakers, in selecting judges that are good constitutional adjudicators, must weigh the value of an independent court against one that simply follows the will of elected officials.

Selection by the elected branches of the entire court, either unilaterally or in concert, may allow policymakers to overcome the delegation dilemma especially if judges are carefully screened beforehand (see Kiewet and McCubbins 1991; Brinks and Blass 2017, 2018). Such selection methods may create direct lines of loyalty between the appointer and the judge, and, as stated above, this could also possibly occur with mixed selection courts if one party or the president dominates the other selection branches (see Epstein and Posner 2016; Garoupa et al. 2021b, 2021c). For example, attitudinal voting on the US Supreme Court suggests that presidential nomination and senate confirmation have resulted in judges who generally vote the party line, at least on highly salient cases.

There is good reason, however, to believe that when the method of judicial selection itself allows more diverse actors to select judges, this may loosen the hold of the legislature and executive on selection (Driscoll and Nelson 2015). The mixed selection system may in certain circumstances also assuage the need for judges to appear loyal to a particular party or branch even when judges do not have life tenure. This appears to be the case on the Chilean CT and the Colombian CC.

If policymakers have specific goals for the role of constitutional courts within politics and society, then mixed selection may provide a means for selecting judges who are more concerned about living up to their constitutional adjudication style rather than showing overt loyalty to a party or particular president. If policymakers are specifically concerned with creating an equilibrium on the court, allowing diversity of views and allowing the court to play an active legislative and judicial role, then the mixed selection method may allow the court to operate in a less partisan manner or one driven by individual judges' loyalty concerns. In other words, while prior scholars have mentioned that more players involved in selection of all judges to a court, as in the case of presidential appointment and senate confirmation (allowing for two veto players), may allow for more moderate judges, a better method is to allow judges to have separate nominating origins, who work within a collegial setting in which judges of any one origin *cannot* hold a majority of seats on the court. Further, for policymakers who are interested in diversity of views on the court allowing for better deliberation and ultimately decisions based on considered viewpoints of those who were historically marginalized, mixed selection could be designed to allow nontraditional actors, such as human rights groups or academics, to choose a certain portion of judges.

9.2.2 *Other Judicial and Legislative Institutions: Indirect Control*

While this book has made a case in support of mixed selection, the ability of courts with this selection method to check political actors depends on other specific rules or institutions. For example, quorum rules allow for court compositions to vary by case, which has been noted by some scholars, but not generally tested empirically. As shown by the results in this book, court composition fluctuations due to quorum rules allow for judges selected by certain actors to hold more seats on certain cases and influence the courts' propensities to veto laws. Chilean policymakers designed the CT to be filled with judges of whom 70 percent were selected by elected actors and 30 percent by nonelected actors, and the Colombian CC sought a court in which 2/3 of the judges were chosen by nonelected actors and one-third by elected actors, all purportedly to provide an equilibrium of different interests on these courts. However, quorum rules in both countries allow the court compositions to deviate from these intentions when the full court is required to decide a certain case and as such may provide certain judges more influence on a case than intended by policymakers.

Constitutional designers should carefully weigh the practical benefits of quorum requirements with their influence on decision-making. While they do allow for some judges to have more influence on cases, if the fluctuations in composition are indeed random, for which I have argued and provided some evidence in support, then this may enhance both the internal independence of judges on a case and the external independence of courts in relation to the other branches. Such rules ensure that judges must regularly readjust their calculations regarding the influence of their vote in court compositions that are periodically shifting. Additionally, allowing for an even number of judges on a case due to the court size (i.e., Chile has ten judges) or smaller quorums (the CC and the CT allow smaller quorums of eight judges to make decisions) also may influence decision-making, especially when additional rules allow the chief justice to break the tie, allowed in Chile, but not Colombia. Institutional designers should be wary of allowing chief justices with such extensive powers especially if divided decisions become more prevalent on a court.

Finally, constitutional designers who are interested in the role of courts in checking the powers of the elected branches and effectuating policy may want to reconsider supermajority legislative voting rules for some kinds of legislation, such as constitutional amendments or organic laws as in Chile. While such supermajority legislative rules may ensure that minority interests can influence policy and that policy itself reflects legislative compromises, such rules greatly constrain the power of constitutional courts as it may be very difficult for a diverse court to have a position outside that of a supermajority of legislators. Other countries may want to carefully consider whether strident supermajority voting rules weaken the policymaking role of courts as shown by the Chilean CT's lower rate of judicial vetoes on organic laws and precepts required to be passed by 3/5 or 4/7 of legislators. If countries are serious about the role of constitutional courts to check the powers of other actors, then they should eliminate these strident supermajority legislative voting rules for most types of legislation.

Policymakers also may have other roles in mind for constitutional courts besides checking powerful actors. For example, one of the reasons Colombia's Constituent Assembly decided to create the CC was in part to uphold rights that were newly expanded and enshrined in the country's new constitution. Mixed selection may enhance such a goal as it limits partisan voting on important individual rights cases as seen on the US Supreme Court. Certain variations of mixed selection also allow selection of judges to constitutional courts by human rights organizations.

9.2.3 *Future Research*

This study has focused on mixed selection as an important theoretic area of interest. However, additional analysis of mixed selection courts is needed using my methodology, which focuses on data analysis at the judge and case level, review of legislative histories, and interviews with judges to determine how this selection method operates in practice in its many variations worldwide. For each mixed selection system analyzed, scholars should inquire about the intent in adopting this selection method. Do policymakers intend to use this selection method to achieve more deliberation, more diversity, and better policymaking by constitutional courts or in some instances are policymakers paying lip service to such goals and manipulating mixed selection to achieve their own goals? Scholars studying mixed selection need to study more closely how the goals of courts and politicians in effectuating policy evolve over time and how mixed selection helps or hinders these developments. More theorizing is required about how variations in mixed selection influence decisions and policymaking.

While I have focused only on abstract constitutional review when the full court is required to meet, additional areas of inquiry are needed to determine the influence of mixed selection on other types of cases, such as those involving concrete review or *tutelas* or *amparos*, which make up a large portion of many constitutional courts' dockets. Many of these different types of review require that only a portion (i.e., half or a third) of the court meets on any particular case. How these panels are chosen and how judges' selecting institution influences decision-making directly and through the presence of other judges with different selectors may be greatly constrained by the dynamics of panel size and whether panels are fixed or fluctuate by case as well as whether such fluctuations are random or based on practical concerns or judges' areas of expertise.

This study has highlighted mixed selection on two high courts to determine how it works in practice. However, we still do not know the normative value of this method compared to other methods of selection and in conjunction with other institutional rules on judicial decision-making or even other types of judicial outcomes such as independence, accountability, and trust. Comparative research is sorely needed to examine the benefits of mixed selection against all other methods on either case outcomes or some other variable of interest. While much additional comparative work is needed to understand the influence of judicial selection and other rules, the advent of more publicly available data and increasingly sophisticated methods for studying such data make this a rewarding area of inquiry.

Appendices

APPENDIX A1 COMPARATIVE OVERVIEW OF CONSTITUTIONAL COURTS WITH MIXED SELECTION

TABLE A.1. *Comparative overview of constitutional courts with mixed selection*[1]

Country Constitution (date last revised) Name of Court	Mixed selection configuration (tenure length, court renewal)
Albania 1998 (rev. 2016) Constitutional Court	9 judges as follows: 3 by the president 3 by the Assembly by 3/5 majority 3 by the High Court (9-year nonrenewable term; 1/3 of Court renewed every 3 years)
Algeria 1989 (reinst. 1996, rev. 2008, 2016)[2] Constitutional Council	12 judges as follows: 4 appointed by the president 2 elected by the president of the People's National Assembly*

(continued)

[1] The sources for the table appear at the end. The left column of the table provides information from the Constitute Project as of February 2022 as to the reviewed constitution including the year of the constitution, its last revision (i.e., rev.) or whether it was reinstated from a prior period (i.e., reinst.). Footnotes appearing in this column describe mixed selection configurations that existed prior to those described in the second column.

[2] Changes in 2008 included the mixed selection of nine judges as follows: three by the president, two by the People's National Assembly, two by the Council of the Nation, two by the Supreme Court, and two by the Council of State.

TABLE A.1 (*continued*)

Country Constitution (date last revised) Name of Court	Mixed selection configuration (tenure length, court renewal)
	2 by the president of the Council of the Nation* 2 by the Supreme Court 2 by Council of State (*These appointers do not have parliamentary capacity nor political party membership) (6-year term; ½ of membership renewed every 4 years)
Andorra 1993 Tribunal Constitucional	4 judges as follows: 2 by the Co-princes (1 each) 2 by the General Council (8-year term, renewable up to 2 times)
Angola 2010 Constitutional Court	11 judges as follows: 4 by the president 4 by the National Assembly by 2/3 majority 2 by the Supreme Judicial Council 1 by competitive submission of curricula under law (7-year term, nonrenewable)
Armenia 1995 (rev. 2005, 2011, 2015)[3] Constitutional Court	9 judges as follows: 3 nominated by president 3 nominated by the government 3 nominated by the General Assembly of Judges (only may nominate judges) All nominations must be approved by the 3/5 of the National Assembly (12-year term (single), judges must retire by age 70)
Austria 1920 (reinst. 1945, rev. 2013) Constitutional Court	14 judges as follows: 8 proposed by federal government, appointed by the president 6 proposed by National Council (of which 3 from outside Vienna), appointed by the president (life tenure)
Belarus 1994 (rev. 2004) Constitutional Court	12 judges as follows: 6 by the president 6 by the Council of the Republic (11-year term, judges must retire by age 70)

3 Prior changes in 2011 included mixed selection of nine judges as follows: four by the president, five by the National Assembly by recommendation of the president with terms until age sixty-five.

Country Constitution (date last revised) Name of Court	Mixed selection configuration (tenure length, court renewal)
Belgium 1831 (rev. 2014) Constitutional Court	12 judges as follows: 6 proposed by the first chamber, appointed by the King, confirmed by 2/3 majority of legislature 6 proposed by the second chamber, appointed by King, confirmed 2/3 majority legislature (6 must be Dutch speaking and 6 French speaking) (life tenure)
Benin 1990 Constitutional Court	7 judges as follows: 4 by the president 3 by the Office of the National Assembly (5-year term, renewed once)
Bosnia & Herzegovina 1995 (rev. 2009) Constitutional Court	9 members as follows: 4 by the House of Representatives of the Federation 2 by the Assembly of the Republika Srpska 3 by the president of the European Court of Human Rights under consultation with the presidency (5-year term, nonrenewable, judges must retire by age 70)
Bulgaria 1991 (rev. 2015) Constitutional Court	12 members as follows: 4 by the National Assembly 4 by the president 4 by a joint meeting of the judges of the Supreme Court of Cassation and the Supreme Administrative Court (9-year, nonrenewable term; renew 1/3 of Court every 3 years)
Burkina Faso 1991 (rev. 2012, 2015)[4] Constitutional Council	10 judges as follows: President of court appointed by president of Faso 3 magistrates of exceptional grade appointed by the president of Faso on proposal of the minister of justice 3 three persons of distinction appointed by the president of Faso having at least one jurist

(*continued*)

[4] Prior changes in 2012 included mixed selection of judges as follows: former heads of state (varies); three magistrates proposed by the Ministry of Justice, appointed by the president, three persons of distinction appointed by the president (at least one jurist); three persons of distinction appointed by the president of the National Assembly (at least one jurist); three persons of distinction appointed by the president of the Senate (at least one jurist).

TABLE A.1 (*continued*)

Country Constitution (date last revised) Name of Court	Mixed selection configuration (tenure length, court renewal)
	3 persons of distinction appointed by the president of the National Assembly having at least one jurist (9-year nonrenewable term; renew 1/3 of Court every 3 years)
Cambodia 1993 (2008) Constitutional Council	9 judges as follows: 3 appointed by the king 3 by the National Assembly 3 by the Supreme Council of the Magistracy (9-year term; renew 1/3 of Court every 3 years)
Cameroon 1972 (2008) Constitutional Council	11 judges as follows: 3 by the president of the republic; 3 by the president of the National Assembly after consultation with the Bureau 3 by the president of the Senate after consultation with the Bureau 2 by the Higher Judicial Council Former presidents of the republic shall be ex officio members of the Constitutional Council for life (6-year renewable term)
Cape Verde 1980 (rev. 1992) Supreme Court of Justice (which includes one constitutional chamber)	5 judges at a minimum as follows: 1 by the president from among judicial magistrates or the public prosecutor's office 1 by 2/3 of present members of the National Assembly from among judicial magistrates, public prosecutors, or national jurists 3 by the Superior Council of Magistrates from judicial magistrates (5-year term)
Central African Republic 2016 Constitutional Court	9 members of which at least 4 are women as follows: 2 magistrates including one woman elected by their peers 2 attorneys including one woman elected by their peers 2 members of a law faculty including one woman, elected by their peers 1 member appointed by the president of the republic 1 member appointed by the president of the National Assembly 1 member appointed by the president of the Senate (7 years nonrenewable; all 9 members renewed in full)

Country Constitution (date last revised) Name of Court	Mixed selection configuration (tenure length, court renewal)
Chad 1996 (rev. 2005, 2018)[5] Constitutional Council	43 members (5 chambers one of which is a constitutional chamber) as follows: 1 president of the court by decree of president after opinion of National Assembly 17 chosen from among the high professional magistrates of which 9 chosen by the president of the republic and 8 by the president of the National Assembly 7 from among the specialists of Administrative Law of which 4 chosen by the president of the republic and 3 by the president of the National Assembly 11 from among the specialists of Budgetary Law and of Public Accounting of which (6 chosen by the president of the republic, 5 by the president of the National Assembly) 7 from among the specialists in Constitutional Law of which 4 chosen by the president of the republic and 3 by the president of the National Assembly. (7 years renewable)
Chile 1980 (rev. 2005)[6]	10 judges as follows: 3 by the president 4 by the National Congress (2 by the Senate (2/3 vote) and 2 by the Chamber of Deputies (2/3 vote) for approval or rejection by the Senate) 3 by the Supreme Court (9-year nonrenewable terms, must retire by age 75; partially renew court every 3 years)
Colombia 1991 (rev. 2015) Constitutional Court	9 judges as follows: 3 proposed by president, confirmed by Senate 3 proposed by Supreme Court of Justice, confirmed by Senate 3 proposed by Council of State confirmed by the Senate

(*continued*)

5 Prior changes in 2005 included mixed selection of nine judges as follows: five (two magistrates and three jurists) by the president of the republic, four (one magistrate and three jurists) by the president of the National Assembly for nine-year non-renewable term.

6 Prior changes in 1989 included mixed selection of seven judges as follows: three by Supreme Court, three by the COSENA, one by president, one by Senate.

TABLE A.1 (*continued*)

Country Constitution (date last revised) Name of Court	Mixed selection configuration (tenure length, court renewal)
	For each judgeship, president, Supreme Court of Justice, and the Council of State propose a list of 3 judges from which the Senate chooses 1 (8-year, nonrenewable terms)
Comoros 2001 (rev. 2009) Constitutional Court	8 judges as follows 1 by the president 3 by vice presidents (one each) 1 by the Assembly 3 by the Island executives (6-year renewable term)
Congo, Dem. Rep. of (Kinshasa) 2005 (rev. 2011) Constitutional Court	9 judges as follows: 3 by president 3 proposed by Parliament, approved by president 3 proposed by the Superior Council of the Magistrature, approved by the president (9-year nonrenewable term; renew 1/3 of the Court every 3 years; on renewal 1 judge per group drawn by lots)
Congo, Republic of (Brazzaville)(rev. 2002, 2015)[7] Constitutional Court	9 judges as follows: 3 by the president 2 by the president of the Senate 2 by the National Assembly 2 by the Supreme Court among its members At least 6 members are notables (4-year renewable term)
Côte d'Ivoire (2016) Constitutional Council[8]	8 judges as follows: A president of the council chosen by the president of the republic A former president of the republic unless waiver 6 councillors (3 of whom are appointed by the president of the republic, 2 by the president of the National Assembly, and 1 by the president of the Senate (councillors 6-year nonrenewable term; ½ of Court renewed every 3 years)

7 Prior changes in 2002 included mixed selection of nine judges as follows: three by president, six by National Assembly appointed by president for nine-year renewable 1/3 every three years.

8 The first Constitutional Council had a different mixed selection method.

Country Constitution (date last revised) Name of Court	Mixed selection configuration (tenure length, court renewal)
Cyprus 1960 (rev. 2013) Supreme Constitutional Court	3 judges as follows: 1 Greek appointed jointly by president and vice president 1 Turk appointed jointly by president and vice president 1 neutral judge who shall be president of the court appointed jointly by president and vice president
Djibouti 1992 (rev. 2010) Constitutional Council	6 judges as follows: 2 by the president 2 by the president of the National Assembly 2 by the Superior Council of the Magistrature (8-year term, nonrenewable)
Ecuador[9] 2008 (rev. 2015) Constitutional Court	9 judges chosen by a qualification commission, which itself is comprised of 3 chosen by the executive, 3 by the legislature, 3 by the Citizen Participation branch and confirmed by the Senate (9-year term without immediate reelection; renew 1/3 of Court every 3 years)
Equatorial Guinea 1991 (rev. 2012) Constitutional Tribunal	5 judges as follows: president of the court appointed by the president 2 proposed by the Chamber of Deputies and appointed by the president 2 proposed by the Senate Deputies and the Senate respectively, appointed by the president (7-year term)
Ethiopia 1994 Constitutional Council of Inquiry (which investigates constitutional cases and submits interpretation to House of the Federation, which decides constitutionality)	11 members as follows: The president of the Federation Supreme Court (who is recommended by the prime minister and appointed by the House of people's representatives) The vice president of the Federal Supreme Court (who is recommended by the prime minister and appointed by the House of people's representatives) 6 appointed by the president of the nation on recommendation by the House of people's representatives 3 designated by the House of the Federation among its member

(continued)

9 This is not a clear case of mixed selection as a commission, in which the three branches choose specific members, chooses the judges.

TABLE A.1 (*continued*)

Country Constitution (date last revised) Name of Court	Mixed selection configuration (tenure length, court renewal)
France 1958 (rev. 2008) Constitutional Council	9 judges as follows: 3 by president 3 by the president of National Assembly 3 by Senate (Former presidents of the republic shall be ex officio life members of the Constitutional Council) (9-year nonrenewable term; renew 1/3 of the Court every 3 years)
Gabon 1991 (rev. 2011) Constitutional Court	9 judges as follows: 3 by the president 3 by the president of the Senate 3 by the president of the National Assembly (7-year renewable term; renew 1/3 of the Court every 7 years)
Georgia 1995 (rev. 2013, 2018) Constitutional Court	9 judges as follows: 3 by the president 3 by Parliament by majority of 3/5 of total number of members 3 by the Supreme Court (10-year nonrenewable term)
Germany 1949 (rev. 2014) Constitutional Court	16 judges as follows: 8 by the Bundestag 8 by the Bundesrat (12-year terms, must retire at age 68)
Greece 1975 (rev. 2008) Supreme Special Court	13 judges as follows: president of the Supreme Administrative Court president of the Supreme Civil and Criminal Court president of the Court of Audit 4 councillors of the Supreme Administrative Court and 4 members of the Supreme Civil and Criminal Court chosen by lots for 2 years 2 law professors chosen by lots when Court must resolve a conflict between courts or between courts and administrative authorities or controversies concerning whether a statute enacted by Parliament is contrary to the constitution if there are conflicting judgments about statutes among the other high courts
Guatemala 1985 (rev. 1993) Constitutional Court	For matters of unconstitutionality, 7 judges as follows: 1 by the plenary of the Supreme Court of Justice 1 by the plenary of the Congress 1 by the president of the republic in the Council of Ministers

Country Constitution (date last revised) Name of Court	Mixed selection configuration (tenure length, court renewal)
	1 by the Superior University Council of the University of San Carlos de Guatemala 1 by the Assembly of the College of Attorneys 2 by a drawing of substitutes (5-year renewable term)
Guinea 2010 Constitutional Court	9 judges as follows: 2 notable persons with 1 by the Bureau of the National Assembly and 1 by the president 3 magistrates by their peers 1 lawyer by peers 1 teacher of the Faculty of Law by peers; 2 representatives of the National Institution of Human Rights (9-year nonrenewable term)
Haiti 1987 (rev. 2012) Constitutional Court	9 judges as follows: 3 by the Executive Power 3 by the National Assembly by 2/3 each chamber 3 by the Superior Council of the Judicial Power Additional requirements divided among appointers regarding background and experience (i.e., magistrates, jurists, and notable persons) (9-year nonrenewable term)
Indonesia 1945 (reinst. 1959, rev. 2002) Constitutional Court	9 judges as follows: 3 nominated by Supreme Court, affirmed by the president 3 nominated by the National Assembly, affirmed by the president 3 by the president (Must retire by age 70)
Iran (Islamic Republic of) 1979 (rev. 1989) Guardian Council	12 judges as follows: 6 *adil fuqaha* by the Leader 6 jurists by the Islamic Consultative Assembly from among the Muslim jurists nominated by the Head of the Judicial Power (no term listed, but replenish every 3 years ½ of each appointer type.
Italy 1947 (rev. 2012) Constitutional Court	15 judges as follows: 5 by the president 5 by the Parliament in joint sitting 5 by ordinary and administrative supreme courts (9-year nonrenewable term)
Kazakhstan 1995 (rev. 2011)	7 judges as follows: 3 by president

(*continued*)

TABLE A.1 (*continued*)

Country Constitution (date last revised) Name of Court	Mixed selection configuration (tenure length, court renewal)
Constitutional Council (subsequent amendment not shown here)	2 by Senate 2 by Majilis (6-year terms; ½ of Court renewed every 3 years)
Korea (Republic of) 1948 (rev. 1987) Constitutional Court	9 judges as follows: 3 by the president 3 proposed by the National Assembly, appointed by the president 3 proposed by the Supreme Court chief justice, appointed by the president (head of court until age 70; other judges 6-year renewable terms until age 65)
Latvia 1992 (reinst. 1991, rev. 2016) Constitutional Court	7 judges as follows: 3 proposed by the Saeima, confirmed by majority of Saeima 2 proposed by the Cabinet, confirmed by majority of Saeima 2 proposed by the plenum of the Supreme Court, confirmed by majority of Saeima (10-year term until age 70)
Lebanon 1926 (rev. 2003–2011) Constitutional Council	10 judges as follows: 5 appointed by parliament by absolute majority 5 appointed by council of ministers by 2/3 majority of members of government (6-year nonrenewable)
Lithuania 1992 (rev. 2006, 2019) Constitutional Court	9 judges as follows: 3 proposed by the president and appointed by the Seimas 3 proposed by the president of the Seimis and appointed by the Seimas 3 proposed by the president of the Supreme Court and appointed by the Seimas (9-year nonrenewable term; renew 1/3 of Court every 3 years)
Luxembourg 1868 (rev. 2009) Constitutional Court	9 judges as follows: President of Superior Court of Justice President of the Administrative Court 2 councilors of the Court of Cassation 5 magistrates appointed by the Grand Duke, on advice of Superior Court and the Administrative Court (not removable)

Country Constitution (date last revised) Name of Court	Mixed selection configuration (tenure length, court renewal)
Madagascar 2010 High Constitutional Court	9 judges as follows: 3 by the president 2 by the National Assembly 2 by the Senate 2 by the Supreme Council of the Magistrature (7-year nonrenewable term)
Mali[10] 1992 Constitutional Court	9 judges as follows: 3 by the president (at least 2 jurists) 3 by the president of the National Assembly (at least 2 jurists) 3 magistrates by the High Council of the Judiciary (7-year term, renewable 1 time)
Mauritania 1991 (rev. 2012) Constitutional Council	9 judges as follows: 4 by the president of the republic 3 by the president of the National Assembly 2 by the president of the Senate (9-year nonrenewable term; renew 1/3 of Court every 3 years)
Mauritius 1968 (rev. 2016) Supreme Court[11]	3 or more appointed by president as follows: 1 chief justice in consultation with the Prime minister 1 Senior Puisne judge, with advice of chief justice Other Puisne judges with advice of judicial and legal service commission (Number of judges determined by parliament)
Moldova (Republic of) 1994 (rev. 2006) Constitutional Court	6 judges as follows: 2 by the Parliament 2 by the president 2 by the Superior Council of Magistrates (6-year term)

(*continued*)

10 The chart shows the mixed selection system under Mali's 1992 Constitution. However, in reaction to a political crisis brought on by the Constitutional Court's tossing out of "30 results from long-delayed parliamentary elections – a move that benefitted Keita's party but triggered protests," the president in 2020 chose all nine justices as part of a compromise to allegedly ease tensions. Al Jazeera, "Mali's Keita appoints Constitutional Court Judges to Ease Crisis" (August 8, 2020).

11 The case of the appointment of justices to the Mauritius Supreme Court is not a clear case of mixed selection as the president appoints all judges, but who is consulted varies by type and number of judges.

TABLE A.1 (*continued*)

Country Constitution (date last revised) Name of Court	Mixed selection configuration (tenure length, court renewal)
Mongolia 1992 (rev. 2001) Constitutional Court or Tsets	9 judges as follows: 3 nominated and appointed by the State Great Hural (Parliament) 3 nominated by the president and appointed by the State Great Hural 3 nominated by the Supreme Court and appointed by the State Great Hural (6-year term)
Montenegro 2007 (rev. 2013) Constitutional Court	7 judges as follows: 2 by proposal of president elected by Parliament 5 by working body of Parliament upon announced public invitation elected by Parliament (12-year terms)
Morocco 2011 Constitutional Court	12 judges as follows: 6 by the King (1 proposed by Secretary General of the Superior Council of the Ulema) 6 of which 3 chosen by the Chamber of Representatives and 3 by the Chamber of Councillors from candidates presented by the Bureau of each Chamber (after 2/3 secret vote of each chamber). Alternative provisions if chambers unable to select members (9-year nonrenewable term; Each category renewed by 1/3 every 3 years)
Mozambique 2004 (rev. 2007) Constitutional Council	7 judges as follows: 1 by the president 5 by the Assembly under proportional representation 1 by the Superior Council of the Judiciary (5-year renewable terms) CIA World Fact Book reports nonrenewable
Myanmar 2008 (rev. 2015) Constitutional Tribunal	9 judges as follows: 3 chosen by the president 3 chosen by the Speaker of the Pyithu Hluttaw 3 chosen by the Speaker of the Amyotha Hluttaw (5-year term)
Niger 2010 (rev. 2017) Constitutional Court	7 judges as follows: 2 notable persons, 1 by the president and 1 by the Bureau of the National Assembly 2 magistrates by their peers (1 of first grade, 1 of second grade) 1 lawyer, elected by his peers

Country Constitution (date last revised) Name of Court	Mixed selection configuration (tenure length, court renewal)
	1 professor-researcher (with doctorate in public law), elected by his peers 1 representative of the associations of defense of human rights and promotion of democracy elected by the singular or the plural of these associations (6-year nonrenewable terms; Renew 1/3 of Court every 2 years)
North Macedonia 1991 (rev. 2011) Constitutional Court	9 judges as follows: 6 by the Assembly by a majority vote of the total number of representatives 3 by the Assembly by a majority vote of the total number of representatives within which "there must be a majority of the votes of the total number of representatives belonging to minority communities in Macedonia" (9-year nonrenewable term)
Portugal 1976 (rev. 2005) Constitutional Court	13 judges as follows: 10 by the Assembly 3 by the Constitutional Court (6 of 13 judges chosen from among judges of remaining courts; 7 of 13 from among jurists) (6-year nonrenewable term)
Romania 1991 (rev. 2003) Constitutional Court	9 judges as follows: 3 by the Chamber of Deputies 3 by the Senate 3 by the president (9-year nonrenewable term)
Serbia 2006 Constitutional Court	15 judges as follows: 5 by the National Assembly (from among 10 proposed by president) 5 by the president (from among 10 proposed by the National Assembly) 5 by the general session of the Supreme Court of Cassation (from 10 proposed by general session of the High Judicial Court and the State Prosecutor Council) (Each proposed list of candidates must have 1 from the autonomous provinces) (9-year term; only 2 terms possible)
Spain 1978 (rev. 2011) Constitutional Court	12 judges as follows: Appointed by the king of which 4 nominated by the Congress by a majority of three-fifths of its members

(*continued*)

TABLE A.1 (*continued*)

Country Constitution (date last revised) Name of Court	Mixed selection configuration (tenure length, court renewal)
	4 nominated by the Senate with the same majority 2 nominated by the Government 2 nominated by the General Council of the Judicial Power. (9-year nonrenewable term)
Tanzania 1977 (rev. 2005) Special Constitutional Court	Selection as follows: ½ appointed by the Government of the United Republic ½ appointed by the Revolutionary Government of Zanzibar (Term replacement)
Thailand[12] 2017 Constitutional Court	9 as follows appointed by the king from the following persons: 3 judges in the Supreme Court holding a position not lower than Presiding Justice of the Supreme Court for not less than 3 years elected by a plenary meeting of the Supreme Court 2 judges of the Supreme Administrative Court holding a position not lower than judge of the Supreme Administrative Court for not less than 5 years elected by a plenary meeting of the Supreme Administrative Court 1 qualified person in law obtained by selection from persons holding or having held a position of Professor of a university in Thailand for not less than 5 years, and currently having renowned academic work 1 qualified person in political science or public administration obtained by selection from persons holding or having held a position of professor of a university in Thailand for not less than 5 years, and currently having renowned academic work 2 qualified persons obtained by selection from persons holding or having held a position not lower than Director-General or a position

[12] The case of the appointment of justices to the Constitutional Court of Thailand is not a clear case of mixed selection as the king appoints all judges, but who is consulted varies by type and number of judges. Further, it is not clear that this Court has meaningful constitutional review powers.

Country Constitution (date last revised) Name of Court	Mixed selection configuration (tenure length, court renewal)
	equivalent to a head of government agency, or a position not lower than Deputy Attorney-General, for not less than 5 years
Timor-Leste 2002 Supreme Court	As follows: 1 by national parliament Rest by Superior Council of the Judiciary (itself selected through mixed selection)
Togo 1992 (rev. 2007) Constitutional Court	9 judges as follows: 3 by the president of which 1 chosen on the basis of their juridical competence 3 by the National Assembly by 2/3 of its members (none are deputies and 1 based on juridical competence) 3 by the Senate with the majority of two-thirds (2/3) of its members (none are senators and 1 based on juridical competence) (7-year renewable term)
Tunisia 2014 Constitutional Court	12 judges as follows: 4 by the president 4 by the Assembly of the Representatives of the People 4 by the Supreme Judicial Council ¾ of all judges should be legal specialists (9-year nonrenewable term)
Turkey 1982 (rev. 2011, 2017)[13] Constitutional Court	15 as follows: – The president appoints: 3 from a list of three candidates for each vacant position nominated by the Court of Cassation among its own members

(*continued*)

[13] Prior to 2011 changes included mixed selection of seventeen judges as follows: two proposed by president and Court of Accounts; appointed by the National Assembly; one proposed by heads of bar associations, appointed by the National Assembly; three proposed by High Court of Appeals, appointed by president; two proposed by the Council of State, appointed by the president; one proposed by the High Military Court of Appeals, appointed by president; one proposed by the High Military Administrative Court, appointed by president, three proposed by the Council of Higher Education, appointed by president, four proposed by high level executives, lawyers, judges, appointed by president for twelve year nonrenewable terms with retirement at sixty-five.

TABLE A.1 (*continued*)

Country Constitution (date last revised) Name of Court	Mixed selection configuration (tenure length, court renewal)
	2 members from a list of three candidates for each vacant position nominated by the Turkish Council of State among its own members 3 (at least two of whom being lawyers) members from a list of three candidates for each vacant position nominated by the Higher Education Council among professors of law, economics or political science, who are themselves not members of the Council 4 members among senior administrative officers, attorneys-at-law, judges, prosecutors, and Constitutional Court clerks with at least 5 years of experience – The Grand National Assembly by secret ballot and with two-thirds majority: 2 from a list of three candidates for each vacant position nominated by the Court of Accounts among its own members 1 from a list of three candidates for each vacant position nominated by the heads of bar associations among attorneys-at-law (12 year nonrenewable term)
Ukraine 1996 (rev. 2016) Constitutional Court	18 judges as follows: 6 by the president 6 by the Congress of Judges 6 by the Verkhovna Rada (9-year nonrenewable term)

Sources: There are several sources for this table. One main source is the Constitute Project website. Elkins, Zachary, Tom Ginsburg, and James Melton. 2021. Constitute: The World's Constitutions to Read, Search, and Compare. Online at constituteproject.org. Additional sources reviewed were: the Venice Commission (Council of Europe), which lists website links for constitutional courts at www.venice.coe.int/webforms/courts/; the CIA, World Factbook, which lists the appointment mechanism for all levels of national courts in a given country at www.cia.gov/library/publications/the-world-factbook/fields/2094.html/; Marjan Mavčič (2018); and, court specific websites, such as that for the Constitutional Council of Lebanon. Many of the countries have reformed their selection methods and this table reflects the status of appointment mechanisms as to the dates of the constitutions in the left-hand column, all reviewed by the author as of February 2022. Not included are draft constitutions in which mixed selection was also contemplated, such as a 2018 draft constitution for Chile (see Chapter 4 for a discussion) and the draft constitution of Yemen (2018).

A1.1 *Determination of Percent of Constitutional Courts with Mixed Selection*

Courts reviewed in order to determine the percentage of constitutional courts with mixed selection as of 2021. There were 68 constitutional or supreme courts with mixed selection out of 130 countries reviewed or 52 percent. The 130 courts reviewed are listed below:

Afghanistan 2004
Albania 1998 (rev. 2016)
Algeria 2020
Andorra 1993
Angola 2010
Argentina 1853 (reinst. 83, rev. 1994) (judicial review created by the court itself)
Armenia 1995 (rev. 2015)
Australia 1901 (reinst. 1945, rev. 2013) (judicial review created by the court itself)
Austria 1920 (reinst. 1945, rev. 2013)
Azerbaijan 1995 (rev. 2016)
Bahrain 2002 (rev. 2017)
Bangladesh 1972 (reinst. 1986, rev. 2014)
Belgium 1831 (rev. 2014)
Belarus 1994 (rev. 2004)
Belize 1981 (rev. 2011)
Benin 1990
Bhutan 2008
Bolivia (Plurinational State of) 2009
Bosnia and Herzegovina 1995 (rev. 2009)
Brazil
Bulgaria 1991 (rev. 2015)
Burkina Faso 1991 (rev. 2015)
Burundi 2018
Cambodia 1993 (rev. 2008)
Cameroon 1972 (rev. 2008)
Cape Verde 1980 (rev. 1992)
Central African Republic 2016
Chad 1996 (rev. 2018)
Chile 1980 (rev. 2015)
Colombia 1991 (rev. 2015)
Comoros 2001
Congo (Democratic Republic of the) 2005 (rev. 2011)
Congo (Republic of the) 2015
Costa Rica 1949 (rev. 2020)
Côte d'Ivoire 2016
Croatia 1991 (rev. 2013)

Cyprus 1960 (rev. 2013)
Czech Republic 1993 (rev. 2013)
Djibouti 1992 (rev. 2010)
Dominican Republic 2015
Ecuador 2008 (rev. 2015)
El Salvador 1983 (rev. 2014)
Equatorial Guinea 1991 (rev. 2012)
Estonia 1992 (rev. 2015)
Ethiopia 1994
France 1958 (rev. 2008)
Gabon 1991 (rev. 2011)
Gambia 1996 (rev. 2018)
Georgia 1995 (rev. 2018)
Ghana 1992 (rev. 1996)
Germany 1949 (rev. 2014)
Greece 1975 (rev. 2008)
Guatemala 1985 (rev. 1993)
Guinea 2010
Guinea-Bissau
Haiti 1987 (rev. 2012)
Honduras 1982 (rev. 2013)
Hungary 2011 (rev. 2016)
India 1949 (rev. 2016)
Indonesia 1945 (reinst. 1959, rev. 2002)
Iran (Islamic Republic of) 1979 (rev. 1989)
Iraq 2005
Israel 1950 (rev. 2013) (judicial review created by the court itself)
Italy 1947 (rev. 2012)
Japan 1946
Jordan 1952 (rev. 2016)
Kazakhstan 1995 (rev. 2017)
Kenya 2010
Korea (Republic of) 1948 (rev. 1987)
Kosovo 2008 (rev. 2016)
Latvia 1922 (reinst. 1991, rev. 2016)
Lebanon
Liberia
Liechtenstein 1921 (rev. 2011)
Lithuania 1992 (rev. 2019)
Luxembourg 1868 (rev. 2009)
Madagascar 2010
Malawi 1994 (rev. 2017)

Mali
Malta 1964 (rev. 2016)
Mauritania 1991 (rev. 2012)
Mauritius
Moldova (Republic of) 1994 (rev. 2016)
Mongolia 1992 (rev. 2001)
Montenegro 2007 (rev. 2013)
Morocco 2011
Mozambique 2004 (rev. 2007)
Myanmar 2008 (rev. 2015)
Namibia 1990 (rev. 2014)
Nepal 2015 (rev. 2016)
Nicaragua 1987 (rev. 204)
Niger 2010 (rev. 2017)
North Macedonia (Republic of) 1991 (rev. 2011)
Pakistan 1973 (reinst. 2002, rev. 2018)
Panama 1972 (rev. 2004)
Paraguay 1992 (rev. 2011)
Peru 1993 (rev. 2009)
Poland 1997 (rev. 2009)
Portugal 1976 (rev. 2005)
Romania 1991 (rev. 2003)
Russian Federation 1993 (rev. 2014)
Sao Tome and Principe 1975 (rev. 2003)
Senegal 2001 (rev. 2016)
Serbia 2006
Sierra Leone 1991 (reinst. 1996, rev. 2013)
Slovakia 1992 (rev. 2017)
Slovenia 1991 (rev. 2016)
Somalia 2012
South Africa 1996 (rev. 2012)
Spain 1978 (rev. 2011)
Sudan 2019
Suriname 1987 (rev. 1992)
Syrian Arab Republic 2012
Taiwan (Republic of China) 1947 (rev. 2005)
Tajikistan 1994 (rev. 2016)
Tanzania (United Republic of) 1977 (rev. 2005)
Thailand 2017
Timor-Leste 2002
Togo 1992 (rev. 2007)
Tunisia 2014

Turkey 1982 (rev. 2017)
Uganda 1995 (rev. 2017)
United Kingdom
United States (judicial review created by the court itself)
Ukraine 1996 (rev. 2016)
Uzbekistan 1992 (rev. 2011)
Venezuela (Bolivarian Republic of) 1999 (rev. 2009)
Zambia 1991 (rev. 2016)
Zimbabwe 2013 (rev. 2017)

APPENDIX A2 CHILEAN CONSTITUTIONAL TRIBUNAL JUDGES' BACKGROUNDS AND CODING (2006–2016)

TABLE A.2. *Chilean Constitutional Tribunal judges' backgrounds and coding (2006–2016)*

Minister Name	Appointing institution	Political associations and prior careers (sources)
Juan Colombo Campbell (1993–2000; 2001–2010)	COSENA	Concertación Evidence: Chosen by President Aylwin of the Concertación to serve on CT from 1993 to 2000. In an interview for the Colegio de Abogados, Colombo emphasized that he supported Aylwin. His career prior to work on the Tribunal included work as a professor, dean, and attorney. Sources: (1) Resume, (2) Entrevista, Alvarado, (3) University of Chile summary of achievements, (4) Mercurio online 2001
José Luis Cea Egaña (2002–2010)	COSENA	No association with political parties Evidence: Career in academia as dean of Academia de Ciencias Policiales de Carabineros. Cea was an abogado integrante for the court of appeals of Santiago. He has no political party affiliations mentioned in news or other sources. Sources: (1) Resume, (2) Interview
Jorge Correa Sutil (2006–2009)	President Lagos	Concertación Evidence: Chosen by President Lagos of the Concertación to serve on the CT; also served as Subsecretary of Interior under Ricardo Lagos. Listed as member of DC (Christian Democrats), a party of the Concertación. Prior career as professor and attorney. Sources: (1) Resume, (2) Cooperativa.cl

Minister Name	Appointing institution	Political associations and prior careers (sources)
Raúl Bertelsen Repetto (2006–2015)	Senate	Right Evidence: Bertelson and Vodanovic were both chosen by the Senate at the same time. Their nominations were part of a "horse trading" deal in which the two main coalitions (the Concertación and Center Right) were able to each choose a candidate. The Right chose Bertelsen, while the Center Left chose Vodanovic. Bertelsen previously served as a member of the Ortúzar Commission, which helped to draft the 1980 Constitution under the military junta. He is reported as having affinity toward one of the Alianza's parties (UDI). Bertelson served as an abogado integrante for the CT prior to becoming a judge. Sources: (1–2) El Mercurio (2005, 2014)
Hernán Vodanovic Schnake (2006–2015)	Senate	Concertación Evidence: Vodanovic and Bertelsen were both chosen by the Senate at the same time. Their nominations were part of a "horse trading" deal in which the two main coalitions (the Right and Center Left) were able to each choose a candidate. Vodanovic served in several government positions under Concertación presidents Allende and Frei. Sources: (1) Resume, (2–3) El Mercurio (2005, 2014)
Mario Fernández Baeza (2006–2011)	Camera/ Senate	Concertación Evidence: Prior to work on the CT, served as a senator for PPD/PS, parties of the Concertación. He served as Under-secretary of Aviation and War under Concertación. presidents Aylwin and Frei. Appointed as minister of National Defense and later General Secretariat of the presidency and German Ambassador under President Lagos of the Concertación. His resume mentions prior positions as an attorney and academic. (Post bench evidence: Fernández Baeza served as Minister of the Interior and Public Security in Michele Bachelet's second term). Sources: (1) Resume, (2) Vargas (2016), (3) Que Pasa (2018)
Marcelo Venegas Palacios (2006–2013)	Camera/ Senate	Right Evidence: Venegas was an assessor to various RN (party of the Alianza) politicians. Beginning in 1990s, he was chief of cabinet for senator Sergio Onofre Jarpa and is

(*continued*)

TABLE A.2 (*continued*)

Minister Name	Appointing institution	Political associations and prior careers (sources)
		known to be close with the president of the RN Carlos Larraín and Senator Sergio Romero. During the military dictatorship, he was Minister for the Instituto de Desarrollo Agropecuario and for the Dirección Nacional de Comunicación Social. He also controlled communications for the CT under the dictatorship. Sources: (1) Resume, (2) El Mercurio (2009)
Marisol Peña Torres (2006–2009, 2009–2018)	Supreme Court	No association with political parties Evidence: This judge has no political party affiliations mentioned in news or other sources. She has stated in a news article that she had no affiliation with any political parties (El Mostrador 2018). Prior to serving on the bench, Peña had an extensive academic career. She was also legal counsel for the division of municipalities of the Comptroller General's office and legal advisor of the General Secretariat of the Government. Sources: (1) Resume, (2) El Mercurio Legal, (3) Interview, (4) El Mostrador (2018)
Enrique Navarro Beltrán (2006–2012)	Supreme Court	No association with political parties Evidence: This judge has no political party affiliations mentioned in news or other sources. Prior position as director of studies of the Supreme Court (2002–2006), professor, and attorney. Sources: (1) Resume, (2) El Mercurio (2006), (3) Carvajal (2012)
Francisco Fernández Fredes (2006–2015)	Supreme Court	Concertación Evidence: Member of the Socialist Party committee. Member of Socialist Salvador Allende's government prior to the military coup. Positions in several Concertación governments as follows: Director of the Service of National Consumers (SERNAC) (1993–1998). National Economic Prosecutor (2000–2001), Commission of Citizen Defense and Transparency of the Secretariat of the Government (2001–2005) Sources: (1) Resume, (2) El Mercurio (2006), (2) El Librero (2015)
Carlos Carmona Santander (2009–2018)	President Bachelet	Concertación Evidence: Chosen by President Michele Bachelet, socialist and member of Concertación. Carmona held

Minister Name	Appointing institution	Political associations and prior careers (sources)
		numerous positions as an academic and in Concertación governments including Fundación Frei (1986–1987); Secretary for Frei (1988–1989), asessor executive (1990–1991), chief division of executive (1994–1995), Subsecretary (1999–2000). Sources: (1) Resume, (2) El Mostrador, (3) Izuierdo Diario
José Antonio Viera Gallo Quesnay (2010–2013)	President Bachelet	Concertación Evidence: Chosen by President Michele Bachelet, socialist, and member of Concertación. Viera previously served as a member of Congress representing the Socialist Party during the Allende government. Viera led the Socialist party in exile in Italy during the dictatorship. He represented the Socialist Party as a congressman (1990–1994) and Senator (1998–2006). Viera served as president of the Chamber of Deputies from 1990 to 1993. He served as minister of secretary general under President Bachelet. Sources: (1) Resume, (2) Biography in Biblioteca del Congreso Nacional
Iván Aróstica Maldonado (2010–2013, 2013–2022)	President Piñera	Right Evidence: Chosen by President Sebastián Piñera of the RN, a party of the Alianza. Worked as fiscal and director of the Caja de Previsión de la Defensa Nacional (from 1984 (under dictatorship) to 1995). Served as chief of juridical division of the Ministry of Interior from 2010 to 2013 under the presidency of Piñera. Prior to the CT, he also was a professor and attorney. Sources: (1) Resume, (2) Izquierda diario (2017)
Domingo Hernández Emparanza (2012–2020)	Supreme Court	No association with political parties Evidence: This judge has no political party affiliations mentioned in news or other sources. Served as attorney for Subsecretary of Health and National Fund of Health and other public administrations; Abogado integrante for Corte Apelaciones of Santiago (1998–2005); Abogado integrante for Supreme Court (2006–2012); supplemental judge of Electoral Tribunal for the region of Santiago. Prior work as professor and dean. Sources: (1) Resume, (2) El Mercurio (2012)

(*continued*)

TABLE A.2 (*continued*)

Minister Name	Appointing institution	Political associations and prior careers (sources)
Gonzalo García Pino (2013–2022)	Camara/ Senate	Concertación Evidence: García Pino held several prestigious positions prior to the CT in successive Concertación governments including: Asesor Jurídico de la División Judicial del Ministerio de Justicia (1991); División de Cultura del Ministerio de Educación (1992); Subsecretaría del Interior (2000–2001); Jefe del Comité Asesor del Ministro de Defensa Nacional (1994–1997); Jefe de la División de Seguridad Ciudadana del Ministerio del Interior (2000–2004); Asesor del Ministro del Interior (2004–2005); Subsecretario de Marina (2005–2006); Subsecretario de Guerra (2006–2010). Prior to the CT, García Pino also worked as a professor and an attorney. Sources: (1) Resume, (2) Carvajal (2012)
Juan José Romero Guzmán (2013–2022)	Camera/ Senate	Right Evidence: Romero served as integrante en Consejo de Concesiones de Obras Publicas under Sebastián Piñera (2010–2013) and was a judge in the Tribunal de Defensa de la Libre Competencia (2008–2013). Prior to being chosen to the CT, he also was a professor and attorney. Source: (1) Resume, (2) Carvajal (2012)
María Luisa Brahm Barril (2013–2022)	President Piñera	Right Evidence: Brahm was chosen by President Sebastián Piñera of the RN, a party of the Alianza. Prior to serving on the CT, she held some positions under the dictatorship such as Fiscalía Oficina de Planificación Nacional (ODEPLAN) (1983–1985) and other positions for ODEPLAN. She served under Piñera's government as Chief of Asesores del Presidente and Integrante del Consejo Directivo de Auditoría Interna General de Gobierno. Prior to the CT, she worked for the Instituto Libertad. Sources: (1) Resume, (2) El Mostrador (2013)
Cristián Letelier Aguilar (2015–)	Senate	Right Evidence: Letelier's nomination was seen as part of a "horse trade" in the Senate in which parties of the Right chose Letelier and those of the Concertación chose Pozo. Letelier served as a Congressman for the UDI (a party of the Alianza or Right (2011–2014)). Prior

Minister Name	Appointing institution	Political associations and prior careers (sources)
		to service on the CT, he also worked as a professor, attorney and asesor jurídico de la Sociedad Nacional de Minería. Sources: (1) Carvajal (2015), (2) Contreras (2015), (3) Salinas (2015)
Nelson Pozo Silva (2015–)	Senate	Concertación Evidence: Pozo's nomination was seen as part of a "horse trade" in the Senate in which parties of the Concertación chose Pozo and those of the Right chose Letelier. News articles at the time of the appointment characterized Pozo as a "militant" of the PS or Socialist Party (party of the Concertación). Prior to the CT, he was a professor and abogado integrante of the Court of Appeals of Santiago (2004–2008) and abogado integrante de la Corte Suprema (2009–2012). He was known as a member of the PS (party of the Concertación). Sources: (1) Carvajal (2015), (2) Contreras (2015), (3) Salinas (2015)
José Vásquez Márquez (2015–)	Supreme Court	No association with political parties Evidence: Vásquez is known as independent having no affiliations with the two main coalitions. Prior to service on the CT he was a judge and president of the Tribunal Ambiental of Santiago. He was director of studies analyzing the Supreme Court from 2006 to 2014. Prior to the CT, he served as attorney, arbiter and professor. This judge has no political party affiliations mentioned in news or other sources. Sources: (1) Resume, (2) El Libero (2015)

Notes. The analysis considers only judges serving on the CT after the constitutional reforms which went into effect in 2006. Prior to constitutional reforms, the Consejo de Seguridad Nacional (COSENA) (a nonelected agency created under Chile's 1980 Constitution composed of the president of the republic, the president of the Supreme Court, presidents of the Senate and Chamber of Deputies, heads of the armed forces and the Controller General) selected two judges. Prior to the reforms, the COSENA chose Ministers Cea and Colombo, who served on the Tribunal until 2010. Colombo had been an abogado integrante previously appointed by President Aylwin from 1993 to 2000.

The coded party associations were confirmed by at least two sources (listed below) based on judges' party affiliation, work with a government of a particular party or staff of a legislator, or service as a legislator. The party of the selecting president was also imputed to the judge in certain cases. Coding judges' political associations was not based on how judges voted on particular cases on the CT such as abortion or other highly contested issues. Pardow and Verdugo (2015) adopted similar coding based on their own research and assessment for the following judges: Cea, Correa Sutil, Bertelsen, Vodanovic, Fernández Baeza, Venegas, Peña, Navarro, Fredes, Fernández Baeza. When an author interview was mentioned this was an interview of the judge in question or someone who discussed the judge. Interviews took place in Santiago in January 2016. Other sources for this analysis included resumes from the Chilean Constitutional Tribunal website and news analyses, articles and commentary at the time of selection, elevation, death, or change of judges' job or composition of the court. Sources for judges' careers are predominantly from their resumes.

Sources for Table A.2:

Alvarado, Jorge Núñez Alvarado. Entrevista a Juan Colombo Campbell, ex presidente del Tribunal Constitucional: Apuntes de un cíclope.

Carvajal, Cinthya. Cristián Letelier y Nelson Pozo, Nuevos Ministros del Tribunal Constitucional, El Mercurio, January 8, 2015, p. A1.

El derecho tiene que avanzar a la realidad y buscar soluciones razonables El Mercurio (May 5, 2012) [Navarro].

Gonzalo García y Juan José Romero ratificados para el Tribunal Constitucional (July 3, 2013).

Contreras, Pablo. 2015. "Designación de dos nuevos ministros del TC: la cocina constitucional.

Colegio de abogado archivo.

https://archivo.colegioabogados.cl/cgi-bin/procesa.pl?plantilla=/v2/cont_actividades_listado.html&idcat=668&titulo_categoria_listado=&nseccion=actividades%2520y%2520noticias%2520%253A%2520%2520%253A%2520Entrevista%2520a%2520Juan%2520Colombo%2520Campbell%252C%2520ex%2520presidente%2520del%2520Tribunal%2520Constitucional%253A%2520Apuntes%2520de%2520un%2520c%25EDclope

Cooperative.cl. Aborto: Correa Sutil defendió al ministro Santelices ante diputados (Martes, 12 de Junio de 2018) [Colombo].

El Librero. El perfil de los seis candidatos que se disputan el cupo de ministro del Tribunal Constitucional (August 27, 2015) [Fredes, Vásquez Márquez].

La Izquierda Diario. Iván Aróstica, el nuevo presidente del Tribunal Constitucional. El ex funcionario de Sebastián Piñera será ratificado como presidente el próximo 28 de agosto (August 13, 2017) [Aróstica, Carmona].

El Mercurio. Senado aprueba a abogados Bertelsen y Vodanovic para Tribunal Constitucional en votación única, los parlamentarios votaron en forma electrónica por la dupla que logró 34 votos a favor y cuatro en contra de la bancada PRSD (November 8, 2005).

Nominación de Corte Suprema: Ex defensor ciudadano va al TC (August 17, 2006) [Fredes].

Senadores ya barajan nombres para suceder a Bertelsen y Vodanovic en el TC (November 23, 2014).

Pleno eligió a dos miembros del Tribunal Constitucional (April 29, 2006) [Navarro].

Corte Suprema eligió a Domingo Hernández como nuevo ministro del Tribunal Constitucional El abogado, quien obtuvo 15 de 21 votos a su favor, reemplazará en el cargo a Enrique Navarro. Lo siguió en la elección Emilio Pfeffer, quien es actualmente abogado integrante de la Corte de Apelaciones de Santiago (May 25, 2012) [Hernández].

El Mercurio.online. Marcelo Venegas fue designado como nuevo presidente del Tribunal Constitucional. Su nombre fue respaldado por todos los miembros de la entidad. Asumirá el cargo el 28 de agosto, en reemplazo de Juan Colombo (August 5, 2009).

El Mercurio Legal. Marisol Peña es elegida como presidenta del Tribunal Constitucional.

El Mercurio online. Juan Colombo nuevo miembro del Tribunal Constitucional. Juan Colombo reemplazará al ministro Mario Verdugo luego que el 28 de noviembre se concretara su alejamiento por haber cumplido 75 años de edad (March 27, 2001).

El Mostrador. María Luisa Brahm acusa "intromisión" y "presión indebida" de El Mercurio en decisiones del TC (September 13, 2013) [Carmona, Brahm].

Marisol Peña: aunque en el TC "la política no debiera reinar, en la práctica sí reina" (June 8, 2018).

Biblioteca del Congreso Nacional. Historia política of parliamentarias. www.bcn.cl/historiapolitica/resenas_parlamentarias/wiki/Jos%C3%A9_Antonio_Viera_Gallo_Quesney

Salinas, Claudio. Senado: Las historias detrás de la sumaria aprobación de dos ministros del TC: Critican acuerdo UDI-PS y acusan a nuevos magistrados de plagio y homofobia. La Segunda online (January 10, 2015) [Letelier, Pozo].

Pardow, Diego and Sergio Verdugo. 2015. "El Tribunal Constitucional chileno y la reforma de 2005. Un Enroque entre Jueces de Carrera y Académicos." *Revista de Derecho* XXVIII (1): 123–144. A 2013 version of the paper in English provides background for these authors' coding choices.

Qué Pasa. Mario Fernández vuelve a clases. El también conocido como "Peta" Fernández volvió a clases. Esto, porque retomó sus actividades académicas como profesor de la Facultad de Derecho de la Universidad de Chile, específicamente en el departamento de Derecho Público (April 13, 2018).

University of Chile announcement. Juan Colombo Campbell Nuevo Profesor Emerito U. de Chile.

Vargas, Felipe. Presidenta Bachelet designa a Mario Fernández como nuevo ministro del Interior y El embajador en Uruguay ocupará el cargo del saliente ministro Jorge Burgos. El mercurio online (June 8, 2016).

APPENDIX A3 COLOMBIAN CONSTITUTIONAL COURT JUDGES' BACKGROUNDS AND CODING (1993–2014)

TABLE A.3. *Colombian Constitutional Court judges' backgrounds and coding*

Magistrate Name	Nominating Institution (Confirming Senate[a])	Political associations coding and prior careers (sources)
Ciro Angarita Barón (1993)	President Gaviria (S1)	Not in analysis. Service prior to 1997.
Eduardo Cifuentes Muñoz (1993–2000)	President Gaviria (S1)	Liberal Evidence: Commentary during appointments and afterward on the ideology of the Court placed this judge as associated with the Liberal Party. Prior to serving on the CC, he worked as an academic and director of investigations for the Bank of Colombia. Sources: (1) Rubiano Galvis (2009), (2) El Tiempo (1992), (3) La SillaVacia (2016), (4) Semana (2015)
José Gregorio Hernández Galindo (1993–2001)	Supreme Court (S1)	Conservative. Evidence: Commentary during appointments and afterward on the ideology of the Court placed this judge as associated with the Conservative Party. Prior to serving on the CC, he was an academic and in the 1980s had government posts as an auxiliary magistrate for the Supreme Court's *sala constitucional* (the predecessor of the CC). Sources: (1) Rubiano Galvis (2009), (2) El Tiempo (1992), (3) La SillaVacia (2016), (4) Elección Visible
Simón Rodríguez (1993)	Consejo de Estado (S1)	Not in analysis. Service prior to 1997.

Magistrate Name	Nominating Institution (Confirming Senate[a])	Political associations coding and prior careers (sources)
Alejandro Martinez Caballero (1993–2001)	President Gaviria (S1)	Liberal Evidence: Commentary during appointments and afterward on the ideology of the Court placed this judge as associated with the Liberal Party. Prior to serving on the CC, he was an attorney and professor. He worked for the Controlería and had been a Deputy for Congress for ANAPO in 1966. He worked as an assessor for la Alianza Democráta M-19 in the Constituent Assembly. Sources: (1) Rubiano Galvis (2009), (2) Semana (2015), (3) La SillaVacia (2016)
Fabio Morón Díaz (1993–2001)	President Gaviria/ SC (S1)	Not in analysis. Service prior to 1997.
Jaime Sanin Greiffenstein (1991–1993)	Supreme Court (S1)	Not in analysis. Service prior to 1997.
Carlos Gaviria Díaz (1993–2001)	Consejo de Estado (S1)	Liberal Evidence: Commentary during appointments and afterward on the ideology of the Court placed this judge as associated with the Liberal Party. Prior to serving on the CC, he was an attorney and professor and served as municipal judge in Rionegro. Gaviria served as senator for the Frente Social y Político a party of the Left. (Post bench evidence: Gaviria ran as a presidential candidate for the Liberal Party against Uribe). Sources: (1) Rubiano Galvis (2009), (2) El Tiempo (1992), (3) La SillaVacia (2016)
Jorge Arango Mejía (1993–1998)	Supreme Court (S1)	Liberal Evidence: Commentary during appointments and afterward on the ideology of the Court placed this judge as associated with the Liberal Party. Prior to serving on the CC, he was a civil judge in la Dorado, a mayor and an ambassador to the Czech Republic. Sources: (1) Rubiano Galvis (2009), (2) El Tiempo (1992), (3) La SillaVacia (2016)

(*continued*)

TABLE A.3 (*continued*)

Magistrate Name	Nominating Institution (Confirming Senate[a])	Political associations coding and prior careers (sources)
Antonio Barrera Carbonell (1993–2001)	Consejo de Estado (S1)	Liberal Evidence: Commentary during appointments and afterward on the ideology of the Court placed this judge as associated with the Liberal Party. Prior to serving on the CC, was an attorney and assessor of the Instituto Colombiano de la Reforma Agraria and a conjuez for the Tribunal Administrativo de Cundiamarca and a conjuez for the Consejo de Estado. Sources: (1) Rubiano Galvis (2009), (2) Resume, (3) El Tiempo, (4) La SillaVacia (2016)
Hernando Herrera Vergara (1993–1999)	President Gaviria (S1)	Liberal Evidence: Commentary during appointments and afterward on the ideology of the Court placed this judge as associated with the Liberal Party. Prior to serving on the CC, he was a magistrate in the Consejo Superior de la Judicatura and a vice minister of communications. Sources: (1) Rubiano Galvis (2009), (2) Resume, (3) El Tiempo (1992), (4) Semana (2015), (5) La SillaVacia (2016)
Vladimiro Naranjo Mesa (1993–2001)	Consejo de Estado (S1)	Conservative Evidence: Commentary during appointments and afterward on the ideology of the Court placed this judge as associated with the Conservative Party. Prior to serving on the CC, he was an academic for various institutions. Assisted in talks with the FARC for the Pastrana government. Sources: (1) Rubiano Galvis (2009), (2) El Tiempo (1992), (3) La SillaVacia (2016)
Alfredo Beltrán Sierra (1998–2006)	Supreme Court (S2)	Liberal Evidence: Considered to have an orientation toward the Liberal Party from various sources. Prior to service on the CC, he was a professor and auxiliary magistrate for the Tribunal Superior de Bogotá. Sources: (1) Rubiano Galvis (2009), (2) Resume

Magistrate Name	Nominating Institution (Confirming Senate[a])	Political associations coding and prior careers (sources)
Jaime Araújo Rentería (2001–2009)	Consejo de Estado (S3)	Liberal Evidence: Commentary noted that he was a member of the Liberal Party. In 1995, he was the choice of the Consejo for the Liberal Party. Prior to service on the CC, he was ambassador for Colombia for the Holy See and magistrate of the Consejo Nacional Electoral. In 1998, he ran as candidate for the Liberal Party. (Additional post bench evidence: In 2009, he ran for candidate from the Liberal Party. In 2018, Araújo was a vice presidential candidate for the Liberal Party). Sources: (1) Rubiano Galvis (2009), (2) La SillaVacia (2016), (3) Lamprea (2009)
Manuel José Cepeda Espinosa (2001–2009)	President Pastrana (S3)	Conservative Evidence: Commentary lists him as a moderate conservative with expertise in constitutional matters. Prior to the CC, he was an assessor for both the Gaviria and Barco administrations (both from the Liberal Party) and Ambassador to UNESCO. He was chosen by President Pastrana of the Conservative Party. Sources: (1) Rubiano Galvis (2009), (2) Resume
Jaime Córdoba Triviño (2001–2009)	Supreme Court (S3)	Liberal Evidence: Commentary places him as a moderate liberal. Prior to service on the CC, he was a professor and attorney. He also was a criminal judge for Bogotá, delegated procurador before the Supreme Court and Defensor del pueblo as well as vice fiscal general of the nation and worked as assessor on some international organizations. Sources: (1) Rubiano Galvis, (2) Resume
Rodrigo Escobar Gil (2001–2009)	Consejo de Estado (S3)	Conservative Evidence: Commentary places him as associated with the Conservative Party. Prior to the CC, he was a professor and attorney. Sources: (1) Rubiano Galvis (2009), (2) La SillaVacia (2012)

(continued)

TABLE A.3 (*continued*)

Magistrate Name	Nominating Institution (Confirming Senate[a])	Political associations coding and prior careers (sources)
Marco Gerardo Monroy Cabra (2001–2009)	President Pastrana (S3)	Conservative Evidence: Commentary places him as associated with the Conservative Party. He was chosen by President Pastrana of the Conservative Party. Prior to the CC, worked in academics and was a civil judge, magistrate of the Superior Tribunal of Bogotá and of the Supreme Court. (Post bench, he was a candidate for position on the International Criminal Court). Sources: (1) Rubiano Galvis (2009), (2) La SillaVacia (2009) (3) Semana (2015)
Luis Eduardo Montealegre Lynett (2001–2004)	Consejo de Estado (S3)	Liberal Evidence: Commentary suggests he was associated with the Liberal Party. He was a criminal judge of Bogotá and vice procurador general of the nation. He was assessor for various governments. (Post bench, he was named fiscal general and a profile of him at that appointment associates him historically with the Liberal Party (see El Espectador 2012). Sources: (1) Rubiano Galvis (2009) (2) El Espectador (2012)
Álvaro Tafur Galvis (1999–2007)	President Pastrana (S3)	Conservative Evidence: Commentary associates him with the Conservative Party. He was nominated by President Pastrana of the Conservative Party. Prior to service on the court, he was a conjuez and magistrate for the Supreme Court, the Consejo de Estado and the Consejo Superior de la Judicature. He also worked as an academic. Sources: (1) Rubiano Galvis (2009), (2) Semana (2015), (3) Elección Visible
Clara Inés Vargas Hernández (2001–2009)	Supreme Court (S3)	Liberal Evidence: Commentary places her as associated with the Liberal Party. Her nomination was supported by the Liberal Party as well. Prior to serving on the CC, she was a civil judge and magistrate of the Superior Tribunal of Bogotá and served as a procuradora delegated by the Supreme Court.

Magistrate Name	Nominating Institution (Confirming Senate[a])	Political associations coding and prior careers (sources)
		Sources: (1) Rubiano Galvis (2009), (2) Lamprea (2009)
Humberto Sierra Porto (2004–2012)	Consejo de Estado (S4)	Liberal Evidence: Commentary associates him with the Liberal Party and his nomination was supported by the Liberal Party and a dissident group from Uribe's coalition. Prior to working on the CC, he was an academic and litigant, assessor of the chamber of deputies and procurador delegado for the Public Function. Sources: (1) Rubiano Galvis (2009), (2) La Silla Vacia (2013), (3) Lewin (2013)
Nilson Elías Pinilla (2006–2014)	Supreme Court (S4)	Conservative Evidence: Commentary suggests he is associated with the Conservative Party and was supported by parties of Uribe's government coalition. Prior to the CC, he was a professor and served as a municipal criminal judge and as a magistrate of the Supreme Court. He also was an assessor of the Bank of the Republic. Sources: (1) Rubiano Galvis (2009), (2) Silla Vacia (2009), (3) La Semana (2015)
Mauricio González Cuervo (2007–2015)	President Uribe (S5)	Conservative Evidence: This judge was considered to be associated with the Conservative Party. Prior to the CC, he had been a professor, vice minister of the interior and vice minister of justice and juridical secretary of the president. Evidence: (1) Rubiano Galvis (2009), (2) La SillaVacia (2009), (3) Semana (2015)
María Victoria Calle Correa (2009–2017)	President Uribe (S5)	Conservative Evidence: This judge is considered associated with the Conservative Party and close to the government at the time of her selection. Prior to work on the CC, she worked as an attorney and was vice counsel of an insurance company and consultant for some municipalities.

(continued)

TABLE A.3 (*continued*)

Magistrate Name	Nominating Institution (Confirming Senate[a])	Political associations coding and prior careers (sources)
		Sources: (1) Rubiano Galvis (2009), (2) La SillaVacia (2009)
Juan Carlos Henao Pérez (2009–2012)	Consejo de Estado (S5)	Liberal Evidence: Commentary suggests that this judge is considered associated with the Liberal Party, which supported his selection to the CC. Prior to work on the CC, he served as an administrative law expert and as a conjuez and auxiliary magistrate for the Consejo de Estado. Sources: (1) Rubiano Galvis (2009), (2) La SillaVacia (2009)
Gabriel E. Mendoza Martelo (2009–2017)	Consejo de Estado (S5)	Conservative Evidence: Commentary suggests that he is considered associated or affiliated with the Conservative Party. His election to the Court was supported by senator Efraín Cepeda who was the president of the Conservative Party. Prior to the CC, he served as a municipal criminal and labor judge and was magistrate for the Administrative Court of the Atlántico and a magistrate for the Consejo de Estado. Sources: (1) Rubiano Galvis (2009), (2–3) La SillaVacia (2009, 2012)
Jorge Iván Palacio (2009–2017)	Supreme Court (S5)	Conservative Evidence: Commentary suggests that he is associated with the Conservative Party. His appointment to the CC was supported by the government coalition. Prior to the CC he was a municipal criminal judge and a magistrate for the Supreme Court as well as a juridic assessor for the Bank of the Republic. Sources: (1) Rubiano Galvis (2009)
Jorge Ignacio Pretelt Chaljub (2009–2017)	President Uribe (S5)	Conservative Evidence: Commentary suggests that he is aligned with the Conservative Party, especially Uribe. His nomination was supported by the president's governing coalition. Prior to the CC, he was a

Magistrate Name	Nominating Institution (Confirming Senate[a])	Political associations coding and prior careers (sources)
		magistrate for the Consejo Nacional Electoral and a conjuez of the Consejo Superior de la Judicatura. He also was a professor. He resigned after a corruption scandal. Sources: (1) Rubiano Galvis (2009), (2) Semana (2015), (3–6) La SillaVacia (2009, 2012, 2017), (7) Lewin (2016), (8) Lewin & Duque (2017)
Luis Ernesto Vargas Silva (2009–2017)	Supreme Court (S5)	Liberal Evidence: Commentary places him aligned more with the Liberal Party than the Conservative Party. Prior to the CC, he was a civil judge and magistrate of the Tribunal Superior de Cundinamarca. Sources: (1) Rubiano Galvis 2009, (2) La SillaVacia (2009)
Luis Guillermo Guerrero Pérez (2012–)	Consejo de Estado (S6)	Conservative Evidence: Commentary places him as a conservative and his selection was supported by the Conservative Party. He defeated another candidate, Carolos Medellín, supported by the Liberal Party. He stated in a news source that he has an affinity toward the ideas of the Conservative Party, but as a constitutional judge he would not represent a political ideology (Silla Vacia 2012). Prior to the CC, he was an asesor jurídico for a university, was secretary general for the Corporación Autónoma para Desarrollo de Nariño, magistrate for the Sala Administrativa for the Consejo Superior de la Judicatura, attorney, and asesor de la Federación Nacional de Cafeteros. Sources: (1) Semana (2015), (2) La SillaVacia (2012, 2017) (3) Lewin (2017)
Alberto Rojas Ríos (2012–)	Consejo de Estado (S6)	Conservative Evidence: Commentary stated although, it was first assumed he was a liberal, as he worked with some judges and other political figures that were aligned with the Liberal Party, he was associated more with the Conservative Party and they supported his

(*continued*)

TABLE A.3 (*continued*)

Magistrate Name	Nominating Institution (Confirming Senate[a])	Political associations coding and prior careers (sources)
		selection to the CC. Prior to the CC, he served as a procurator and vice procurator general, academic and attorney. He also worked as a conjuez for the CC prior to his elevation. Sources: (1) Semana (2013), (2–3) La Silla Vacia (2013, 2016)
Gloria Stella Ortiz Delgado (2014–)	Supreme Court (S6)	Conservative Evidence: Commentary suggests, she was selected with assistance from the Conservative Party. Prior to the CC she was an attorney for a university and had many years of experience in the judicial branch including as an auxiliary judge, attorney and auxiliary magistrate for the CC. Sources: (1) Lewin (2017), (2) Acosta and Gómez (2014), (3) Unidos por la vida (2015)

Notes. The coded party association was confirmed by at least two sources (listed) based on judges' party associations, work with a government of a particular party or legislator or staff for a legislator. The party of the selecting president was also imputed to the judge in certain cases, such as in the cases of Pastrana's three presidential appointees. The party association was not based on how judges voted on particular cases on the CC such as abortion or other highly contested issues. Other sources for this analysis included resumes from the Colombian Constitutional Court, news analyses, articles, and commentary during confirmation, elevation, or death. Sources for judges' careers are predominantly from Rubiano Galvis (2009) and Elección Visible.

[a] The confirming senates are referred to as S1 to S6 as follows: S1 (1991 to July 1994), S2 (July 20, 1994 to July 1998), S3 (July 20, 1998 to July 2002), S4 (July 20, 2002 to July 2006), S5 (July 20, 2006 to July 2010) and S6 (July 20, 2010 to July 2014).

Sources for Table A.3:

Acosta, Ricardo Cáceres and Marlene Gómez. Senado Elige a Gloria Stella Ortiz como magistrada de la Corte Constitucional (Notice of the Senate, May 7, 2014).

El Espectador. Así es Eduardo Montealegre, el nuevo fiscal (March 22, 2012).

El Tiempo. Seis Liberales para la Corte Constitucional (1992).

La Silla Vacia. Partido Liberal se distancia del magistrado Alberto Rojas (August 29, 2013) [Rojas, Sierra Porto, Montealegre, Gaviria].
Carlos Gaviria Díaz: Ex candidato presidencial (July 13, 2016).
Jaime Araújo Rentería (July 13, 2016).

Alberto Rojas Ríos, Magistrado de la Corte Constitucional (July 13, 2016).
Carlos Gaviria Díaz. Ex candidato presidencial (July 13, 2016) [Gaviria, Martínez, Hernández, Naranjo, Morón, Cifuentes, Arango, Herrera, Barrera].
La Nueva Corte es más conservadora que la anterior y de menor perfil, pero no es de bolsillo de Uribe (March 25, 2009) [Pinilla, Mendoza, Pretelt, Calle, González, Monroy, Escobar Gil, Henao].
Luis Guillermo Guerrero, nuevo magistrado de la Corte Constitucional (August 14, 2012).
Jorge Pretelt Chalub, Ex magistrado de la Corte Constitucional (May 2, 2017).
Lewin, Juan Esteban. Terna para la Corte constitucional sin constitucionalista: un favorito, una sorpresa y una penalista (March 6, 2013) [Sierra Porto, Guerrero].
Pretelt, un conservador suspendido con votos conservadores (August 24, 2016).
Pretelt, la encarnación de un proyecto político conservador (March 9, 2015).
El Senado define hoy si la Corte se vuelve más conservadora (May 3, 2017) [Pretelt, Ortiz].
Montoya, Ana María. "Si no vas al Senado, No te Eligen Magistrado: Instituciones Informales y Criterios de Selección de los Magistrados de la Corte Constitucional Colombiana en el Senado (1992–2009)." *Colombia Internacional* 79: 155–190 (2013).
Rubiano Galvis, Sebastian. 2009. "La Corte Constitucional: Entre la Independencia Judicial y la Captura Política. In *Mayorías sin Democracia: Desequilibrio de Poderes y Estado Derecho en Colombia 2002–2009.*
Semana. 2013. El polémico nuevo magistrado Alberto Rojas fue elegido tras dos semanas de "propaganda negra" (April 10, 2013).
El magistrado que puede cambiar toda la corte (October 14, 2015) [Cifuentes, Herrera, Martinez, Cepeda, Tafur, Monroy, Pretelt, Guillermo, Pinilla, González, Mendoza].
Unidos de la Vida. Magistrada Gloria Stella Ortiz impone el aborto e ideología de género (December 14, 2015) (article was not used for this judge's position on abortion, but rather commentary of the Conservative Party supporting her selection).

References

Abadie, Alberto, David Krukker, Jane Herr, and Guido Imbens. 2004. "Implementing Matching Estimates for Average Treatment Effects." *The Stata Journal* 4(3): 290–311.

Abraham, Henry J. 1999. *Justices, Presidents, and Senators: A History of the U.S. Supreme Appointments from Washington to Clinton*. New York: Rowman & Littlefield.

Achury, Susan. 2019. "The Impact of Formal Authority in Latin American Constitutional Justice." Unpublished doctoral dissertation on file with the University of Houston.

Adolph, Christopher. 2013. *Bankers, Bureaucrats, and Central Bank Politics: The Myth of Neutrality*. New York: Cambridge University Press.

Agüero, Felipe. 2003. "Chile: Unfinished Transition and Increased Political Competition." In *Constructing Governance in Latin America*, 2nd edition, eds. Jorge I. Domínguez and Michael Shifter. Baltimore: Johns Hopkins University Press. 292–320.

Alarie, Benjamin, and Andrew J. Green. 2017. *Commitment and Cooperation on High Courts: A Cross-Country Examination of Institutional Constraints on Judges*. Oxford: Oxford University Press.

Alemán, Eduardo, and Patricio Navia. 2016. "Presidential Power, Legislative Rules, and Lawmaking in Chile." In *Legislative Institutions and Lawmaking in Latin America*, eds. Eduardo Alemán and George Tsebelis. Oxford: Oxford University Press. 92–121.

Amaral-García, Sofia, Nuno Garoupa, and Veronica Grembi. 2009. "Judicial Independence and Party Politics in the Kelsenian Constitutional Courts: The Case of Portugal." *Journal of Empirical Legal Studies* 6: 381–404.

Archer, Ronald P., and Matthew S. Shugart. 1997. "The Unrealized Potential of Presidential Dominance in Colombia." In *Presidentialism and Democracy in Latin America*, eds. Scott Mainwaring and Matthew S. Shugart. Cambridge: Cambridge University Press. 110–159.

Asch, Solomon. 1952. *Social Psychology*. Englewood Cliffs, NJ: Prentice-Hall.

Ashenfelter, Orley, Theodore Eisenberg, and Stewart J. Schwab. 1995. "Politics and the Judiciary: The Influence of Judicial Background on Case Outcomes." *The Journal of Legal Studies* 24: 257–281.

Austen-Smith, David. 2011. "Economic Methods in Positive Political Theory." *The Oxford Handbook of Political Science Online*. www.oxfordhandbooks.com/view/10.1093/oxfordhb/9780199604456.001.0001/oxfordhb-9780199604456-e-039.

Austen-Smith, David, and Jeffrey S. Banks. 2010. *Positive Political Theory I: Collective Preference*. Ann Arbor: University of Michigan Press.

Bagashka, Tanya, and Lydia Tiede. 2018. "Explaining Dissensus on the Bulgarian Constitutional Court." *East European Politics* 34: 418–439.

Banks, William C., and Edgar Alvarez . 1991. "The New Colombian Constitution: Democratic Victory or Popular Surrender?" *The University of Miami Inter-American Law Review* 23: 39–92.

Barcikowski, Robert. 1981. "Statistical Power with Group Mean as the Unit of Analysis." *Journal of Educational Statistics* 6(3): 267–285.

Barros, Robert. 2002. *Constitutionalism and Dictatorship*. Cambridge: Cambridge University Press.

Baum, Lawrence. 1997. *The Puzzle of Judicial Behavior*. Ann Arbor: University of Michigan Press.

2006. *Judges and Their Audiences: A Perspective on Judicial Behavior*. Princeton: Princeton University Press.

BBC. 2017. "Poland Court Bill: Parliament Votes for Judicial Reforms." BBC (July 20), www.bbc.com/news/world-europe-40670790

Beim, Deborah, and Jonathan P. Kastellec. 2014. "The Interplay of Ideological Diversity, Dissents, and Discretionary Review in the Judicial Hierarchy: Evidence from Death Penalty Cases." *The Journal of Politics* 76: 1074–1088.

Bello. 2021. "After the Storm: A Constitutional Convention Offers Chile a Chance of a New Social Contract." *The Economist* (March 20), 32.

Bentsen, Henrik Litleré. 2018. "Court Leadership, Agenda Transformation, and Judicial Dissent: A European Case of a 'Mysterious Demise of Consensual Norms'." *Journal of Law and Courts* 6: 189–213.

Bergara, Mario, Barak Richman, and Pablo T. Spiller. 2003. "Modeling Supreme Court Strategic Decision-Making: The Congressional Constraint." *Legislative Studies Quarterly* 28: 247–280.

Bernal, Carlos. 2013. "Unconstitutional Constitutional Amendments in the Case Study of Colombia: An Analysis of the Justification and Meaning of the Constitutional Replacement Doctrine." *International Journal of Constitutional Law* 11: 339–357.

Bickel, Alexander M. 1986. *The Least Dangerous Branch: The Supreme Court at the Bar of Politics*. New Haven, CT: Yale University Press.

Blackwell, Matthew, Stefano Iacus, Gary King, and Giuseppe Porro. 2009. "CEM: Coarsened Exact Matching in Stata." *The Stata Journal* 9: 524–546.

Blair, Clifford, J. Higgins, Mary Topping, and Allan Mortimer. 1983. "An Investigation of the Robustness of the t Test to Unit of Analysis Violations." *Educational and Psychological Measurement* 43: 69–80.

Bowen, Terry, and John M. Scheb. 1993. "Reassessing the 'Freshman Effect': The Voting Bloc Alignment of New Justices on the United States Supreme Court, 1921–90." *Political Behavior* 15: 1–14.

Boyd, Christina, Lee Epstein, and Andrew Martin. 2010. "Untangling the Causal Effects of Sex on Judging." *American Journal of Political Science* 54: 389–411.

Brinks, Daniel, and Abby Blass. 2017. "Rethinking Judicial Empowerment: The New Foundations of Constitutional Justice." *International Journal of Constitutional Law* 15: 296–331.

2018. *The DNA of Constitutional Justice in Latin America: Politics, Governance, and Judicial Design, Comparative Constitutional Policy*. Cambridge: Cambridge University Press.

Brock, William A., and Steven N. Durlauf. 2007. "Identification of Binary Choice Models with Social Interactions." *Journal of Econometrics* 140: 52–75.

Brouard, Sylvain, and Christoph Hönnige. 2017. "Constitutional Courts as Veto Players: Lessons from the United States, France and Germany." *European Journal of Political Research* 56: 529–552.
Brudney, James, S. Schiavoni, and Deborah Merrit. 1999. "Judicial Hostility toward Labor Unions? Applying the Social Background Model to a Celebrated Concern." *Ohio State Law Journal* 60: 1675–1771.
Bushnell, David. 1993. *The Making of Modern Colombia: A Nation in Spite of Itself*. Berkeley: University of California Press.
Caldeira, Teresa P. R., and James Holston. 1999. "Democracy and Violence in Brazil." *Comparative Studies in Society and History* 41(4): 691–729.
Cameron, A. Colin, Jonah B. Gelbach, and Douglas L. Miller. 2011. "Robust Inference with Multi-way Clustering." *Journal of Business and Economic Statistics* 19: 238–249.
Cameron, Charles. 2002. "Judicial Independence: How Can You Tell It When You See It? And Who Cares?" In *Judicial Independence at the Crossroads: An Interdisciplinary Approach*, eds. Stephen B. Burbank and Barry Friedman. Thousand Oaks: Sage. 134–147.
Cameron, Charles M., and Lewis A. Kornhauser. 2017a. "Theorizing the U.S. Supreme Court." *Oxford Research Encyclopedia of Politics*, online. http://dx.doi.org/10.1093/acrefore/9780190228637.013.264.
2017b. "Rational Choice Attitudinalism?" *European Journal of Law and Economics* 43: 535–554.
Carey, John. 2002. "Parties, Coalitions, and the Chilean Congress in the 1990s." In *Legislative Politics in Latin America*, eds. Scott Morgenstern and Benito Nacif. Cambridge: Cambridge University Press. 222–253.
Carothers, Thomas. 1999. *Aiding Democracy Abroad: The Learning Curve*. Washington, DC: Carnegie Endowment for International Peace.
Carroll, Royce, and Mónica Pachón. 2016. "The Unrealized Potential of Presidential Coalitions in Colombia." In *Legislative Institutions and Lawmaking in Latin America*, eds. Eduardo Alemán and George Tsebelis. Oxford: Oxford University Press. 122–147.
Carroll, Royce, and Lydia Tiede. 2011. "Judicial Review of the Chilean Constitutional Tribunal." *Journal of Empirical Legal Studies* 8(4): 856–877.
2012. "Ideological Voting on Chile's Constitutional Tribunal: Dissent Coalitions in the Adjudication of Rights." *Journal of Human Rights* 11: 85–105.
Cepeda Espinosa, Manuel José. 1985. "Las Relaciones entre el Presidente y La Corte durante la Emergencia Económica: Un Semidiós Enfrentando a un Monstruo." In Manuel José Cepeda Espinosa, ed., *Estado de Sitio y Emergencia Económica*. Bogotá: Contraloría General de la República, 43-71.
2004. "Judicial Activism in a Violent Context: The Origin, Role, and Impact of the Colombian Constitutional Court." *Washington University Global Legal Studies Law Review* 3: 529–700.
2019. "Responsive Constitutionalism." *Annual Review of Law and Social Science* 15: 21–40.
Cepeda Espinosa, Manuel José, and David Landau. 2017. *Colombian Constitutional Law: Leading Cases*. Oxford: Oxford University Press.
Coleman, James S. 1990. *Foundations of Social Theory*. Cambridge, MA: The Belknap Press of Harvard University Press.
Conlisk, John. 1980. "Costly Optimizers versus Cheap Imitators." *Journal of Economic Behavior and Organization* 1: 275–293.
Contreras, Dante, and Kirsten Sehnbruch. 2014. "Social Policies: From Social Debt to Welfare State?" In *Democratic Chile: The Policies of a Historic Coalition 1990–2010*, eds. Kirsten Sehnbruch and Peter Siavelis. Boulder, CO: Lynne Rienner. 243–262.

Correa Sutil, Jorge. 1993. "The Judiciary and Political System in Chile: The Dilemmas of Judicial Independence during the Transition to Democracy." In *Transition to Democracy in Latin America: The Role of the Judiciary*, ed. Ivan Stotzky. Oxford: Westview Press. 89–106.

Correa Sutil, Jorge, and María Molina Osorio. 2015. "¿Año de Incertezas? Indicios de Potencial Inestabilidad en la Jurisprudencia del Tribunal Constitucional Durante el 2014. *Anuario de Derecho Público* 1: 97–140.

Couso, Javier. 2004. "The Politics of Judicial Review in Chile in the Era of Democratic Transition, 1990–2002." In *Democratization and the Judiciary: The Accountability Function of Courts in New Democracies*, eds. Siri Gloppen, Roberto Gargarella, and Elin Skaar. London: Frank Cass.

2011. "Models of Democracy and Models of Constitutionalism: The Case of Chile's Constitutional Court, 1970–2010." *Texas Law Review* 89(7): 1517–1536.

Couso, Javier, and Alberto Coddou. 2010. "La Naturaleza Jurídica de la Acción de inaplicabilidad en la Jurisprudencia del Tribunal Constitucional: un Desafío Pendiente." *Estudios Constitucionales* 8(2): 389–430.

Couso, Javier, and Lisa Hilbink. 2011. "From Quietism to Incipient Activism: The Institutional and Ideological Roots of Rights Adjudication in Chile." In *Courts in Latin America*, eds. Gretchen Helmke and Julio Ríos-Figueroa. Cambridge: Cambridge University Press. 99–122.

Couso, Javier, Domingo Lovera Parmo, Matías Guiloff, and Alberto Coddou. 2011. *Constitutional Law in Chile*. The Netherlands: Wolters Kluwer.

Cross, Frank B., and Emerson H. Tiller. 1998. "Judicial Partisanship and Obedience to Legal Doctrine: Whistleblowing on the Federal Courts of Appeals." *Yale Law Journal* 107: 2155–2176.

Dahl, Robert. 1957. "Decision-Making in a Democracy: The Supreme Court as a National Policy-Maker." *Journal of Public Law* 6: 279–295

Danelski, David. 1960. "The Influence of the Chief Justice in the Decisional Process of the Supreme Court". Presented at the Annual Meeting of the Political Science Association, New York.

1986. "Causes and Consequences of Conflict and Its Resolution in the Supreme Court." In *Judicial Conflict and Consensus: Behavioral Studies of American Appellate Courts*, eds. C. Lamb and S. Goldman. Lexington: University of Kentucky Press. 21–49.

Dargent, Eduardo. 2009. "Determinants of Judicial Independence: Lessons from Three 'Cases' of Constitutional Courts in Peru (1982–2007)." *Journal of Latin American Studies* 41: 251.

Dargent, Eduardo, and Paula Muñoz. 2011. "Democracy against Parties: Party System Deinstitutionalization in Colombia." *Journal of Politics in Latin America* 3(2): 43–71.

Dix, Robert H. 1987. *The Politics of Colombia*. New York: Praeger.

Dobkin, Donald S. 2007. "Court Stripping and Limitations on Judicial Review of Immigration Cases." *Justice System Journal* 28: 104.

Domínguez, Jorge I., and Michael Shifter. 2003. *Constructing Democratic Governance in Latin America*, 2nd ed. Baltimore: The Johns Hopkins University Press.

2013. *Constructing Democratic Governance in Latin America*, 4th ed. Baltimore: The Johns Hopkins University Press.

Douglas, William O. 1948. "Address to the American Bar Association." In *Judges on Judging: Views from the Bench*, ed. D. O'Brien. Washington, DC: CQ Press.

Drake, Paul W., and Iván Jaksić. 1995. "Transformation and Transition in Chile, 1982–1990." In *The Struggle for Democracy in Chile*, eds. Paul Drake and Iván Jaksić. Lincoln, NE: University of Nebraska Press. 1–17.

1999. *El Modelo Chileno: Democracia Y Desarrollo En Los Noventa*. Santiago, Chile: LOM Ediciones.

Driscoll, Amanda, and Michael J. Nelson. 2015. "Judicial Selection and the Democratization of Justice: Lessons from the Bolivian Elections." *Journal of Law and Courts* Spring: 115–148.

Duce, Mauricio and Riego, Cristián. 2009. "La Prisión Preventiva en Chile: El Impacto de la Reforma Procesal Penal y de sus Cambios Posteriores." Santiago: CEJA. 151–212.

Duque Daza, Javier. 2006. "Partidos Divididos, Dirigencia Fragmentada: Los Partidos Liberal y Conservador Colombianos 1974–2006." *Convergencia* 13(41): 173–209.

2011. "Redefinición de las Reglas de Juego. Las Reformas al Sistema Electoral Colombiano como un Caso de Volatilidad Institucional, 1991–2011." *Papel Político* 16(2): 421–460..

2015. "¿ Presidentes Legislando? Las Facultades Legislativas en el Presidencialismo Colombiano 1991–2014." *Revista Estudios Socio-Jurídicos* 17(1): 79–123.

Elacqua, Gregory, and Pablo González Soto. 2014. "Education: Freedom of Choice or Enterprise." In *Democratic Chile: The Politics and Policies of a Historic Coalition, 1990–2010*, eds. Kirsten Sehnbruch and Peter M. Siavelis. Boulder, CO: Lynne Rienner. 281–305.

Ely, John Hart. 1980. *Democracy and Distrust: A Theory of Judicial Review*. Cambridge: Harvard University Press.

Epperly, Brad. 2017. "Political Competition and De Facto Judicial Independence in Non-democracies." *European Journal of Political Research* 56(2): 279–300.

Epstein, Lee, and Jack Knight. 1998. *The Choices Justices Make*. Washington, DC: Congressional Quarterly Press.

2013. "Reconsidering Judicial Preferences." *Annual Review of Political Science* 16: 11–31.

Epstein, Lee, and Eric A. Posner. 2016. "Supreme Court Justices' Loyalty to the President." *The Journal of Legal Studies* 45(2): 401–436.

Epstein, Lee, William Landes, and Robert Posner. 2011. "Why (and When) Judges Dissent: A Theoretical and Empirical Analysis." *Journal of Legal Analysis* 3: 101–137.

2013. *The Behavior of Federal Judges: A Theoretical and Empirical Study of Rational Choice*. Cambridge, MA: Harvard University Press

Eskridge, William, Jr. 1991a. "Overriding Supreme Court Statutory Interpretation Decisions." *Yale Law Journal* 101: 331–455.

1991b. "Reneging on History? Playing the Courts/Congress/President Civil Rights Game." *California Law Review* 79: 613–684.

Faundez, Julio. 1980. "The Defeat of Politics: Chile under Allende." *Boletín de Estudios Latinoamericanos y del Caribe* 28: 59–75.

1997. "In Defense of Presidentialism: The Case of Chile, 1932–1970." In *Presidentialism and Democracy in Latin America*, eds. Scott Mainwaring and Matthew Shugart. Cambridge: Cambridge University Press. 300–319.

2007. *Democratization, Development, and Legality: Chile, 1831–1973*. New York: Palgrave Macmillan.

Feld, Lars P., and Stefan Voigt. 2003. "Economic Growth and Judicial Independence: Cross-Country Evidence Using a New Set of Indicators." *European Journal of Political Economy* 19: 497–527.

Fernández, Adriela, and Marisol Vera. 2012. "The Bachelet Presidency and the End of Chile's Concertación Era." *Latin American Perspectives* 39: 5–18.

Figueroa, Dante. 2013. "Constitutional Review in Chile Revisited: A Revolution in the Making." *Duquesne Law Review* 51: 387–419.

Finkel, Jodi. 2004. "Judicial Reform in Argentina in the 1990s: How Electoral Incentives Shape Institutional Change." *Latin American Research Review* 39: 56–80.

Fischman, Joshua. 2011. "Estimating Preferences of Circuit Judges: A Model of Consensus Voting." *Journal of Law and Economics* 54: 781–809.

2015. "Interpreting Circuit Court Voting Patterns: A Social Interactions Framework." *The Journal of Law, Economics, and Organization* 31: 808–841.

Flemming, Roy B., and B. Dan Wood. 1997. "The Public and the Supreme Court: Individual Justice Responsiveness to American Policy Moods." *American Journal of Political Science* 41: 468–498.

Fontana, David. 2011. "Docket Control and the Success of Constitutional Courts." In *Comparative Constitutional Law*, eds. Tom Ginsburg and Rosalind Dixon. Cheltenham: Edward Elgar. 624–641.

Fox, Donald T., and Anne Stetson. 1992. "The 1991 Constitutional Reform: Prospects for Democracy and the Rule of Law in Colombia." *Case Western Reserve Journal of International Law* 24: 139–163.

Franz, Tobias, and Andrei Gómez Suárez. 2019. "Why Is Colombia Striking for Change." London School of Economics, Latin America and Caribbean blogs (December 16).

Friedman, Barry. 2004. "The Importance of Being Positive: The Nature and Function of Judicial Review." *University of Cincinnati Law Review* 72: 1257–1303.

2005. "The Politics of Judicial Review." *Texas Law Review* 84: 257–337.

2006. "Taking Law Seriously." *Perspectives on Politics* 4(2): 261–276.

Fuentes, Claudio A. 2014. "Democratizing Chile through Constitutional Reforms." In *Democratic Chile: The Politics and Policies of a Historic Coalition*, 1990–2010, eds. Kirsten Sehnbruch and Peter Siavelis. Boulder, CO: Lynne Rienner. 69–102.

Gaceta Especial Sala Constitucional. 1993. *La reforma constitucional de 1991. Tomo 1*. Santafé de Bogotá.

Gamboa, Ricardo, and Mauricio Morales. 2018. "Chile's 2015 Electoral Reform: Changing the Rules of the Game." *Latin American Politics and Society* 58: 126–144.

García-Jaramillo, Santiago, and Francisco Gnecco-Estrada. 2016. La teoría de la sustitución: de la protección de la supremacía e integridad de la constitución, a la aniquilación de la titularidad del poder de reforma constitucional en el órgano legislativo, 133 Vniversitas, 59–104.

García Odgers, Ramón, and Pablo Bravo-Hurtado. 2018. "Reforms on Court Management in Chile." Presented at the Conference on Judicial Management from Comparative Perspective, Tianjin China (August 2018).

Garlicki, Lech. 2007. "Constitutional Courts versus Supreme Courts." *International Journal of Constitutional Law* 5: 44–68.

Garoupa, Nuno, and Tom Ginsburg. 2015. *Judicial Reputation*. Chicago: University of Chicago Press.

Garoupa, Nuno, and Veronica Grembi. 2015. "Judicial Review and Political Partisanship: Moving from Consensual to Majoritarian Democracy." *International Review of Law and Economics* 43: 32–45.

Garoupa, Nuno, Fernando Gómez-Pomar, and Veronica Grembi. 2013a. "Judging under Political Pressure: An Empirical Analysis of Constitutional Review Voting in the Spanish Constitutional Court." *Journal of Law, Economics and Organization* 29(3): 513–534.

2013b. "Political Influence and Career Judges: An Empirical Analysis of Administrative Review by the Spanish Supreme Court." *Journal of Empirical Legal Studies* 9(4): 795–826.

Garoupa, Nuno, Rebecca Gill, and Lydia Tiede, eds. 2021a. *High Courts in Global Perspective Evidence, Methodologies, and Findings*. Charlottesville: University of Virginia Press.

Garoupa, Nuno, Marian Gili, and Fernando Gómez-Pomar. 2021b. "Mixed Judicial Selection and Constitutional Review: Evidence from Spain." *European Constitutional Law Review* 17: 1–27.

2021c. "Loyalty to the Party or Loyalty to the Party Leader: Evidence from the Spanish Constitutional Court." *International Review of Law and Economics* forthcoming doi:10.1016/j.irle.2021.105999.

Garretón, Manuel Antonio. 1993. "La Redemocratizacón en Chile: Transición, Inauguración y Evolución." *Estudios Interdisciplinarios de América Latina y el Caribe* 4(1): 5–25. http://eial.tau.ac.il/index.php/eial/article/view/1248.

Gely, Rafael, and Pablo T. Spiller. 1990. "A Rational Choice Theory of Supreme Court Statutory Decisions and the Applications to the *State Farm* and *Grove City* Cases." *Journal of Law, Economics and Organization* 6: 263–300.

George, Tracey E. 2001. "Court Fixing." *Arizona Law Review* 43(1): 9–62.

2008. "From Judge to Justice: Social Background Theory and the Supreme Court." *North Carolina Law Review* 86: 1333–1367.

Giles, Micheal, Virginia Hettinger, and Todd Peppers. 2001. "Picking Federal Judges: A Note on Policy and Partisan Selection Agendas." *Political Research Quarterly* 54: 623.

Gilman, Howard. 1993. *The Constitution Besieged: The Rise and Demise of Lochner Era Police Powers Jurisprudence*. Durham: Duke University Press.

Ginsburg, Tom. 2003. *Judicial Review in New Democracies: Constitutional Courts in Asian Cases*. Cambridge: Cambridge University Press.

Goff, Brian. 2005. "Supreme Court Consensus and Dissent: Estimating the Role of the Selection Screen." *Public Choice* 122: 483–499.

González Schmessane, Andrea. 2017. "Jueces recurren a la Comisión Internacional DDHH en busca de Independencia Judicial." Emol.com (March 15). www.emol.com/noticias/Nacional/2017/03/15/849509/Jueces-recurren-a-la-Comision-Internacional-de-DDHH-en-busca-de-independencia-judicial.html.

Gottschall, Jon. 1986. "Reagan's Appointments to the U.S. Courts of Appeals: The Continuation of a Judicial Revolution." *Judicature* 70: 48–54.

Grossman, Guy, Oren Gazal-Ayal, Samuel D. Pimentel, and Jeremy M. Weinstein. 2016. "Descriptive Representation and Judicial Outcomes in Multiethnic Societies." *American Journal of Political Science* 60: 44–69.

Gutmann, Amy, and Dennis Thompson. 1996. *Democracy and Disagreement*. Cambridge, MA: Harvard University Press.

Haas, Liesl, and Merike Blofield. 2014. "Political Reform and Gender Equality." In *Democratic Chile: The Politics and Policies of a Historic Coalition, 1990–2010*, eds. Kirsten Sehnbruch and Peter Siavelis. Boulder, CO: Lynne Reinner. 119–142.

Haggard, Stephan, and Robert R. Kaufman. 1995. *The Political Economy of Democratic Transitions*. Princeton: Princeton University Press.

Haggard, Stephan, and Matthew McCubbins, eds. 2001. *Presidents, Parliaments, and Policy*, Political Economy of Institutions and Decisions. Cambridge: Cambridge University Press.

Hammergren, Linn. 2002. "Do Judicial Councils Further Reform? Lessons from Latin America." In *Rule of Law Series* #28. Washington, DC: Carnegie Endowment of International Peace.

2007. *Envisioning Reform: Improving Judicial Performance in Latin America*. University Park: Pennsylvania State University Press.

Hanretty, Chris. 2014. "The Bulgarian Constitutional Court as an Additional Legislative Chamber." *East European Politics & Societies* 28(3): 540–558.

Hanssen, F. Andrew. 2004. "Learning about Judicial Independence: Institutional Change in the State Courts." *Journal of Legal Studies* 33: 431–473.

Heiss, Claudia, and Patricio Navia. 2007. "You Win Some, You Lose Some: Constitutional Reforms in Chile's Transition to Democracy." *Latin American Politics and Society* 49: 163–190.

Helmke, Gretchen. 2002. "The Logic of Strategic Defection: Court–Executive Relations in Argentina under Dictatorship and Democracy." *American Political Science Review* 96: 291–303.

Helmke, Gretchen, and Mitchell Sanders. 2006. "Modeling Motivations: A Method for Inferring Judicial Goals from Behavior." *American Journal of Political Science* 68(4): 867–878.

Herron, Erik, and Kirk Randazzo. 2003. "The Relationship between Independence and Judicial Review in Post-Communist Courts." *The Journal of Politics* 65: 422–438.

Hettinger, Virginia, Stefanie Lindquist, and Wendy Martinek. 2003. "Acclimation Effects and Separate Opinion Writing in the U.S. Courts of Appeals." *Social Science Quarterly* 84: 792–810.

Hilbink, Lisa. 2007. *Judges beyond Politics in Democracy and Dictatorship: Lessons from Chile*. Cambridge: Cambridge University Press.

2012. "The Origins of Positive Judicial Independence." *World Politics* 64: 587–621.

Hirschl, Ran. 2000. "The Political Origins of Judicial Empowerment through Constitutionalization: Lessons from Four Constitutional Revolutions." *Law & Social Inquiry* 25: 91–149.

2004. *Towards Juristocracy: The Origins and Consequences of the New Constitutionalism*. Cambridge, MA: Harvard University Press.

Hönnige, C. 2009. "The Electoral Connection: How the Pivotal Judge Affects Oppositional Success at European Constitutional Courts." *West European Politics* 32(5): 963–984.

Ho, Daniel E., Kosuke Imai, Gary King, and Elizabeth A. Stuart. 2007. "Matching as Nonparametric Preprocessing for Reducing Model Dependence in Parametric Causal Inference." *Political Analysis* 15(3): 199–236.

Holden, Richard, Michael Keane, and Matthew Lilley. 2021. Peer Effects on the United States Supreme Court. *Quantitative Economics* 12(3): 981–1019.

Hong, Joon Seok. 2019. "Signaling the Turn: The Supermajority Requirement and Judicial Power on the Constitutional Court of Korea." *The American Journal of Comparative Law* 67: 177–217.

Howard, Bob, and Jeffrey Segal. 2004. "A Preference for Deference? The Supreme Court and Judicial Review." *Political Research Quarterly* 57(1): 131–143.

Hox, Joop. 2018. *Multilevel Analysis: Techniques and Application*. New York: Taylor and Francis.

Iaryczower, Matias, and Matthew Shum. 2012. "The Value of Information in the Court: Get It Right, Keep It Tight." *American Economic Review* 102: 202–237.

Iaryczower, Matías, Pablo T. Spiller, and Mariano Tommasi. 2002. "Judicial Independence in Unstable Environments, Argentina 1935–1998." *American Journal of Political Science* 46: 699–716.

International IDEA (International Institute for Democracy and Electoral Assistance). 2017. "Judicial Appointments." Constitution Building Primers.

Jaros, Dean, and Bradley C. Canon. 1971. "Dissent on State Supreme Courts: The Differential Significance of Characteristics of Judges." *Midwest Journal of Political Science* 15: 322–346.

Kapiszewski, Diana. 2012. *High Courts and Economic Governance in Argentina and Brazil.* New York: Cambridge University Press.

Kastellec, Jonathan P. 2007. "Panel Composition and Judicial Compliance on the U.S. Courts of Appeals." *Journal of Law, Economics, and Organization* 23: 421–441.

Keck, Thomas M. 2007. "Party, Policy, or Duty: Why Does the Supreme Court Invalidate Federal Statutes?" *American Political Science Review* 101: 321–338.

Kelemen, Katalina. 2013. "Dissenting Opinions on Constitutional Courts." *German Law Journal* 14(8): 1345–1372.

Kelsen, Hans. 1928. "La Garantie Juridictionnelle de la Constitution." *Revue du Droit Public* 44: 197–257.

1942. "Judicial Review of Legislation: A Comparative Study of the Austrian and American Constitution. *The Journal of Politics* 4: 183–200.

Kiewiet, D. Roderick, and Mathew McCubbins. 1991. *The Logic of Delegation: Congressional Parties and the Appropriations Process.* Chicago: The University of Chicago Press.

Kornhauser, Lewis. 1992. "Modeling Collegial Courts I: Path-Dependence." *International Review of Law and Economics* 12: 169–185.

Krackhardt, David. 1998. "Endogenous Preferences: A Structural Approach." In *Non-Rational Aspects of Organizational Decision Making*, eds. Jennifer Helpern and Robert N. Stern. Ithaca: Cornell University Press. 239–247.

Lagos, Ricardo. 2012. *Southern Tiger: Chile's Fight for a Democratic and Prosperous Future.* New York: Palgrave Macmillan.

Lamprea, Everaldo. 2010. "When Accountability Meets Judicial Independence: A Case Study of the Colombian Constitutional Court's Nominations." *Global Jurist* 10: 1–38.

Landau, David. 2005. "The Two Discourses in Colombian Constitutional Jurisprudence: A New Approach to Modeling Judicial Behavior in Latin America." *George Washington International Law Review* 37(3): 687–744.

2014. "A Dynamic Theory of Judicial Role." *Boston College Law Review* 55: 1501–1562.

2015. "Beyond Judicial Independence: The Construction of Judicial Power in Colombia." Doctoral dissertation, Harvard University, Graduate School of Arts & Sciences. School of Arts & Sciences. http://nrs.harvard.edu/urn-3:HUL.InstRepos:14226088

2016. "Political Support and Structural Constitutional Law." *Alabama Law Review* 67(4): 1069–1124.

Landes, William, and Richard Posner. 1975. "The Independent Judiciary in an Interest-Group Perspective. *Journal of Law and Economics* 18(3): 875–901.

Langer, Laura, and Paul Brace. 2005. "The Preemptive Power of State Supreme Courts: Adoption of Abortion and Death Penalty Legislation." *Policy Studies Journal* 33: 317–340.

LaRosa, Michael J., and Germán R. Mejía. 2013. *Colombia: A Concise Contemporary History*, updated 1st ed. Lanham, MD: Rowman & Littlefield.

2017. *Colombia: A Concise Contemporary History*, updated 2nd ed. Lanham, MD: Rowman & Littlefield.

Law, David S. 2011. "Why Has Judicial Review Failed in Japan?" *Washington University Law Review* 88: 1425–1466.

Levitsky, Steven, and Lucan Way. 2010. *Competitive Authoritarianism: Hybrid Regimes after the Cold War.* Cambridge: Cambridge University Press.

Levy, Marin K. 2017. "Panel Assignment in the Federal Courts of Appeals." *Cornell Law Review* 103: 65–116.

Linz, Juan J., and Alfred Stepan. 1996. *Problems of Democratic Transition and Consolidation: Southern Europe, South America, and Post-Communist Europe.* Baltimore: The Johns Hopkins University Press.

Liptak, Adam. 2020. "John Roberts Was Already Chief Justice. But Now It's His Court. *New York Times* (June 30). www.nytimes.com/2020/06/30/us/john-roberts-supreme-court.html (last accessed July 2020).

Londregan, John. 2001. "Appointment, Reelection, and Autonomy in the Senate of Chile." In *Legislative Politics in Latin America*, eds. Scott Morgenstern and Benito Nacif. Cambridge: Cambridge University Press. 341–376.

Luna, Juan Pablo. 2021. "Chiles Fractured Democratic Consensus." In *Divisive Politics and Democratic Dangers in Latin America*, eds. Thomas Carothers and Andreas Feldmann. Washington, DC: Carnegie Endowment for International Peace. 13–17.

López, Ramón. 2014. "Fiscal Policy: Promoting Faustian Growth." In *Democratic Chile: The Policies of a Historic Coalition 1990–2010*, eds. Kirsten Sehnbruch and Peter Siavelis. Boulder, CO: Lynne Rienner. 199–220.

López, Santiago. 2005. "Partidos Desafiantes en América Latina: Representación Política y Estrategias de Competencia de las Nuevas Oposiciones." *Revista de Ciencia Política* (Santiago) 25(2): 37–64.

Losada, Rodrigo, and Nicolás Liendo. 2016. "El Partido "Centro Democrático" en Colombia: Razones de su Surgimiento y Éxito." *Análisis Político* 29(87): 49–51.

Loveman, Brian. 1994. "Protected Democracies and Military Guardianship: Political Transitions in Latin America, 1978–1993." *Journal of Interamerican Studies and World Affairs* 36(2): 105–189.

2007. "The Transition to Civilian Government in Chile, 1990–1994." In *The Struggle for Democracy in Chile*, eds. Paul Drake and Iván Jaksić. Lincoln, NE: University of Nebraska Press.

Mac-Clure, Lucas. 2011. "Tribunal Constitucional y los Derechos: La Discusión Pendiente." In *Frente a La Mayoría: Leyes Supramayoritarias Y Tribunal Constitucional En Chile*, eds. Lucas I. Sierra and Lucas Mac-Clure. Santiago, Chile: Centro de Estudios Públicos (CEP), Corporación de Estudios para Latinoamérica (CIEPLAN), Libertad y Desarrollo, Proyectamérica. 171–274.

MacGregor Burns, James. 2009. *Packing the Court: The Rise of Judicial Power and the Coming Crisis of the Supreme Court*. New York: Penguin Press.

2010. *Packing the Court: The Rise of Judicial Power and the Coming Crisis of the Supreme Court*. London: Penguin Books.

Magaloni, Beatriz. 2003. "Authoritarianism, Democracy and the Supreme Court: Horizontal Exchange and the Rule of Law in Mexico." In *Democratic Accountability in Latin America*, eds. S. Mainwaring and C. Welna. Cambridge: University of Cambridge Press.

Mainwaring, Scott, and Matthew Shugart. 1997. *Presidentialism and Democracy in Latin America*. Cambridge: Cambridge University Press.

Manski, Charles F. 1993. "Identification of Endogenous Social Effects: The Reflection Problem." *Review of Economic Studies* 60: 531–542.

2000. "Economic Analysis of Social Interactions." *Journal of Economic Perspectives* 14:115–136.

Marks, Brian A. 1989. "A Model of Judicial Influence on Congressional Policymaking: Grove City College v. Bell." Unpublished dissertation, Washington University.

Mavčič, Arne Marjan. 2018. *Constitutional Review Systems around the World*. Lake Mary, FL: Vandeplas.

McCubbins, Matthew, Roger Noll, and Barry Weingast. 1995. "Politics and Courts: A Positive Theory of Judicial Doctrine and the Rule of Law." *Southern California Law Review* 68: 1631–1681.

2006. "Conditions for Judicial Independence." *Journal of Contemporary Legal Issues* 15: 105.

2007. "The Political Economy of Law." In *Handbook of Law and Economics*, vol. 2, eds. Mitchell Polinsky and Steven Shavell, 2 vols. Amsterdam: Elsevier. 1654–1738.

McGuire, Kevin T. 1995. "Repeat Players in the Supreme Court: The Role of Experienced Lawyers in Litigation Success." *Journal of Politics* 57(1): 187–196.

El Mercurio. 2017. "Discusión por aborto: Amplitud llama a no politizar el Tribunal Constitucional La directiva del partido de oposición realizó esta petición luego de que los parlamentarios de Chile Vamos anunciaran que acudirían a este organismo en caso de que se apruebe la despenalización de la interrupción del embarazo en tres causales." www.emol.com/noticias/Nacional/2017/07/22/867963/Representantes-de-Amplitud-llaman-a-no-politizar-el-Tribunal-Constitucional.html

Merhof, Katrin. 2015. "Building a Bridge between Reality and the Constitution: The Establishment and Development of the Colombian Constitutional Court." *International Journal of Constitutional Law* 13(3): 714–732.

Merryman, John, and Rogelio Pérez-Perdomo. 2007. *Th Civil Law Tradition: An Introduction to the Legal Systems of Europe and Latin America*. Stanford: Stanford University Press.

Miles, Thomas J., and Cass R. Sunstein. 2006. "Do Judges Make Regulatory Policy? An Empirical Investigation of Chevron." *University of Chicago Law Review* 73: 823–882.

Mohor, Alejandra, and Víctor Covarrubias. 2007. *El Nuevo Procedimiento Penal en Chile*. Santiago, Chile: RIL Editores.

Montes, Juan Esteban, and Tomás Vial. 2005. "The Role of Constitution-Building Processes in Democratization: Case Study Chile." In *The Role of Constitution-Building Processes in Democratization*. Stockholm, Sweden: International Institute for Democracy and Electoral Assistance (International IDEA).

Montoya, Ana. 2013. "'Si no Vas al Senado, No te Eligen Magistrado': Instituciones Informales y Criterios de Selección de los Magistrados de la Corte Constitucional Colombiana en el Senado (1992–2009)." *Colombia Internacional* 79: 155–190.

Moreno, Erica, Brian Crisp, and Matthew Shugart. 2003. "The Accountability Deficit in Latin America." In *Democratic Accountability in Latin America*, eds. Scott Mainwaring and Christoper Welna. Cambridge: Cambridge University Press. 79–131.

Morgenstern, Scott, and Benito Nacif, eds. 2002. *Legislative Politics in Latin America*. Cambridge: Cambridge University Press.

Muñoz León, Fernando. 2014. "Morning-After Decisions: Legal Mobilization against Emergency Contraception in Chile" *Michigan Journal of Gender and Law* 21(1): 123–175.

Myerson, Roger B. 1998. "Population Uncertainty and Poisson Games." *International Journal of Game Theory* 27: 375–392.

2002. "Comparison of Scoring Rules in Poisson Voting Games." *Journal of Economic Theory* 103: 217–251.

Naurin, Daniel, and Øyvind Stiansen. 2020. "The Dilemma of Dissent: Split Judicial Decisions and Compliance with Judgments from the International Human Rights Judiciary." *Comparative Political Studies* 53: 959–991.

Navarro Beltran, Enrique. 2011. "El Control De Constitucionalidad De La Leyes En Chile (1811–2011)." *Cuadernos del Tribunal Constitucional* 43: 31.

Navia, Patricio, and Ricardo Godoy. 2014. "The Alianza's Quest to Win Power Democratically." In *Democratic Chile: The Politics and Policies of a Historic Coalition, 1990–2010*, eds. Kirsten Sehnbruch and Peter Siavelis. Boulder, CO: Lynne Rienner. 43–48.

Nunes, Rodrigo. 2010. "Ideational Origins of Progressive Judicial Activism: The Colombian Constitutional Court and the Right to Health." *Latin American Politics and Society* 52(3): 67–97.

O'Brien, David M. 2011. *Storm Center: The Supreme Court in American Politics*, 9th ed. New York: W.W. Norton.

Oppenheim, Lois Hecht. 2007. *Politics in Chile: Socialism, Authoritarianism, and Market Democracy*, 3rd ed. Boulder, CO: Westview Press.

Orren, Karen, and Stephen Skowronek. 2004. *The Search for American Political Development*. New York: Cambridge University Press.

Ostberg, C. L., and Matthew Wetstein. 2007. *Attitudinal Decision Making in the Supreme Court of Canada*. Vancouver: University of British Colombia Press.

Pachón, Mónica, and Matthew S. Shugart. 2010. "Electoral Reform and the Mirror Image of Inter-party and Intra-party Competition: The Adoption of Party Lists in Colombia." *Electoral Studies* 29(4): 648–660.

Pardow, Diego, and Sergio Verdugo. 2015. "El Tribunal Constitucional chileno y la reforma de 2005. Un Enroque entre Jueces de Carrera y Académicos." *Revista de Derecho* XXVIII(1): 123–144.

Pellegrina, Lucia, and Nuno Garoupa. 2013. "Choosing between the Government and the Regions: An Empirical Analysis of the Italian Constitutional Court Decisions." *European Journal of Political Research* 52(4): 431–480.

Peña, J. 2017. "Los 10 miembros del Tribunal Constitucional que podrían decidir el futuro del proyecto de aborto: Los senadores y diputados de Chile Vamos recurrirán a la instancia para impugnar una de las iniciativas clave del Gobierno, tras ser aprobada en el Senado y que hoy votará la Cámara." July 22. www.emol.com/noticias/Nacional/2017/07/20/867549/Los-10-miembros-del-Tribunal-Constitucional-que-veran-el-proyecto-de-aborto-en-tres-causales.html (last accessed July 21, 2020).

Peress, Michael. 2009. "Small Chamber Ideal Point Estimation." *Political Analysis* 17: 276–290.

Peterson, Steven A. 1981. "Dissent in American Courts." *Journal of Politics* 43: 412–434.

Pfeffer, Emilio. 2005. *Reformas Constitucionales 2005*. Santiago, Chile: Editorial Jurídica.

Popova, Maria. 2010. "Be Careful What You Wish For: A Cautionary Tale of Post-Communist Judicial Empowerment." *Democratizatsiya* 18: 56–73.

Posada-Carbó, Eduardo. 2013. "Colombia: Democratic Governance Amidst an Armed Conflict." In *Constructing Democratic Governance in Latin America*, 4th ed., eds. Jorge I. Domínguez and Michael Shifter. Baltimore: The Johns Hopkins University Press. 233–254.

Prillaman, William. 2000. *The Judiciary and Democratic Decay in Latin America: Declining Confidence in the Rule of Law*. Westport, CT: Praeger.

Pritchett, C. Herman. 1948. *The Roosevelt Court*. New York: Macmillan.

Ramos, Natalie A. 2019. "Explainer: Chile's Constitutional Conundrum – To Change or Not to Change?" Reuters (November 6). www.reuters.com/article/us-chile-protests-explainer/explainer-chiles-constitutional-conundrum-to-change-or-not-to-change-idUSKBN1XG2WV (last accessed February 7, 2022).

Rampf, David, and Diana Chavarro. 2014. "The 1991 Colombian National Constituent Assembly: Turning Exclusion into Inclusion, or a Vain Endeavour?" Inclusive Political Settlements, Paper 1. Berlin. Reprint.

Ramseyer, J. Mark, and Eric Rasmusen. 2001. "Why Are Japanese Judges So Conservative in Politically Charged Cases?" *American Political Science Review* 95: 331–344.

Rettberg, Angelika. 2021. "From Old Battles to New Challenges in Colombia. In *Divisive Politics and Democratic Dangers in Latin America*, eds. Thomas Carothers and Andreas Feldmann. Washington, DC: Carnegie Endowment for International Peace. 18–21.

Richards, Mark J., and Herbert M. Kritzer. 2002. "Jurisprudential Regimes in Supreme Court Decision-making." *American Political Science Review* 96(June): 305–320.

Ríos-Figueroa, Julio. 2011. "Institutions for Constitutional Justice in Latin America." In *Courts in Latin America*, eds. Gretchen Helmke and Julio Ríos-Figueroa. New York: Cambridge University Press. 27–54.

Rodríguez-Raga, Juan Carols. 2011. "Strategic Deference in the Colombian Constitutional Court, 1992–2006." In *Courts in Latin America*, eds. Gretchen Helmke and Julio Ríos-Figueroa. New York: Cambridge University Press. 81–98.

Rogers, James. 2001. "Information and Judicial Review: A Signaling Game of Legislative-Judicial Interaction." *American Journal of Political Science* 45: 84–99.

Rosenn, Keith. 1992. "A Comparison of the Protection of Individual Rights in the New Constitutions of Colombia and Brazil." *University of Miami Inter-American Law Review* 23: 23.

Rowland, C. K., and Robert A. Carp. 1996. *Politics and Judgment in Federal District Courts*. Lawrence: University of Kansas Press.

Sadurski, Wojciech. 2008. *Rights before Courts, a Study of Constitutional Courts in Postcommunist States of Central and Eastern Europe*. Dordrecht, The Netherlands: Springer.

2019. *Poland's Constitutional Breakdown*. Oxford: Oxford University Press.

Safford, Frank, and Marco Palacios. 2002. *Colombia: Fragmented Land, Divided Society*. New York: Oxford University Press.

Salinas, Daniel, and Pablo Fraser. 2012. "Educational Opportunity and Contentious Politics: The 2011 Chilean Student Movement." *Berkeley Review of Education* 3. http://dx.doi.org/10.5070/B83110044.

Schanzenbach, Max M., and Emerson H. Tiller. 2008. "Reviewing the Sentencing Guidelines: Judicial Politics, Empirical Evidence and Reform." *The University of Chicago Law Review* 75: 715–760.

Scherer, Nancy. 2004. "Blacks on the Bench." *Political Science Quarterly* 119(Winter): 665–675.

Schwartz, Alex, and Melanie Murchinson. 2016. Judicial Impartiality and Independence in Divided Societies: An Empirical Analysis of the Constitutional Court of Bosnia-Herzegovina. *Law and Society Review* 50(4): 821–855.

Schwartz, Herman. 2000. *The Struggle for Constitutional Justice in Post-Communist Europe*. Chicago: University of Chicago Press.

Scribner, Druscilla. 2011. "Courts, Power and Rights in Argentina and Chile." In *Courts in Latin America*, eds. Gretchen Helmke and Julio Ríos-Figueroa. New York: Cambridge University Press. 248–277.

Segal, Jeffrey, and Harold Spaeth. 2002. *The Supreme Court and the Attitudinal Model Revisited*. Cambridge University Press. Cambridge.

Segal, Jeffrey, Chad Westerland, and Stefanie Lindquist. 2011. "Congress, the Supreme Court, and Judicial Review: Testing a Constitutional Separation of Powers Model." *American Journal of Political Science* 55(1): 89–104.

Sehnbruch, Kirsten, and Peter M. Siavelis. 2014. "Political and Economic Life under the Rainbow." In *Democratic Chile: The Politics and Policies of a Historic Coalition, 1990–2010*, eds. Kirsten Sehnbruch and Peter M. Siavelis. Boulder, CO: Lynne Rienner. 1–14.

Selznick, Philip. 1994. *The Moral Commonwealth*. Berkeley: University of California Press.

Shapiro, Martin. 2004. "Judicial Review in Developed Democracies." In *Democratization and the Judiciary: The Accountability Function of Courts in New Democracies*, eds. Siri Gloppen, Roberto Gargarella, and Elin Skaar. London: Frank Cass. 7–26.

Shapiro, Martin, and Alec Stone Sweet. 2002. *On Law, Politics, and Judicialization*. Oxford: Oxford University Press.

Sheppele, Kim. 2011. "Hungary's Constitutional Revolution." *New York Times* (December 19).

Shor, Miguel. 2009. "An Essay on the Emergence of Constitutional Courts: The Cases of Mexico and Colombia." *Indiana Journal of Global Legal Studies* 16: 173–194.

Siavelis, Peter. 1997. "Continuity and Change in the Chilean Party System: On the Transformational Effects of Electoral Reform." *Comparative Political Studies* 30(6): 651–674.

1999. Continuidad y Transformación del Sistema de Partidos en una Transición 'Modelo'." In *El Modelo Chileno: Democracia Y Desarrollo En Los Noventa*, eds. Paul W. Drake and Iván Jaksić. Santiago, Chile: LOM Ediciones.

2000. *The President and Congress in Post-Authoritarian Chile: Institutional Constraints to Democratic Consolidation*. University Park: The Pennsylvania State University.

2002. "Exaggerated Presidentialism and Moderate Presidents: Executive-Legislative Relations in Chile." In *Legislative Politics in Latin America*, eds. Scott Morgenstern and Benito Nacif. Cambridge: Cambridge University Press. 79–113.

2013. "Chile: Beyond Transitional Models of Politics." In *Constructing Democratic Governance in Latin America*, 4th ed., eds. Jorge I. Domínguez and Michael Shifter. Baltimore: The Johns Hopkins University Press. 204–232.

2014. "From a Necessary to a Permanent Coalition." In *Democratic Chile: The Politics and Policies of a Historic Coalition, 1990–2010*, eds. Kirsten Sehnbruch and Peter Siavelis. Boulder, CO: Lynne Rienner. 15–42.

Sierra, Lucas I. 2011. "La Supramayoría en la Potestad Legislativa Chilena como Anomolía Democrática." In *Frente a La Mayoría: Leyes Supramayoritarias Y Tribunal Constitucional En Chile*, eds. Lucas Sierra and Lucas Mac-Clure. Santiago, Chile: Centro de Estudios Públicos (CEP), Corporación de Estudios para Latinoamérica (CIEPLAN), Libertad y Desarrollo, Proyectamérica. 13–170.

2012. "Quórum Legislativo de Supramayoría y Tribunal Constitucional en Chile." In *Violencia, Legitimidad y Orden Público, SELA*. Buenos Aires: Libraria Ediciones. 281–296.

Silva, Enrique C. 2008. *El Tribunal Constitucional de Chile (1971–1973)*, 2nd ed. 38: 159.

Skidmore, Thomas E., and Peter H. Smith. 2001. *Modern Latin America*, 5th ed. Oxford: Oxford University Press.

Smith, Peter H. 2012. *Democracy in Latin America: Political Change in Comparative Perspective*, 2nd ed. Oxford: Oxford University Press.

Smith, Rogers M. 1988. "Political Jurisprudence, The 'New Institutionalism' and the Future of Public Law." *American Political Science Review* 82(March): 89–108.

Solum, Lawrence. 2005. "Judicial Selection: Ideology versus Character." *Cardozo Law Review* 26: 659–689.

Songer, Donald, and Julia Siripurapu. 2009. "The Unanimous Decisions of the Supreme Court of Canada as a Test of the Attitudinal Model." *Canadian Journal of Political Science* 42: 65–92.

Songer, Donald, Ashlyn Kuersten, and Erin Kaheny. 2000. "Why the Haves Don't Always Come Out Ahead: Repeat Players Meet Amici Curiae for the Disadvantaged." *Political Research Quarterly* 53(3) 537–556.

Spiller, Pablo and Rafael Gely. 1992. "Congressional Control of Judicial Independence: The Determinants of U.S. Supreme Court Labor Relations Decisions." *Rand Journal of Economics* 23(4): 463–492.

Spitzer, Matthew, and Eric Talley. 2011. "Left, Right, and Center: Strategic Information Acquisition and Diversity in Judicial Panels." *The Journal of Law, Economics, and Organization* 29: 638–680.

Staton, Jeffrey K. 2004. "Judicial Policy Implementation in Mexico City and Mérida." *Comparative Politics* 37(October): 41–60.

2010. *Judicial Power and Strategic Communication in Mexico*. Cambridge: Cambridge University Press.

Stone Sweet, Alec. 1992. *The Birth and Development of Judicial Politics in France*. New York: Oxford University Press.

2000. *Governing with Judges: Constitutional Politics in Europe*. Oxford: Oxford University Press.

2002. "Constitutional Courts and Parliamentary Democracy." *West European Politics* 25(2): 77–100.

2012. "Constitutional Courts." In *Oxford Handbook of Comparative Constitutional Law*, ed. Michel Rosenfeld and András Sajó. Oxford: Oxford University Press.

Stotzky, Irwin. 2004. "Lessons Learned and the Way Forward." In *Democratization and the Judiciary*, eds. Siri Gloppen, Roberto Gargarella, and Elin Skaar. London: Frank Cass. 144–146.

Tiede, Lydia. 2006. "Judicial Independence: Often Cited, Rarely Understood." *Journal of Contemporary Legal Issues* 15: 129–161.

2012. "Chile's Criminal Law Reform: Enhancing Defendants' Rights and Citizen Security. *Latin American Politics and Society* 54(3): 65–93.

2016. "The Political Determinants of Judicial Dissent: Evidence from the Chilean Constitutional Tribunal." *European Political Science Review* 8: 377–403.

2020. "Mixed Judicial Selection and Constitutional Review." *Comparative Political Studies* 53(7): 1092–1123.

Tiede, Lydia, and Aldo Ponce. 2014. "Evaluating Theories of Decision-Making on the Peruvian Constitutional Tribunal." *Journal of Politics in Latin America* 6(2): 134–164.

Tiede, Lydia, Robert Carp, and Kenneth Manning. 2010. "Judicial Attributes and Sentencing Deviation Cases: Do Sex, Race, and Politics Matter?" *Justice System Journal* 31(3): 249–272.

Tsebelis, George. 2002. *Veto Players: How Institutions Work*. Princeton: Princeton University Press.

Turkewitz, Julie, and Sofía Villamil. 2021. "Children Trapped by Colombia's War, Five Years after Peace Deal." *New York Times* (March 27, 2021). www.nytimes.com/2021/03/27/world/americas/colombia-children-war-FARC.html.

Ulmer, Sydney. 1973. "Social Background as an Indicator to the Votes of Supreme Court Criminal Cases: 1947–56 Terms." *American Journal of Political Science* 17(3): 622–630.

Unah, Isaac, and Ange-Marie Hancock. 2006. "U.S. Supreme Court Decision-making, Case Salience, and the Attitudinal Model." *Law and Policy* 28: 295–320.

Valenzuela, Arturo. 1994. "Party Politics and the Crisis of Presidentialism in Chile: A Proposal for a Parliamentary Form of Government." In *The Failure of Presidential Democracy: The Case of Latin America*, eds. Juan J. Linz and Arturo Valenzuela. Baltimore: Johns Hopkins University Press. 91–150.

Valenzuela, Eugenia Somarriva. 2006. "Criterios De Hermenéutica Constitucional Aplicados Por El Tribunal Constitucional: Contribución Del Tribunal Constitucional a La Institucionalización Democrática." *Cuadernos del Tribunal Constitucional* 31: 11–125.

Vanberg, Georg. 2005. *The Politics of Constitutional Review in Germany*. New York: Cambridge University Press.

2015. "Constitutional Courts in Comparative Perspective: A Theoretical Assessment." *Annual Review of Political Science* 18: 167–185.

Vanden, Harry, and Gary Prevost. 2015. *The Politics of Latin America: The Power Game*, 5th ed. New York: Oxford University Press.

Varas, Augusto. 2014. *El Gobierno De Piñera (2010–2014)*. Santiago, Chile: Catalonia.

Varol, Ozan O., Lucia Pellegrina, and Nuno Garoupa. 2017. "An Empirical Analysis of Judicial Transformation in Turkey." *The American Journal of Comparative Law* 65(1): 187–216.

Venice Commission (European Commission for Democracy through Law). 2007. "Vademecum on Constitutional Justice." CDL-STD(1997)020. Strasbourg, France: Venice Commission.

2015. "Compilation of Venice Commission Opinions, Reports and Studies on Constitutional Justice." Vol. CDL-PI(2015)002. Strasbourg, France: Venice Commission.

Verdugo, Sergio. 2017. "Birth and Decay of the Chilean Constitutional Tribunal (1970–1973)." *International Journal of Constitutional Law* 15(2): 469–494.

Verdugo, Sergio, and Jorge Contesse. 2018. "The Rise and Fall of a Constitutional Moment Lessons from the Chilean Experiment and the Failure of Bachelet's Project." *Int'l J. Const. L. Blog*, March 13, 2018.

Vial Correa, Gonzalo. 2006. *Tribunal Constitucional de Chile: Historia y Trayectoria 1971–2006*. Santiago, Chile: La Fundación CAP auspició la publicación de esta obra.

Villarraga Sarmiento, Álvaro. 2009. *Biblioteca de la Paz- 1990–1994: Acuerdos con el EPL, PRT, MAQL y CRS- Diálogos con la CGSB. Tomo III*. Bogotá: Gente Nueva Editorial.

Vitale, David. 2014. "The Value of Dissent in Constitutional Adjudication: A Context-Specific Analysis." *Review of Constitutional Studies* 19: 83–108.

Voeten, Erik. 2007. "The Politics of International Judicial Appointments: Evidence from the European Court of Human Rights." *International Organization* 61(4): 699–701.

2008. "The Impartiality of International Judges: Evidence from the European Court of Human Rights." *American Political Science Review* 102(4): 417–433.

Voigt, Stefan, Jerg Gutmann, and Lars P. Feld. 2015. "Economic Growth and Judicial Independence, a Dozen Years On: Cross-Country Evidence Using an Updated Set of Indicators." *European Journal of Political Economy* 38: 197–211.

Von Doepp, Peter. 2006. "Politics and Judicial Assertiveness in Emerging Democracies: High Court Behavior in Malawi and Zambia." *Political Research Quarterly* 59: 389–399.

Weeks, Gregory. 2014. "The Military and Twenty Years of the Concertación." In *Democratic Chile: The Politics and Policies of a Historic Coalition, 1990–2010*, eds. Kirsten Sehnbruch and Peter Siavelis. Boulder, CO: Lynne Reinner. 103–118.

Weingast, Barry. 1997. "The Political Foundations of Democracy and the Rule of Law." *American Political Science Review* 91: 245–263.

Weinshall, Keren, Udi Sommer, and Ya'acov Ritov. 2018. "Ideological Influences on Governance and Regulation: The Comparative Case of Supreme Courts." *Regulation and Governance* 12: 334–352.

Whittington, Keith E. 2000. "Once More unto the Breach: Post behavioralist Approaches to Judicial Politics." *Law and Social Inquiry* 25(2): 601–634.

2005. "'Interpose Your Friendly Hand': Political Supports for the Exercise of Judicial Review by the United States Supreme Court." *American Political Science Review* 99(4): 583–596.

2014. "The Least Activist Supreme Court in History? The Roberts Court and the Exercise of Judicial Review." *Notre Dame Law Review* 89(5): 2219–2252.

Wilson, Bruce M. 2009. "Rights Revolutions in Unlikely Places: Costa Rica and Colombia." *Journal of Politics in Latin America* 1(2): 59–85.

Wohlfarth, Patrick C. 2009. The Tenth Justice? Consequences of Politicization in the Solicitor General's Office. *Journal of Politics* 70: 224–237.

Index

For EU product safety concerns, contact us at Calle de José Abascal, 56–1°, 28003 Madrid, Spain or eugpsr@cambridge.org.

www.ingramcontent.com/pod-product-compliance
Lightning Source LLC
LaVergne TN
LVHW011526200926
848484LV00001B/167

* 9 7 8 1 3 1 6 5 1 2 3 1 9 *